Giovanni Morelli, Constance Jocelyn Ffoulkes

**Italian painters**

Giovanni Morelli, Constance Jocelyn Ffoulkes

**Italian painters**

ISBN/EAN: 9783337637712

Printed in Europe, USA, Canada, Australia, Japan

Cover: Foto ©ninafisch / pixelio.de

More available books at **www.hansebooks.com**

# ITALIAN PAINTERS

# ITALIAN PAINTERS

*CRITICAL STUDIES OF THEIR WORKS*

## By GIOVANNI MORELLI

(IVAN LERMOLIEFF)

## THE BORGHESE AND DORIA-PAMFILI GALLERIES IN ROME

TRANSLATED FROM THE GERMAN BY

### CONSTANCE JOCELYN FFOULKES

WITH AN INTRODUCTION BY

## THE RIGHT HON. SIR A. H. LAYARD, G.C.B., D.C.L.

CORRESPONDING MEMBER OF THE INSTITUT DE FRANCE
MEMBER OF THE PRUSSIAN ORDER OF MERIT
TRUSTEE OF THE NATIONAL GALLERY, ETC.

*WITH ILLUSTRATIONS*

LONDON
JOHN MURRAY, ALBEMARLE STREET
1892

# CONTENTS.

# LIST OF ILLUSTRATIONS.

## FULL-PAGE ILLUSTRATIONS.

## WOODCUTS IN TEXT.

## Errata.

Page 86, paragraph 12, line 2, *for* 578 *read* 425.

„ 95, note 4, line 8, *for* Turin Academy *read* Turin Gallery.

„ 119, line 1, *for* Abozzo *read* Abbozzo.

„ 121, note. line 7, and elsewhere, *for* Roselli *read* Rosselli.

„ 198, line 25, *for* of about 1554 *read* of 1554.

„ 279, line 8, *for* Signor *read* Count.

# INTRODUCTION.

I have been asked to write an introduction to the following translation from the German, by Miss Jocelyn Ffoulkes, of the well-known studies on early Italian painting by the late Senator Giovanni Morelli, published by him under the pseudonym of 'Ivan Lermolieff.' A close friendship, extending over nearly forty years, with that remarkable and highly-gifted man, with whom I was in constant correspondence, and to whom I owe, to a great extent, such acquaintance as I have with Italian art, enables me to speak with some confidence of his character, his views, and his work. I the more willingly avail myself of this opportunity to say something with respect to them as they have been misunderstood, and, I fear, sometimes maliciously misrepresented. I feel, indeed, almost called upon to do so in consequence of a personal attack upon my departed friend which appeared in the 'Fortnightly Review' of last October, from the pen of Dr. William Bode, the director of the Berlin gallery, a gentleman of some repute as a 'professional art-critic,' and the leader of that small band of connoisseurs who reject the opinions and method of Morelli. It was hoped by Morelli's friends that, when the grave had closed over him, the controversy in which he had been engaged with the German professor would have ceased; and certainly a generous and chivalrous opponent would have been silent over his tomb. Not that he would have been in any way hurt or offended by Dr. Bode's attack upon him. It would, on the contrary, have afforded him no small amusement. He was not in the habit of noticing mere scurrilous abuse, although he was never backward in answering, with merciless logic, those who, engaged in the same pursuits as himself, differed from him in opinion, and sometimes expressed their dissent with unnecessary warmth. He adopted, it is true, a bantering and somewhat sarcastic tone in his criticisms on his opponents, calculated to cause offence, and this is, perhaps, to be regretted. His banter and his irony were, however, consistent with his assumed character of an ignorant Russian, who sought instruction in art from those who professed to be the highest authorities on the subject, but whom Morelli believed to be pretentious pedants, little acquainted with its true principles, and who consequently were guilty of egregious and misleading mistakes. But he avoided personalities. It was the class, not the individual, against which his shafts were directed, and he fought like a gentleman with a polished rapier, and not like a clown with a bludgeon. He never condescended to ill-mannered vituperation, and with his amiable and kindly nature he would have shrunk from causing pain to any human being. Dr. Bode denounces him as a 'Swiss physician who was educated in Germany, and had of late taken his seat in the Senate at Rome, and who had strung together into a theory his experiences as an

old and lucky hand at collecting,' and as a ' quack doctor '
who 'extolled his method with an air of infallibility.'
Morelli's irony, when playfully turned against those professors and experts who, whilst pretending to infallibility,
have added spurious works to the institutions over which
they preside, was no doubt keen and cutting. That it
touched and vexed those who felt that they had exposed
themselves to it is sufficiently proved by the tone and
temper of the article in the ' Fortnightly Review.' But
it is somewhat surprising that the director of a renowned
German gallery should thus seek to revenge himself upon
his critic after his death. That the taunts launched by
Herr Bode and others against Morelli are not only unfounded, but contrary to the truth, those who knew my
friend are well aware. How little he deserved to be called
a 'Romanised Swiss,' a 'quack doctor,' and a mere 'amateur,'
will be seen by the following sketch of his life and labours.

Giovanni Morelli is said to have been descended from a
Protestant family which had fled from the south of France
to escape the persecution to which the Huguenots were
exposed in the reign of Louis XIV., and had sought refuge
in Geneva. Such is the statement of the Marquis Visconti
Venosta in a touching obituary notice of his deceased
friend, contributed to the ' Perseveranza ' newspaper; and
he must have had good grounds for making it, although
I am assured that there is no evidence to support it.
Morelli himself affirmed that his ancestors were members of
an illustrious Venetian patrician family, who had professed
the Lutheran faith at the beginning of the sixteenth century,
and had been compelled to fly from Venice to the south of

France.   To escape detection they assumed the name of
Morelli, which was that of one of their servants.   His
father, a native of Woeschbach, on the Lake of Constance,
crossed the Alps and settled at Verona, where he successfully engaged in some industrial enterprises, and became
President of the Chamber of Commerce.   He married a
lady of Bergamo of a Protestant family of the name of
Zavaritt.   His son was born at Verona on February 25,
1816; but, having been left an orphan at an early age, was
taken by his mother to her native city, where he was
brought up.   As he dwelt there for many years of his
life, Morelli came to consider himself a native and citizen
of Bergamo, for which picturesque and famous city he
ever retained the most lively attachment.   He was accustomed to boast, in his pleasant manner, that he was a
thorough Bergamesque, with some of the good qualities
and most of the peculiarities which form the comic side
of the character of that sturdy race.

Morelli was destined for the profession of a physician,
and after receiving his preliminary education in German-
Switzerland was sent, when twenty years of age, to Munich
to complete it—for in those days the Italian colleges were
closed to Protestants.   'The young Italian,' says a writer
in the 'Quarterly Review,'[1] 'soon gave proof of his many-
sided attractiveness.   The Rector, Ignatius Döllinger, immediately took to him, advised him to study comparative
anatomy, accepted him as his pupil, and finally as his
assistant; Von Schubert, the Professor of Natural History,

[1] See 'Giovanni Morelli: the Patriot and Critic,' in the *Quarterly
Review* for July 1891.

looked equally kindly upon him and encouraged him to frequent his house; Frederick Rückert, the poet, conceived an ardent friendship for him, and read him his unpublished verses; and, as a crowning tribute, Genelli, the sculptor (painter), engaged on the subject of Prometheus, persuaded him to stand for his model.' After passing his medical examination he went to Berlin, where he was admitted into the best literary and scientific society, and was especially welcomed by Bettina von Arnim, who was deeply interested in him. It was thus that he attained a complete mastership of the German language, in which his published works are written. The late Count Usedom, the well-known diplomatist, and subsequently at the head of the museum of Berlin, once observed to me, speaking of Morelli, 'he has not only taught us art—he has taught us our language.'

After accompanying Agassiz in some of his glacier expeditions in Switzerland, Morelli spent some time at Paris, continuing his scientific studies. It was there, I believe, that the great collections of the Louvre first induced him to turn his attention to the fine arts, and led him to visit Rome and Florence with the object of seeing the famous galleries in those cities.

Morelli, a true Italian, with his generous and noble nature, could not be other than an Italian patriot. When, therefore, the revolutionary movement broke out in Italy, in 1848, he abandoned medicine, which he never practised, and hastened to take part in the events which led to the expulsion of the Austrians from Lombardy. He placed himself at the head of a corps of volunteers formed at Bergamo, and distinguished himself by his enterprise and bravery, storming the Austrian barracks at Monza, and one of the gates of Milan. The rare qualities of the young man, his great intelligence, his courage and fervent patriotism, were soon recognised by the national provisional government established at Milan, which included amongst its members some of the most eminent men in Italy. Availing themselves of his intimate acquaintance with the German language and with the German character, they sent him to represent them at the national German Parliament then assembled at Frankfort. When there he wrote and published, in the form of a pamphlet, entitled 'Worte eines Lombarden an die Deutschen,' an eloquent appeal to the Germans for their aid and sympathy in the struggle for independence and unity then taking place in his native land—a struggle in which the Germans themselves were engaged. In it he dwelt upon the friendship which should exist between two nations both equally cultured, both endowed with the most splendid traditions of art and literature, and consequently, both equally worthy of liberty. It is somewhat curious that amongst the arguments he used to enforce this appeal was one founded upon the superiority achieved by both races in the realms of art. I cannot refrain from quoting the following striking and prophetic passage from it :—

'In those days when the most virulent of hatreds—that of religion—divided our respective countries, the noble Raphael was in friendly correspondence with Albert Dürer, Galileo with Keppler. Thus, too, in those years when our most illustrious men languished in chains in the dungeons of Spielberg, Goethe addressed kindly and respectful letters to Manzoni. That love for the sublimest of arts and for pure science, which seems to have been more liberally bestowed by Providence as an heritage upon the Italian and German races than upon any others, thus kept them united when savage instincts led powerful rulers to find their advantage in throwing the bloody torch of discord between them. The world nevertheless does not stand still: it moves onwards, although slowly, and at every advancing footstep the light becomes clearer within and around. Through the darkness of barbarism we already see the dawn which foretells a bright day to all nations. And when that day appears, art and science and a flourishing commerce will closely unite Germany and Italy, and a common culture and prosperity will assure the happiness of both nations.'

It will be thus seen that at an early period of his life Morelli had turned his attention to the fine arts—and especially to the Italian masters—and that he had a high appreciation of the intellectual development of Germany, and of the best qualities of the German race. An answer is thus conclusively given to those who, like Dr. Bode, sneer at him as a mere 'amateur,' who had recently picked up his knowledge of art by frequenting the shops of dealers in pictures and antiquities, as well as to those who attribute his somewhat severe criticisms on German directors of picture-galleries, and on German professional art-critics, to a hatred of Germany and the Germans. To this latter accusation he has himself given the following answer in his address to the German people, from which I have already quoted: 'He who appeals to you in the name of his fellow-countrymen has passed amongst you six of the best years of his youth. Ties of the most intimate friendship and of the deepest gratitude bind him to the comely land to which he owes the cultivation of his heart and of his intellect, and to which he would give the name of his second country if that love of country which is the most sublime, the most ardent, sentiment of man could brook division.' He had, it is true, a deep hatred of pedantry and pretension wherever he detected them. If he denounced the claim to infallibility and the blunders of German professors, he was not less hard upon his own countrymen when they exposed themselves to similar treatment. At the same time, he never hesitated to admit that the study of the fine arts was pursued in Germany with far more industry and scientific method than in Italy or elsewhere in Europe, although he was led to believe that there was a want of method in their manner of dealing with works of art, which offended his independent judgment and the scientific turn of his mind. However antipathetic some pedantic and self-sufficient German professor might be to him, he had the most profound contempt for the directors of Italian galleries and for Italian professional connoisseurs, part of whose business it is to certify to the genuineness of spurious pictures, and to help the dealer in imposing upon the credulous foreigner. He took a malicious pleasure in holding both up to ridicule, which he was in the habit of doing with infinite humour and wit.[2]

Morelli's political mission to Frankfort being without

[2] I remember once going with him to see a picture which its owner attributed to Luino, and with respect to which he desired to have Morelli's opinion. After looking at it for a moment Morelli said very gravely,

result, he returned to Italy, and hastened to Venice, then besieged by the Austrians, and took an active part in the defence. After the fall of the city and the re-establishment of the Austrian rule in Lombardy, convinced that the future of Italy was with Piedmont, he joined that group of illustrious statesmen who had gathered round Cavour, and were the founders of their country's unity and independence. He became the valued friend of the poet Manzoni, of Gino Capponi, the patriot-historian of his native Florence, of the dramatist Niccolini, of Marco Minghetti, the future prime minister of United Italy, and of other prominent liberal leaders, with whom he carried on an active correspondence, parts of which have been published, and bear high testimony to his statesmanlike views as to the condition and prospects of Italy at a time of general illusions, to his political foresight, and to the wisdom and moderation of his opinions; for he had no confidence in, or sympathy for, extreme revolutionists, who were eager to plunge their country into fresh troubles, regardless of the means which they employed, and of the blood which they caused to be shed. This feeling may be traced in the occasional bantering allusions to the advanced radical and republican parties which occur even in his treatises on art. Nevertheless, when in 1865 the war with Austria was renewed, Morelli placed himself at once under Colonel Guicciardi, who, at the head of a body of volunteers, was engaged in defending the Valtellina against an Austrian

---

'Lui-no,' with a slight emphasis on the 'no.' The owner was delighted, and boasted that his picture had been pronounced genuine by the great connoisseur.

invasion. In this mountain warfare he distinguished himself by his intrepidity, activity, and military qualities. I joined him when he was so engaged at Bormio. He had promised to organise a bear hunt for me, which, however, from the failure of the chief performer to appear, never came off.

I made Morelli's acquaintance in the house of Sir James Hudson, the British Minister at Turin, who had the greatest regard and esteem for him. The British Legation was then a privileged place of meeting for Cavour and his political friends, and the most distinguished liberals from all parts of the Peninsula. Morelli was admitted to their counsels, and took part in the great work in which they were engaged—that of preparing the way for the redemption of their country. But he had no taste for politics, which in Italy, at that time, and perhaps necessarily, comprised intrigues and conspiracies repugnant to a man of his upright and honourable character. He turned to art as a solace and a source of occupation to divert his thoughts from the sufferings of his native land under the cruel rule of the stranger. He devoted himself to its study with the earnestness and thoroughness of a German, and the acuteness and imagination of an Italian. He made himself acquainted not only with the contents of the principal galleries in Europe, but there was scarcely a village church in Italy containing a picture of any note which he did not visit, sometimes travelling on horseback or on foot in remote and even dangerous parts where there were no roads, and meeting with many adventures, which he would relate in his lively and graphic manner.

When I first met him he was already recognised by

those who knew him, and were acquainted with the ardour
and success with which he had pursued his studies, as the
highest authority in matters connected with Italian art.
He had formed a friendship with Mr. Mündler, a distinguished German connoisseur, at one time connected with
our National Gallery, to which he rendered signal services ;
and with Sir Charles Eastlake, who, accompanied by
Mr. Mündler, was assiduous in visiting public and private
collections in Italy in the interests of that great institution
of which he was the director. Sir Charles gladly availed
himself of Morelli's knowledge and advice. On the other
hand, Morelli formed the highest opinion of Sir Charles's
taste and critical judgment in matters of art, and of his
extensive acquaintance with its history and literature. The
value he attached to Mr. Mündler's opinions as a critic and
connoisseur is shown by the frequent reference he makes to
him in his works, and by his readiness to accept the views
and decisions of even a German, when he believed them
to be well-founded, and not arrogantly and dogmatically
expressed.

Morelli's means did not permit him to be a collector,
but he possessed in his house at Bergamo a few pictures
of considerable merit, which his intimate knowledge of the
Italian masters had enabled him to discover in the hands
of dealers and others who were ignorant of their value. He
once told me that one of the greatest sorrows he had
experienced in life was when, as a young man having been
induced to gamble, he lost a sum of money which he was
only able to pay by selling a picture by Mantegna, which
he had been fortunate enough to 'pick up,' and which he

highly prized. The choice and interesting collection of pictures which he bequeathed to the city of Bergamo had been for the most part left to him by a friend, who, however, had collected them under his advice.

In January 1860, King Victor Emanuel, in recognition of Morelli's distinguished services to the national cause, named him a citizen of the Sardinian kingdom. In April 1861 he was chosen to represent Bergamo in the Italian Chambers, and was re-elected to three subsequent Parliaments. His election was the more remarkable as he was a Protestant. The bishop of the city was amongst his warmest supporters, which proved the general esteem felt for his character; and one of the highest eulogiums upon him, after his death, appeared in the local organ of the clerical party, which extolled his justice, impartiality, and toleration in matters of religion and the interest he took in questions concerning the welfare of his Roman Catholic fellow-citizens. He joined the party—the 'Right' as it is termed—which was led by the men who had been followers of Cavour, and who adhered to the views and principles of that great statesman. But he was unwilling to take any active part in politics, although always ready to give his advice to his political friends, by whom he was constantly consulted. It was to his favourite subject—the fine arts— that he devoted himself, thinking that he might be more useful to his country by doing so than as a professional politician. He consequently availed himself of an early opportunity to call the attention of the Chambers to the neglect with which the public galleries and museums in Italy were treated, to the gross ignorance displayed by

those who were in charge of them in naming and classifying their contents, and to the fraudulent manner in which
pictures and works of art belonging to religious and other
public institutions were sold to dealers, to be sent out
of Italy. To put a stop to this flagrant abuse Morelli
induced the Minister of Public Instruction, in 1862, to
appoint a commission, of which he was named a member,
to prepare a law for the conservation of works of art—a law
which bears his name, and forbids the heads of such institutions, under severe penalties, to alienate what was justly
to be considered public property. He has been accused of
wishing to prevent the sale, and exportation from Italy, of
works of art belonging to private individuals. But so far
from such being the case, no one condemned more strongly
than he did the illiberal and shortsighted regulations, pro-
mulgated by the Italian Government, to prevent the owners
of pictures from disposing of them to private persons or
to public galleries, and forbidding their exportation—regulations which only cause trouble to honest people, and give
occasion to the employment by unscrupulous persons of
fraudulent means for evading them. Morelli was proud of
seeing the art in which his countrymen had excelled, and to
which Italy owed so much of her renown, worthily represented in foreign collections, and pictures were not unfrequently purchased for them on his recommendation. It was
only when some work by a very rare and important painter
was about to leave the country that he interfered. Thus,
when the owners of the Manfrin gallery at Venice were about
to sell to the Berlin museum one of the very few genuine
works by Giorgione, he urged the Italian Government

to exercise their right of pre-emption by acquiring it. On their declining to do so, on the ground of want of funds, he induced his friend, the late Prince Giovanelli, to advance the money and to keep the picture, on condition of ceding it to a national institution when the Government was able to refund the price paid for it—a condition which the prince was unwilling, after he had been offered many times the amount, to fulfil.

In consequence of Morelli's representations a commission had been appointed by the Italian Government, in April 1861, of which he was named the president, to make a register of all works of art possessed by public institutions in Umbria and the Marches, with power to visit churches, convents, and monasteries, in which such works were believed to exist, for the purpose of making a list of and describing them. Those who attempted to sell or remove them were threatened with severe penalties. With this commission Signor Cavalcaselle was associated, as secretary I believe, and from the facilities which he was thus afforded of seeing and examining pictures, and from the teachings of his distinguished chief, he acquired much of the knowledge which enabled him to publish, in conjunction with Mr. Crowe, his well-known works upon the Italian schools of painting.

The power thus conferred upon Morelli to visit even convents of women, from which men were strictly excluded, gave rise occasionally to amusing incidents, which he was fond of relating. I happened to accompany him on one of these visits. He had heard that there existed in a convent a signed picture by a somewhat rare master—Marco Marziale—which he was desirous of examining.

We knocked at the door, and a nun came to a small
lattice to inquire our business. When told of it, she
declared that it was quite impossible for us to be admitted.
Morelli having informed her of his authority to enter, she
went to consult the superior, who shortly afterwards appeared, and, yielding with a good grace to the requirements
of the law, directed the door to be unlocked. We entered
a long corridor into which opened the cells occupied by the
nuns. On its walls were hung very indifferent pictures,
representing subjects of classical mythology, little fit for
the eyes of chaste recluses. Morelli inquired of the superior,
in his arch manner, whether they represented the branch
of art which was principally studied by the inmates of the
monastery; adding that it was not such pictures that he
expected to find in it, but pious representations of the
Madonna and Saints. The old lady replied that these
pictures had been there from time immemorial. 'There
can be no possible objection to your disposing of them,'
observed Morelli gravely, 'and perhaps the sooner you get
rid of them the better.' She then led us into a parlour in
which we found the picture of which we were in search.
By this time Morelli had so captivated our guide by the
charm of his manner and conversation, that she insisted
upon entertaining us with sweetmeats and liqueurs.

Morelli next turned his attention to the reform of the
administration of the Italian museums and galleries. He
endeavoured to obtain the appointment to them of more
competent directors than those who had been named to
the office, chiefly through political or personal favour and
intrigue. When his political friends were in power they

wished him to hold a position which would have given him
the supreme direction of all such public institutions, and
he was warmly urged to accept it. But he declined to
undertake a task which, he was convinced, would have
exposed him to constant vexation, and in which he would
have had to contend in vain with intrigue, jobbery, and
favouritism of every description. He was then offered the
more limited office of director of the Florence galleries,
which he also refused. His remonstrances, however, as to
the neglect with which the Italian galleries were treated,
and as to the ignorance displayed by those who had the charge
of them in the naming and classifying of pictures, produced
some effect. It is difficult to conceive what this ignorance
was—and in some instances still is. Spurious works and
manifest copies were ascribed to the greatest masters. No
distinction was made between the different schools of painting. Pictures, whose authors would have been evident to the
merest connoisseur, were attributed to painters with whom
in manner they had no connection whatever, and who
belonged to entirely different schools. The student sought
in vain for instruction; and the public was only misled.
The directors of some galleries were shamed by Morelli's exposure into making changes, and his remonstrances have
led to improvement; but the confusion and ignorance which
still prevail may be judged of by published catalogues, and
by the manner in which the pictures are in some places
exhibited, as, for instance, in the Correr museum at Venice,
where highly interesting works of the old masters are
jumbled up with productions of the last and present century
of the vulgarest and most common-place description, hung

on a level with the eye, whilst those of the fifteenth and sixteenth centuries are, in Academy phrase, 'skied' and beyond the reach of examination.

Another of Morelli's suggestions, adopted by the Government, is the entrance fee to the galleries and museums paid by visitors, who had previously been exposed to constant annoyance from the attendants and others connected with them, asking for 'buona mano.' From this source funds were to be furnished for the purchase of works of art for the national collections, which in some instances have been judiciously applied to the purpose, but which in others have been wasted owing to the want of intelligence of their directors.

In the later years of his life Morelli dwelt principally at Milan, where he occupied a modest apartment, which contained his choice collection of pictures. He was, however, frequently absent, visiting, over and over again, Germany, France, and England, to study the galleries and private collections of pictures and drawings in those countries. He attended the meetings of the Chambers at Rome when business of importance, or any question in which he was interested, and on which he considered that his vote might be useful to his political friends and to the party to which he belonged, was under discussion. After his elevation to the Senate, which took place in 1873, it was less necessary for him to take an active part in public affairs, and he could devote more time to his favourite pursuit. Although for many years he had been a most diligent and assiduous student of · the fine arts, it was not until he was nearly sixty that he ventured to publish

any of the results of his researches.    His modest and
retiring nature restrained him from doing so, until he
hoped that he had attained to some maturity of experience
and judgment.    His first publication consisted of a series
of essays which he contributed in 1874, 1875, and 1876,
under the assumed name of 'Ivan Lermolieff,' to a German
periodical, 'Lützow's Zeitschrift für bildende Kunst.' They
were written in German, and purported to be a critical description of pictures in the celebrated Borghese gallery at
Rome; but they dealt with many interesting questions
relating to the history of Italian painting, and to the works
of the early Italian masters.    These essays, from the
originality of the writer's views, his profound knowledge
of his subject, and the boldness of his criticisms, caused a
lively sensation in the German artistic world, and much
curiosity as to the writer, who, however, successfully
preserved his incognito.    The success that they achieved
induced him to publish in 1880 a volume containing
remarks and criticisms on the contents of the galleries of
Munich, Dresden, and Berlin, and on the works of the
old Italian masters in general.    Like his first essays,
it was written in German, with the title of 'Ein kritischer
Versuch von Ivan Lermolieff ins Deutsche übersetzt von
Johannes Schwarze.' [3]    Morelli thus retained his pseudonym,
and the whole title was a mystification.   'Lermolieff' was
an anagram of his own name with a Russian termination.
'Johannes Schwarze,' John Black, was Morelli himself—

---

[3] A translation in English by
Mrs. Richter was published in 1883,
under the title of *Italian Masters in
German Galleries : a Critical Essay*
*on the Italian Pictures in the
Galleries of Munich, Dresden and
Berlin, by Giovanni Morelli, member
of the Italian Senate.*

his name being a diminutive of ' Moro ' (black)—and the place in Russia from which he pretended to come (Gorlaw) was a small property (Gorli) he possessed in the Brianza, also with a Russian termination. I have heard that a conscientious and erudite German professor spent much time in a fruitless search for the place in Russian maps.

The criticisms which this book contained on the directors of these galleries, and its exposure of the way in which spurious works and copies of pictures by the great Italian masters had been unhesitatingly accepted by them as originals, and had consequently been imposed as such upon an ignorant and credulous public, caused an explosion of wrath in Germany against Morelli, who was speedily detected under his assumed name. He was denounced as an impostor with a mere superficial knowledge of art, and his suggestions and criticisms were treated by great professional art-authorities with indignant contempt. But he took no notice of the attacks upon him, confident that the truth would prevail in the end. It was not long before his confidence was justified. The wrath of the irate German professors gradually cooled, and Morelli secured a triumph which it has been given to few men of letters to enjoy. Some of his most violent opponents became his pupils, catalogues of German galleries had to be rewritten to alter the attribution of pictures according to his views,[4] and even Dr. Bode, considered in Germany a great authority, was not slow, I suspect, in availing himself of Morelli's

[4] For instance, the able and conscientious director of the Dresden gallery adopted no less than 46—out of 56—of his suggestions, only reserving the remainder for further consideration.

criticisms and suggestions.   The 'Lermolieff mania,' as the
learned doctor sarcastically terms it in his article in the
'Fortnightly Review,' had set in, and Morelli came to be
recognised in Germany, and in all European countries, by
those who were competent to judge, as the greatest connoisseur and critic of Italian art of his or, indeed, of any
other time.

To the very end of his life Morelli was indefatigable in
visiting public and private collections and in studying their
contents.   The picture gallery in the Imperial Palace at
St. Petersburg and those of Copenhagen and Stockholm
were, I believe, the only ones of any importance that he
had not seen.   He was frequently in London, and was intimately acquainted with our splendid national collection,
which he considered the most complete in Europe in the
representation of the Italian schools of painting, and consequently the most instructive to the student.   He specially
approved the judgment and care with which the pictures
had been selected and their arrangement and classification,
which, he considered, reflected the greatest credit upon those
who had had its direction and management.   He enjoyed
the friendship of its three consecutive directors, Sir Charles
Eastlake, Sir William Boxall, and Sir Frederick Burton,
all of whom set the highest value upon his knowledge and
critical judgment, and were ever ready to profit by his
advice.   In 1872 he spent some time with me in Spain,
visiting the churches and galleries of Madrid, Seville,
Granada, and other Spanish cities.   Besides adding to his
knowledge of art, he furnished, I have reason to believe,
valuable information to King Victor Emanuel as to the

prospects of his son Amadeo, who was then on the Spanish throne. In the fine gallery of the Prado, in which he spent many long days, he made several interesting and important discoveries, amongst others that of a fine picture by Giorgione, which had previously been ascribed to Pordenone, and one by Lorenzo Lotto, which passed for a work by Titian.

Morelli not only turned his attention to pictures by the old Italian masters; he made a most careful and minute study of their original drawings and sketches. He maintained that the information derived from such a study afforded the best means of identifying the authors of pictures which had for the most part been so 'restored' and repainted, and even rubbed down to the very priming in the process, that, although little of the original work might remain, yet in the forms of parts of the human frame and in the mode of treatment the master might still be traced. For the whole race of picture cleaners and restorers Morelli had an intense and almost amusing detestation, as if they were not only his personal enemies, but the enemies of those great masters whom he so deeply venerated, and whose works they had without pity destroyed, or so transfigured that serious wrong was done to their memories. And he was justified in this feeling, as the mischief and havoc caused by the cleaner and restorer are incalculable and irremediable.

In pursuing this branch of his studies he had examined almost every collection of the drawings of the old Italian masters in Europe, and had formed an important one himself. He intended to conclude the work, of which

the two volumes translated into English now about to be
published form the first part, by a third which was to
treat of the Berlin gallery. An additional volume was to
be specially devoted to the subject of the original drawings
and sketches of the Italian painters, his criticisms and
suggestions with respect to which would, I am disposed to
believe, have formed the most important and original
portion of his great work. It is deeply to be regretted—
although it may be fortunate for Herr Bode—that death
prevented the execution of his design.

The discoveries made by Morelli in pursuing his studies
and researches are innumerable, and some are of the
highest importance to the art-student, who should always
have his works at hand. Amongst his many suggestions
may be mentioned the attribution to Pintoricchio of the
drawings from the famous so-called 'Raphael's Sketch-
book,' preserved in the Venice Academy—an attribution,
however, which the directors of that gallery have not
thought fit to accept. Morelli's announcement that they
were not by Raphael, but by Pintoricchio, was at first
received with ridicule by well-known writers on the great
Umbrian painter. How dared a mere 'amateur' call in
question Raphael's studies contained in his own sketch-
book, and the authenticity of which had been recognised by the highest authorities, dead and living, and
proved by the most unquestionable evidence! Morelli
showed to demonstration that no such evidence existed,
and that several of these sketches were studies for existing
works by Pintoricchio, which had been executed by that
painter whilst Raphael was an infant, or before he was

born. The name of 'Raphael's Sketch-book' had been simply invented by one Bossi, a Milanese artist and collector, living in the first half of this century, who, having acquired what he considered a priceless treasure, boldly pronounced the drawings to be by Raphael, and as such sold them to the Austrian Government for the Venice Academy. Those who maintained their authenticity against Morelli first commenced a retreat by admitting that some of them might be by Pintoricchio, whilst others were undoubtedly by Raphael—it is somewhat curious that the two painters, one a man of middle age and the other an infant, should have used the same sketch-book!—and that some again were studies by masters of the Florentine school, by Polla-juolo, Luca Signorelli, and I know not whom.[5] Beaten out of this position by Morelli, they have for the most part been compelled to allow that he was right in ascribing all of them to Pintoricchio. This 'Sketch-book' has been the foundation of many theories respecting Raphael's life and works, which are now consequently exploded. A drawing, believed to be from it, for the little picture of Apollo and Marsyas, which belonged to the late Mr. Morris Moore, and which he sold for a large sum to the Louvre, upon the condition, very improperly acceded to by the authorities connected with that institution, that it should always be exhibited as a genuine work by Raphael, furnished that gentleman with what he considered triumphant evidence of

---

[5] Amongst the sketches said to have been taken from the so-called Raphael's 'Sketch-book' exhibited in the Venice Academy, there are two (on one sheet) undoubtedly by Raphael; but they formed no part of this volume, and are on paper of a different size.

its authenticity. But it did not even form part of the 'Sketch-book,' and is on paper of different size and fabric from that used by Pintoricchio, and is not executed, as his sketches are, in pen and ink. Morelli attributed both sketch and picture to Perugino.

It would take up too much space to recapitulate the numerous discoveries—for such indeed they may be called— made by Morelli in the European picture galleries, and which are described in his published works. I may, how- ever, mention that he was the first to point out, and prove, that the celebrated reclining Magdalen in the Dresden Museum, which had been accepted by learned professional art-critics and connoisseurs as a genuine work by Correggio, and had been the admiration of the public as such, could not possibly be by that master; but only at most the copy of a lost picture by him, or, perhaps, even an original work by some Flemish painter of the time and school of Vanderwerf; and that a Venus of the utmost beauty, which had been hung almost out of sight in the same gallery—as a copy by Sassoferato of a picture by Titian (!)— was a genuine work by Giorgione, and was to be ranked amongst the finest productions of this great artist. In this case his sagacious judgment was confirmed by a curious piece of evidence. Giorgione's 'Sleeping Venus' had been described by an anonymous writer of the sixteenth century as being in the possession of the Venetian patrician family of Marcello. To it, this writer states, Titian had added a Cupid seated at her feet. The absence of this Cupid in the Dresden picture was held to be fatal to Morelli's attribution. In the archives of the gallery, how-

-ever, has since been found a document which proves that when the picture was bought the missing Cupid still existed, but in so damaged a condition that it was thought best to remove it altogether. This marvellous work, which Titian and other great masters of the period took as their model for their numerous reclining and sleeping Venuses and nude female figures, now forms one of the principal treasures of this famed collection, and is duly honoured by being suitably hung. It was Morelli, too, who first assigned to Titian the fine picture of " The Daughter of Herodias " in the Doria-Pamfili gallery—one of the master's most delightful works—which had previously been attributed to Pordenone.

Another remarkable instance of the sagacity of Morelli was his discovery—in establishing which he was much engaged during the latter years of his life—that many so-called originals by Raphael, Leonardo da Vinci, and other painters of the best period of Italian art in public and private galleries, were copies or imitations of their works by highly skilled Flemish artists, who studied in Italy, and made a traffic of them. They have deceived even the practised eye of so eminent a connoisseur as Dr. Bode.

I may mention a further instance of Morelli's almost intuitive recognition of the author of a painting, and of the correctness of his judgment. Last year a collection of pictures was to be offered for sale by auction at Cologne. Small and ill-executed photographs of those of the Italian schools were sent to him. He detected amongst them at once two of importance—one by Bazzi or Sodoma, and one by Giulio Romano. He wrote to me on the subject, and urged me to go to Cologne to see them, which I was unable to do. He then called the attention of two of his German friends to them. On his advice, although he had never seen them, the one he attributed to Bazzi was purchased by Herr Habich of Cassel—himself a successful collector and one of Morelli's followers—and proved to be so fine an example of this rare and original painter that, at Morelli's request, Herr Habich generously ceded it to the Brera at Milan, of which it is now one of the principal ornaments. The 'Giulio Romano,' acquired by Miss Hertz, proved to be a charming work of his early time, when he was under the direct influence of his great master. Although German professional experts and connoisseurs, including, I believe, Dr. Bode, had flocked to Cologne to examine this collection and to attend the sale, they had failed to detect these works, which would have formed a most valuable addition to any public gallery. I give illustrations of both of them. Morelli may further be said to have rehabilitated, if he did not discover and resuscitate, several painters of great merit, whose names had been almost forgotten, and whose works were attributed to other masters. Amongst them may be mentioned Bernardino de' Conti, Ambrogio Preda or de Predis, and Giovanni Pedrini or Gianpietrino—who have been confounded with Leonardo da Vinci—and Romanino and Cariani, whose works had been ascribed to Giorgione and Palma Vecchio.

Morelli was no less successful in his criticisms on the history of Italian painting than he had been in the identification of the works of the Italian masters. He proved that

MADONNA AND CHILD WITH LAMB.  SODOMA.

To face p. 26.

"Virgin and Child." By Giulio Romano.

*(In the possession of Miss Hertz.*

*To face p.* [26] *of Introduction.*

in many cases it consisted of mere traditions, not only
unsupported by evidence, but opposed to patent facts.
He condemned Vasari, of whose literary abilities, however,
he was fully sensible, for having inserted in his biographies
of the Italian painters vague gossip and mere reports
respecting them, which had reached him second-hand, and
for having been too frequently influenced in his judgments of their works and character by personal enmity or
dislike, or by a desire to extol the merits of those who
came from his own part of the peninsula, at the expense
of others of equal if not superior merit—a common
form of Italian patriotism. A striking instance of this
tendency of Vasari is furnished by his unjust treatment of
Pintoricchio, one of Morelli's favourite masters, whose character he has successfully vindicated, and to whose great
merits he has called attention, proving that he was the
author of works attributed to other painters, such as two
frescoes in the Sistine chapel—the "Baptism of Christ"
ascribed to Perugino, and the "Journey of Moses," given
to Luca Signorelli—and frescoes in the Library of the
Duomo at Siena assigned to Raphael.[6] One of Morelli's
most valuable contributions to art-history is his exposure
of the erroneous statements of Vasari concerning the
early life and education of Raphael, which have misled all
subsequent biographers of the painter. He proved that
not Pietro Perugino, as alleged by that writer, and as
generally supposed, had been his first master, but Timoteo
Viti, whom Vasari had made his pupil. He supported

---

[6] See *Italian Masters in German Galleries*, pp. 265-269.

this view by such a mass of evidence and such conclusive arguments that it has now been generally accepted.

It is, I think, to be regretted that Morelli insisted upon publishing his later works under his pseudonym of 'Lermolieff,' although he allowed Mrs. Richter to give his name in her translation of his 'Italian Masters in German Galleries' as that of the author of the original work. Knowing him as I did, I can understand why he used it when he first appeared as an author. He had a kind of horror of 'appearing in print.' Moreover, his love of fun and his delight in mystifying pretentious pedants induced him to assume the character of an ignorant and simple 'son of the Steppe,' who, having commenced in his own country the study of art, sought in Germany and Italy instruction from learned professors and professional art-critics. He soon finds that their teachings are full of contradictions, and are manifestly absurd even to his own inexperienced judgment. Thinking for himself, and his eyes having been opened by an intelligent but unprofessional Florentine art-critic, he, with much humour, and sometimes, it must be admitted, with cutting, and perhaps needless, sarcasm, exposes the ignorance of those who pretend to be infallible teachers and guides in matters of art, and have sometimes the arrangement and direction of great public galleries. Having succeeded in his object, and having been detected in his disguise, he might have thrown it off and appeared in his true name. But he resisted the persuasions of his friends who endeavoured to prevail upon him to do so.

He commenced writing, and continued to write, in

German—a language as familiar to him as his own—
because he felt that it was in Germany that the study of
art was the most generally and seriously pursued, whilst in
Italy the subject was one which created little interest, and was
in the state which Signor Frizzoni, his friend and pupil, has
defined as ' civiltà cinese '; and because it was in Germany
that were to be found the chief opponents of his views.
He was, moreover, desirous of showing German critics that
in Italy there were persons able to discuss matters of art
on the ground which they were disposed to claim as exclusively their own.

I must now shortly refer to what Morelli terms his
' Principles and Method.' He has himself defined them in
an imaginary dialogue—his favourite mode of expressing
his views—between the Russian seeker after knowledge
and an aged Tuscan gentleman with whom he casually
makes acquaintance when in the Florence galleries. This
gentleman, who, as an ' amateur,' has devoted himself to
the study of art, and much despises professors and professional art-critics, maintains that to form an opinion upon
the authenticity of a picture, to judge of its merits, and
to determine first the school of painting to which it belongs,
and then by whom painted, it is not merely necessary to
collect a number of facts concerning the life of the presumed author, to discover the exact dates of his birth and
death, and to point out the misstatements of Vasari and
other writers with respect to him. His identification and
the genuineness of the work attributed to him should
depend upon scientific analysis, upon an accurate knowledge, derived from long and careful study, of his manner

and style, and especially of his delineation of the different
parts of the human body—or what Morelli denominates
'his treatment of form'—and of his peculiar sense of
colour.    In addition, the student should endeavour to
associate himself in spirit with the painter to whom he
would ascribe a work, and to ascertain whether the mental
disposition of the master would have led him thus to treat
his subject.   This he terms 'the experimental method'
such as employed by Darwin in his scientific researches.
He warns the student not to be led away by first impressions, and not to depend upon mere guess-work, or upon
traditions and doubtful documentary evidence.   He exposes
the worthlessness of many such traditions which had long
been accepted as indisputable facts—such as the attribution
of the so-called " Fornarina," in the Tribune of the Uffizi at
Florence, and other pictures in that collection, to Raphael.
He exemplifies the danger of trusting to documentary
evidence by various instances, such as that of a distinguished searcher in the Florence archives, who, because he
had found that Fra Diamante, a very inferior follower of
Filippo Lippi, had painted at Rome a picture representing
"Christ delivering the Keys to Peter," at once jumped to
the conclusion that the celebrated fresco in the Sistine
chapel of the same subject by Perugino—a master of a
totally different school—was really by this almost unknown
artist, and hastened to announce his great discovery.

The accusation brought against Morelli by Herr Bode,
that he disparaged, and held up to contempt, Messrs. Crowe
and Cavalcaselle is unfounded.   He fully recognised their
industry in collecting facts relating to early Italian art

and the services which they have rendered to its history.
But he disagreed with them as to the manner in which they
made use of the data they had collected, or in what he
termed their 'method.' He was wont, when in a joking
mood, to say of them, and of others whose diligent researches in the Italian archives have led to the discovery
of numerous facts relating to the early Italian painters,
that they were like truffle-dogs, which found the truffles,
but did not know how to make use of them when found.
In his later works Morelli has expressed, it is true, much
dissatisfaction with the manner in which Signor Cavalcaselle has discharged his official duties as director of the
art department in the Ministry of Public Instruction—
attributing to him the destruction of the frescoes by
Mantegna at Mantua and of other important early wall-
paintings, in consequence of the incompetency, if not something worse, of the men he has employed to restore them.

Dr. Bode ventures to write in the article to which I
have referred that Morelli, as 'a surgeon,' having had his
attention directed to the form of the human body, 'issued
a catalogue of the ears, noses, and fingers, the former
property of Sandro (Botticelli), Mantegna, Raphael, Titian
& Co., and with this schedule in hand every lover of art is
to patrol the picture galleries, when he will be able to single
out unerringly the different masters in spite of all the
wretched mistakes of the directors.' I am surprised that
a man of Dr. Bode's intelligence and, it may be presumed,
sense of truth should have committed himself to such a
statement. It proves how keenly he feels the justice of
Morelli's criticisms with respect to himself. It is true that

Morelli attached much importance to the study of 'form,'
and of the manner in which painters were accustomed to
delineate the different parts of the human frame, as one
of the clues to assist a student in identifying the author
of a picture—as a specialist in handwriting identifies the
author of a written document by the peculiar forms of
some of the letters.   He says himself of his method, in the
introduction to the second volume of this work, ' it has been
asserted in Germany that I profess to recognise a painter
and to estimate his work solely by the form of the hand,
the finger-nails, the ear, or the toes.   Whether this statement is due to malice or to ignorance I cannot say; it is
scarcely necessary to state that it is incorrect.   What I
maintain is, that the forms, more especially those of the
hand and ear, aid us in distinguishing the works of a master
from those of his imitators, and control the judgment which
subjective impressions might lead us to pronounce.'   This
mode of judging as to the authenticity of a picture has
now been generally adopted by serious art-critics and
students, as furnishing a valuable, but certainly not the
only, test to those who know how to avail themselves of it.

Morelli possessed all the qualities required in a connoisseur and critic—a most extensive knowledge not only of
the history of his own country and of others, but of the
local history of almost every city and province in Italy,
considerable scientific acquirements, an intimate acquaintance with nearly all the public and private collections in
Europe, a marvellous memory, which enabled him to remember even the smallest details of a picture that he had
once seen, the place it occupied if hung in a gallery, and

the number it bore, a wonderfully trained eye, unwearied industry, a most refined taste, and a passionate love for all that is truly great and beautiful. Yet 'the professional critic,' generally an incompetent and unsuccessful artist, sneered at him as 'an amateur.' He has himself answered the sneer in an amusing dialogue which he pretends to have overheard between two gentlemen standing before the well-known double portrait by Raphael of Beazzano and Navagero, usually known as "Bartolo and Baldo," in the Doria-Pamfili gallery at Rome. One of these gentlemen, a learned professor from Berlin, whom we have little difficulty in identifying, does not hesitate to pronounce dogmatically that the picture is a copy; the other—Morelli in the garb of an Austrian baron—maintains its genuineness by arguments, to which his antagonist can only reply by a contemptuous shrug of the shoulders. 'My dear Baron,' said he, 'you must admit that you are only an amateur, and have no claim to be a professional art-critic.' 'Professional or not,' replied the other warmly, 'I hold that amateurs who have a real love of art, and who, like myself, have a collection of their own, are quite as much entitled to express an opinion on a work of art as—nay, even better entitled to do so, than—so-called professional critics, who really care no more about a picture than the anatomist cares about the dead body he is dissecting.' Morelli further, in his 'Principles and Method,' thus modestly describes his own qualifications: 'I should never claim for myself either knowledge or endowments sufficient to warrant my setting myself up above my fellows. Yet, considering the years of honest study I have devoted to the subject, I think I

have at least as much right to express my opinion as
the scores of superficial writers on art in Italy and elsewhere, especially when I see how charlatans manage to pass
themselves off as critical judges of Italian art.'

Whilst adhering tenaciously to opinions which he had
formed after long study and mature consideration, he was
ever open to conviction, and ready to abandon or modify
them when persuaded that they were erroneous.   He
willingly listened to those who differed from him, although
their knowledge and experience might be infinitely inferior
to his own.   His readiness to receive young men, to pour
out to them the treasures of his knowledge when he saw
that they were in search of truth, and were inspired by a
genuine love of art, and his polished courtesy to strangers—
amongst them many German students and professors—who
sought his advice, were remarkable and lovable traits in
his character.   They endeared him to all who were brought
into contact with him.   He was a true 'capo-scuola.'
Never was a man more beloved and esteemed by his friends
and pupils, and never was there a more delightful companion.   To visit with him a picture gallery, or to examine
a collection of the drawings of the old masters, was an
intellectual treat which those who have enjoyed it are not
likely to forget.   The patience and clearness with which
he imparted his views, his wit and humour, the droll
manner in which he would illustrate his meaning by racy
Italian proverbs and popular sayings, his extensive knowledge, and his memory stored with facts of all kinds,
rendered him the most agreeable and instructive of teachers.
The accomplished author of the article in the 'Quarterly

Review,' to which I have referred, who knew Morelli well, describes him as a man of ' rare, grand, complete character, a patriot and a statesman, gifted, highly cultivated, genial and enlightened, noble in mind and person, and with an individual charm which all, men and women alike, who knew him will acknowledge.' It is not surprising that a man so endowed should have had a host of devoted friends and followers in his own country and abroad. Marco Minghetti, the statesman and Italian Prime Minister, became his pupil, and wrote a life of Raphael in accordance with his views. The Marquis Visconti Venosta, the Minister for Foreign Affairs, explained Morelli's theories on Italian art and taught his method in several able articles contributed to the Italian art-journals of most authority. The fascination which he exercised over women was something extraordinary, and amongst his most attached and warmest friends were some of the most highly-endowed and charming of his countrywomen. He was ever a welcome guest in the most cultivated circles and in the houses of the best families of Italy—in those of the Roman Princes, and of the ancient aristocracy of the Milanese. The Emperor and Empress Frederick, who had long known him, delighted in his society, and had for him the highest regard. On the other hand, for the noble-hearted emperor Morelli had a profound veneration, and for the artistic knowledge and taste, and for the varied acquirements and amiable character, of the empress the truest admiration. Even the German professors and ' gallery-directors,' against whom, I am afraid, he took a malicious pleasure in poking fun, which according to Herr Bode ' embittered their

lives,' ended by yielding to his charm, and became his
sincere friends, and even, in some instances, his enthusiastic disciples. Amongst them may be mentioned the
distinguished critics and connoisseurs Herr Woerman, the
director of the gallery of Dresden, the late Dr. Thausing,
the learned curator of the 'Albertina' at Vienna, Eisen-
mann, Lützow, Dr. Richter, and many others. Robert
Browning, the poet, to whom I introduced Morelli, was
charmed by his conversation, and pronounced his books to
be amongst the most delightful and instructive that he had
ever read ; and Browning, from his knowledge of the early
Italian painters and of their works, had some claim to be a
judge.

During the winter of 1890-91 Morelli suffered from
a distressing difficulty of breathing, which he attributed
to asthma and a bronchial attack. About the end of February I received a letter from him which caused me much
anxiety. He told me that his medical adviser had found
that his heart was seriously affected, and had ordered him
complete rest, forbidding all mental as well as physical exer-
tion. I wrote at once to his friend Dr. Frizzoni, to ask whether
there were grounds for alarm. His answer confirmed the
account that Morelli had given me of himself. A day or
two later I received a letter from this gentleman, written at
Morelli's dictation, asking me to examine a picture in the
Venice Academy which he believed to be an old copy of a
lost original by Giorgione. From his description, I had no
difficulty in finding it. My reply reached him on his death-
bed. In his wanderings he constantly talked of his favourite
painter, whose name was almost the last word upon his lips.

Morelli died on February 28, 1891. As a senator he would have been entitled to a public funeral, and the people of Milan and Bergamo would have hastened to show their respect and esteem for their illustrious fellow-citizen by doing honour to his remains. But his modest nature was opposed to all display. He requested by his will that he should be quietly and privately buried in the public cemetery of Milan at five o'clock in the morning—an hour at which only a few relations and attached friends were likely to be present. His wishes in this respect were strictly attended to.

Expressions of sorrow at his death came from all parts of Italy. The Minister of Public Instruction, Signor Villari, the eminent historian of Savonarola and Macchiavelli, sent the following touching telegram to the Marquis Visconti Venosta: 'I am deeply grieved by the death of the Senator Giovanni Morelli, my dearest friend, the valiant soldier of his country, the learned and original illustrator of Italian art. I request you to represent the Ministry at the funeral of the illustrious departed.' The town-council of Bergamo at once met to testify their sorrow at the death of their adopted citizen, who had brought fame to their city, and to express their regret that in obedience to his desire they were unable to do him further honour by attending his funeral. Signor Farini, the President of the Senate, in announcing to that body the decease of their colleague, thus spoke of him amidst general and unusual signs of sympathy and approval. 'Although his nature forbade his taking part in the daily struggles of political life, he was never absent from solemn debates concerning the highest interests of the State. A true appreciation of facts, moderation

without weakness, a firm faith in his own principles and in
his friends, guided his conduct in the two branches of the
Legislature. . . . Modesty, fortitude, rectitude, gave to the
life of Morelli a wonderful moral completeness.   His will,'
the President added, 'was an epilogue worthy of his lofty
character, his generous heart, and his patriotism.'   By this
will he bequeathed his choice collection of pictures to the city
of Bergamo, a considerable sum to its charities, and 100,000
francs to be invested, the accumulated interest of which was
to be given every three years to the youth—a native of the
city or province of Bergamo—who had most distinguished
himself in scientific studies; the prize to be 5,000 lire, to
go towards completing his studies in one of the German
Universities.   His valuable collection of drawings he left to
Dr. Gustavo Frizzoni; whom he also appointed custodian
of the pictures he had bequeathed to the city of Bergamo.
As Dr. Frizzoni is in possession of the materials which
Morelli had collected for his third unpublished volume,
and for that on the drawings of the old masters, it is to be
hoped that he will be able to complete his master's work.

I know of only three portraits of Morelli : one a drawing
in chalk by the Empress Frederick, which has been reproduced in the ' Archivio Storico dell' Arte ' for March and
April 1891, and two by the celebrated German painter
Lenbach, which convey some idea of his features but none
of his character.[7]

That the translation of Morelli's last work now published
will prove a most valuable contribution to the history of
Italian art I cannot doubt.   No one could engage in a study

[7] A photograph taken of him after death well represents his noble features.

of Italian painting, or could pretend to connoisseurship, or could even fully enjoy the pictures of the great Italian masters, without availing himself of it as a guide and text-book. A highly competent critic, Mr. Claude Phillips, has justly observed [8] that it would be as absurd to return to a pre-Morellian period of criticism, as it would be to study natural science without profiting by the discoveries of Darwin, and has written of his last work that it is worthy to take its place as a succinct, but none the less invaluable, book of reference, an acquaintance with the conclusions of which will be indispensable to those who pretend to any systematic study of Italian art in its greatest and more representative phase. The fame of Morelli as the most accomplished of art-critics and connoisseurs will increase as time rolls on, and his name will be honoured when those of his detractors will only be remembered by the blunders which they committed and which he exposed.

Such was Morelli, the 'quack doctor' and 'Romanised Swiss' of the German professor, but the gifted critic and true patriot of his own countrymen and of those who are capable of appreciating his worth.

A. H. LAYARD.

VENICE: *December* 1891.

[8] See *The Academy* of May 3, 1890.

c

# PREFACE.

THE present work relates principally to two Roman galleries and to pictures in Italy; in time I hope to supplement it by two further volumes, dealing with the galleries of Munich, Dresden and Berlin, and though each volume may be regarded as independent and complete in itself, the three together will form a single work, comprising all my 'Critical Studies on Italian Painters,' added to and in part rewritten.

The notice of the Borghese gallery is a much-altered and revised edition of some articles, which originally appeared in Von Lützow's 'Zeitschrift für bildende Kunst,' in the years 1874, 1875, and 1876. If report is to be trusted, they were more favourably received at the time of their publication by the younger, and consequently less biased, students of art than I had any reason to expect, considering the dryness of the subject; but I never doubted for a moment what would be the opinion of older critics with regard to them. I might have predicted that they would either pay no attention to my views and suggestions, or would dismiss them with an incredulous smile, if indeed—a not unprecedented occurrence—they did not claim them as their own. It was therefore to the younger generation of art-students, Russian, German, and English, that I hoped to appeal in these essays, and also to those few persons who visit Italy in order to fit themselves for the scientific study of art, and who might desire their judgment to be free and independent in a picture gallery, instead of allowing it to be guided by others. I should never, however, have thought of reprinting these papers, had not indulgent readers of my book on 'Italian Masters in German Galleries,' which appeared some years later but has long been out of print, urged me to republish it together with the articles on the Borghese gallery. I felt disposed more readily to accede to their request as, since they were written, I am conscious of having made some progress in knowledge of art, and am thus enabled to rectify mistakes that I may have previously committed. The articles have now been almost entirely rewritten; a notice of the Doria gallery has been added, and pictures in other Roman and Italian collections have been incidentally mentioned. I have also endeavoured, in a kind of introduction, entitled 'Principles and Method,' to give my younger fellow-students an account of the curious circumstances which first led me to become an art-critic. Practically, therefore, this volume may be regarded as a new work. This introduction, it should be observed, is not intended for persons well-versed in the history of art, and may be omitted by them. What I have said on former occasions must be repeated here, namely, that, far from regarding my own opinions and judgments as infallible, I am quite ready to admit that, even in this new and revised edition, I may have committed mistakes; but, as in the attribution of Italian pictures confusion still reigns supreme, and is seemingly on the increase, I think I may be permitted to state my views, and to give my readers an opportunity of testing them. The entire responsibility for the opinions I have expressed, however, rests with me; hence, in order that the student may always know with whom he has to deal, every picture and drawing renamed by me is marked throughout this work with a cross. (†)

If, in course of time, it is evident that my attributions are incorrect, the blame will attach to me alone; if, on the other hand, they stand the test and prove sound, the merit will be due to me— that is to say, to the experimental method which I recommend. Some of my opponents in Italy, indeed, maintain that this method is by no means new, but was adopted by Padre Lanzi, and by the brothers de Goncourt of Paris. I will not question this statement, for, as there is nothing new under the sun, it may eventually transpire that this identical method was well known to some Chinese art-historian three or four thousand years ago ; only it appears to me that, whatever the method may be, everything depends upon the way in which it is applied. But, supposing my opponents to be correct in their assertions, how comes it, I would venture to ask, that the erroneous names formerly borne by many pictures in the galleries of Europe, and now for the most part corrected at my suggestion, were not rectified years ago by Padre Lanzi, the brothers de Goncourt, and others? And, moreover, were this statement well-founded, how is it that some of my other opponents, more especially in Germany, have sought to make this method for the decisive identification of the author of a picture appear ridiculous, by proclaiming that I am insensible to every deeper quality in a work of art, and regard only its external features, laying particular stress upon the form of the hand, the ear, and even, *horribile dictu*, of the finger-nails? As in the human eye we discriminate between long and short sight, so among those who study art we find that there are some who have eyes to see, and others whom the most powerful of glasses would not benefit in the slightest degree, because there are practically two kinds of sight—physical and mental. The first is that of the public at large, and writers on art have at all times traded on the boundless credulity of this class; the second belongs to a very few intelligent and unprejudiced artists and students of art. Endowed with natural capacity, it is the privilege of the latter, after long and careful study, to discern in the features, in the form and movement of the hand, in the pose of the figure—in short, in the whole outward frame—the deeper qualities of the mind; while the other class of observers, even should they happen to notice these particulars, would look upon them as meaningless. The right understanding of the outward form in a work of art, to which I attach especial importance, is not accorded to everyone. This outward form in the representation of the human figure is by no means accidental, as many contend, but is determined by inward conditions; whereas the mannerisms of some artists are simply the result of chance or habit. The typical, or fundamental, form (*Grundform*) of hand and ear is characteristic in the works of all independent masters, and affords valuable evidence for identifying them, while mannerisms may, at most, serve to distinguish those of painters wanting in individuality.

Among those critics who have openly combated my theories and my judgments on pictures, the one most deserving of notice, both on account of his official position and of his energy and activity, is Dr. William Bode, director of the Berlin gallery, who enjoys a considerable reputation in his own country and in Paris.

I may have secret foes, more relentless perhaps, as Dr. Bode has observed, than himself; let me hope so at least, for I hold that, under existing circumstances, writings on art which do not raise a storm of opposition can have little real merit. Dr. Bode attacks me, among other reasons, because I venture to differ from Messrs. Crowe and Cavalcaselle, his teachers and guides, and to characterise their writings as misleading. He accuses me, as a former student of medicine, of being a mere empiric; and further, though following me closely in my own studies, he affirms that I have no knowledge of Leonardo da Vinci or of the Milanese school and its principal representatives—Sodoma, Boltraffio, Gianpietrino, Solario, Ambrogio de Predis, and Bernardino de' Conti; that I am equally ignorant of Timoteo Viti and Raphael in the Umbrian school, of the Pollajuoli, Verrocchio, and Raffaellino del Garbo in the Florentine, and of Jacopo de' Barbari and Mantegna in the Venetian. In short, he would give his readers to understand that I am a mere interloper, wholly unqualified to speak on the subject of Italian painting, and that my superficial teaching ' must necessarily lead to the most fatal dilettanteism.' From his point of view Dr. Bode is no doubt in the right; for, if my theories and opinions are correct, then

his must of necessity be radically wrong, and
*vice versâ*, as in everything we are unfortunately
diametrically opposed. What appears black to me
is white to him, and pictures which in his eyes are
masterpieces of art, in mine are, as a rule, simply
feeble works of the school. Yet neither of us is
guided by party feeling, but solely by a love of truth,
and we each estimate and describe things exactly
as we see them. This curious psychological
problem may perhaps be explained, partly by
the diversity of our individual training—Dr. Bode
having originally been destined for the law and I for
a medical career—and partly by the action and influence of climate and surroundings. Karl Ritter, the
most celebrated geographer of our day, has pro-
pounded a theory that the human species in its
most perfect form is developed in North Germany ;
if this were the case, Dr. Bode would, of course, if
only from the accident of birth, have a considerable
advantage over me. As, however, the eminent
North-German geographer's argument cannot, I think,
be accepted as conclusive, and should, moreover, be
taken in a general and not in an individual sense,
I will say no more on the subject. 'Every one has his
fancy,' and every one, I may add, thinks he knows
best. This being the case, it does not require much
foresight to predict, that the confusion resulting
from such conflicting opinions about the same pictures

d

must be disastrous to the study of Italian art. I
would advise Dr. Bode therefore to follow my example, and to refer the decision of all such points on
which we cannot agree to intelligent and unprejudiced arbiters, qualified for the task. Whatever be their verdict, we may console ourselves
with the thought that the scientific study of art,
which we both have so much at heart, will eventually
be furthered by these means. Hence, in the following
studies I have quoted Dr. Bode's views, as expressed
by him in the fifth edition of Burckhardt's 'Cicerone,'
placing them side by side with my own opinions.

When mention is made of the works of Messrs.
Crowe and Cavalcaselle, I refer to the original
English edition of 'A New History of Painting in
Italy'[1] and of 'A History of Painting in North
Italy.'[2] When I quote Passavant's 'Raphael' it is
from the French edition—'Raphael d'Urbin et son
père G. Santi, par J. D. Passavant. Édition française,
refaite, corrigée, et considérablement augmentée par
l'auteur, et revue et annotée par M. Paul Lacroix.'[3]

For quotations, &c. from Vasari, Le Monnier's
Florentine edition has always been used.[4]

One word more respecting the illustrations in this
work. Some of my readers may consider that they
are too few in number, others that they are too many.

---

[1] 3 vol . London, 1866.
[2] 2 vols. London, 1871.
[3] 2 vols. Paris, 1860.
[4] 13 vols. 1846.

It was no easy task for me to keep within the limits which a book of this kind should not overstep. My choice was, of course, mainly guided by the idea that the illustrations were to render the meaning of the text as plain as possible to the reader. I confined myself, therefore, to such as appeared to me strictly necessary, assuming that they who intend to make a more serious study of the forms would go to the works of art themselves. For the purpose of the book, the number of illustrations is, I think, sufficient.

I take this opportunity of expressing my gratitude to Dr. J. P. Richter, and to my publisher Herr Brockhaus. The former was good enough to look through my manuscript, and to point out various deficiencies; he also undertook to make a full and complete index—a task which he has admirably fulfilled. The latter spared neither trouble nor expense to meet my views, and it is due to his knowledge of the subject that the illustrations are so satisfactory.

IVAN LERMOLIEFF.

Gorlaw: *October* 1889.

## NOTICE TO THE READER.

W<small>HILST</small> this volume was passing through the press the Borghese gallery was removed to the Villa Borghese outside the walls of Rome; the pictures have been re-arranged and re-numbered, and some are no longer to be found in the collections. Considerable changes have also taken place in the Doria-Pamfili gallery. The Translator has obtained, through the kindness of the Rev. H. W. Pullen, the information required to enable her to make the necessary alterations in Signor Morelli's references to pictures in these two collections. Those mentioned by him which have disappeared have been marked with a *.

It is reported that the celebrated " Violin Player " attributed to Raphael, and other well-known pictures formerly in the Sciarra-Colonna gallery, have been sold and sent out of Italy.

Unfortunately the process of re-arrangement and re-numbering of pictures has recently been going on to a greater or less extent throughout the galleries of Europe, and it has been impossible for the translator to readjust them in all cases; but Signor Morelli's descriptions are so lucid that she does not anticipate that the reader will have any difficulty in identifying the various pictures to which he refers.

# PRINCIPLES AND METHOD.

*Dans les choses du monde presque toute question n'est qu'une question de méthode.*—LA BRUYÈRE.

As I was leaving the Pitti one afternoon, I found myself descending the stairs in company with an elderly gentleman, apparently an Italian of the better class. I had frequently noticed him in the galleries, either alone or with several younger companions, and his unusual intelligence in observing and discussing pictures had often struck me. On that particular afternoon I was greatly impressed by all I had seen : by the splendour of the rooms, by the masterpieces of art, more especially a landscape by Rubens which I had studied just before leaving, and by the beauty of the gardens with their pines, cypresses, and ilex groves. As we left the palace, I could not refrain from expressing to this gentleman my admiration of Brunelleschi's stately pile.

'I never should have believed,' I added, 'that so magnificent an edifice could have been erected under a Republic.'

'And why not?' inquired my companion smiling. 'Do you suppose that art is dependent on the form of government? Provided outward circumstances be favourable, I should imagine that art, like religion, will flourish equally under republican or despotic rule. As you seem to appreciate our great architect,' he continued, 'may I invite you to accompany me to the Villa Rucciano, also built by

B

Brunelleschi for his wealthy fellow-citizen, Luca Pitti? It is not far off, and the evening is fine and balmy.'

I thanked him for his kind proposal, and observed that, being a Russian, and in Italy for the first time, I had never heard of the Villa, which was not even mentioned in my guide-book.

'Guide-books,' he remarked in a slightly ironical tone, 'are written for the great body of tourists who have no desire to be overdone with sightseeing. Travelling in these days is regarded more as a duty than as a pleasure. The modern tourist's first object is to arrive at a certain point; once there, he disposes of the allotted sights as quickly as possible, and hurries on resignedly to fresh fields, where the same programme is repeated. In the way we live nowadays, a man has scarcely time to collect his thoughts. The events of each day glide past like dissolving views, effacing one another in turn. There is thus a total absence of repose, without which enjoyment of art is an impossibility.'

'Too true unfortunately,' I rejoined; 'I myself travelled from Munich to Florence, viâ Verona and Bologna, and did not stop to see either of these places even superficially, though no doubt they are both full of interest. As an excuse, I must plead that the endless books on art and æsthetics, which I read in Germany and Paris, had given me such a positive distaste for the subject and all connected with it, that I came to Italy vowing not to visit a single church or picture gallery. Florence, however, soon forced me to abandon this resolution.'

'Then you were formerly an admirer of art, and it was your sojourn in Germany and Paris which gave rise to this aversion to it?'

'Distaste, perhaps, but scarcely aversion,' I rejoined.

'Brought on probably by too much reading,' said my

new friend. 'The truth is, art must be seen, if we are to derive either instruction or pleasure from it.'

'A very different view is taken in Germany, my dear sir,' said I. 'There people will only read, and art must be brought to public notice, not through the medium of brush or chisel, but through that of the printing press.'

'Unhappily,' resumed the Italian, 'we live in an age when writing and publishing are epidemic in Europe; when every one appears to think it his bounden duty to proclaim his own ignorance in this manner.'

'Yes,' I said, 'these unfortunate people ruin their eye-sight and fritter away the best part of their time in reading and writing, and how few among them understand the art of living!'

'Climatic conditions may have something to do with this psychological phenomenon,' observed my guide; 'raw foggy days, and long cold evenings, are an incentive to men to study, and Germany, from its geographical position, is peculiarly fitted to be the parent of a nation of thinkers, writers, and readers, just as sea-girt lands develop a race of merchants and sailors. In my youth—now, alas! long past—I spent some years in Germany. I have a great regard for the Germans; they are a most estimable and learned race, and no other nation under the sun has applied itself with equal ardour to the study of our great painters. Their weak point is, that they write far too much about them, and, worse still, publish their writings too hastily, unmindful of the counsel of Horace to Piso: *nonumque prematur in annum*, though it appears to me that these words apply to writers on art, even more than to poets. A bad poem is like an empty nut, we simply throw it away and there is an end of it; but the publication of erroneous views and false criticism concerning works of art does in-calculable harm: they are taken up and repeated by the ignorant multitude, and the author, if only from sheer vanity, will not recall his words.'

'You are perfectly right,' I said; 'such superficial writers always appear to me the impersonation of vanity.'

'These youthful seekers after knowledge,' he continued, 'come flocking over the Alps, and you may see them any fine morning armed with red and brown guide-books, hungering and thirsting for information, and taking stock of churches and galleries with irrepressible ardour. It is positively delightful to watch them! And you may occasionally find amongst them really competent connoisseurs, who can appreciate our old masters far better—to our shame be it said—than we ourselves, who live on the spot.'

'For Heaven's sake!' I cried, 'don't speak to me of art-connoisseurs. I read so many controversial publications about them when in Germany, that I am sick of the subject. You must know,' I added, seeing that my friend seemed startled by my vehemence, 'that the professors who bring out volumes on the history of art are the bitterest foes of the connoisseurs, while the painters in their turn abuse both. It has been said, sarcastically, that the art-connoisseur is distinguished from the art-historian by knowing something of early art. If he happens to be of the better sort he abstains from writing on the subject. On the other hand, the art-historian, although writing much upon art, really knows nothing about it; whilst the painters who boast of their technical knowledge are neither competent critics nor competent historians.'

The Italian, who apparently had never heard of this paper war in Germany, laughed heartily at my description, but observed, as he paused for an instant to muse on the matter, that the subject seemed likely to foster an interesting controversy. Then he went on his way for a time in thoughtful silence, till, reaching a green spot near the Arno, he suggested that we should sit down and rest. It was a beautiful autumn evening; the dark slender tower of the Palazzo Vecchio shot up proudly into the sky; in the distance lay the blue hills of Pistoia and Pescia, bathed in golden light.

As we sat down, he began again: 'You say that in Germany and Paris art-historians do not acknowledge art-connoisseurs, and *vice versâ* ?'

'No, no,' I said, 'art-connoisseurs say of art-historians that they write about what they do not understand; art-historians, on their side, disparage the connoisseurs, and only look upon them as the drudges who collect materials for them, but who personally have not the slightest knowledge of the physiology of art.'

'It appears to me,' said my companion, 'that the French and German professors have been rather hasty in their judgment, and have hardly given the matter due attention. The controversy is one of very long standing, and by no means without interest, but deserves unbiased and impartial criticism. What is an art-connoisseur after all,' he added, 'but one who understands art ?'

'Decidedly so, to judge by the name,' I said. 'An art-historian, on the other hand,' I continued, 'is one who traces the history of art from its earliest development to its final decay, and who describes the process to us. Is it not so ?'

'It certainly ought to be,' rejoined the Italian. 'But in order to write or discourse about the development of any subject, we ought first to be thoroughly acquainted with it. No one, for instance, would dream of writing on physiology without having first mastered anatomy.'

'Of course not,' I replied.

'The botanist is bound to understand plants,' he proceeded, 'and the zoologist animals, so as to be able to distinguish a fig from a pumpkin at a glance, or the young lion from the domestic cat ; in the same way the art-historian must be well acquainted with architecture, sculpture, and painting if he would gain a clear idea of his subject, and give his listeners or readers a correct summary of it.  An early writer has observed : " He who climbs a mountain before becoming familiar with the plain is unable to say, when he reaches the top, whether the trees he looks down upon are olives, cypresses, poplars, or willows ; whether the character of the landscape, in short, is southern or northern."  I take it, therefore, that we must first know something of the plain, if we are to form a general impression of, or to describe, the country around, as seen from a height.   Otherwise our description would be merely a string of empty, pointless phrases and high-sounding platitudes, which would apply equally to any other landscape.'

'You may say the same of most of the books dealing with the history of art,' I rejoined.

'In former days, I admit, this was the case all over Europe,' said the Italian.  'The history of art was then commonly taught by men absolutely devoid of any real feeling for art, mostly æsthetic *literati* or pedantic archæologists, who had gleaned all their information from the writings of their predecessors, or had picked it up from the discourses of the professors in the academies.  But nowadays, I hear, things are very different in England and France, and especially in Germany, where every university has its art-professorship filled by distinguished and learned men, who year by year train up a certain number of able scholars to follow in their steps.'

'Alas! far too many,' I replied.  'Even in Germany, that hotbed of learning, your type of professor is the exception and not the rule, and even there the text, "by their fruits ye shall know them," is by no means inapplicable.

Take, for example, the man whose enthusiasm for art has been stimulated in the lecture-hall—how does he behave in a picture gallery ? Very much like a rustic in a menagerie ; or, if he be one of the learned and cultivated, he approaches the pictures in a kind of æsthetic abstraction, not knowing exactly what to make of them. The lecturer's elaborate definition of the " beautiful " debars one scholar from seeing any beauty in the painting before him, whether by Titian or Correggio. The different names of the artists so bewilder another, that he finds it impossible to think of the pictures at all. The unfortunate youth is struggling vainly to recollect whether he is to rank Perugino above Botticelli, or Titian above Giorgione, and *vice versâ* ; and you must remember that I am only speaking now of the most cultivated classes. As to the general public who throng picture galleries, all they care for in painting and statuary is to compare the counterfeit with its prototype, true to the principle that art should be nothing but the ape of nature. Needless to add, that for a portrait by Denner or Seibold; these worthy people would pass by a Titian or a Holbein hanging near.'

'Unfortunately,' observed my companion, 'this is very much the case with us, though every educated man ought to have gathered enough from his instructor to enable him to appreciate a picture, or a statue, as much as a good poem or novel.'

'How can you expect this, my dear sir,' I broke in, 'if the teacher himself is ignorant of the language of art ; if he crams his audience with a series of æsthetic platitudes, and can produce nothing for their benefit but a string of dry names and dates, and untrustworthy biographies ? I should have thought that his first duty would be to point out to his pupils the characteristic features in a work of art. They should be taught to feel at home among the dry, archaic, *quattro-centisti* painters, and to hold intelligent converse with them. By this means their enjoyment would be heightened when they came to see the glorious works of Raphael, Titian, Giorgione, or Correggio. How is it that, even in Germany, educated people know so little what to make of the great Albert Dürer? Simply because they have not learnt to see; because Dürer's mode of expressing himself—angular and often unlovely as it is, yet always full of character—is unintelligible to them.'

'All this is very depressing,' said the Italian, 'but I should have said it was only in Italy, where the proverb *inertia est sapientia* still holds good, that education was so backward, and that everywhere else in Europe, and especially in Germany, great strides had been made in knowledge of art, just as much as in other sciences. I fear, however,' he added, smiling, ' that you take pleasure in painting the case blacker than it really is. It is easy to understand that *dilettanti*, not only in Italy but in France, Russia, England and Germany, should prefer the sweets of material enjoyment, both in art and literature, to the pure delight which real knowledge has to offer, for only through prolonged and arduous toil is that to be attained. We cannot possibly hope to understand a work of art unless we have first succeeded in analysing it, and from the analysis have passed to the synthesis; though such refinement of perception is not to be expected of the multitude. The educated public in Germany, however, is a very large body, larger than that of all the other countries of Europe put together, and I scarcely think that they would read so many books on art unless they hoped to derive from them something beyond mere satisfaction to the senses, and——·

'My dear sir,' I interrupted, ' an educated man, who has

the patience to wade through the ponderous tomes on art, which are annually recommended to his notice, knows about as much of the subject by the time he has got to the end of them as he knew at the beginning; this, at least, is my personal experience. He may have revelled in the fine writing, and no doubt may have acquired quite a stock of new painters' names, and a string of the latest and most approved art-terms, with which to do great execution at the next social gathering; but, beyond that, all these names and dates, these well-turned sentences and fine theories, are mere empty nothings, and practically worthless.'

'If I am to believe you then,' said the Italian, 'really competent professors of the history of art are very scarce in Europe, and for the simple reason that men still go on in the old groove—studying art from books only, instead of from the works of art themselves.'

'This may be one reason,' I replied; 'the superficial dabbler, who causes confusion and anarchy in science, just as much as in politics, owes his existence to the pernicious influence of many inferior teachers.'

'Very true,' returned my companion; 'I have always felt that men who set up to teach others should first get a clear idea themselves of the works which practically constitute art, should study these works, be they of painting, sculpture, or architecture, with intelligence, analyse them, distinguish between good and bad specimens —in a word, should thoroughly understand them.'

'I suppose you refer to what may be termed "art morphology," that is, to the understanding of the outward forms in a work of art; and in a measure, I allow that you are right. But a German art-philosopher would tell you that the idea existed in the mind of the artist long before the visible part of his work took shape; that the task of

c

the art-historian is to grasp, fathom, and explain this idea—the main problem he has to solve being, how to attain to a fundamental understanding of a work of art. The historian himself would tell you that the history of art should direct attention, not so much to the works of art themselves, as to the culture of the people under whose influence and auspices these works originated.'

'Then, in that case,' rejoined the Italian, 'setting aside the fact that it is almost impossible to penetrate to the inward part of anything without being first acquainted with its outward conditions, the history of art may be said to resolve itself into a physiological treatise on art on the one hand, and a history of civilisation on the other; both excellent branches of philosophy in their way, but scarcely adapted to promote a taste for art, or to further its knowledge. I do not deny that the causes of certain changes in style can only be satisfactorily explained by reference to the history of culture, though such cases are not so common as is usually asserted. You must not suppose, however,' he added promptly, 'that I am not fully aware how desirable it is for a professor to lead his scholars from time to time into higher regions of thought, and, for the nonce, to leave alone the study of form and technical execution. I consider that the instructor should then direct the attention of his pupils, not to the details, but to the work as a whole; should explain to them the links connecting the epochs of development in art, and should teach them finally to rise above mere facts, and to measure their value. Such flights, however, should only be taken within proper limits and at a favourable moment: otherwise the scholar is apt to relapse into the old error of approaching a work of art with preconceived notions, of seeing in it his own ideas, instead of allowing it to speak for itself. A question earnestly and intelligently asked of a painting or statue will undoubtedly evoke an answer. The first thing, therefore, for a scholar to learn is, how to put that question with intelligence. Thus we come back again to the main point, that the basis of all art study is the form and the technic. Observation and experience,' he added, 'are the foundation of every science: *Per varios usus artem experientia fecit, exemplo monstrante viam.*'

'All this sounds well enough,' I answered, 'and may be very desirable, but you do not appear to consider the expenditure of time and money your method is likely to entail. In all probability it would scare away most beginners from the study of art—for who could afford to become an art-historian at that rate?—and hundreds of persons would thus be deprived of their daily bread.'

'We will leave "daily bread" entirely out of the question,' said my companion drily. 'Those who treat art or science as a milch cow, which is to furnish them with the means of subsistence, had better turn banker, lawyer, innkeeper, or chemist. The pursuit of art as I understand it does, undoubtedly, require long years of study; but I think you rather overrate the pecuniary cost. As the botanist lives among his fresh or dried plants, the mineralogist among his stones, the geologist among his fossils, so the art-connoisseur ought to live among his photographs and, if his finances permit, among his pictures and statues. This is his world, and here he learns to see with the trained and cultivated eye of an artist, for *visus, qui nisi est verus, ratio quoque falsa sic omnis.* Yet, for all this, he must never neglect the study of nature. To understand a work of art thoroughly he must be an artist himself—that is to say, he must learn to look at all around him with an artist's eye.'

'You expect too much from a young connoisseur,'

said I, 'and I think lay yourself open to attack. Let me ask you one thing: how do you expect a beginner in the study of art to distinguish the photograph of a genuine work from that of a spurious painting? for in these days good and bad, weeds and flowers, are all photographed promiscuously.'

'Why,' returned the Italian, 'of what use are lectures on the history of art if not to make us think and see for ourselves; to teach us how to distinguish true from false, important from worthless? Why do we go to school? Not merely to be told by word of mouth what we could read for ourselves at home with infinitely less trouble; but in order that the stirring and suggestive words of the teacher may inspire us with enthusiasm for art; that we may learn, by the examples he brings forward, how to discriminate merit in a work of art, and to recognise the characteristic features of each master, his peculiarities in the choice and conception of his subject, in the representation of form, and in the harmony of colour.'

'But we have already seen,' I remarked, 'that the teacher, such as you would have him to be, is very difficult to find, and I think that on the whole you are too exacting in what you require from art-historians. How can anyone in our short life attain to a comprehensive knowledge of all the old masters, and least of all a professor or a director of a gallery, who, in addition to all his other labours, has to bring out his books and catalogues? How, in the name of reason, is he to find time to examine and test everything himself, and moreover to extend his studies even to second- and third-rate painters; and how, unless he be a connoisseur himself, is he to decide whether the discoveries of others are of any value or not? for you must bear in mind that there are quite as many ciphers among connoisseurs as among art-historians. No! what we have a right to

require of them is, that they should be conversant with the
founders and principal masters of each school, and be
able to discriminate between their genuine works and those
of their pupils and imitators, so as not to fall into the
errors, common enough in these days, of making Michael
Angelo responsible for statues, and Verrocchio, or even
Leonardo, for paintings, which, when examined with the
eye of common sense, prove to be nothing but feeble works
of the school.'

'What you say is fair enough,' returned my companion;
'the question is, whether one condition can be attained
without the other. We can only judge of a man's nature
and merits aright by comparing him with others—either
with his superiors or his inferiors. Let us take a very
common case : suppose your art-historian visits a picture
gallery mainly to study Titian; would it be possible for
him, if he be really in earnest, to neglect the works which
he meets with at every turn, by the great forerunners
and contemporaries of the master? I should imagine
that his thirst for knowledge would naturally lead him
from the study of Titian's works to those of the Bellini, of
Carpaccio, Giorgione, Lorenzo Lotto, Pordenone, Palma,
&c. But setting this aside, you allow, do you not, that
every art-historian is bound to know enough about the
great representatives of each school to distinguish them
from their pupils and imitators with some amount of
certainty ?'

'Yes,' I replied, 'that seems little enough to expect.'

'And do you suppose,' said my companion, stopping
and looking at me with a smile, 'that it is such a simple
matter ? The study of the works of Raphael or Leonardo
presupposes a thorough acquaintance with all the other
Italian schools. To gain a more intimate knowledge of
these two great artists, to form a right judgment of

their merits, and to be able to indicate what special benefits
they conferred on their schools in point of conception,
representation, and technic, we must both study every
example of the school whence these masters emanated,
and must learn to estimate the merits of their predecessors and contemporaries, as well as of their immediate
scholars.  Unless our judgment rests on this sure and solid
foundation, it will always remain one-sided and deficient,
and we cannot lay claim to any real understanding of
art.'

'But, my dear sir,' I broke in, 'the elaborate and tedious
course of study which you appear to think incumbent on
an art-historian would end by turning him into a mere
connoisseur, and would leave him no time at all for studying the history of art itself.'

The Italian smiled.  'You have hit the right nail on
the head,' he said; 'true enough, your art-historian will
gradually disappear (no great loss either, you will admit),
and in due course of time, as the larva develops into the
butterfly, the connoisseur will emerge from his chrysalis
state.'

This triumphant rejoinder caused me rather an unpleasant surprise.  'I cannot agree with you here,' I said,
'and as a proof that you are in the wrong, or, at all events,
that you expect far too much from art-historians, let me
mention two of the most recent publications about Raphael,
which have appeared respectively in Paris and Berlin—
the two great centres of all historical research in matters
of art.  The first is a magnificent volume, and was received
with acclamation, not only in Paris, but I may almost say
throughout the whole civilised world.  The second, the work
of a professor of art at Berlin, was greeted with rapturous
applause, at all events on the banks of the Spree.  Both
writers are art-historians of the first water, but by no

means connoisseurs; indeed, both would be mortally offended if you were to characterise them as such, for even to look at pictures irritates them.'

The Italian burst out laughing. 'I should never dream of such a thing,' he said. 'No, no, my dear sir,' he continued with growing excitement, 'it is only after profound and earnest study that a lover of art develops, gradually and insensibly, into a connoisseur, and finally into an art-historian, provided he has it in him, which of course is a *conditio sine quâ non*. Every young man may begin life with the intention of becoming a priest, a lawyer, a professor, an engineer, a land-surveyor, or a doctor; if he be well off he may even aspire to become a deputy to the Parliament; but it would be simply ludicrous if a youth of twenty or twenty-four were to say: 'I am going to be an art-critic, or perhaps even an art-historian.'

'And yet,' I observed, 'this is what constantly occurs, especially when a man has been unsuccessful in other professions.'

'Such cases are of no great consequence,' said my companion, 'so long as they are the exception and not the rule; they will occur in every department of knowledge, in science as well as in art. But, to resume our discussion. All that I wish to contend is that the germ of the art-historian, if it exist at all, can only develop and ripen in the brain of the connoisseur; in other words, it is absolutely necessary for a man to be a connoisseur before he can become an art-historian, and to lay the foundations of his history in the gallery and not in the library.'

'The view you take is the one that has always appeared to me the most rational,' said I; 'namely, that no one should take up the study of art who has not a very decided capacity for it, and that the study of the works of art

themselves can alone fit a man for the task of writing a
history of art. Theoretically a man may be possessed of
the highest cultured taste and yet be devoid of a spark
of real feeling for art. *Exempla sunt odiosa.*'

'True enough,' said my companion; 'yet nearly all
recent writers on art in Italy are "æsthetes," and for
the most part of an extremely uninteresting race. The
aim and object of their writings is to dazzle and mislead
the reading public by fine language, high-flown descriptions
of the pictures, and more or less *piquant* analogies.
There may be some who appreciate this kind of thing,
but a reader who is really in earnest will soon find that
there is no lasting benefit to be gained from it; it only
bores him and blunts his perceptions. Italian art-historians, more especially local investigators, and persons
employed by Government in public institutions and galleries, cling to tradition with the most dogged pertinacity,
no matter how puerile and absurd it may be.'

'I can assure you,' said I, 'this state of things is not
peculiar to Italy, it is just as bad in Russia. If you have
managed to secure any official post, it would be as much as
your place was worth to cast any slur upon tradition. You
would completely ruin yourself by trampling on the
cherished prejudices of all your patrons and clients.'

'Tradition is not to be altogether despised,' said the
Florentine; 'I only wish to protest against its being taken
for gospel and made to stifle the voice of criticism. As an
aid to identifying works of art, it has certainly little claim
to be trusted. How many absurd tales about men and
events, even in the history of our own times, after being
freely circulated, have been invested with the halo of
tradition! How often, again, has not recent criticism
exposed the falsity of legends which have come down to us
as "tradition," and has rooted them out from the history

of nations where they had flourished for so long. Years of experience have taught me to regard this fungus-growth of tradition, which surrounds so many works of art, and the personality of so many old masters, with extreme suspicion, and I think my distrust is not altogether unfounded. For the origin of these traditions is not far to seek. Often it may be traced to carelessness or to party-feeling, occasionally even to man's natural tendency to invest the most trivial incidents concerning himself with interest, misrepresenting, and even sometimes distorting them past recognition, by exaggeration or the reverse. The value of such traditions in the history of all nations is not great, and in the history of art it is even of less importance. A few examples may serve to convince you that this kind of testimony, so dear to art-historians, is only to be accepted with the greatest caution. According to tradition, the painter Andrea del Castagno murdered his friend and fellow-worker, Domenico Veneziano, till a document, discovered by Signor Milanesi, the well-known director of the Florence archives, proved beyond a doubt that the supposed murderer died before his victim. Tradition, again, relates that Leonardo da Vinci expired in the arms of the art-loving Francis I. It has, however, been incontestably shown that on the day of Leonardo's death the French king was not near the spot where the master breathed his last, and probably had other things to do than to perform the last offices for the dying painter. Tradition, using Vasari as a mouthpiece, proclaimed that Raphael's father had himself commended his son to Perugino. Tradition told how Giovanni Bellini, disguised as a senator, watched Antonello da Messina at work, and thus stole his secret of painting with oil as a vehicle; how Raphael made the drawings for the frescoes of his master Pintoricchio in the library at Siena; and, finally, how the much-extolled study of a beautiful Roman girl in the Barberini Gallery was the portrait of Beatrice Cenci, painted from life. As to the ridiculous names still borne by many pictures, thanks to tradition, I will not comment upon them, as I should infallibly bore you by so doing.'

'Very likely,' I replied.

'In these days,' he resumed, 'a more intelligent and unbiased method of criticism has done something towards dispelling some of these pointless and even childish fabrications; but much still remains to be done. For the present we may leave this comparatively subordinate study alone, and go back to our former theory—that the history of art can only be studied properly before the works of art themselves. Books are apt to warp a man's judgment, though at the same time I am quite ready to admit that good reproductions and representations of the art of the Egyptians, the Hindoos, the Assyrians, Chaldeans, Phœnicians, Persians, &c., and of the earliest examples of Greek art, are of the greatest value from an educational point of view, and as a means of deepening and increasing our feeling for art. But the art which we can best understand and appreciate is that which stands in the closest relation to our own era of civilisation, and books and documents will not suffice for studying it; we must go to the works of art themselves, and, what is more, to the country itself, tread the same soil and breathe the same air, where they were produced and developed. For does not Goethe say? "Wer den Dichter will verstehen muss in Dichters Lande gehen."'

' Your theory, then,' I observed, 'is that a true knowledge of art is only to be attained by a continuous and untiring study of form and technic, that no one should venture into the domain of the history of art without being first an art-connoisseur. All your arguments may be correct enough, but

my own studies are too elementary for me either to agree with,
or to differ from, you at present. One thing, however, I may
confidently affirm, namely, that all the art-historians and
connoisseurs whom I have met in Europe would treat with
contempt your theories. They would tell you that he
whom Nature had destined for a true art-historian or
critic, need not think of troubling himself about the details
upon which you lay so much stress; in his eyes it would
be sheer waste of time, and would simply deaden his intellect to do so. The *general impression* produced upon him
by a work of art, be it picture or statue, is quite sufficient to
enable him to recognise the master at the first glance, and
beyond this general impression or intuition, and tradition,
he only needs the testimony of a *written document* to arrive
at complete certainty as to its author. All other ex-
pedients could, at most, be of service only to those who know
nothing of their business—like the life-belt to the man who
cannot swim—if, indeed, they do not make confusion worse
confounded in the study of art, and foster " the most fatal
dilettanteism." '

'The same objections are raised here,' replied the
Italian, 'against the study of form and technic—that is,
against analytical research; and the loudest protests are
made by those who have neither the disposition, nor the capacity, for studying anything thoroughly. I know persons, by
no means deficient in intelligence or culture, who consider
that understanding a subject means degrading it, and are as
violently opposed to the study of form and technic in works
of art as are priests, for the most part, to physical science.
Let us weigh the matter dispassionately. You say, if I
have rightly understood you, that art-historians in Germany
and Paris only attach importance to intuition, and to documentary evidence, and regard the study of works of art as
purposeless and a waste of time. It is quite possible, I admit,

that the general impression or intuition may often be sufficient to enable an astute and well-trained eye to *guess* at
the authorship of a work of art. But the Italian proverb
is frequently verified in these cases: "l'apparenza in-
ganna"—appearances are deceitful. I maintain, therefore,
and could support my assertion by any amount of evidence, that, so long as we trust only to the general impression for identifying a work of art, instead of seeking
the surer testimony of the forms peculiar to each great
master with which observation and experience have made
us familiar, we shall continue in the same atmosphere of
doubt and uncertainty, and the foundations of the history
of art will be built as heretofore on shifting sands. According to these writers then, art-criticism, like art itself, is
inborn; is that so?'

'Yes,' I replied, 'this certainly is the view taken by
many leading critics in the present day.'

'Such theories should, I think, be taken *cum grano*,'
said my companion. 'Artistic talent is inborn in so far that
very many people come into the world without a spark of
disposition either for art or for science; but even with sufficient ability no one will attain to any results in either
branch without study, and unless surrounding circumstances be favourable. One man may be endowed with
considerable talent for art, another with a greater capacity
for science; but without study and unremitting practice
both will remain dunces. Our greatest masters—Ghiberti,
Pollajuolo, the Bellini, Correggio, and others,—and Raphael
himself—were, for the most part, the sons of artists, and
were destined and trained from their earliest youth for an
artist's career. Without this home influence many of them,
even Raphael perhaps, might have found their vocation in
trade, or in a scientific calling; and so it is with connoisseurs. They must undoubtedly have, above all things, the

perceptive faculty, and, besides, an eye for colour, and a feeling for beauty of form, and must not be addicted to philosophical crotchets; but, for all that, inborn feeling, which with practice becomes intuition, will not suffice for the science of art unless trained and developed by a study of the works of art themselves. Leonardo da Vinci said: "Fuggi i precetti di quelli speculatori, che le loro ragioni non sono confermate dalla sperientia"—"Beware of the teaching of these theorists because their reasoning is not confirmed by experience."[1] I can speak from personal experience. Educated in this country, where unfortunately such maxims have long been rife, I must plead guilty to having held the same views which you describe as prevalent in Germany and Paris—for we have been accustomed to take our cue from beyond the Alps. For years I thus groped about in the dark, trusting solely to intuition and regarding my own judgment as infallible, and I was very wroth if I happened to come across anyone who presumed to differ from me, for our judgment is governed far more by our will than by our reason. But repeated failure ended by discouraging me, and I then began to examine pictures more carefully, and to compare the painters one with another, with the result that I believe I have at length found a path which, if rightly pursued, will eventually lead us to the truth. A closer study of form and technic soon convinced me, to my great satisfaction, that this is the only road which in most cases—I will not say in every case—leads to the goal. As a matter of fact, all art-historians, from Vasari down to our own day, have only made use of two tests to aid them in deciding the authorship of a work of art—intuition, or the so-called general impression, and documentary evidence; with what result you have seen for yourself. You say that,

---

[1] See *Leonardo da Vinci* by J. P. Richter, ii. 304.

after reading much literature on art and art-criticism in Paris and Germany, you came to the conclusion that every critic thinks it necessary to set up a theory of his own.'

'Yes, unhappily this is the case,' I replied; 'all these books and pamphlets had the effect of setting me against the study of art.'

'I allow,' continued my companion, 'that a general impression is sometimes sufficient to determine whether a work of art be Italian, Flemish, or German; and, if Italian, whether of the Florentine, Venetian, or Umbrian school; and that intuition alone may occasionally enable a practised eye to identify the author of a painting or statue (even the most ordinary art-dealer possesses this kind of shrewdness), for in all intellectual matters the general conditions govern the particular. If this main question be settled, and it be assumed that the painting, or drawing, belongs to the early Florentine school, we must then make up our mind whether it be by Fra Filippo Lippi, Pesellino, Sandro Botticelli, or Filippino Lippi, or by one of the many imitators of these masters. Further, if the general impression convinces us that the painting is of the Venetian school, we must then decide if it be of the school of Venice itself or that of Padua, or, again, if it belong to that of Ferrara, or to that of Verona, &c. To arrive at a conclusion (often by no means an easy matter) the general impression is not sufficient. I have myself experienced the difficulty. Do we not find many a picture by Giovanni Bellini, even in public collections, attributed to Mantegna? Quite recently, one in the Uffizi was even ascribed to Basaïti (No. 631), and in the gallery at Verona one, still more strangely, was transferred to the Florentine school (No. 77, Sala Bernasconi). Again, do we not find early works by Correggio assigned now to Titian (Uffizi, No. 1002), now to Francia (Pavia); pictures by Fra

Bartolommeo ascribed to Albertinelli (Louvre, 1115); by
Giulio Romano to Bagnacavallo (Louvre, 1438); and by
Botticelli to Filippino Lippi (English National Gallery);
Sodoma confounded now with Leonardo da Vinci, now with
Sebastiano del Piombo, and even recently with Jan Scorel
(Frankfort); while in the Albertina [2] and at Pesth (Roxana)
his works are given to Raphael? Only by gaining a
thorough knowledge of the characteristics of each painter
—of his forms and of his colouring—shall we ever succeed
in distinguishing the genuine works of the great masters
from those of their pupils and imitators, or even from
copies; and though this method may not always lead to
absolute conviction, it, at least, brings us to the threshold.'

'That may be,' said I, 'but you must recollect that every
human eye sees form differently.'

'Exactly so,' said the Italian, 'and, for this very
reason, every great artist sees and represents these forms
in his own distinctive manner; hence, for him they become characteristic. For they are by no means the
result of accident or caprice, but of internal conditions.
You had better say,' he continued, smiling, 'that most
persons, and pre-eminently art-historians, and " art-philo-
sophers " as you call them, do not see these various forms
at all. Preferring, as their practice is, mere abstract
theories to practical examination, it is their wont to look
at a picture as if it were a mirror, in which, as a rule, they
see nothing but the reflection of their own minds. It is no
easy matter, I admit, to see form correctly—I might almost
say to feel it aright; this is partly due to the physical con-
formation of the eye; but I feel convinced that, with application and perseverance, a man of ability may attain to a
good deal. Every kind of study takes time, and our most

---

[2] The fine red chalk drawing in the Albertina has now been rightly
attributed to Sodoma.

precious endowments are not a free gift of the gods, but must be won through toil and sacrifice. The Greeks knew this, and Leonardo da Vinci himself often exclaimed when at work: " *Tu, o Dio, ci vendi tutti li beni per prezzo di fatica* "—(Thy blessings, O God, we receive not as a free gift, but we earn them by toil). For myself, I am bound to confess that twenty years of study scarcely carried me beyond the first principles of the language of form. But of course, in this, as in every other science, it depends upon the capacity of the individual whether the progress be slow or rapid. Unfortunately I only took up this interesting study comparatively late in life, when the organs of sight are not as keen as they once were, and when memory is apt to play us tricks. Like the language of a nation, the phraseology of form and colour can only be properly learnt and understood in the land of its birth. There is not the slightest doubt about that. National prejudices affect our mental vision as well as our physical sight; but in a foreign country we must gradually divest ourselves of home prepossessions. We must be in harmony with the intellectual atmosphere, as well as with the outward conditions, of the land we are in, if we are ever to feel at one with its people and its products.'

'Art and science,' I interrupted, 'are the heritage of all mankind, and acknowledge no nationality.'

'No doubt,' said the Italian, 'though the saying is one which again must be taken *cum grano*, for I maintain that each nation has its distinctive conception of science, art, and religion. Every country swears by its own lawyers, by its own philosophers, and even by its own picture-restorers, and has far more confidence in their wisdom than in that of foreigners.'

'And do you wish to make out,' I cried in amazement, 'that it takes nearly a lifetime to learn this language of form ? Well, all I can say is, that you will not make many converts to your views.'

'No matter,' replied the Italian indifferently; 'there is no need for anyone to climb the mountain who has neither inclination nor capacity for the task. Let him stay at its foot in luxurious idleness, and jeer at those who are toiling upwards if he will. For such as these the great masters assuredly did not paint. Can we possibly understand all the subtleties of poetry without first mastering the language of the poets ?'

'Perhaps not,' I said, 'but the general public will never take to your so-called language of form. The multitude can hardly distinguish between an intellectual countenance in nature and a commonplace one; at most they may notice that one man has a wart on his forehead, that another has a hare-lip, a snub-nose, or perhaps blue eyes; but they scarcely observe anything further.'

'I am perfectly well aware,' said my companion, 'that the full enjoyment of art is reserved only for a select few, and that the many cannot be expected to enter into all the subtleties, whether of the art of the Greeks and Romans, or of Dante, Shakespeare, Ariosto, Goethe, Giotto, Masaccio, Leonardo da Vinci, Giorgione, Raphael, Dürer, or Correggio. An unusually high degree of culture is requisite for this; but I contend that by means of a better system of education than that introduced by the Jesuits throughout Europe, a higher standard might be attained than is at present possible.'

'I suspect that your select few have always been remarkably rare,' said I. 'Every age has its manners, its customs, and its art. The general public, whose mental horizon is bounded by the narrow limits of their own epoch, may be incapable of understanding the art of former times ; but they are, on the other hand, fully competent to appre-

D

ciate the art of the present day—battle-pieces, *genre*, landscape, the representation of animals and still-life, the socialistic novel, and, above all, the illustrated newspapers. As to the works of the old masters, they are usually so much damaged, that I believe good copies would prove just as attractive to the public, that is to the uninitiated, as the originals themselves.'

'If not more so,' replied my companion quietly. 'I am quite of your opinion on that score. The nearer the copyist, who, of course, reproduces the original after his own manner, approaches to the taste and feeling of our own day, the greater will be the appreciation of his work by the public. Correggio's Magdalen, and the Holbein Madonna at Dresden, are instances of this, and I could cite many others equally striking.'

'I have long had the same opinion,' I said warmly, 'of the people one comes across in picture galleries.'

'We have rather drifted away from our subject,' said the Italian as he rose from the bench. 'I think, however, we are pretty well agreed, both as to the value of what is termed "tradition," and as to the state of indecision in which the general impression leaves us when we wish to identify an old picture.'

'Say, rather, we are entirely agreed,' I rejoined. 'I suppose, however, that you respect documentary evidence ?'

'Written documents,' he replied, 'are only of value in the hands of a scientifically trained and competent critic; in those of a novice in the study of art, or of a keeper of archives who understands nothing of the subject, they are not only useless, but misleading.'

'Do you mean to say,' I exclaimed, 'that you are even going to cast doubts upon the value of records which all art-historians prize so highly ?'

'The only true record for the connoisseur,' he replied

calmly, 'is the work of art itself. You may think this a bold and sweeping assertion, but I can assure you that it is not so, and I can prove it by several examples. Is there any document more likely to inspire confidence, more apparent to every spectator, than that bearing the master's own name on a picture, which we call in Italian a *cartellino*?'

'Well,' I replied, 'if every painting were signed with its author's name, there would certainly be no great merit in being a connoisseur.'

'There I cannot agree with you,' said the Italian; 'art-historians and gallery-directors are still duped by records and *cartellini*, just as in the good old days, when passports were an absolute necessity, the police were taken in by the greatest scoundrels. I could mention dozens of forged *cartellini*, of old standing and of recent date, on pictures in some of the principal galleries; the following, however, may suffice for the present. In the Doria gallery in Rome, and in the Louvre, you will find pictures by Niccolò Rondinelli of Ravenna, given to Giovanni Bellini,[3] and described and extolled as such by art-historians, misled by a forged signature. Paintings by other pupils and imitators of the master also bear the name of Giovanni Bellini; for instance, a small Madonna in the Borghese gallery,[4] and a 'Pietà' in the Poldi-Pezzoli collection at Milan,[5] two 'Madonnas' in the gallery at Padua,[6] and a 'Pietà' in the collection at Bergamo.[7] Again we find Andrea del Sarto's monogram on pictures which can only be regarded as feeble copies of originals by that great master —notably in the Doria-Pamfili and Borghese galleries. Recently, a much-darkened and unattractive painting of

---

[3] See Crowe and Cavalcaselle, *History of Painting in North Italy*, vol. i. 185, 3.

[4] *Ibid.* i. 193, 3.

[5] *Ibid.* i. 144, 1.

[6] No. 755 and No. 1273 (Legato Crescini).

[7] Crowe and Cavalcaselle, i. 143,3.

the school of Perugia, in the Turin gallery, has been taken
by many a superficial and uncritical writer for the work of
Timoteo Viti, merely because of its forged signature ; hence
this charming painter of Urbino was condemned as unworthy to have been the master of Raphael.    The great
window in the church of S. Giovanni in Monte, at Bologna,
is another proof of the value of documentary evidence ; it
represents St. John the Evangelist, and bears the initials,
C. A. F.    No one who has the least acquaintance with the
Ferrarese school can fail to recognise in it the serious spirit
and massive forms of Francesco Cossa, which differ so widely
from those of Lorenzo Costa, as well as his characteristic
drapery with its peculiar folds.    Nevertheless art-historians
and  guide-books[8]  alike  ascribe  Cossa's  work  to  Lorenzo
Costa, and why ?    Because they are incapable of reading
the painting itself, and thus of interpreting the " written
document" aright ; perhaps, too, because Vasari constantly
confounded Cossa, of whom he knew little, with Costa, a
younger Ferrarese painter, of whom he knew rather more.
On another Ferrarese painting, representing St. Sebastian,
has been inscribed by some forger the name " Laurentius
Costa " in Hebrew characters.    Everyone accordingly assigned the picture to this master, though a practised eye
would have seen at a glance that it was by Cosimo Tura,
of whom, moreover, it is a most characteristic example.
I could enumerate many more such " documents," which
have been wrongly interpreted by the unlearned, and many
signatures which were inscribed upon pictures even centuries ago with intent to deceive.    Art-historians consider
that their antiquity attests their genuineness ; and base
profound and elaborate dissertations upon them.'

 ' The less we understand of a subject,' I observed, ' the

---

* Signor Corrado Ricci, the author      agrees with me, and cites this window
of the latest guide-book of Bologna,    as the work of Francesco Cossa.

louder and more emphatic will be the admiration we express for it.'

'Now,' continued my companion, 'I must mention another kind of document—those in archives, which are constantly being reclaimed from dust and oblivion by diligent and praiseworthy inquirers. Keepers of archives, in Italy and Belgium especially, have been most indefatigable in their search for documents relating to artists and their works. Many of these records have already been, and no doubt may still be, the means of throwing light on obscure points, and of discovering the names of hitherto unknown artists. Art-history owes a debt of gratitude to these persons, among whom I may mention Gaye, a Danish writer of great learning and considerable knowledge of art; Signor Gaetano Milanesi; the late Michelangelo Gualandi of Bologna; the late learned Marchese Campori; Adolfo Venturi of Modena, a young author of merit; Signori Braghirolli and Bertolotti of Mantua; and the late Signor Cechetti of Venice, a most careful and intelligent writer, whose recent death is much to be regretted. On the other hand, many of these documents, interpreted by archivists in their own way, have been the means of propagating the gravest errors. It is, of course, hardly necessary to add that these records only make mention of large and important works executed for churches, or by order of princes. Paintings in public and private collections are for the most part small easel pictures, and documents relating to their authorship and pedigrees will scarcely be forthcoming. We are thrown either upon tradition, or upon the general impression when we have to pass judgment on them, and as the intuitive faculties differ in each individual, the conclusions arrived at must necessarily be of the most varied nature. I will cite a few examples to show you that I have not exaggerated. About 1840 a large fresco of the

"Last Supper" was discovered at Florence, in the suppressed convent of S. Onofrio, under a coating of whitewash. Writers on art, connoisseurs, and painters formed different opinions with regard to it; some even went so far as to ascribe it to Raphael, and it was engraved as his work by the late Signor Jesi. More judicious critics pronounced it to be of the school of Perugia. One day, however—in the Strozzi library, if I mistake not—a painter came upon a document from which it appeared that, in 1461, Neri di Bicci, an indifferent Florentine artist, had been commissioned to paint a "Last Supper" in the convent of S. Onofrio. *Eureka!* cried the happy finder, and immediately published his precious document. The more intelligent connoisseurs turned the discovery into ridicule. Indeed one of the best known and most distinguished archivists in Italy considered it so absurd, that he thought it his duty to make an example of the discoverer by publicly taking him to task. At the same time he availed himself of the opportunity to express his own individual opinion that it was the work of Raffaellino del Garbo, a later Florentine painter, and a pupil of Filippino Lippi. But by doing so he showed that his own knowledge of art was on much the same level as that of the painter who, on the strength of his document, had maintained that Neri di Bicci was the author of the fresco.'

'And to whom is the fresco now attributed?' I asked.

'Passavant gave it to Giovanni Spagna, Signor Cavalcaselle to Gerino da Pistoia; both critics therefore considered it to be by a pupil of Perugino.'

'And what is your opinion of these attributions?'

'I too believe it to be the work of a pupil of Perugino, who was inspired by a Florentine engraving of the fifteenth century, and executed the painting from drawings by his master. It may be by Giannicola Manni, Perugino's well-known assistant. But we need not trouble ourselves with these questions of detail now. Let me give you another still more striking instance of the very problematic value of a document in the hands of a man who does not understand the phraseology of art. The same distinguished archivist I mentioned just now, who has rendered good service in his particular branch of research, had the misfortune to discover a document some years ago in our city archives, which records that Fra Diamante, an inferior painter of the middle of the fifteenth century, the pupil and assistant of Fra Filippo Lippi, was commissioned to paint a fresco in the Vatican, of "Christ delivering the keys to St. Peter." Jubilant at his great discovery, he gave vent to his mingled excitement and scorn in the following terms : "How little you art-critics know of your business ! From Vasari downwards you have all ascribed the large fresco in the Sistine chapel representing "St. Peter receiving the keys" to Perugino, and you profess to see his manner in it. But let me tell you that you are quite on the wrong tack ; for it is not the work of an Umbrian at all, but of our Florentine, Fra Diamante. Be as incredulous as you like, but you will be bound to believe me in the end. Here it is in black and white in my document, as clear as noonday, and before such evidence criticism and strife must cease."'

'As I have not been in Rome I cannot say anything about this fresco,' said I. 'Do you consider it to be the work of Perugino ? '

'His best work,' replied the Italian emphatically, with an air of complete conviction.

'I must confess,' I observed, 'that you have persuaded me of this much, that the work of art itself is, after all, the only trustworthy evidence for purposes of identification. You must allow, however, that the technic may be of great service to a trained eye in distinguishing one master from

another.   In Germany there is a school of connoisseurs who
consider a knowledge of the technical qualities of a painting
a most important point, if indeed it is not the chief guide
in determining its authorship.'

'It is rather a bold venture,' said the Italian with a
laugh, 'to pretend to recognise the technical qualities,
such as the several pigments employed, in pictures of the
fifteenth and sixteenth centuries, which, for the most part,
are entirely disfigured by repainting.  Since the days of
the French artist Largillière, however, it has become the
fashion to do so with many painters and connoisseurs,
and even with some art-historians.  No wonder, therefore,
that the more sensible among modern painters should
ridicule the pretensions of some recent writers on art.  All
these gratuitous suppositions as to method only serve to
throw dust in the eyes of a credulous public.  Ask any
honest and competent picture-restorer, and——'

'Are there any in existence ?' I interrupted.

'They certainly are, as we Italians say, as rare as white
flies,' he replied, smiling ; 'yet I have had the good fortune
to meet with a few in my time, and not one of them ever
ventured confidently to say what particular colours or
varnishes the painter had made use of; they could hardly
even decide whether the picture was painted entirely in
*tempera* or finished with glazes of oil.'

Evening had now closed in, and we found ourselves
again at the Ponte Vecchio.  My companion, who lived in
the Via S. Frediano, prepared to bid me good-bye, regret-
ting, at the same time, that his lengthy dissertation should
have prevented us from reaching the Villa Rucciano, which
was to be the object of our walk.  I thanked the old gentleman for his kindness, and for the trouble he had taken to
explain his views upon many a vexed question in the realm
of art-criticism, and asked him whether he would be dis-

posed to accompany me on the following day to the Uffizi
and the Pitti, should he have nothing better to do.

'With the greatest pleasure,' he replied, 'but you must
not look upon me as an authority, or upon my judgment as
infallible. I would never claim for myself either knowledge or endowments sufficient to warrant my setting
myself up above my fellows. Yet, considering the years of
honest study I have devoted to the subject, I think I have
at least as much right to express an opinion as the scores
of superficial writers in Italy and abroad, especially when I
see how many charlatans manage to pass themselves off as
critical judges of Italian art.'

And so we parted, having arranged an hour for meeting
on the morrow in the Tribune.

The following morning at the appointed time I mounted
the steep flights of stairs leading to the Uffizi gallery, and
in the Tribune I found my new friend awaiting me. He
greeted me cordially, probably flattering himself that he
was going to make an easy convert of me to his theories
about art.

'There are a good many pictures here,' I said, looking
round, 'bearing the name of Raphael—one, two, three,
four, five, actually six; will you be so good as to illustrate
by them the practical value of your theory of form?'

'A very natural request,' said the Italian, smiling;
'but, supposing the forms in these six pictures ascribed to
Raphael should not resemble the master's typical forms—
nay, supposing they should not even coincide with each
other—what would you say then?'

'That a theory which breaks down at the first test can
have no practical value,' I answered promptly.

'As you confess yourself an amateur, and acknowledge
that you have not yet learnt to see,' he said, 'I had no

right to expect any other answer. My opponents denounce my theory in the same way; but the question is, would a thoroughly qualified critic consider that they are justified in doing so? I think not. When two Greek scholars fail to agree about the meaning of a passage in the classics, the reason may be that one has more discernment than the other. The reader may side with the more able or with the less competent exponent, whichever is the more congenial to him, yet he would never doubt for a moment that both were equally well versed in the Greek grammar.'

'Of course not,' I answered.

'Very well,' continued my companion, 'yet this is by no means the case with art-historians and art-critics so-called. The first superficial writer on art who happens to notice my theory treats it with lofty scorn, notwithstanding that it is based both on long experience and on profound research. He rejects my views with his wonted assurance, though unable to produce a single reason for so doing, and being himself without the requisite knowledge and capacity for understanding my method. The public, who have the greatest respect for everything in print, have no discrimination—resembling the peasant, who, when a parrot called out to him " Good morning," from a window, took off his hat to it. They of course know not which opinion to accept —mine, the result of a prolonged study of the grammar of art, or that of the improvised art-critic, who either sweepingly condemns my conclusions, or even occasionally gives them out as his own discoveries!

' For a beginner like yourself,' he continued after a pause, and in a calmer tone, 'it would be advisable first to study some of the *quattro-centisti* ; for instance, Antonio Pollajuolo, Signorelli, Fra Filippo Lippi or his pupil Sandro Botticelli, for in the works of these early masters the bones and muscles are less hidden by the flesh, and the distinctive and characteristic forms of each master are therefore more apparent, than is the case with the painters of the *cinque-cento*, especially with Raphael, whose refined feeling for beauty always led him to conceal as much as possible what was bony or angular, without impairing the character of the form. I will, however, comply with your request as far as I can; but before examining the six pictures ascribed to Raphael, I should like to draw your attention to two others which are attributed to Fra Filippo Lippi in the catalogue, though I consider one of them to be the work of his pupil Sandro Botticelli.'

I followed my active guide into the next room, where we found a small picture, No. 1179, representing St. Augustine in his study.

'Look at this painting carefully,' he said, as he placed me before it in the best light. 'Among Sandro Botticelli's characteristic forms I will mention the hand, with bony fingers—not beautiful, but always full of life; the nails, which, as you perceive in the thumb here, are square with black outlines, and the short nose with dilated nostrils, which you see exemplified in Botticelli's celebrated and undisputed work hanging close by—" The Calumny of Apelles " (No. 1182). Note, too, the peculiar lengthened folds of the drapery, and the transparent golden red colour in both pictures. If you like, you may also compare the nimbus round the head of St. Augustine, with the glories of other saints in *authentic* works of the same period by the master, and you will, I think, be forced to acknowledge that the painter of the " Calumny," and of the large "Tondo" (No. 1267 *bis.*) in the next room, must also have been the author of this St. Augustine.'

This matter-of-fact way of identifying works of art by the help of such external signs savoured more of an anatomist, I thought, than of a student of art, and was moreover

entirely opposed to the usually accepted method. Nevertheless I answered : 'You seem to be right in your conjectures ; but how is it that the picture came to be ascribed
to Fra Filippo and not to Botticelli ?'

'Because those who named the pictures in this gallery
were only guided by the general impression, and were not
in the habit of comparing the works by different masters
of the same school ; the principal reason, however, was that
Vasari, in his life of Fra Filippo, records that the Frate
painted a "St. Augustine in his Study" for Bernardo
Vecchietti.'

'As if no other artist could have treated the subject !'
I exclaimed.

'Exactly,' said my companion, evidently well pleased.
'You see, therefore, in this case again, how little is the
value of a written document or of tradition, when we are not
capable of questioning the work of art itself as to its author.'

'But now,' said I, 'in order to convince me fully, you
must be good enough to show me an authentic picture by
Fra Filippo, that I may compare it with this St. Augustine.'

'Come with me,' he answered, and taking my arm he led
me into the last room in that part of the gallery, and
showed me a Madonna adoring the Infant Saviour, whom two
Angels support (No. 1307).[9]

'In this picture,' he remarked, 'you must first observe
the dissimilarity in the tone of the colours. Compare the
light blue of the Madonna's mantle with the darker scale of
colour in Botticelli's works ; then the forms with those in
Botticelli's paintings—the hand, the ear, the nose, the head,
the drapery—and afterwards give me your candid opinion.'

I examined Fra Filippo's work as closely as I could,

---

[9] An old copy of this picture, entirely disfigured by repainting, is in the collection of Prince Torlonia, in Rome ; and a drawing, a palpable forgery, is in the Uffizi (Case 39, 184). Messrs. Crowe and Cavalca-selle, however, describe it as an 'admirable drawing' (ii. 347-8).

and indeed as I had never before studied any picture, and finally I was obliged to admit that the painter of it could not possibly have executed the " St. Augustine." My companion appeared satisfied, and took me back into the Tribune, where Raphael's charming " Madonna del Cardellino " first riveted our attention. The picture attracted me more than any of the other works by Raphael in this room, and seemed to me overflowing with youthful tenderness and grace. I could not refrain from expressing my admiration of it to my amiable cicerone.

'I entirely agree with you,' he said ; ' this picture has always struck me as one of the most charming of Raphael's early works, and I have studied nearly all his Madonnas. For the present, however, we will not think of the æsthetic value of the painting, but, keeping to our method, consider the forms only ; the hand and ear, for instance. Look at this Raphaelesque type of ear in the children. See how round and fleshy it is ; how it unites naturally with the cheek and does not appear to be merely stuck on, as in the works of so many other masters ; observe the hand of the Madonna with the broad metacarpus and somewhat stiff fingers, the nails extending to the tips only. You will find this type of hand in other authentic contemporary works of Raphael, for instance, in the " Marriage of the Madonna," in the Brera ; the " Madonna de' Tempi " at Munich ; the small Madonna belonging to Lord Cowper, and in others.'

'For goodness' sake,' I cried, ' leave such unsightly things as nails out of the question. The German and French critics would inevitably ridicule you if you were to tell them that even the nails were characteristic of a great master.'

'Everything may be turned into ridicule,' replied the Italian rather testily, ' especially by people who understand nothing of the subject. And, may I ask, are the nails more

unsightly than any other part of the human frame, in the
eyes of an anatomist ?    May not the form and shape of the
nails be of service to us in discriminating between a
northern (Flemish or German) and an Italian picture;
between a work by Mariotto Albertinelli, and one by his
prototype Fra Bartolommeo ; in recognising the hands of
Bernardino de' Conti, of Bartolommeo Montagna, and of
other masters, and in distinguishing them from those
of their contemporaries [1] and fellow-workers ?    But, out
of consideration for you and your German and French
friends,' he added, ' I will leave the " unsightly " nails out of
the question, and direct your attention only to the nobler
parts of the human frame.    I must now beg you to compare
the forms which we have just noted in this painting
by Raphael, with those in a picture hanging close by,
called the " Madonna del Pozzo " (No. 1125).    Is not the
ear quite different in form, and the hand with its short
stumpy fingers ?    Are the children of the same type
as in Raphael's painting ?    And does the hard and somewhat over-smooth colouring at all resemble Raphael's
flesh-tints, which are still discernible in the " Madonna del
Cardellino," notwithstanding the injury it has suffered
from restoration ? '

   ' Certainly not ; I can see all this plainly,' I replied
at once ; 'and how different is the landscape, with its
peculiar treatment of trees and shrubs, from Raphael's !

---

[1] To cite a few out of many instances, we find in Oxford a sheet
containing, amongst other studies,
the head of a young man and
a hand, ascribed to Raphael and
reproduced as such in the publications of the Grosvenor Gallery
(No. 19). It is just this hand, however, which reveals the northern
master, for the thumb-nail is of a
form which we never find in Italian
pictures, though it frequently occurs
in northern paintings. It resembles
a section of an octagon more than
anything else, and appears as if it
had had three clean cuts with the
scissors. At Chatsworth we also
find a study of two hands, which,
notwithstanding their decidedly
northern character, are ascribed
to Parmeggianino.

THE SO-CALLED "FORNARINA." BY S. DEL PIOMBO.

*(In the Uffizi.)*

To face p. 32.

How unpleasing is the grouping of the figures, and how ugly the position of the Madonna's right leg—Raphael would certainly have had more feeling for line ! The scale of colour, too, is very unlike that in the " Madonna del Cardellino." '

'This painting,' pursued my companion, 'was pronounced by Passavant, by Mündler, and finally even by Messrs. Crowe and Cavalcaselle, to be unworthy of Raphael ; and is it not a disgrace to the authorities of the gallery that they should still allow the master's name to appear upon it ? '

'And to what painter do all these critics ascribe it ? '

'Wicar, Passavant, and Signor Cavalcaselle gave it, very rightly, I think, to Franciabigio.'

'As critics and non-critics are apparently agreed that it is not by Raphael, we need not pursue the question any further. Will you now tell me your opinion about the " Fornarina," which hangs beside it ? '

'Willingly,' he replied. 'First I must tell you that this picture long passed as a Giorgione ; but in the beginning of this century Puccini, then the director of the gallery, to whom the attribution to Raphael of the " Madonna del Pozzo " is due, imagined that he could detect in this portrait the features of the mythical " Fornarina," and therefore attributed it to Raphael. Later and more intelligent critics, however, have assigned it to the school of Giorgione.'

'I know too little of Raphael's manner,' said I, 'to venture on an opinion in the face of modern criticism. But I must tell you frankly that, at the first glance, the picture seemed to me pervaded by a breath of Raphael.'

'A breath indeed ! ' said the Italian ; 'like all amateurs you are simply guided by the general impression. To a critical mind this " breath of Raphael " indicates little or nothing. Still, I will allow that at a distance the type of this Roman woman recalls several heads in Raphael's

works. Why is Titian so frequently confounded with
Palma Vecchio by amateurs? Because the two painters
used the same, or very similar, Venetian models. Observe
the forms in this picture more closely: the fleshy arm, the
imperfect modelling of the mouth, the position of the fingers
so unlike Raphael, and the black shadows which you will
not find in a single painting by the master, either of his
Florentine or Roman period; and if you look at the few traces
of original colour remaining in this portrait, you will certainly
be obliged to modify your first impression. The stiff and
somewhat academic hand is certainly not treated in the
manner of Giorgione and still less in that of Raphael; the
accessories, and the date 1512 in gold, also show that it is
not by the latter master, for after the "Entombment" of
1507, I do not know of any authentic work by him bearing
a date.'

'Surely the "Violin Player" in the Sciarra-Colonna
gallery is of 1518,' I remarked. 'I only know it from the
engraving, but I believe I am not mistaken in saying that
it is dated 1518.'

'You are quite right,' said the Italian, 'but the date
appears to me later than the painting,[2] and the name
of Raphael was not given to it for many years after
the master's death. Vasari makes no mention of the
picture. The stone parapet against which the young man
leans, and on which is the misleading date, the modelling
of the face and the treatment of the fur, all recall the
school of Giorgione. If you compare this delightful picture
of the "Violin Player" with the so-called portrait of
the "Fornarina," and with various heads in the altar-
piece in S. Giovanni Crisostomo at Venice, I think you will
agree with me, that the "Violin Player" is an early work

---

[2] Baron Rumohr asserted that the date, 1518, was painted in the 'im-
pasto ' (iii. 137).

by Sebastiano del Piombo,[3] and cannot be by Raphael.
Stone parapets, such as we see here, only occur in Venetian
portraits; for instance, in the so-called " Bella di Tiziano,"
by Palma Vecchio, also in the Sciarra gallery; in a female
portrait by Bernardino Licinio, of 1524, belonging to the
Andreossi family at Milan, and in other portraits. But
to return to this " Fornarina." About 1512 Raphael
painted his celebrated " Madonna di Foligno." Compare
the hands in that painting with the hand of this woman;
you cannot fail, I think, to see the great dissimilarity between them even though you have not yet applied yourself
to the study of form. Look too at the liquid colouring,
purely Venetian, not in the face, which is entirely repainted,
but in the bodice with its tones of light blue and dark red;
such chords of colour do not occur in any of Raphael's paintings, nor indeed in those of any contemporary Florentine,
though we find them in several works of Fra Sebastiano's
Venetian period; for instance, in his large picture here, the
" Death of Adonis " (No. 592), which the catalogue ascribes
to Moretto, and in the lunettes by him in one of the lower
rooms of the Farnesina at Rome. Compare too the treatment of the fur, with that in a male portrait in the Pitti (No.
409), and I think you must be convinced that both this " Fornarina " and the " Violin Player " are by Fra Sebastiano del
Piombo, and have nothing whatsoever to do with Raphael.'

'And does the form of hand in this portrait really
coincide with that in all Fra Sebastiano's authentic works?'
I asked.

'By no means,' replied the Italian, seemingly rather
astonished at this question. 'Sebastiano del Piombo's
forms are very different in the various epochs of his artistic

---

[3] If I am not mistaken, it was
Professor Springer who first cast
doubts on this " Raphael," and suggested Sebastiano del Piombo as the
possible author of the portrait.

E

career. For I consider that he, like Girolamo Genga, is to be regarded as one of the first of the Eclectics. As the influence of Signorelli drew Genga after him, so Sebastiano, though first swayed by Raphael, was afterwards led out of his natural course by Michael Angelo. In an early work, the "Pietà," belonging to Sir Henry Layard at Venice, he follows in the steps of Cima da Conegliano, and his forms and types are severe like those of that master. Later, he felt the overpowering influence of the great Giorgione, and his types, forms, and method of painting then recall this master, as in the altar-piece I mentioned to you just now, in S. Giovanni Crisostomo, and in the four Saints in the Church of S. Bartolommeo di Rialto at Venice (SS. Bartholomew, Sebastian, Sinibaldo, and Louis), and finally in the "Violin Player" of the Sciarra gallery.[1]

[1] In the collection at Lille there is a characteristic drawing representing a Faun (see wood-cut; Braun, No. 39) which dates from

FAUN BY SEBASTIANO DEL PIOMBO.

About 1510 Agostino Chigi summoned him to Rome, and probably through him Sebastiano made acquaintance with the young Raphael, then rapidly becoming the prime favourite of the Roman patrons of art. It is not surprising, therefore, that the types and forms in Sebastiano's works of that period should have some affinity with those of Raphael, which we fancy we can detect in this "Fornarina" of 1512, and in a fine male portrait in the Scarpa collection at La Motta.[5] After 1512, Sebastiano, unfortunately for his art, formed a friendship with Michael Angelo, who was then inclined to be rather jealous of Raphael's growing fame, and his forms and types then become altogether Michael-Angelesque. Soon after this date, if I mistake not, Sebastiano painted a second portrait, formerly at Blenheim, and now in the Berlin museum —sometimes called the "Fornarina" and sometimes "Dorothea"—at one time also ascribed to Raphael. The landscape in this picture is still quite Giorgionesque; but the type of hand, with unnaturally long fingers, has something of Michael Angelo. And now, if it does not weary you, I should like to give you my opinion (rather a startling one, perhaps) about another much talked-of work by Raphael.'

I consented, not wishing to offend my loquacious companion, though, to tell the truth, I was beginning to feel I had had almost enough of his long-winded dissertations.

'If I have not made a great mistake,' he proceeded, 'I

this epoch of Sebastiano's career; it is wrongly attributed to Titian. The form of hand is still Giorgionesque; that of the ear is identical with the form we find in paintings of his first Roman period (1511–1513).

[5] This splendid, though some-what repainted, portrait passes as the likeness of Tibaldeo by Raphael. I think it more probably represents Raphael himself, at the age of twenty-six or twenty-seven, and that it was painted by Sebastiano—at that date his great admirer.

should say that the "St. John the Baptist," seated on the trunk of a tree, in the Louvre (No. 1500), which no doubt you have often admired as a Raphael, is also one of the first works which Sebastiano painted in Rome from a sketch by his new friend and patron Michael Angelo. It was probably executed to rival Raphael's painting of the same subject, of

"ST. JOHN THE BAPTIST"
IN THE LOUVRE.

which there is a school copy in the Tribune here (No. 1127). In the "Fornarina" we perceive the imitation of Raphael, while the "St. John" in the Louvre appears to me to mark Sebastiano's transition from his Raphaelesque to his Michael-Angelesque manner. The action and the pose of the figure, as well as the expression, recall some of Michael Angelo's giant forms on the ceiling of the Sistine chapel—for instance the two nude youths above the Erythræan Sibyl.[6] The form and the bend of the second finger is quite Michael-Angelesque; the landscape on the other hand is still Venetian, and differs entirely from Raphael's ideal landscapes.[7]

[6] There are several drawings at Chatsworth by Sebastiano; one as-

EAR OF SEBASTIANO DEL PIOMBO.

cribed to Giorgione, and another to Titian; a third, in indian ink, represents one of the prophets in S. Pietro in Montorio at Rome. In this last, the form of ear coincides exactly with that of the "St. John the Baptist" in the Louvre. Another fine drawing of Sebastiano's Michael-Angelesque period is in the Louvre (photographed by Braun, No. 424).

[7] Dr. Bode, I may add, asserts that the "Fornarina" in the Barberini gallery and the "Dorothea" in Berlin have much in common. According to him the former dates from 1509 or 1510, Sebastiano's decorative works in the Farnesina from 1509, and the "Dorothea" from 1511

'Now,' he continued, taking my arm and directing my whole attention again to the portrait of the "Fornarina," 'the form of the hand here is nothing but the transition from Giorgione to Raphael; it is an academic hand, devoid of character. But I will not weary you with more of these hyper-critical observations, as no connoisseur of Raphael of any repute in these days would be likely to favour Puccini's view.'

TWO FIGURES FROM THE CEILING OF THE SISTINE CHAPEL.

'I am not competent,' I remarked, 'to give an opinion on such a knotty point, but all your reasons for combating the views of those who ascribe the portrait to Raphael have not yet succeeded in effacing my first impression.'

At this confession the Italian seemed a little put out; finally, however, he owned that I was not so much in the wrong, and that these kind of eclectic pictures were not suited to the studies of beginners. 'Now look,' he said,

—the latter being a year earlier, therefore, than the "Fornarina" in the Tribune (*Kunstfreund*, No. 15, p. 228). The question in dispute has been discussed by Dr. Julius Meyer, in a brilliant article in the *Jahrbuch der k. preussischen Kunstsammlungen*, No. 1, 1886. I consider that this writer was originally on the right track, but was misled by the theories of his friend and colleague, Dr. Bode.

'at this other female portrait close by, No. 1120, bearing
Raphael's name.   It is finely conceived and splendidly
modelled, but unfortunately so much repainted that we can
only form an opinion of it from the scale of colour in the
dress, and from the drawing of the face, and more especially
of the hand, with the first finger extended.   It is still a
striking portrait, notwithstanding its damaged condition,
and is undoubtedly the work of an important Florentine
master.   First of all, look at the form of the left hand, with
the outstretched finger.   Does it bear any resemblance to
the hand of the "Fornarina," or to that of the "Madonna
del Cardellino"?   If you were to compare it with the hand
of Maddalena Doni in her portrait in the Pitti, you would
be still more puzzled to know why Passavant should have
instanced these hands as distinctive of the manner of
Raphael,[8] for I can see no likeness in them to the hands in
any one of Raphael's authentic works. The whole character
of the portrait is that of the *quattro-cento*; if it were really
Raphael's work, it must necessarily have been executed
earlier than the portraits of the Doni in the Pitti.'

'To whom do you ascribe it?' I asked, in order to
show some interest in all these hair-splitting explana-
tions.

'That is a difficult question to answer,' he replied.
'I must confess that the picture does not give me sufficient
clue to warrant my attributing it to any particular master
with confidence.   Only charlatans and novices in the study
have a name ready for every work of art. And now, before
leaving the Tribune and crossing to the Pitti to examine
Raphael's forms in the pictures there attributed to him,
let me draw your attention to Titian's characteristic form
of hand and ear, in his fine portrait of the prelate Becca-
delli (No. 1116).   You must not lose patience, if I detain

* Passavant, *Raffael d'Urbin*, ii. 41.

you with what may appear to you trivial and even absurd. It is my object to make you notice everything in a work of art, and in time you will come to see that even details, in themselves insignificant, may lead us to the truth, especially in the works of subordinate painters. Look at the hand in this portrait, particularly at the ball of the thumb, which is too strongly developed, and at the round form of the ear. In all his *early* works, and in most of those of his *middle period* till between 1540–1550, Titian adheres to the same round form of ear—for instance, in

the "Three Ages," and the "Holy Family" in the Bridgewater collection (the latter picture being wrongly attributed to Palma Vecchio); in the "Daughter of Herodias" in the Doria-Pamfili gallery; and in No. 633 of the Uffizi. This peculiarity in the ball of the thumb also frequently occurs in his other paintings

THE BALL OF THE THUMB IN TITIAN'S WORKS.

and in his drawings. As the master is constantly confounded with Giorgione (Pitti and Madrid), Pordenone (Doria gallery), Paris Bordone (Capitoline gallery), and even with Andrea Schiavone (Dresden gallery, No. 168),[9] these few hints may be of service to you in judging of disputed pictures, for Titian's hand and ear differ considerably from those we find in paintings by the masters I have just mentioned.'

'You may be right,' I said, with ill-concealed impatience, 'but for the present do let us keep to Raphael's forms, which I am just beginning to understand; otherwise my brain will be so confused with ears, hands, and nails, that I shall be positively incapable of seeing the pictures at all!'

[9] See Crowe and Cavalcaselle, *Life of Titian*, ii. 478.

The Italian laughed, but gave in to me, and we left the
Tribune for the Pitti.

'We will go at once to the Madonna called "del Granduca,"'
he said as we entered the first room, 'though it might more
appropriately be named "del Duca," as in all probability it
was painted at Urbino (in 1504) for the Duke Guidobaldo;
but this is of no great consequence.'

On reaching the picture, my guide pointed out the oval
of the Madonna's face, which, he said, recalled Raphael's
first master Timoteo Viti, far more than his later instructors Pintoricchio or Perugino. 'The expression and the
pose of the head,' he added, 'are quite in the manner of
Timoteo.' Then, of course, we looked at the hands, which,
though very like those of the "Madonna del Cardellino,"
were, he declared, more bony and more suggestive of the
quattro-cento. 'And the ear of the child,' he continued,
'does it not remind you forcibly of the ears of the children
in the "Madonna del Cardellino"? Observe the round
fleshy form, and see how it grows out, so to say, from the
cheek. It is lamentable,' he added, with a shrug of the
shoulders, 'that the mantle of the Madonna should have
been so badly cleaned by an ignorant restorer. It is now
no longer blue, but green, and has entirely lost its original
lustre. Can you see any resemblance between this hand
and that of the "Madonna del Pozzo," or of the female
portrait, No. 1120, in the Tribune?'

'Even I can now see,' I rejoined, 'that the master who
drew and painted this hand did not execute the hands in
the pictures in the Tribune. The difference both in conception and modelling is most striking.'

My companion smiled approvingly, and we then went
back into the first room to look at a portrait called the
"Donna Gravida" (No. 229), which, according to the catalogue, is the work of an unknown master.

'Passavant,' he said, 'rightly ascribes this female portrait to Raphael; but in my opinion places it too late in the master's career, namely, in 1507. If I am not mistaken, it dates from the same period as the portraits of the Doni, about 1505; the hands are precisely of the same form as in those portraits. The face, especially the left side, has suffered so much at the hands of the restorer that Raphael's touch is now hardly perceptible. But keep the form of the hands in your mind's eye, and let us go at once to the portraits of the Doni.'

On seeing the likeness of Maddalena Doni, I could not refrain from exclaiming: 'You are right! exactly the same conception, the same treatment of the sleeve, the same broad hand with short stumpy fingers, the same nails, and the same rather uninteresting, inanimate expression. The landscape, too, coincides with that in the "Madonna del Cardellino."'

My guide was quite pleased with my ready acquiescence in his views, and rubbed his hands with satisfaction at my progress, as he termed it, in comprehending the forms. 'And does not the position of the arms,' he asked me, 'and the whole conception, remind you of another celebrated female portrait which no doubt you have often admired in the Louvre?'

'Indeed it does,' I replied; 'of course you mean the "Mona Lisa," by Leonardo da Vinci?'

'*Colto nel segno*—you have hit the mark,' he cried. 'We may therefore conclude that when Raphael painted these portraits in 1505, he had often been in Leonardo's workshop. Now, having looked at these five early works by Raphael,' continued my instructor, 'we will turn to another painting in this gallery, which also dates from his Florentine period—the large altar-piece (No. 165) ordered by the Dei family, but which Raphael had to leave unfinished when summoned to Rome by Pope Julius II.'

My cicerone first called my attention to the fact that in later times this picture had been painted over by an unskilful restorer, so that in its present condition the original outlines are hardly to be recognised. 'But this will not materially interfere with our studies of form,' he remarked. ' First of all look at the hand and ear. I must tell you, however, that Raphael painted this picture in the summer of 1508, about three years later than those we have just examined.

' I am delighted to find the same round fleshy ear as in the five other pictures,' I said, ' but the form of the hands appears to me rather different.'

'Quite right,' he replied; ' Raphael never remained stationary, but was always making progress in his art. In the main, however, the form of hand is the same as in all his later paintings; but you must recollect that in this picture the hands have been quite disfigured by the restorer.'

' It appears to me,' I observed after a pause, ' that it recalls Fra Bartolommeo's large work in the first room (No. 208), and even the one here (No. 159), in the composition, the architectural background, the arrangement of the drapery, and even in the types of the two flying angels.'

' I quite agree with you,' he returned, ' and it proves, I think, that it was only at this date, in 1508, that a more intimate relation sprang up between the young Raphael and Fra Bartolommeo. Note also the two singing angels at the foot of the throne—a " motive " which is quite Venetian. Fra Bartolommeo may have introduced it in Florence from the city of the Lagoons.'

From this room we went into the ' Sala di Marte,' to the " Madonna della Seggiola " (No. 79).

'In this celebrated picture,' he said, 'you will notice that, while the form of ear is, in the main, identical with that in the works of Raphael's Peruginesque and Florentine periods, the hand is not so natural as in the two female portraits (Nos. 229 and 59), in the "Madonna del Cardellino," and in several paintings of his Peruginesque epoch; for example, the "Ecce Homo" in the Tosio gallery at Brescia, the St. Sebastian in the gallery at Bergamo, and a drawing for an angel playing a viol (for the "Coronation of the Madonna") in the British Museum (Braun 70). The hand, in the "Madonna della Seggiola," is no longer of the *bourgeois* type, faithfully reproduced from nature, but is of that elegant and refined form, which Raphael adhered to throughout his Roman period. Even here the metacarpus is still broad and rather flat, after the manner of his first master, Timoteo Viti; but the fingers are tapering, and it is a well-shaped, you may say an ideal, female hand. This "Tondo" was probably painted about 1513 or 1514. In all Raphael's works from this period to his death you will find the same conventional form of hand, both in the few paintings which proceeded from his own brush, and in those which his pupils executed from his cartoons. Among others, I may instance the Madonna in the Bridgewater gallery, and the beautiful portrait of the woman he loved.'

'And where is the true portrait of this woman?' I asked.

'In this gallery,' he replied, 'in one of the cabinets in which we have already been.'

We went to it at once, and my enthusiastic companion placed me in the best light for seeing it. The face produced a powerful impression upon me, so sparkling is it with life.

Before such a masterpiece I had no inclination to think of the tiresome study of hands and ears. 'Truly,' I exclaimed in my enthusiasm, 'such a woman was worthy of Raphael's love, and it must have been her face which inspired the "Madonna di San Sisto."'

'Most connoisseurs in all parts of the world would probably agree with you, always excepting the Florentine directors of this gallery,' said the Italian with a cynical smile, 'who still continue to call this portrait the "Donna Velata," and to ascribe it to an unknown painter. One point, however, on which critics cannot agree is, whether it be an original or only a copy.'

'Good heavens!' I cried amazed, 'you don't mean to say that anyone can take this strikingly beautiful work for a copy? Critics who look upon this countenance, with its marvellous vitality, as a mechanical reproduction must indeed have strange notions about art!'

At this moment a young man approached us, and, greeting my companion, observed in a significant tone, as he adjusted his spectacles: 'What must the original of this portrait have been, when even the copy makes so great an impression upon one!'

I noticed that at these words the colour mounted to my companion's face, but he only observed drily, 'Then you also consider this portrait to be a copy?'

'All connoisseurs in the world are agreed upon this point,' rejoined the other emphatically.

'And you are a professor of painting at the Academy!' said my friend with undisguised irony.

'Yes, and as a professor of painting I am in a position to set you right if you are in any doubt about the matter,' he proceeded with consummate assurance. 'You must know,' he continued, 'that no connoisseur of Italian art either in Germany, the centre of learning, or in Paris, will accept this picture as an original nowadays. Just look at the touches of the Venetian, or, if you prefer

THE "DONNA VELATA."  BY RAPHAEL.

*(In the Pitti.)*

*To face p. 52.*

it, the Bolognese copyist, on the cheek and on the
brow!'

This seemed to be the last straw for my companion.

'We are neither in learned Germany nor infallible Paris
at the present moment,' he said very decidedly, 'but
in Florence, and before the picture itself. Let me tell you
first of all,' he continued in a calmer tone, 'that this
portrait, which, according to Vasari's testimony, belonged to
the Botti family, was still in their possession in 1677, and
there Cinelli saw and described it as an original. If it were
a Bolognese copy we must assume that it was made at
a still later period, and after the picture had left the
Botti collection. And what Bolognese of that date, I
should like to know, would have been capable of making
such a copy? Look at all the copies by Crespi and
Donduzzi and see how black in the shadows they have
become; moreover, if it only dated from the last, or
even from the seventeenth, century it ought to be in
a far better state of preservation, whereas the colour has
scaled off in so many places that the very priming is
visible. And what do you suppose became of the original?
Even in the eighteenth century a painting by Raphael was
not so easily lost sight of. No! no! I am too old to be taken
in by the baseless, arbitrary assertions of some muddle-
headed foreign professor. How do you propose to prove
that the touches in the face are from the brush of a
Bolognese artist? Do they differ so materially from those
in the "Madonna di San Sisto" at Dresden? Only a highly
imaginative mind could discover the strokes of the brush at
all, for the face has been greatly over-cleaned, and the
painting has been retouched in many parts—in the forehead, in the nose, on the right cheek, and in the neck and
throat; even the background, which was originally brown,
has been daubed over by the restorer.'

' Yes, I admit all this,' murmured the professor.

'And is this not another proof, if such were needed, that it is not a copy? Just look at the painting with your own eyes, my dear sir, and never mind what the critics in Berlin and Paris see fit to tell us about it.   A copyist, indeed ! to have painted those eyes, with their wonderful expression, that proud mouth, that noble brow—never !' [1]

At these impassioned words the professor silently slipped his spectacles into his pocket and vanished into the next room.

' I don't wonder,' said I, when he had disappeared, ' at your being exasperated by such opinions, especially when they come from a professional artist.   Until now I had never seen this picture, and knew it only from photographs.   I am but an amateur, yet I have never been able to understand how anyone could regard such a gem as a copy, least of all connoisseurs who pretend to be infallible judges of art.'

' We shall find,' said my friend, ' this same essentially Roman type in the Magdalen in the altar-piece with S. Cecilia in the gallery of Bologna.   Raphael executed this picture in 1516 for the Cappella dell' Olio in the church of S. Giovanni in Monte, and about that time he may have immortalised the features of his beloved in the portrait before us. Passavant thought that, according to his custom at that time, he left the execution of the dress and of the hand to one of his assistants.   This supposition is probable enough I think, but the superb and queenly head could only have been executed by Raphael himself.   Five or six years

---

[1] The late Mr. Mündler wrote of this portrait (*Beiträge zu J. Burckhardts Cicerone*, p. 41) : ' My first impression of this picture grew stronger every time I saw it. Raphael appears to me to be proclaimed by every touch ; for who but he could have attained to such unequalled nobility and charm ?   The left eye, for instance, is a perfect miracle of drawing, chiaroscuro, and artistic treatment.'

THE " FORNARINA."

*(In the Barberini Gallery, Rome*

*To face p. 55.*

later, when the great master was no more, she was
again portrayed by one of his scholars, probably by
Giulio Romano. That portrait is now in the Barberini
gallery ascribed to Raphael. In it we see the once noble-
looking woman completely transformed. She is not only
older, but has degenerated; the painter, moreover, has
represented her in such a debased and repulsive manner
that she looks positively disreputable. See,' he continued,
going closer to the portrait, 'how thoroughly Raphaelesque
is the form of ear.'

'My dear sir,' I exclaimed, 'spare me these details of
hands and ears before such a picture. In the presence of art
like this it is utterly impossible to think of these things.
Raphael's spirit has cast its magic spell over me, and I cannot descend to that prosaic level requisite for studying forms
and details in a work of art.'

After I had taken a long look at this splendid work,
my long-suffering guide suggested that we should go to
another portrait of about the same period of the master's
career. So we returned to the 'Sala d'Apollo,' where
hangs the celebrated likeness of Leo X., with the Cardinals
Giulio de' Medici and Luigi Rossi.

'Much the same treatment of drapery,' I observed.

'And the same round fleshy ear,' he added. 'I could tell
you a good deal about this famous portrait,' he continued,
'but we will content ourselves now with noting that the ear
is identical in form with that in the other authentic works
by Raphael which we have seen to-day. In this also the
hands and the accessories were probably by his assistants.'

'Although the "Fornarina" is supposed to have
been of the people,' I observed, 'how proud and noble she
looks, compared with this high-born Pope! Had the
painter not endeavoured to ennoble him by the richness of
the details—the illuminated breviary, the magnifying glass,

the beautifully chased golden hand-bell, the rich ecclesiastical habit, the turkey carpet—this aristocratic Medici
might pass for a wealthy publican.'

The Italian smiled, and carried me off to the ' Sala di
Saturno,' where we paused for a moment before the spirited
portrait of Julius II.

' See what a contrast,' he said, ' between this Pontiff and
his successor, Leo X. Like the " Fornarina," he too was
of the people. His fine countenance betokens a powerful
and commanding character, his deeply furrowed features
denote passionate emotion, noble pride and conscious
strength, and were cast in a very different mould from
those of the crafty, sensual, phlegmatic Medici.'[2]

' Few pursuits are so interesting to an art-historian,' I
remarked, ' as the study of portraits.'

' Undoubtedly,' he replied, 'if the historian himself be
interesting, which unfortunately is very seldom the case.
To understand Italian history it is absolutely necessary
to study portraits, both male and female; for some portion of the history of the period is always written in those
faces, if we only know how to read it. If you compare
the portrait of this so-called " Donna Velata " with that
of the high-born Maddalena Doni, or of Eleonora Gonzaga
della Rovere, known as the " Bella di Tiziano " (No. 18 in
this gallery), you will see at once that the ideal had completely died out among the aristocracy at the time of the
Renaissance, while among the people a healthy vitality
and moral vigour still prevailed.'

After this digression into the history of culture, my
companion took me to look at the " Vision of Ezekiel," a

[2] The portrait in the Tribune
may possibly be the original, though
it is much disfigured by repainting.
According to Vasari, the Castle of
Urbino contained both Raphael's
portrait of Julius II. and a copy of
it by Titian (?). It is said that both
of them were brought to Florence
from Urbino

small painting hanging on the opposite wall. I knew it well from the engraving and had always admired the composition—at once so attractive and so impressive.

'If I remember rightly,' I observed, 'Vasari says that Raphael painted this picture for the Hercolani family of Bologna.'

'Yes,' he replied; 'hence by way of saying something quite original, several northern critics have asserted that, like the "Donna Velata," this picture was a late copy executed by some Bolognese artist.'

'And what has become of Raphael's original?' I asked.

'We must leave that question for these great authorities to answer,' he replied. 'The little picture is splendidly executed, but I also am of opinion that it is not by Raphael. The Hand of the Almighty, the scale of colour, the ears of the angels, and especially their thick upper lips, are all, I think, characteristic of Giulio Romano, Raphael's favourite pupil; nevertheless, in the beautiful composition, the spirit of the master himself is seen in all its freshness and life. It probably dates, as several art-critics consider, from 1517.'

'If you are right,' I observed, 'Giulio Romano must have been capable of imitating the technic and the forms of his master and prototype so closely as to deceive us, for it would never have occurred to me to cast doubts on the authenticity of this picture.'

'And yet,' said my guide, 'nearly all the easel paintings of Raphael's last period, from 1516 to his death, were executed in great part by his scholars and assistants, and chief among them was Giulio Romano. At that date the master himself was so much in request as painter, architect, and archæologist, that it would have been wholly impossible for him to fulfil all the commissions that poured in from every side, even had he been endowed with four hands instead of two, and had each day been composed of twenty-four working hours instead of twelve.'

Not over-well pleased to be told that I was not to regard this picture, which had such charm for me, as entirely by Raphael, I moved on to the portrait of a Cardinal on the same wall (No. 171). 'I suppose you will tell me that this splendid portrait of a prelate with a cast in his eye is not by Raphael either, but only by one of his pupils?' I said with a laugh.

'And what if I tell you that the painting is not even Italian,' he said, also laughing, 'but only a copy by a foreigner of an original by Raphael!'

'If your experimental method is to lead to such results,' I exclaimed, 'then it would be best for the world to know as little as possible of it; and to forget what it does know as speedily as may be.'

'In all probability this will be the case,' said the Italian good-humouredly. 'But suppose we examine this cele-brated portrait a little more closely. The liquid character of its painting recalled the method of the German masters to Passavant;[3] he even thought that Raphael might have been under the influence of some of Holbein's pictures when engaged upon it, which, however, I may observe incidentally, was a chronological impossibility. But there can be no doubt that the technic of the painting is not Italian; this must strike every connoisseur. Look at the hard fixed eye and badly modelled mouth, at the thumb of the right hand which is completely out of drawing, and at the crude colours of the book. You must acknowledge that no great master could have painted this portrait. However, to relieve your mind of all uncertainty, I may as well tell you at once, that the original is still in the possession of the Inghirami

[3] i. 175.

family at Volterra, and though ruined by modern restoration, it is still recognisable in parts as the work of Raphael.'

Of course there was nothing more to be said after this, and I was forced to give in, though I must confess that my guide's destructive criticism was as displeasing to me as were fire-arms to Ariosto's Orlando.

'On the opposite wall,' he continued, 'there is another portrait of a Cardinal (158), which is still given to Raphael, though Passavant rightly pronounced it the work of a scholar.' When I examined it I had no difficulty in perceiving that the eyes and the left hand were badly modelled, and that the ear was not of that round fleshy form which we had been noticing in Raphael's genuine portraits. 'Another similar work of the school, representing Cardinal Passerini, is in the Naples Museum,' he said, as, glancing at his watch, he prepared to leave. And I also was of opinion that for the present this one lesson was quite enough. So we parted.

I remained in Florence some weeks longer, and made use of the time to follow up the teaching of my guide by studying form in painting, sculpture, and architecture. I soon came to the conclusion, however, that such a dry, uninteresting, and even pedantic, study may be all very well for a 'former student of medicine,' and might even be of service to dealers and experts, but in the end must prove detrimental to the truer and more elevated conception of art. And so I left Florence dissatisfied.

On my return to Kasan I heard, to my surprise, that Prince Smaranzoff's celebrated collection of pictures, principally Italian of the best period, was shortly to be sold by auction. My first art-studies had been made in this gallery, as the château was only a few versts from the town, and I had often been there in my youth. I still had a lively recollection of the six Madonnas by Raphael which it contained, and I now felt a strong desire to see and study the pictures again before they were scattered to the four winds.

One bright December morning, therefore, I ordered my sleigh and started in high spirits. I found the splendid rooms swarming with Russians and foreigners—dealers, art-connoisseurs, and directors of galleries. They were all examining the pictures one by one, with the greatest interest, and, as I thought at first, with immense knowledge, going into raptures first over one, then over another; identifying here a Verrocchio, there a Melozzo da Forli—even a Leonardo da Vinci—at the first glance. I listened curiously to their analytical remarks about the fine technical qualities of the Venetian pictures, and the excellent state of preservation of the Raphaels, and marvelled; but what was my astonishment, when at length I was able to approach, and critically to examine, all these Madonnas, with which I also had been enchanted some years before! The Raphaels in the Pitti were still fresh in my memory, and I could not refrain from testing these works of art by the method the Italian in Florence had taught me. I could hardly believe my eyes, and felt as if scales had suddenly fallen from them. The Madonnas, one and all, now appeared to me equally stiff and uninteresting, the children feeble if not positively absurd; as to the forms, they had not a trace of Raphael. In short, these pictures, which only a few years before had appeared to me admirable works by Raphael himself, did not satisfy me now, and on closer inspection I felt convinced that these much-vaunted productions were nothing but copies, or perhaps even counterfeits. The works attributed to Michael Angelo, Verrocchio, Leonardo da Vinci, Botticelli, Lorenzo Lotto, and Palma Vecchio, made exactly the same impression upon me. I was overjoyed to find how satisfactory were the results of my hitherto short and superficial studies, even though the knowledge I had gained was so far only of a negative character. As I drove home, I determined to leave Gorlaw and return as speedily as possible to Germany, Paris, and Italy, in order to study in the galleries with renewed zeal, in accordance with the method the Italian had indicated to me, and which I had, at first, been inclined to disparage.

I therefore spent a year, partly in Germany, and partly in London and Paris, and then proceeded to Italy, sanguine of success in my studies.

This time I greeted the dark cypresses and pines, and the sunny sky above them, with unmitigated delight. After devoting some months to the local schools of Lombardy and of the Venetian territory, as well as to the study of the Italian language and literature, I turned my steps towards Tuscany, that paradise of art. My first thought on reaching Florence was to seek my former guide in order to express my gratitude to him for the trouble he had once taken to instruct me. I applied first to the inspector of the gallery, supposing that he would be the most likely person to tell me if this indefatigable student of pictures were still in Florence, and where he might be found. I was much amazed when this Government official met my question with the cold rejoinder, that he had a great antipathy to this old heretic with his mania for renaming pictures, and had nothing whatever to do with him. 'Moreover,' he added, ' he is a declared enemy of liberty ; if you wish to find him you must apply to a *Codino*.' [4]

After many inquiries I at length succeeded in discovering an individual who was able to give me some

---

[4] A person belonging to the old or reactionary party in politics is so nicknamed.—(Trans.)

information about him—an apothecary, a lean, cadaverous fellow, with a long nose and keen dark eyes. Could he tell me if the old man were still alive, I asked.

'Unless he died quite recently,' he replied grimly, 'he is still in the land of the living.'

'And do you know where he is to be found? Some time ago,' I added, 'he lived in the Via S. Frediano.'

'Yes, I know;' replied my surly informant, 'but some months since he quitted Florence altogether and retired into the country. I heard,' he pursued with a sneer, 'that he grew tired of his fellow-men, because they were not all made after his pattern. He keeps aloof from everyone, excepting a few of his old political friends.'

'Yet when I knew him,' I hazarded, 'he appeared cheerful and sociable enough.

'He never had any conscience,' said the apothecary venomously, 'and was always opposed to law and order. All these Italian anarchists and would-be reformers of the world are in reality vain and insolent egotists, devoid of religion and of veneration for the powers that be. No wonder that they should end by becoming misanthropes! God forgive them the havoc they have wrought in our beautiful land!'

From these caustic remarks I inferred that my gaunt informant belonged to the clerical, while my former cicerone must evidently have been of the patriotic, party. But I felt some surprise that a man who, a comparatively short time before, had been such an enthusiast for art and science, and especially for the regeneration of his country, had thus suddenly sunk into obscurity.

I thanked the crabbed apothecary and parted from him as speedily as possible. As I went home I fell to meditating upon the transitoriness of our joys and sorrows in this world.

After a sojourn of two years in Tuscany I reached the Eternal City at last. Here for many months I have studied art in churches and galleries, and, finally, I have conceived the presumptuous idea of imparting some of the results to the young students of art in my own country.

I trust that they will receive these attempts in the same spirit of good-will in which they are offered.

# THE BORGHESE GALLERY.

*'One day telleth another.'*

IN these democratic days, when the banner of universal equality has been planted even on the mouldering walls of Rome—the centre and stronghold of Ultramontanism—we must expect that, with the gradual abolition of entail and hereditary right, things so hateful to the democracy, the various art-collections belonging to the great Roman families and many a little gem from the Vatican will before long be dispersed.[1] While these galleries, therefore, still remain intact, it seems desirable to take a survey of the choicest and best known among them, and critically to discuss the masterpieces they contain. The task is neither easy nor particularly agreeable, and I should have shrunk from incurring so heavy a responsibility, at the commencement of my career, had not my prolonged sojourn in Rome convinced me that the abilities of distinguished Italian critics, in the present day, instead of being devoted to art, might be employed more profitably to themselves on politics, or archæology, or on any other subject. The authorities,

---

[1] The fulfilment of Signor Morelli's prediction appears to be impending. The Borghese gallery has already been transferred from the Borghese Palace in the city to the Borghese Villa without the walls, and one of its famous pictures—the so-called portrait of Cesare Borgia, wrongly ascribed to Raphael—has been sold, and has left the country. The law abolishing entail and primogeniture must inevitably lead to the impoverishment and breaking-up of the great historic families of Italy, and consequently to the dispersion of those collections which have afforded delight and instruction to many generations.—(Trans.)

therefore, will scarcely take it amiss, I trust, if I avail myself of this tempting opportunity to test the value of my own studies, which have at least the merit of conscientiousness, however limited my powers. Considering how wearisome is the task of compiling a catalogue, how insignificant indeed in the eyes of most people, it is hardly to be expected that art-historians, or directors of galleries with their manifold duties, should occupy themselves with trivialities of this description. Such work is for those who, like myself, can only aspire to be regarded as students in the realm of art-criticism, while it is the privilege of those who are philosophers and historians to soar unfettered into other and more exalted spheres. Thus reasoning, I gradually overcame my natural diffidence and let my vanity have full play. May the Gods preserve this audacious venture from the fate of the frog in the fable!

I thought it advisable to make these few prefatory remarks, as I wish it to be clearly understood that this work is only the more or less unpretending effort of a student; and that in attempting to identify works of the great Italian masters, whenever the attributions of the catalogue appear to me untenable, I have merely sought to put my own powers of criticism to the test. This, and this alone, is the task I have set myself.

Such an undertaking is only likely to interest those who are disposed to make similar studies in the Roman galleries, so long as they continue to exist. As my conclusions occasionally differ from those traditionally and universally accepted, every one must exercise his own judgment as to which of the two opinions, if either, is the more worthy of acceptance. Even my mistakes, and there will be no lack of them, may thus be of use to some, and may aid them in their search after truth. The daring assertion of Mr. Wornum, an Englishman, who first declared the Holbein

Madonna in Dresden to be a copy, was at first stigma-
tised as rank heresy by all orthodox German art-critics;
eventually, however, his view received the most unqualified
recognition, and was confirmed by those critics who had
met in the capital of Saxony to pronounce judgment on the
picture. For the present I shall confine myself to discussing two of the most important picture galleries in Rome,
the Borghese and the Doria-Pamfili. This, however, will
not deter me, when opportunity offers, from casting an
occasional glance at other Italian collections. Respecting
the origin of these galleries I can furnish no reliable
information, and, as far as I know, all the guide-books
are silent on this subject. For the study of the works
of art themselves, at least as I understand it, this is a
matter of no importance. Most of these collections, if
I am not mistaken, owe their origin to the taste for art—
according to some, to the Spanish love of display—in the
seventeenth century. The nucleus of the Borghese gallery
was formed by Cardinal Scipione Borghese in the beginning
of that century; the remaining collections, with the exception
of the Colonna and the Chigi, were of later origin. The
Barberini gallery, subsequent to the annexation of the
Principality of Urbino by the Papal See, received considerable additions from the Castle of Urbino at the hands of
Pope Urban VIII. Later, it had the misfortune to be
divided into two parts, one of which fell to the Barberini-
Colonna family, the other to the house of Sciarra-Colonna.

In the hanging and arrangement of the pictures in these
galleries, no system was, as a rule, adopted; everything was
subordinated to the size and shape of the picture, and even
occasionally to that of the frame, a proceeding unfortunately
only too common in Italy. Thus the paintings may be said
to be distributed through, rather than arranged in, the
rooms. The Borghese gallery is a notable exception, and

owes its present arrangement to Commendatore Rosa, for
many years its custodian, and subsequently a distinguished
archæologist. He has thus shown that he is of opinion
that works of art should be hung according to their
schools. The names affixed to most of the pictures in
these collections, as well as in all the public galleries of
Italy, date from the end of the sixteenth or beginning of
the seventeenth century—from a period, therefore, when
art-criticism was, as a rule, the province of a few acade-
micians and picture-collecting prelates, whose verdicts,
delivered between two pinches of snuff, were regarded as
final and indisputable. Through long years of unchequered
peaceful existence, they have been piously upheld by the
easy-going public, and even by the majority of art-historians.
To criticise them now would be sacrilege in the eyes of
the orthodox, and so in a measure it is, for it might
dispel the cherished illusions of many æsthetic dreamers.[2]
This thought might have caused me pain had I not reflected
that my words, not being intended for them, would never
be likely to reach their ears. I certainly have no desire
to shake the belief of students and tourists in theories
which they regard as infallible, for woe betide the great
European collections should the hitherto confiding public
begin to look sceptically upon its catalogues and red
guide-books. The museums and galleries would soon be
nearly deserted, æsthetic enjoyment would cease, and it is
doubtful whether universal culture, so-called, would be
advanced. Of all this, however, there is not the slightest
fear, and taking the highest view of the subject, it is in
fact completely immaterial, whether a work of art gives me
pleasure or instruction under one name or another ; the

---

[2] Pascal remarks somewhere:
' La coutume fait toute l'équité par
cette seule raison qu'elle est reçue ;
c'est le fondement mystique de son
autorité ; qui la ramène à son
principe l'anéantit.'

point is, that it does give me pleasure—that is to say, that it appeals to my sense of enjoyment, or, as the Germans would put it, that it causes the tenderest chords and fibres of my soul to vibrate. Fortunately for humanity at large, this occurs day by day in all the picture galleries of Europe, in spite of the many mistakes which pedantic art-critics strive to discover in the catalogues. A painting, once said a professor of æsthetics, is like a flower of the field—pure and refined natures delight in it, and care not whether learned botanists classify it among the Rosaceæ or the Malvaceæ. And now, without wasting further words, let us enter the Borghese gallery, which merits the honour of our first visit, for notwithstanding the severe losses it has sustained in the course of its long existence, in my estimation at least, it still ranks first among all the other private collections in the world. The report recently circulated, that the Russian Government had offered 25,000,000 francs for it, was merely spread in order to give some idea of its inestimable worth, and thereby to afford the public a clear and undeniable proof that the pictures in these rooms were really of great pecuniary value, and consequently worthy of its admiration. In my critical discussion of this gallery I shall not follow the sequence of the numbers in the catalogue. This method, though not the most practical, is probably the most logical, and will facilitate matters for those few persons who may be disposed to follow me in this survey.

### Rooms I., II., and III.[3]

The first room contains, almost exclusively, pictures by masters who from the date of their birth belong to the

---

[3] Since the transfer of the gallery to the Villa Borghese the numbers of the rooms and of the pictures have been changed. The new numbers of the pictures are given in the text.—(Trans.)

fifteenth century, but whose labours extend over many years of the sixteenth, such as Sandro Botticelli, Francesco Raibolini, Pintoricchio, Pier di Cosimo, Lorenzo di Credi, Giovan Antonio Bazzi, and others—painters, therefore, who belong to that category which Padre Lanzi was wont to term the most modern of the ancients or the most ancient of the moderns: a definition characteristic alike of his time and of his order. Before, however, examining the several paintings, I wish to say a few words to M. Charles Blanc, a celebrated French art-critic,[4] with respect to a maxim cited by him, and accepted by most art-historians and connoisseurs of our day. They may also serve as a criterion of the method which I have pursued.

'Plus les maîtres sont grands plus leur âme est engagée dans leurs ouvrages,' he justly remarks, though not with much originality, in one of his articles in the 'Gazette des Beaux-Arts' for 1861, entitled "Une Peinture de Léonard de Vinci," in which he seeks to prove that a "St. Sebastian," sold by its owner, M. Moreau, to the Emperor of Russia for 60,000 francs, could be nothing but a genuine work by Leonardo. 'Pour juger de l'authenticité d'un tableau,' he continues, 'il importe de connaître l'esprit du peintre plus encore que ses procédés, car les procédés s'apprennent, le faire se transmet et s'imite, mais l'âme ne saurait se transmettre ; elle est essentiellement inimitable. Ainsi, à l'inverse (! ?) de la plupart des connoisseurs qui regardent principalement dans l'œuvre d'un artiste aux habitudes de son pinceau, j'aimerais mieux m'enquérir avant tout de la tournure de son esprit. L'esprit de Léonard, ou plutôt son génie, était singulièrement complexe,' &c. &c. And because the *génie* of Leonardo was so complex, M. Blanc thought he might attribute to him this " St. Sebastian," a reproduction of which he appended

---

[4] This gifted but superficial writer on art is since dead.

to his article. What would M. Blanc have said if I had replied, 'Mon cher Monsieur Blanc, I too, like you, believe myself to have, if not fathomed, at least studied "la tournure, le génie singulièrement complexe," of Leonardo to the best of my ability; but in addition to these studies of the master's personality, which is ever present in a true work of art, and is indeed that which speaks to us out of the painting and touches the heart, in addition to these psychological studies, I repeat, I have never neglected the study of the *procédés*, the *faire*, of the master, being well aware, from long experience, what tricks imagination is apt to play us. And because it has been my wont, in my art studies, to give heed to the spirit as well as to observe the form, I believe I may confidently reply: This "St. Sebastian" which you extol as a work by Leonardo is, in my opinion, assuredly not the work of the great Florentine.' To judge from the bad illustration, it appears to me to be the work of one of his scholars, in all probability of Cesare da Sesto; if indeed it is permissible from a very poor engraving, to discuss a painting and to pass judgment upon it at all. But for the present, this is of little consequence. I merely wish to show that every student of art labours under the delusion that he has himself thoroughly grasped the distinctive manner and the spirit of the particular master about whom he writes—nay, indeed, that he has grasped and fathomed them better than any one of his predecessors. Art-historians, since the time of Vasari, have all followed this same broad and pleasant, but slippery and perilous, road, and for this very reason so little progress has been made. For surely, no sane man could ever be disposed to regard in the light of a science that art dilettanteism, which has recently made itself heard in every key throughout Europe, and has found expression in ponderous volumes, pamphlets, and lectures, to the delight especially of the ladies. He could only look upon it as a harmless amusement pursued by clever men with wit and brilliancy, and by incompetent writers foolishly.

It is to be hoped therefore, that the followers of M. Blanc will see that the so-called study of 'la tournure de l'esprit, de l'âme' of a master, will help us very little, when we wish to decide the authorship of a work of art with more or less scientific certainty.[5] It was in following this same course, that is, judging only by the general impression, that the late Count Lepel in 1825 went so far as to doubt the genuineness of the Sistine Madonna in the Dresden gallery. As the principal reason for his scepticism, the Count asserted that words cannot easily be found to define art, which stirs and works upon the feelings. And taking his stand upon this slippery maxim, he pronounced the "Madonna di San Sisto" to be a work of the school of Raphael, possibly by Timoteo della Vite, while Hofrath Aloysius Hirt wished to make out that it was by Fattore.[6] For my part, I feel daily more and more convinced that it is only through unremitting study of form that one may gradually attain to understanding and recognising the spirit which gives it life. Such studies, however, are not a matter of weeks, months, or even years.

'Every genuine work of a painter,' says an Indian art-

---

[5] The same French writer who was so intimately acquainted with the 'tournure de l'esprit' of Leonardo da Vinci gives us another striking example of the danger of trusting only to one's natural intuition, however shrewd that may be, in the opinion he expressed of a pen and ink sketch the Thiers collection in the Louvre. Anyone capable of attributing so coarse and even repulsive a forgery to Leonardo da Vinci, would have done better to select any other subject for his dissertations rather than 'l'âme, la tournure de l'esprit' of the great Florentine.

[6] See Graf von Lepel, *Verzeichniss der Werke Raffael's.*

critic, 'will answer thee if thou comprehendest how to question it. If it give thee no answer, then know that thy question was either without intelligence, or the soul, the spirit, the being of the master dwelleth not in that work.' Consequently, I may add, it was either a copy or a production of the school. And if, in support of this view, I find myself obliged, as it were, to particularise certain material signs and forms (which after all are not so material, or so accidental, as they may perhaps appear to some), I trust my indulgent readers will not misunderstand me. Leonardo da Vinci, in his Codex Atlanticus, long ago observed: 'Chi si promette dalla sperienza quel che non è in lei si discosta dalla ragione,' which may be rendered thus: 'He who expects from the experimental method more than it can give, lacks wisdom.'

No one who is at all acquainted with the study of Italian art will deny, that to discriminate between the works of master and pupil is not always so easy as it may appear: to distinguish, for instance (as we are about to speak of the Florentine school) a work by Masolino from one by Masaccio,[7] a painting by Filippino Lippi when young from one by Sandro Botticelli, an early production by the latter from one by Fra Filippo Lippi, or a good early work by Raffaellino del Garbo from a weak painting by Filippino; all works of the same school and the same general character. For, as Masolino was the prototype of Masaccio, and Fra Filippo the master of Botticelli, so this latter was the master of Filippino, who, in his turn, had Raffaellino del Garbo for his pupil. It even occasionally happens that a later painter of the *quattro-cento* is confounded with a

[7] In the Brancacci chapel at Florence, as well as in San Clemente in Rome, Masolino is confounded with Masaccio by Messrs. Crowe and Cavalcaselle (i. 521, 528), and also by Dr. Bode (*Cicerone*, ii. 563, 564).

much earlier one. To cite a few examples : in the Florence Academy, two paintings (representing respectively St. John the Baptist and the Magdalen, Nos. 37 and 39), which are undoubtedly by Filippino, were first attributed to Masaccio, consequently to Fra Filippo's prototype, and afterwards to Andrea del Castagno ; while a St. Jerome (No. 38), which hangs between the two, also a work by Filippino, is still ascribed by the authorities to Andrea del Castagno.[8] It would be easy to cite further instances of the same kind from other schools, as a proof that even art-critics of authority do not always succeed in distinguishing, with any certainty, the works of a pupil from those of the master, or *vice versâ*, when they judge them from the so-called æsthetic standpoint of the ' tournure de l'esprit, l'âme,' of the painter, or when they rely solely on the ' general impression.'

Even long years of practice and constant study do not always enable a man to distinguish an original from a good work of the school ; striking proofs of this are afforded us in the public galleries of France and Italy, and more especially of Germany. The present writer must however disclaim all pretensions to having himself understood the ' tournure de l'esprit, l'âme,' of any great Italian painter. Assuredly he would never be so presumptuous, for often enough it has seemed to him as though, after prolonged years of study of the Italian masters, he had scarcely conquered the first principles of the language of art.

On one point, however, there is not, and cannot be, any longer the slightest doubt in his mind—that in pursuing such studies it is essentially through the medium of ' form ' that we must penetrate to the spirit, in order,

---

[8] Some years before Professor Sidney Colvin was appointed to the British Museum, a drawing by Filip- pino was there attributed to Masaccio (vol. xxxiv. numbered 1860, 6, 16, 64).

through the spirit, to win our way back to a truer knowledge of the 'form' itself.[9]   Such a philosophical precept
sounds something like a truism, and may therefore appear
not altogether worthless to the modern reading public, in
whose eyes such things find favour as a rule.   For myself,
however, I can testify from long experience that its practical application is by no means so easy as it appears,
and moreover costs no little time and trouble.   What, for
instance, is the 'form' in a picture, through which the
spirit of the master—'l'âme, la tournure de l'esprit'—
finds expression?   Surely not the pose and movement
of the human frame alone, nor the expression, type of
countenance, colouring, and the treatment of the drapery?
These are undoubtedly important parts of 'form,' but do
not constitute the whole form.   There still remain, for
instance, the hand, one of the most expressive and characteristic parts of the human body, the ear, the landscape
background if there be any, and the chords, or so-called
harmony, of colour.[1]   In the work of a true artist all these
several parts of the painting are characteristic and distinctive, and therefore of importance, for only by a thorough
acquaintance with them is it possible to penetrate to 'l'âme,
la tournure de l'esprit'—to the very soul of the master.
The character, or style, in a work of art originates simul-

---

[9] 'La natura incomincia col
ragionamento e termina coll' espe-
rienza,' was the teaching of Leonardo
da Vinci.

[1] I cannot refrain from quoting
a passage from that interesting book
*The Life and Letters of Louis
Agassiz*, ii. 566. 'His initiatory
steps in teaching special students
were not a little discouraging, *observation* and *comparison* being, in his
opinion, the intellectual tools, most
indispensable to the naturalist (and,
I may add, to the art-connoisseur
also).   His first lesson was one in
*looking*.   He gave no assistance, he
simply left his student with the
specimen, telling him to use his
eyes diligently, and report upon
what he saw, &c., the professor
requiring the pupil not only to distinguish the various parts of the
animal, but to detect also the relation of these details to more general
typical features.'

taneously with the idea, or, to put it more plainly, it is the artist's idea which gives birth to the 'form' and hence determines the character or style. Copyists can never have any character or style, for 'form' in their works is not due to their own idea. Nor is this all. As most men, both speakers and writers, make use of habitual modes of expression, favourite words and sayings, which they often employ involuntarily and sometimes even most inappropriately, so almost every painter has his own peculiarities, which escape him without his being aware of it. It does even happen that an artist reproduces certain of his own physical defects in his work.[2] Anyone, therefore, intending to study a painter more closely and to become better acquainted with him, must take into consideration even these material trifles (a student of calligraphy would call them flourishes), and know how to discover them; for this purpose, of course, an examination of one, or even of several, of the master's paintings does not suffice; but a wider acquaintance with works of every period of his artistic career is absolutely necessary.

The study of all the individual parts, which go to make up 'form' in a work of art, is what I would recommend to those who are not content with being mere dilettanti, but who really desire to find a way through the intricacies of the history of art, and to attain, if possible, to a scientific knowledge of art. For, as there is a language expressed by

---

[2] Leonardo da Vinci says in chap. xliii. of his *Trattato della Pittura*: 'Quel pittore che avrà goffe mani, le farà simili nelle sue opere, e così gli interverrà in qualunque membro, se il lungo studio non glielo vieta.' And in chap. lxv. he again remarks, that painters frequently fall into the error of reproducing their own physical defects in the figures they paint, and he strongly deprecates such a practice: 'conciossiach' egli è mancamento, che è nato insieme col giudizio: perchè l'anima è maestra del tuo corpo, e quello (that is *mancamento*) del tuo proprio giudizio è che volontieri si diletta nelle opere simili a quelle che essa (that is *l'anima*) operò nel comporre il tuo corpo.'

letters, so there is also a language which expresses itself in form. A child unconsciously learns its mother-tongue by lisping it after its nurse, and finds in this imperfect speech all that is requisite for its limited needs; so, too, the general impression left by a work of art on the public at large is amply sufficient for all its requirements. As the child grows older, however, he must be sent to school in order to master grammar, if he is ever to be capable of reading and appreciating the great writers of his own country. The same applies to the student of art; unless he become familiar with its language he will never be able fully to understand a work of art, and consequently to enjoy it.

Let me endeavour by an example to render my imperfectly expressed ideas more intelligible to my readers. I have already observed that, after the head, the hand is the most characteristic and expressive part of the human body. Now most painters, and rightly enough, put all the strength of their art into the delineation of the features, which they endeavour to make as striking as possible, and pupils, for this part of their work, often appropriated ideas from their masters. This is rarely the case in the representation of the hands and ears; yet they also have a different form in every individual. The types of Saints and the mode of treating the drapery are usually common to a school, having been transmitted through the master's works to his pupils and imitators; while, on the other hand, every independent master has his own special conception and treatment of landscape, and what is more, of the form of the hand[3] and ear. For every important

---

[3] Except the face, probably no part of the human body is more characteristic, individual, significant, and expressive than the hand; to represent it satisfactorily has ever been one of the chief difficulties which artists have had to contend with, and one which only the greatest have been completely successful in overcoming. Of this, both painting and sculpture afford us ample proof. I have given a few examples of characteristic hands.

painter has, so to speak, a type of hand and ear peculiar to himself.[4] On comparing the hands in the earlier works

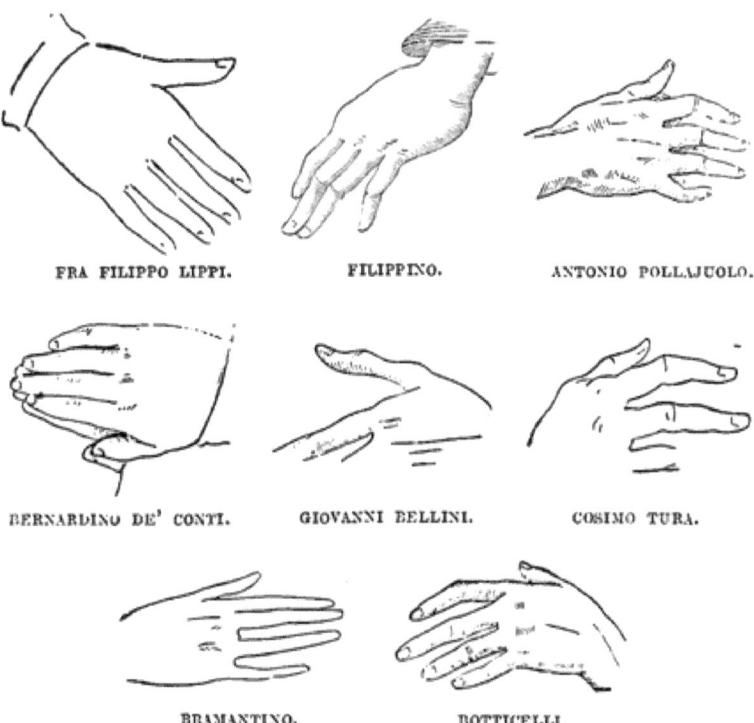

FRA FILIPPO LIPPI.　　FILIPPINO.　　ANTONIO POLLAJUOLO.

BERNARDINO DE' CONTI.　　GIOVANNI BELLINI.　　COSIMO TURA.

BRAMANTINO.　　BOTTICELLI.

[4] Some of those who most disagree with me contend that a variety of forms of hand and ear often occur in the same painting by one master; but this I cannot allow. Goethe has observed somewhere or other: 'In der Dämmerung wird auch die deutlichste Schrift unsichtbar.' My opponents have most likely taken a picture of the school, or even a feeble copy, for an original. I must here reiterate that the *typical form* (*Grundform*) of hand and ear peculiar to each of the great masters is not only to be found in all their pictures, but even in the portraits which they painted from life. In proof, I may cite the following examples: (1) Fra Filippo's portrait of himself in a picture in the Florence Academy (hand and ear). (2) The so-called portrait of Pico della Mirandola, No. 1154, in the Uffizi (hand), and that of a goldsmith in the Corsini gallery at Florence (hand), both by Sandro Botticelli. (3) The portrait of Pandolfini in Filippino's altar-piece in the Badia at Florence (hand and ear). (4) A male portrait by Raffaellino del Garbo in the choice collection of Sir Henry Layard at Venice (hand). (5) The portraits by Raphael of Navagero and Beazzano in the Doria gallery in Rome

of Raphael—from about 1504 to 1505—with those in the works of P. Perugino and Pintoricchio, we shall perceive

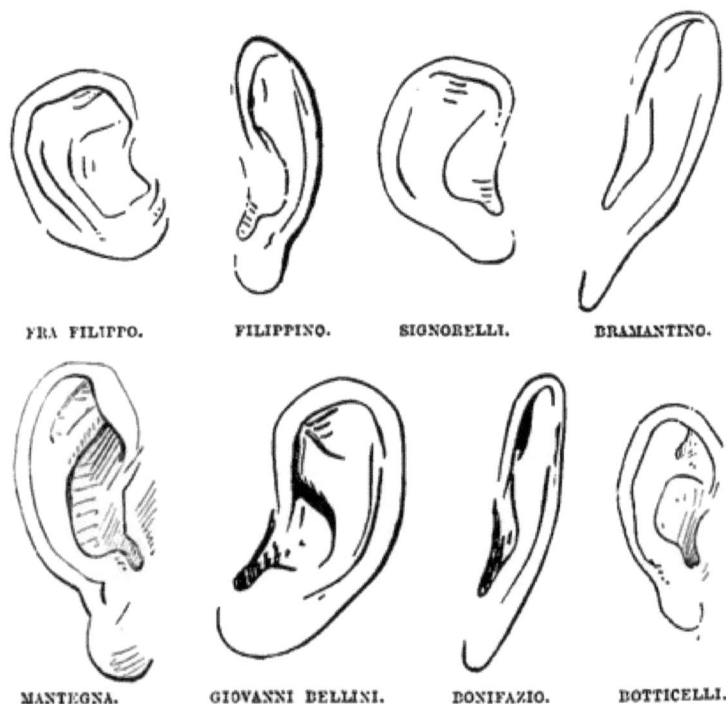

FRA FILIPPO. FILIPPINO. SIGNORELLI. BRAMANTINO.

MANTEGNA. GIOVANNI BELLINI. BONIFAZIO. BOTTICELLI.

a very decided difference between the pupil and his masters. In his Florentine period, especially in the

(ear), those of Pope Leo X. and the so-called "Donna Velata" in the Pitti (ear). (6) The portraits of two Vallombrosan monks by Perugino in the Florence Academy (ear). (7) The portraits of the Gonzagas by Mantegna in the so-called 'Camera degli Sposi' in the Ducal Palace at Mantua, and that of a Cardinal, No. 9, in the Berlin Museum (ear). (8) The portrait of Massimiliano Sforza by Bernardino de' Conti in the Brera (hand and ear). (9) The portraits by L. Lotto in the Brera, at Hampton Court and in the gallery at Vienna (hand). (10) The portrait of a Knight of Malta by Giorgione in the Uffizi (hand). (11) The portrait of Andrea Doria in the Doria gallery, by Sebastiano del Piombo of his Michael-Angelesque period (hand). (12) A portrait of a man in the Tosi gallery at Brescia (No. 32) by Girolamo Romanino (ear). These examples, which I could easily multiply, may perhaps induce my opponents to moderate their somewhat hasty judgments.

"Madonna di casa Tempi" (Munich), the "Madonna del Granduca" (Pitti), the "Madonna del Cardellino" (Uffizi), the "Madonna" belonging to Lord Cowper at Panshanger, the portraits of Maddalena Doni and the so-called "Donna gravida" in the Pitti, &c., the metacarpus is broad and flat, the fingers somewhat lifeless, and the whole hand has rather a homely and commonplace character. After 1509, when Raphael came into contact with a higher class of society in Rome, his treatment of the hand became more refined—as in his cartoon for the "School of Athens" in the Ambrosiana at Milan—till gradually he attained to the elegant, aristocratic form seen in the "Madonna di casa d' Alba," the "Madonna della Seggiola," the "Galatea," &c. In all those works by Raphael in which the *execution is entirely his own*, the ear, like the hand, is always characteristic, and differs in form from the ears of Timoteo Viti, Perugino, Pintoricchio, and others.

After these cursory and introductory remarks on the importance of the several parts in general, and of the hand in particular, in the works by masters of the good period, let us examine more closely the hands of the three Florentine painters, Fra Filippo, Sandro Botticelli and Filippino Lippi. Fra Filippo practically imitated in his hands his prototypes, Fra Angelico [5] and Masaccio, and adhered to the same form to the end of his life. Even his contemporaries, as Vasari relates, found fault with this hand,[6] and its form is certainly not beautiful, being stumpy, awkward, and badly modelled. Fra Filippo's ear, too, is round and clumsy in form, and usually curved inwards. As Rome contains too few

[5] Perhaps nowhere is the influence of Fra Angelico on the young Fra Filippo more strikingly apparent, than in a "Tondo" in the collection of Sir Francis Cook at Richmond.

[6] See Vasari, Lemonnier's edition, iv. 120: 'dove da Carlo Marsuppini gli fù detto, che egli avvertisse alle mani che dipingeva perchè molto le sue cose erano biasimate.'

works by this master for purposes of study, I should advise
anyone who wishes to verify my statements to visit the three
Florentine galleries, which contain over half a dozen
paintings by him. Rome, however, still possesses two
panels by this important painter, one in the Doria-Pamfili
gallery, the other in the Lateran collection. The former
represents on a gold ground the "Annunciation" (*);
the B. Virgin is seated at a *prie-dieu*, before her is the
Archangel holding a lily. The church of S. Lorenzo
at Florence, and the Pinacothek at Munich contain
similar subjects by the master. Fra Filippo's painting in
the Lateran is a Triptych: in the centre is the Coronation
of the Virgin; on the right are two Olivetan monks presenting to her the donor of the picture, Carlo Marsuppini of
Arezzo; in the background are three angels playing on
musical instruments, and on the left are two other monks,
who likewise present one of the faithful to the Mother of
God. This Triptych, which has suffered greatly from repainting, was brought to Rome from Arezzo through the
instrumentality of the picture dealer Baldeschi, and sold to
Pope Gregory XVI. With the exception of Fra Filippo's
works in Rome, Florence, Prato and Spoleto, and two
panels representing the four Fathers of the Church, in the
Academy of Turin, no other works by him are known to
me in Italy.[7]

Botticelli's hands, on the contrary, are very bony and
plebeian, and the nails broad and square, with sharp dark
outlines. These characteristic hands, together with the
large nostrils, the movement and the elongated folds of the
drapery, and the brilliant transparency of colour, in which

[7] The small Madonna and Child
in the gallery of S. Maria Nuova at
Florence, attributed to Fra Filippo,
is only a work of his school, though
classed by Dr. Bode (ii. 572) in the
same category as the fine and genuine
work by the Frate in the Uffizi, No.
1307. An old copy of this latter
picture belongs to Prince Torlonia at
Rome.

a golden cherry-red predominates—while in the paintings of Fra Filippo the prevailing tones are pale blue
and pale grey—make Botticelli's paintings easy to distinguish from those of his imitators.[8] In Filippino's hands,
finally, the structure of the fingers is both peculiar and unpleasing. The juncture with the metacarpus is so sharply
defined that it has not the appearance of a natural growth ;
the fingers look as if they had been screwed into their
places, and are long, wooden, and nerveless. As the scale
of colour differs in the works of these three analogous
painters, so also they deviate strongly from each other in
their landscape backgrounds, and even the form of the
nimbus in their pictures is dissimilar. The landscape of
Fra Filippo, and of his pupil Francesco Pesellino, resembles
that of his contemporaries, and, like Fra Angelico's, consists principally either of a series of rounded hills or of
pointed rocks ; Botticelli, on the other hand, idealised his
landscapes, representing jagged rocks, and often winding
river banks or inlets of the sea. Filippino studied his
landscapes more from nature, and usually represented
the hilly, wooded scenery of Tuscany ; they are also
darker in tone than those of Botticelli. Raffaellino del
Garbo, his talented pupil, had a refined feeling for landscape, and his backgrounds are better composed and in
warmer and more delicate tones than those of his master.
To obtain a thorough knowledge of these three painters
their works in Florence should be studied, for the Roman
collections contain but few examples of their art. Filippino
is represented in Rome by a good panel picture in the second
room of the Sciarra-Colonna gallery, and by frescoes in the

---

[8] Most directors of galleries, who
are wont to follow tradition and to
identify a painting only from a
superficial general impression, almost
invariably confuse Botticelli's genuine works and the productions of
his scholars and imitators.

church of S. Maria sopra Minerva. These latter well-known paintings have, in our time, been most unscrupulously 'restored,' that is *disfigured*, under the very eyes of the Minister of Public Instruction. A like fate has recently befallen Raphael's fresco at Perugia, Titian's frescoes in the ' Scuola del Santo' at Padua, and more especially Mantegna's, in the Palazzo Ducale at Mantua, under the auspices of the Government Inspector-General, Signor G. B. Cavalcaselle.

---

## THE TUSCANS.

AFTER these preliminaries of undue length, let us turn to the pictures themselves. The " Tondo " No. 348 in the Borghese gallery is ascribed to the Florentine Sandro Botticelli; we will therefore begin by considering the pictures by Tuscan masters in these rooms.

### ALESSANDRO FILIPEPI, called BOTTICELLI.

Botticelli, b. 1446, d. 1510, is to be regarded as the pupil of Fra Filippo Lippi, and was undoubtedly one of

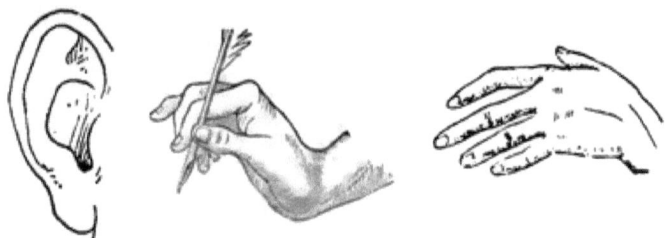

EAR AND HANDS OF BOTTICELLI.

the most gifted and individual among the painters of Italy in the second half of the fifteenth century. The " Tondo " ascribed to him represents the Madonna·

with the Infant Saviour, and angels on either side. The composition, and possibly even the cartoon, belong in all probability to the master himself; the execution, however, can only be ascribed to one of his assistants. I fail to discover in this picture either Botticelli's peculiarly life-like manner of depicting the emotions, or that transparency of colour which distinguishes his works from those of his many imitators. The hands, again, though of the master's typical form, with bony unpleasing fingers, square nails, and black outlines, are absolutely lifeless, and the hair is treated without intelligence. A comparison between this picture and the splendid circular panels in the Uffizi ought to convince every one open to conviction.[9] Naturally, however, as Mephistopheles observed to the student: 'Each man learns only what he can.'

The only genuine works in Rome by this vigorous Florentine are the fine frescoes in the Sistine chapel, and an excellent picture belonging to Prince Mario Chigi—the Madonna with the Child, to whom an angel presents a sheaf of corn. The small painting in the last room of the Colonna gallery[1]—the Madonna with the Child in her arms—and the "Annunciation" in the Barberini collection,[2] both ascribed to him, are only poor productions of his school. As works of his school, and of more or less successful imitators, are attributed to the master himself, I shall take this opportunity of enumerating a few of these miscellaneous productions for the benefit of

[9] Messrs. Crowe and Cavalcaselle (ii. 425) and Dr. Bode (ii. 580) accept this picture as an original.

[1] It seems incredible that a little picture in the last room of the Colonna gallery, representing St. James, should be attributed to Melozzo da Forli. It is manifestly a copy, by a feeble northern painter, of a figure by some follower of Botticelli. The hook-shaped fold in the mantle should be noted, among other peculiarities, as distinctively northern in character.

[2] Messrs. Crowe and Cavalcaselle (ii. 350, note) would attribute this little picture to Marco Zoppo.

those who wish to learn.   Even in Italy they are still shown
to the public as originals by Botticelli, and are accepted
as such by art-historians, both Italian and foreign, professional and unprofessional.   Detailed comparison is the
only sure means by which a student may hope to attain
to a fuller understanding and appreciation of this great
painter, so virile, yet so attractive and full of feeling, and
may learn to distinguish his genuine works from those
which are falsely attributed to him.   The following pictures
are, in my judgment, wrongly ascribed to Botticelli :

### In the Uffizi Gallery.

1. An allegorical figure, No. 1299.   (Crowe and Cavalcaselle ii. 417).[3] (†)

2. " The Annunciation," No. 1316, from a sketch (?)
by the master. (†)

3. The Madonna offering a pomegranate to the Holy
Child, No. 1303. (†)   (Dr. W. Bode, in the ' Cicerone '
ii. 579, calls it an early work of Botticelli.)   The form of
the hand and ear is not that of the master, the body of
the Child is far too weak in modelling, and the expression
and movement of both figures far too lifeless for Botticelli.

### In the Pitti Palace.

4. The Madonna surrounded by angels, No. 348. (†)
(Crowe and Cavalcaselle ii. 424; Dr. Bode agrees with
them.)

5. The so-called portrait of " la bella (?) Simonetta " (?),
No. 353. (†) (Crowe and Cavalcaselle ii. 424; and Dr. Bode
agrees.   The latter, however, observes rightly that this
portrait is ' without special charm.')

---

[3] As already stated in the pre-
face, attributions first given by
Signor Morelli are indicated by a
cross.

6. The Holy Family, No. 357 (Crowe and Cavalcaselle ii. 424). (†)

*In the Accademia delle belle Arti.*

7. The three Archangels with Tobias (Vasari v. 111, 2).[4] (†)

8. The Madonna enthroned with SS. Cosmo and Damiano (Vasari v. 123). (†)

*Formerly in the Oratory of S. Jacopo di Ripoli.*

(Now removed to the school of 'La Quiete.')

9. The Coronation of the Madonna in the presence of

[4] This inferior picture came from the Church of S. Spirito, as a Botticelli, to the Academy, where it was renamed Antonio del Pollajuolo. Messrs. Crowe and Cavalcaselle cite it as the joint work of the brothers Piero and Antonio Pollajuolo. Recently Dr. Bode has expressed the opinion that it is by Andrea Verrocchio, and moreover 'one of the most important panels of the *quattro-cento.*' As the Berlin critic alleges that in studying works of art I have 'practically neglected their deeper meaning for their outward characteristics,' I shall not comment further upon his estimate of this work. I would merely draw attention to the fact that the forms in this picture bear no resemblance to those in Verrocchio's sculptures, nor to those in the Baptism of Christ, or even in pictures which Dr. Bode ascribes to Verrocchio in Berlin and London. As for the '*Sandarakfirniss*' which he mentions as important and characteristic both in the "Baptism" and the "Tobias and the Angel," it may be observed in the works of many other contemporary Florentines; in those, for instance, of the school of Botticelli, of the Pollajuoli, and of Cosimo Roselli. With regard to No. 20 in the Florence Academy (a feeble work again representing Tobias and the Angel), which Dr. Bode believes to be also by Verrocchio and 'executed entirely in *tempera,*' I feel bound once more to differ from him. I would take this opportunity of protesting against the injustice done to an artist of the importance of Verrocchio, in ascribing to him works of so little merit, and of cautioning students against estimating works of art from the standpoint of the so-called '*Geistige Gehalt,*' which is always more or less dependent upon subjective and individual impressions. Thus the Florentine commission 'for the preservation of works of art' (composed almost entirely of painters) have recently bestowed the name of Verrocchio upon a worthless production (No. 1,278 *trs.*) by some Tuscan artist of the second half of the fifteenth century, and have assigned to it a prominent position in the Uffizi, instead of leaving it in its proper place in the depôt of the gallery, whither their predecessors had banished it.

many Saints. (†) (In the edition of the 'Cicerone' of 1879, p. 545, Dr. Bode regarded this work as an original by Botticelli; in the later edition, however, to my great satisfaction, he agrees with me and mentions it only as a work of the school—p. 580 *ibid.* Messrs. Crowe and Cavalcaselle would have us regard it as a 'careful production of Botticelli's fine time,' ii. 424.)

### In the Church of S. Felice.
#### (First altar on the left.)

10. Panel representing SS. Antony, Roch, and Catherine; by a pupil of Botticelli who was influenced by Filippino, but decidedly not by Filippino himself. (†) (Dr. Bode, ii. 581, ascribes it to Filippino.)

### In the Oratory of S. Ansano.
#### (Near Fiesole.)

11. Four small panels, pronounced by the Florentine editors of Vasari (v. 124) to be 'undoubted' works by Botticelli.

### In the Corsini Gallery at Florence.

12. "Tondo," representing the Madonna surrounded by angels (Crowe and Cavalcaselle ii. 578, and Dr. Bode ii. 580). (†) The same collection, however, possesses a genuine, though much over-cleaned work by Botticelli in the portrait of a goldsmith, resembling the sadly disfigured portrait of a medallist in the Uffizi. (†)

### In the Turin Gallery.

13. The three Archangels with Tobias, No. 98. (†)

14. The Madonna with the Infant Saviour, the little St. John and an Angel, No. 99. (†)

15. A small allegorical work representing " The Triumph

of Chastity," No. 369 (Crowe and Cavalcaselle ii. 426);
the fettered Cupid recalls Filippino, the maidens following
the triumphal car are more in the style of Botticelli.[5] (†)

*In the Poldi-Pezzoli Collection at Milan.*

16. "The Pietà." (†)

This collection, however, possesses a genuine, though unfortunately much restored, Virgin and Child by Botticelli;
at Milan we find another most exquisite Madonna and
Child by the master in the Ambrosiana, and three genuine
works in the Morelli collection,—the history of "Virginia,"[6]
a "Salvator Mundi," and the original portrait of Giuliano
de' Medici, of which the Berlin gallery possesses a school
copy formerly in the collection of Prince Strozzi at
Florence.

But enough for the present of Botticelli's imitators
whose works, good, bad, and indifferent, are recommended
to the public by the catalogues, and so too, as a matter of
course, by guide-books, as originals by the master. In conclusion, I may mention a few of his drawings in which
this great artist's peculiarities of expression and representation may be studied.

---

[5] The Marchese Adorno, at
Genoa, possesses four small works
by this Florentine master, who was
probably a fellow-scholar with
Filippino; a sixth—"The Combat
between Cupid and Chastity "—has
recently been bought by the English
National Gallery. These six paintings appear to have formed a series
of decorative panels for furniture.
Dr. Bode attributes them to Botticelli (ii. 579).

[6] This picture may have been one
of those which, according to Vasari,
the master painted for Giovanni
Vespucci: 'con molte figure vivissime
e belle.' It contains about fifty
figures, all equally spirited in conception and careful in execution, and
each one indispensable to the harmony of the whole. I could name
scarcely another work in which
Botticelli's great artistic qualities, as
well as his defects, are so strikingly
apparent as in his masterly representation of this tragic scene. (The
picture referred to is now in the
gallery at Bergamo.)

*In the Uffizi Collection.*

Case 41 : St. John the Baptist, pen, indian ink, and solid white.

Case 43 : St. Jerome, silver point and white.

*In Mr. John Malcolm's Collection in London.*

An allegorical female figure with *putti*, red chalk (Braun, No. 21). From this drawing a pupil of Botticelli painted the well-known picture which passed from M. Reiset's collection into that of the Duc d'Aumale. (Messrs. Crowe and Cavalcaselle regard this picture as an original, ii. 429.)

## LORENZO DI CREDI.

The " Tondo " No. 433, in the Borghese Gallery, is by a younger contemporary of Sandro Botticelli, Lorenzo di Credi (Lorenzo di Andrea di Credi, born at Florence 1459, died there 1537), who might be styled the Carlo Dolce of the fifteenth century, and who as an artist was the complete opposite of Botticelli. The popularity of the circular form for paintings, more especially in Florence, seems to have been due to Luca della Robbia's terra-cotta " Tondi." The picture represents the Madonna with the Infant Saviour on her knee. He is seated on a cushion blessing, with His right hand, the little St. John, and holding in His left some fruit; with a landscape background. On the parapet, to the right of the Madonna, Lorenzo introduced some flowers in a glass, painted from nature with miniature-like care and consummate skill; the treatment indeed is quite Flemish in its conscientious accuracy.[7] This pic-

---

[7] According to Vasari (Lemon-nier's ed. vii. 17) Leonardo da Vinci introduced a similar vase of flowers in a painting of his early period: ' Fece poi Lionardo una nostra Donna in un quadro, che era appresso papa Clemente VII., molto eccellente e fra l' altre cose, che v' eran fatte, con-traffece una caraffa piena d'acqua con alcuni fiori dentro, dove oltre la

ture, one of Lorenzo's most successful works, is in *tempera*, and was probably executed in the last ten years of the fifteenth century. The colours are very bright, the modelling of the Child recalls Verrocchio's *putto* in the court of the Palazzo Vecchio at Florence, as also the *putti* in a genuine pen and ink drawing by Verrocchio in the Louvre (Room X., exhibited on a screen). (†)

In his early days Lorenzo may have applied himself more to sculpture, that is to modelling, than to painting, which accounts for Verrocchio having, in his last will and testament, addressed a petition to the Signoria at Venice requesting that they would entrust to his assistant Lorenzō the completion of the Colleoni statue.

In the Borghese gallery there is another, and rather smaller, "Tondo" (No. 439), also ascribed in the catalogue to Lorenzo di Credi. Herr Jansen, however, in his monograph of Sodoma saw fit to attribute it to that master. The picture represents the Madonna and St. Joseph adoring the Infant Saviour, who lies on a cushion on the ground; with a landscape background. On comparing the two works it will be immediately apparent that, while the composition and drawing recall Lorenzo di Credi, the scale of colour is much deeper than is usual with this master, and reminds one more of the colouring of Botticelli and Signorelli. Neither the hand nor the ear, nor the folds of the drapery, correspond

---

meraviglia della vivezza, aveva imitato la rugiada dell' acqua sopra, sì che pareva più viva che la vivezza.' Vasari evidently describes the painting from hearsay, and the passage may not improbably refer to this Borghese picture, which, it would seem, was already regarded as the work of Leonardo in Vasari's day. It is not surprising, therefore, that Amoretti should have mentioned it as such in his monograph of Leo-

nardo (Memorie storiche su la vita, gli studi e le opere di Lionardo da Vinci, scritte da Carlo Amoretti, Milano, 1804), or that the Florentine editors of Vasari (vii. 17) should, as usual, have followed blindly in the steps of others. How often in books dealing with art are we not reminded of the parable, which that excellent painter old Bruegel depicted so inimitably in his picture in the Naples Museum !

with the distinctive forms in authentic works by Lorenzo di Credi.  High lights, such as those on the bridge of the nose, on the upper lip and on other parts, are never met with in Lorenzo's paintings, and appear to me characteristic of another master.  The chords of colour and the

elongated folds point more perhaps to Signorelli than to Botticelli ; the general arrangement of the drapery, however, approaches Botticelli in the main, while the remainder of the picture, especially the landscape, points to Lorenzo.  I should, therefore, ascribe this excellent work to a skilful Florentine painter,

EAR OF LORENZO
DI CREDI.

who probably learnt of Botticelli, but who later followed Lorenzo closely, and was perhaps employed in his workshop; and I am glad to find that Messrs. Crowe and Cavalcaselle are of a similar opinion [8] (iii. 412). By this master, whom we will call Tommaso, we shall find works both good and indifferent in other places : in the Pitti (No. 354) under the name of Lorenzo di Credi (†) ; in the collection of the Cav. C. Giuntini in Florence (†) ; in

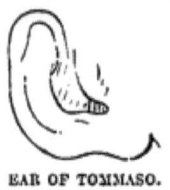

the gallery at Modena under the name of Lippo Fiorentino (No. 43) (†) ; at Milan in the possession of the brothers Prinetti-Esengrini (†), and in the collections of Dr. Gustavo Frizzoni and of the author.[9]  There

EAR OF TOMMASO.

are no other genuine works by Lorenzo di Credi in Rome, except one of his later period in the Capitoline gallery.  In the Colonna gallery (Room I.) we find a small picture of the Madonna with the Child on her knee, to whom she offers some strawberries, which

[8] Dr. Bode (ii. 585) agrees with the Borghese catalogue and pronounces this painting, which on account of its colouring reminds him partly of Leonardo and partly of Signorelli, to be the work of Lorenzo di Credi.

[9] Now in the gallery at Bergamo.

is there simply attributed to a Lippo (?), but which was pronounced by a German writer on art (Mündler, ' Beiträge zu J. Burckhardt's Cicerone,' p. 4) to be a charming work by Lorenzo di Credi. In my opinion, however, it is by an early imitator of Lorenzo, and I am inclined to think by a Fleming, (†) the same probably as, or at least contemporary with, the painter on whom, in the Dresden gallery, the name of Leonardo da Vinci was too hastily bestowed. Lorenzo's best works may be seen in the Uffizi, the Florentine Academy, the Pinacothek at Turin (No. 356), and the Louvre (No. 1264). At Palermo, in the church dell' Olivella, there is also a Madonna by him under the name of Raphael. (†) In his fine work in the Borghese gallery the landscape and the peculiar form of the car and the hand—the latter with the somewhat stiffly bent fingers which Lorenzo nearly always introduces—should be specially noticed; for they are characteristic of the master and recur in all his genuine works. Students will then see for themselves that the feeble painting attributed to him in the Uffizi (No. 1287) can only be by some assistant or imitator, who made use of the master's cartoon.[1] (†) The colours in the landscape are not those of Lorenzo di Credi, the hand and ear do not correspond with his forms, and the heads are wanting in life and expression. This picture, however, receives special mention from Dr. Bode (ii. 585).

---

[1] In addition to Lorenzo's pictures, I would recommend the following drawings for purposes of study: the Cartoon in the Florence Academy; a drawing in the Uffizi (No. 476, Case 125); several in red chalk in the Louvre (Reiset catalogue, Nos. 199, 200, 202 — No. 200 is a good example of the master's distinctive form of ear); a pen drawing in the British Museum (Braun 26), and the portrait of an old man at Chatsworth, under the name of Daniele da Volterra (Braun No. 30). This latter admirable drawing, in which Lorenzo di Credi's characteristic form of ear is also apparent, represents, if I am not mistaken, Mino da Fiesole (died 1486). It should be compared with the portrait of Mino which precedes Vasari's biography of that sculptor. (†)

## LUCA SIGNORELLI.

This great and powerful painter, the forerunner of
Michael Angelo, is only represented in Rome by his fresco
in the Sistine chapel, and by a little Holy Family in the
Casino Rospigliosi.   A second small picture by him, formerly
in the possession of the Patrizi family in Rome, has recently
been sold by them, with all their remaining art-treasures,
and is now in the Berlin gallery; it represents the Visitation.   On the left he has introduced Zachariah, with the
little St. John in his arms; and on the right St. Joseph
with the Infant Saviour on his knee.   The picture, signed
LUCHAS SIGNORELLVS DE CORTONA, is probably a late work
by the master.   The long narrow panels of saints in
the Lateran collection, some of which are ascribed to
Signorelli and some to the school of Murano, I believe to
be by Cola dell' Amatrice (†), a coarse exaggerated painter
of Ascoli, belonging to the later school of Carlo Crivelli.
Those who wish to become more familiar with Signorelli
should above all study his frescoes in the cathedral of
Orvieto.   These masterpieces appear to me unequalled in
the art of the fifteenth century; for to no other contemporary painter was it given to endow the human frame
with a like degree of passion, vehemence, and strength.
The frescoes in the cloisters of Mont' Oliveto are good
examples of Signorelli's art; so too are the large altar-
piece in the sacristy of the cathedral at Perugia, and the
processional standard in the Palazzo Municipale at Borgo
S. Sepolcro.   At Cortona, Volterra, and Urbino we also
find characteristic pictures by the master.   Two very
interesting early works by him are in the Brera at Milan:
"The Scourging of Christ" and a Madonna and Child.   At
Florence we find a large altar-piece and a predella in the
Academy, some excellent easel pictures and a predella in

the Uffizi, a small panel in the Pitti, the portrait of a man in the Torrigiani collection, and several beautiful Madonnas in the Ginori and Corsini galleries.

With Signorelli, as with all other great masters, the form of hand and ear and the landscape are all charac-teristic.[2]  His drawings are found in all the most important collections of Europe; one is in the Uffizi (Case 459, No. 1246), and no less than seven in the Louvre (Nos. 340–346, Braun 140, 141).  The one, however, which was presented to that collection as a Signorelli by the late Mr. Morris Moore (No. 347, Braun 142) is

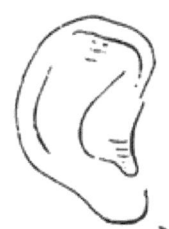

EAR OF SIGNORELLI.

palpably nothing but a coarse copy, or even a forgery. (†) In the British Museum I also saw three good drawings by him (Vol. 32), and one in the Library at Windsor under the name of Masaccio. (†)

Signorelli's drawings are, as a rule, roughly sketched with charcoal; but he occasionally employed black or red chalk.  All those just mentioned seem to me to prove that Antonio del Pollajuolo had a greater influence over Signorelli than has hitherto been supposed, and the fact that A. del Pollajuolo's two drawings, Adam and Eve, in the Uffizi, are there attributed to Signorelli, is a further proof of this. (†)

## GIROLAMO GENGA.

This painter, who had the misfortune to become Signorelli's pupil and assistant, shared the fate which later befell all the pupils, or rather imitators, of Michael Angelo—he became the caricature of his prototype.  And how would it have fared with the pliable, impressionable

---

[2] The master's characteristic form of hand and ear may be studied in No. 1291 in the Uffizi.

nature of the young Raphael, had he too fallen under the uncompromising, one-sided guidance of Signorelli, as some of his biographers erroneously assumed that he did, instead of under that of the gentle and graceful Timoteo Viti?

Girolamo Genga's example furnishes us with a very instructive reply to this question. He too came from Urbino, and was unquestionably endowed with great talents. An examination of his paintings and drawings shows how rapidly he degenerated under the crushing influence of his great master, Signorelli. In the "Martyrdom of St. Sebastian," in the Uffizi (No. 1205), which I consider an early work by Genga of about 1498–99 (†)—though it is there exhibited as by an unknown artist, and is attributed by Messrs. Crowe and Cavalcaselle (iii. 370) to Domenico and Orazio Alfani — the imitation, or rather the aping, of Signorelli is as yet scarcely apparent, but in the paintings and drawings of his later years, this strikes us in all its crudeness. Some of them I will enumerate here:

1. In the two frescoes (Nos. 375, 376) in the Academy of Siena, which came from the Palazzo Petrucci—one representing Æneas with his father Anchises, the other "A Ransom of Prisoners"—the composition is certainly by Signorelli, but they were undoubtedly executed by his pupil and assistant Genga.[3] A small sketch in Indian ink by Genga for the "Ransom of Prisoners" is in the Lille collection (†) (Braun 102), under the name of Jacopo Francia. In the same collection we find another drawing by Genga (†) in pen and ink (Braun 133), but under the name of Giulio Romano, representing the "Continence of Scipio."

---

[3] Dr. Bode regards them as genuine works by Signorelli (ii. 603). The St. Barbara in the Poldi Collection at Milan is also by a scholar and not by Signorelli himself, and so too is No. 19 in the Florence Academy, the Magdalen at the foot of the Cross, in a rocky landscape. (†)

2. The gallery of Siena contains two Madonnas by Genga, one, No. 340, under the name of Girolamo del Pacchia,[4] (†) the second, No. 38ª, placed in the 'Florentine School.' (†) In the picture gallery at Lille, we find a work by Genga (†) described as of the 'École italienne primitive.' It represents the Madonna adoring the Holy Child, who is supported by St. Joseph, and embraces the little St. John ; on the right are two Shepherds. In the Opera del Duomo at Siena is a large "Resurrection" (once forming the shutters of the organ), which was executed by Genga in 1510. Some writers have confounded Genga with Sodoma in this painting, which, it appears to me, has also been the case in his portrait of a man in the Pitti (No. 382).[5] (†)

In addition, I must mention Genga's principal work, painted about 1517–18, for the High-Altar of the church of S. Agostino at Cesena, now in the Brera. The predella belonging to it is in the gallery at Bergamo, and the drawing for it in the Uffizi under the name of Raphael (†) (photographed by Philpot, No. 2610), while the large red chalk drawing for the painting in the Brera is in the Louvre (Braun, No. 223). Another drawing in black chalk, bearing an equally high-sounding name, but which is extremely characteristic of Genga, I saw some years ago in the interesting collection of Mr. Heseltine in London. The subject was the Madonna and Child, with the little St. John. (†) Genga, though greatly extolled by his friend Vasari, was nevertheless, owing to the influence

---

[4] This Sienese painter must originally have been influenced by Genga, then by Albertinelli, and later more especially by Sodoma. Del Pacchia is himself constantly confounded with Andrea del Brescianino, as for instance in No. 115 of the Turin Academy, which is by the latter. (†)

[5] A Holy Family in this collection (No. 349) is, however, attributed to Genga. It appears to me to be an old copy after Filippino Lippi, and certainly has nothing to do with Genga.

of his master Signorelli, the painter who most contributed
to the approaching decline of art in Italy.

The Florentine school of the fifteenth century, which
was influenced to some extent by Paolo Uccello, and later
by Domenico Veneziano, and which numbered among its
principal representatives Alesso Baldovinetti, Cosimo
Roselli, Domenico Ghirlandaio, Mainardi and Granacci, is
unrepresented in the Roman collections by any important
works.[6]  Following the old numbers, we came to a much
damaged picture (∗), ascribed to Paris Alfani of Perugia,
which might be attributed with greater probability to
Franciabigio. (†)   The Florentine painters of the first
decades of the sixteenth century, such as Franciabigio,
Giuliano Bugiardini, Francesco Granacci, Ridolfo del Ghirlandaio, &c., are often confounded in official catalogues
and consequently in other books. This is pardonable,
however, as these artists, having no decided character of
their own, followed, as is customary with such hybrid
natures, first one important master and then another,
endeavouring to imitate and to reproduce the style of each.
The manner and the defects thus assimilated become characteristic of these painters, and should be observed; for
though of no great importance, such a study has its charm,
and is by no means lost labour, since it educates the eye
and enables us to distinguish the works of these secondary
artists with some degree of certainty.   Mr. Mündler,
who recognised in this picture the hand of Bugiardini,
was at all events strictly consistent in his criticism, as
he pronounced the "Annunciation" in the Turin gallery,
and the so-called "Madonna del Pozzo" in the Tribune

---

[6] Two panels in the Colonna
gallery attributed to Domenico
Ghirlandaio, are not by him, but
only of his school. Dr. Bode (ii.
586) ascribes them to Pier di
Cosimo. (!)

of the Uffizi, to be by the same hand.[7]  I also am of
opinion that these works are by the same master ; but I
should substitute the name of Franciabigio for that of
Bugiardini.

## GIULIANO BUGIARDINI.

There are only three paintings by this master still
to be found in the public collections in Rome.  One in the
Colonna gallery (Room I.) is signed IVLIANI. FLORENTINI.
OPVS, and has been greatly damaged by restoration ; the
second, with the forged signature of Andrea del Sarto,
is in the Corsini gallery (Room III., No. 9) ;[8] the third
by Giuliano (?) is in the Borghese gallery (No. 443)
ascribed to the 'School of Raphael,' the subject being
the Madonna with the Child and the little St. John.  In
the Pinacothek at Bologna there are three good works[9]
by Bugiardini, and in the church of S. Maria delle Grazie
at Milan a St. John the Baptist signed with his name.
Among other points of difference between this painter
and Franciabigio, it may be mentioned that Bugiardini
has a more liquid touch in laying on his colours, and
his flesh-tints have less 'smalto' than is usual in the
paintings of Franciabigio.  For some time Bugiardini was
in the workshop of Albertinelli and under his influence—
that he became his imitator is clear from a painting of the
Holy Family in the Turin gallery (No. 106).

[7] Dr. Bode (ii. 682) ascribes the
" Madonna del Pozzo " to Ridolfo del
Ghirlandaio.

[8] Vasari relates that, in order
to help his friend Bugiardini out
of a difficulty, Michael Angelo made
a sketch for him, from which he
painted his picture of the " Martyrdom of St. Catherine," for the Rucellai chapel in the church of S. Maria
Novella at Florence.  This rough
sketch is now in the library of the
Corsini Palace in Rome (Col. 157,
G. 7, No. 125, 514).

[9] A Madonna, and a Madonna
and Child with Saints, both signed,
and a " St. John the Baptist," without signature.

## FRANCIABIGIO.

Like Bugiardini, Franciabigio (b. 1482, d. 1525) was (according to Vasari) first a follower of Mariotto Albertinelli; but he probably spent part of his apprenticeship in the workshops of Granacci and Pier di Cosimo. This is proved by his way of dealing with his subject, his manner of treating drapery, and his landscape backgrounds, which recall those of Pier di Cosimo. Later, it is true, he shows a decided leaning to Andrea del Sarto, who had been his fellow pupil with Pier di Cosimo. This connection with Andrea is especially noticeable in the works of his later years. Among the earlier works of Franciabigio, which show the influence of Albertinelli, may be mentioned the "Annunciation" at Turin; the altar-piece painted by him for the church of S. Giobbe at Florence, which now hangs in the second room of the Uffizi; the small "Calumny of Apelles" (No. 427) in the Pitti; and the picture in the Borghese gallery (No. 177) representing the "Marriage of St. Catherine." [1] (†)

The following pictures in the Uffizi are, I should say, of his middle period: the "Tondo" (1224) (†) with the Holy Family and the little St. John, there attributed to Ridolfo del Ghirlandaio (Dr. Bode thinks it by the latter painter); the picture representing the "Temple of Hercules" (1223); a small Madonna and Child (No. 92) in the first corridor, and another falsely attributed to Raffaellino del Garbo; (†) and the episodes from the life of Joseph, Nos. 1282 (*) and 1249 (*), once in the second room, (†)

---

[1] Dr. Bode (ii. 680) is of the same opinion. He further ascribes the entirely repainted female portrait in the Pitti (No. 140), known as the "Nun of Leonardo da Vinci," to Franciabigio — a verdict I cannot accept. Anyone at all acquainted with Perugino's type of hand will have no hesitation, I think, in pronouncing this portrait to be his work. (†)

ascribed in the catalogue to Pontormo.[2]   The following works, showing in a marked degree the influence of Andrea del Sarto, I should also place in Franciabigio's middle period : the fresco in the entrance-court of the SS. Annunziata and the two frescoes in the ' Scalzi,' at Florence ; three male portraits which have darkened considerably, one in the Pitti (No. 43), one at Windsor, and a third, formerly in the possession of the heirs of the Marchese Gino Capponi, which has recently been sold and is now in Germany.   A Madonna in the Pinacothek at Bologna (No. 294), again under the name of Pontormo, I consider to be also of about the same period. (†)

The following appear to me to be of his third and last epoch.   The so-called "Madonna del Pozzo" in the Tribune; a fine circular panel representing the Madonna and Child in the Palace of Prince Corsini in the Via del Prato at Florence ; the "Letter sent by the hand of Uriah" in the Dresden gallery (No. 75) ; a fine male portrait in the Berlin Museum ; the fresco of the Last Supper in the ' Calza ' at Florence ; and a fresco in the villa of Poggio a Caiano near Florence. Franciabigio died in 1525 ; his life therefore covers about the same space of time as that of Raphael.   His name was not Marcantonio, as stated in all catalogues, even in that of the Pitti, since the time of Baldinucci, but Francesco (in patois Francia) Bigi ; his father's name was Christopher, hence his monogram, an F, an R, a C, and a P, *i.e.* FRanciscus Christophori (the son of Christopher) Pinxit.[3]

---

[2] Studies for this panel (1249), rightly assigned to Franciabigio, are among the drawings in the Uffizi (Philpot 1506).   The landscape, the form of hand and ear, which differs from that of Pontormo, as well as the types of the heads, induced me to ascribe these paintings to Franciabigio rather than to Pontormo; I also fail to discover in them Pontormo's characteristic drawing of the eyes deeply sunk in their sockets.   For all these points a comparison between Franciabigio's picture No. 1223 and these two paintings is desirable.

[3] The Louvre has a good drawing by Franciabigio (Braun 93), another is at Lille under the name of Raphael (Braun 91). (†)

Granacci, Franciabigio and Pontormo—three nearly contemporary painters—are, as we have seen, constantly confounded in their small predella pictures (even by connoisseurs), for there is a family likeness between them. Granacci, the elder of the three (b. 1477), must, at one time, have exercised a more or less considerable influence over his younger contemporaries. In the six predella pictures by Granacci in the Florence Academy, representing the martyrdoms of SS. Catherine, Apollonia, Agnes, and other Saints, the types of heads bear some resemblance to those of Pontormo, while the landscape differs considerably from that of the latter and of Franciabigio. In Granacci's large picture, in the same gallery, the heads of the flying angels are almost identical in type with heads in Franciabigio's panels in the Uffizi (1249 and 1282). It seems incredible that, in his Holy Family in the Pitti (†) (No. 345), Granacci should have been confounded with Baldassare Peruzzi even by Dr. Bode, who again, in this case, appears to have trusted Messrs. Crowe and Cavalcaselle more than his own eyes.[4]

A picture belonging to the Marchese Covoni in Florence is, perhaps, Granacci's best work. It represents the Madonna with the Infant Christ on her left arm, and a book in her right hand; at her feet kneel SS. Thomas, Zenobio, and Francis; above her are two angels. This painting was executed in 1505, by order of Maria Francesca di Zenobio de' Girolami, for the church of S. Gallo.

Before proceeding to discuss the works of Franciabigio's best known pupil, Francesco Ubertini, we will examine the little portrait No. 436. This is a copy of an

---

[4] In order to leave themselves a loophole of escape, Messrs. Crowe and Cavalcaselle prudently observe, 'this is a Siennese work, without the exact stamp of Peruzzi' (iii. 401-2). Alinari of Florence has published a good photograph of this picture.

excellent painting, which the catalogue of the Uffizi describes as the portrait of "Alessandro Braccesi, segretario di Balia," and attributes to Lorenzo di Credi (No. 1217)—an ascription so wide of the mark that I was amazed to find that Messrs. Crowe and Cavalcaselle (iii. 412) had not questioned it.[5] It seems to me that this portrait is far too spirited in conception and too warm in colouring for Lorenzo di Credi, and I have not the slightest hesitation in pronouncing it to be a good early work by Pietro Perugino (†) of about the same period (1485–90 perhaps) as the so-called "Nun of Leonardo" in the Pitti Palace, and worthy of close study. Messer Alessandro Braccesì was inscribed as 'Notaro della Signoria' as early as 1474, and he must therefore have been over twenty at that period, while the portrait represents a boy of about fourteen or fifteen. The naming of the person represented, equally with that of the painter, appears therefore in this case, as in so many others, to be purely arbitrary, and to have been based solely on a general impression.

## BACCHIACCA.

Nos. 425, 427, 440, 442, and 463 all belong to the same master, namely to Francesco Ubertini, called Bacchiacca, (†) who, as a rule, is but little known.[6] They represent episodes from the life of Joseph—subjects which were apparently very popular in Florence for the adornment of the nuptial chamber in the third decade of the sixteenth century. Bacchiacca is several times mentioned by Vasari, though only incidentally, in the biographies of Perugino, Granacci, Franciabigio, Aristotele da San Gallo, and others. As an artist he is by no means wanting in talent, and his

[5] Dr. Bode follows in their steps (ii. 586).

[6] The new director of the Bor-ghese gallery has accepted my ascriptions for these pictures.

works, as a rule, are rare.    I shall therefore devote more
time than a general survey of a picture gallery would seem
to warrant to this not uninteresting painter, who is less
known in the history of art than he deserves to be, and
whose works are frequently met with in different collections,
under the illustrious names of Dürer, Raphael, Leonardo,
and Michael Angelo.

Francesco Ubertini must have been born about 1494,
in Florence.   According to Vasari (xiii. 165), Angelo Bronzino's large painting of 1552, "The Descent into Hades"
(now in the Uffizi, No. 1271), contains portraits of Pontormo,
Giovan-Battista Gello, and Bacchiacca.   In this picture he
appears to be a man of about sixty; a few years later,
in 1557, he died in Florence.   He had two brothers, one
of whom, Baccio, was a pupil and assistant of Perugino;
the other, Antonio, distinguished himself in his day as a
worker in tapestry.

We gather from Vasari, who knew Bacchiacca personally, and esteemed him both as a man and an artist, that,
with his brother Baccio, he also studied for some time under
Pietro Perugino, probably about 1505–1506 ; and that he
afterwards joined Franciabigio and very likely spent the
latter years of his apprenticeship with him, possibly working
as Franciabigio's assistant until the death of that master
in 1525.   According to Passavant, the brothers, Baccio and
Francesco, left Florence for Perugia in order to receive instruction there in the art of painting from Perugino.   It
appears to me, however, more probable that the two Florentines should have visited Perugino's workshop in Florence,
for in the first decade of the sixteenth century this painter
was more in that city than in Perugia.   It is evident,
I think, that later Bacchiacca borrowed much from his
friend, Andrea del Sarto, and, in his last period, from
Michael Angelo.   In his manner of posing his figures, of

drawing the hands, of arranging the draperies, and, more especially, in his landscape backgrounds—which, as a rule, are very careful in execution—it appears to me that the influence of Andrea del Sarto, rather than that of Perugino, or even of Franciabigio, is apparent, though the latter was himself so closely connected with Andrea. From Franciabigio, however, Bacchiacca may have taken his smooth colouring and cold flesh tones.

After the death of Franciabigio, Bacchiacca appears to have gone to Rome, at all events he was there about 1525, and lived on terms of intimacy with Giulio Romano, Francesco Penni, and Benvenuto Cellini ; and the latter mentions him at the beginning of his autobiography. Vasari extols, and rightly, the great care and finish of his small figures, which rarely exceeded a span in height. He further praises the arabesques, with animals and foliage taken from nature, with which Bacchiacca decorated the chamber of Duke Cosimo de' Medici, and adds that he furnished many cartoons for the ducal tapestries. In the collection of the ' Arazzi ' at Florence there are three large tapestries worked with gold, representing the twelve months of the year, in which, it seems to me, I can discern the spirit of Bacchiacca and his distinctive and characteristic forms. (†) In all probability these are the tapestries which were woven by the Fleming Rost from cartoons by Ubertini (see Vasari).

Bacchiacca is also said to have been an excellent animal painter ('era ottimo pittore in ritrarre tutte le sorti d'animali '), and certainly the animals in some of his pictures (for instance, in the one in the Giovanelli collection at Venice) are admirable. As I have studied this little-known master with considerable interest, I may perhaps be permitted to enumerate in chronological order certain of his works which I venture to think I have discovered in the course of my artistic wanderings. I should be well satisfied if these slight notices might induce some art-historian to take up the study of this master, and to produce an historical portrait of him, for Bacchiacca appears to me to be a remarkable painter, who occasionally surprises us by flashes of genius and by his unaffected grace.

I will first, however, mention some of the characteristics by which his works may easily be distinguished from those of his contemporaries, who nearly approached him.

1. In the foreground of his landscapes he nearly always introduces a wedge-shaped rock of a light grey colour, overgrown with trees and bushes (this may be seen in one of the pictures in this gallery, No. 463), and in the middle distance a town with numerous towers.

2. His hands have long bony fingers.

3. Like his master, Franciabigio, he shows a predilection for blue.

4. He first laid in the hair in brown, and added the details with glazes of a yellowish colour; a method to be studied in this picture, No. 463.

5. Like all hybrid artists, Bacchiacca has no characteristic form of ear. It is sometimes rounder, sometimes longer in form, according to the model which he happened to have before him at the time.

6. The close-fitting sleeves which he gives to his female figures show a number of stiff cross-folds in the fore-arm, and usually reach below the knuckles—a peculiarity probably due to his study of Lucas van Leyden's engravings, from which Bacchiacca borrowed various details.

7. In his draperies we often find a fold in the shape of a V. This occurs, for instance, on the upper part of the right arm of the "Vierge au Sein" belonging to Professor Nicole at Lausanne; several times in a painting belonging to Don Giacomo Bertoldi, a priest of Carpenedo near Mestre; in the picture in the Palazzo Giovanelli, and also in draw-

LA VIERGE AU SEIN.  BY BACCHIACCA.

To face p. 105.

ings in the author's collection,[7] in the Louvre, and elsewhere.

I should assign the following works to Bacchiacca's
earliest, or Peruginesque, period :

(a) A small painting (No. 55) representing the " Noli
me tangere," which, with the following, is in the Christ
Church collection at Oxford. (†)

(b) The "Raising of Lazarus," in presence of his sisters
Martha and Mary, who kneel before our Lord. Both pictures recall the school of Perugino. (†)

(c) A small painting, which, some years ago, was still
in the possession of Don Giacomo Bertoldi, and which was
attributed by him, with the assent of several Venetian art-
critics, to Raphael. In this picture, representing the
Madonna seated in a landscape between St. Elisabeth and
the little St. John, and holding the Child on her knee, the
composition is still that of an inexperienced artist. The
pose of the Madonna recalls the school of Perugino, while
the landscape and the scale of colouring already show a
decided leaning to the manner of his second master,
Franciabigio. (†)

(d) The "Vierge au Sein, récemment découverte "—a
small picture entirely repainted, which was hawked about
Europe by its owner, Professor Nicole of Lausanne, in the
vain hope of finding a credulous purchaser. It appears to
me to be also by Bacchiacca, and of a somewhat later
period. The composition of this painting, which, as is
often the case, is more easily understood in the photograph
than in the defaced original, bears some resemblance to
that in the preceding picture. The Madonna holds the
Child to her breast ; to the left is the little St. John. The
landscape background is of the master's characteristic type,
with wedge-shaped rocks, and a town with numerous towers

---

[7] Now in the Frizzoni collection at Milan.

I

in the middle distance. The composition, as well as the
pose of the Madonna, recalls the "Madonna del Pozzo" by
Franciabigio in the Uffizi. It is, perhaps, too much to say
that the hand of the master is still perceptible in a picture
which has been so entirely disfigured by repainting; nevertheless I am firmly convinced that I am not mistaken,
either in this case, or in that of the three preceding pictures.

In the last years of Bacchiacca's first period, which extended to about the year 1518, I should place the following
pictures :

(e) The small and interesting "Adam and Eve" in the
collection of Dr. G. Frizzoni, which was formerly regarded
as a Giulio Romano, and subsequently, when in a Roman
collection, was attributed to Peruzzi. For this remarkable little painting, which leaves much to be desired in
the drawing, Bacchiacca made use of a small cartoon by
his master Perugino, representing Apollo and Marsyas—the
pupil transforming Apollo into Eve, and Marsyas into
Adam. Perugino's well-known painting executed from this
cartoon is now in the Louvre (Salon Carré) under the name
of Raphael, a name arbitrarily placed upon it by its former
possessor. The cartoon itself (†) which is quite in the style
of Perugino's drawing at Oxford of the Archangel with
Tobias (University collection, Robinson's catalogue, No. 16),
is in the Venice Academy—there, too, of course, under the
name of Raphael.

In Bacchiacca's middle period—from about 1518–1536
—I should place the following :

(ƒ) The charming portrait in the Louvre (No. 1506)
of a boy resting his head on his right hand and looking
out of the picture with a joyous, child-like expression.
As it bears the illustrious name of Raphael, it attracts
universal attention, and appeals to the public as a matter
of course. It has been constantly engraved. Bailly in his

"PORTRAIT OF A BOY." BY BACCHIACCA.

*(In the Louvre.)*

*To face p.* 106.

"ADAM AND EVE." BY BACCHIACCA.

*(In the Frizzoni Collection, Milan.)*

*To face p. 106.*

APOLLO AND MARSYAS.

*(A Drawing by* PERUGINO *in the Venice Academy.)*

*To face p. 106.*

inventory of 1709–1710 refers to it in the following terms : 'Tableau estimé de Raphael, réprésentant son portrait.' Years ago this attractive portrait appeared to me to be the work of some Florentine painter of the first half of the sixteenth century, and gradually the conviction grew upon me that this Florentine was unquestionably Bacchiacca. I was led to this conclusion both by the form of hand and by the technical treatment of the hair (glazes of a yellow tone on a brownish ground)—a treatment which I have had occasion to observe in other works by him ; for example, in the one belonging to Dr. Frizzoni. The left eye in this portrait is out of drawing. In later times the picture was enlarged.

(*g*) To this period also belongs the panel in the Uffizi (No. 1296), representing scenes from the life of St. Ascasius, which formed the predella of the altar-piece by Franciabigio, his master, in the church of S. Lorenzo in Florence. Bacchiacca apparently derived some of the figures in this composition from Lucas van Leyden's engravings—a custom very prevalent at that time among other artists. Franciabigio and Pontormo, for instance, constantly made use of Dürer's engravings for their compositions—a fact mentioned by Vasari.

(*h*) The carefully executed panel in the Dresden gallery (No. 80)—which in many points recalls Franciabigio—probably belongs, with the following pictures, to this period :

(*i*) " The Baptism of Christ," in the Berlin Museum.

(*k*) The picture representing the "Death of Abel " in the Morelli collection.[8]

(*l* and *m*) The two panels with episodes from the life of Joseph which are now in the National Gallery, London.[9]

---

[8] Now in the public gallery at Bergamo.

[9] Studies for these two pictures are in the Louvre, Nos. 352 and 353 of the Reiset catalogue. A fragment of a drawing for one of them is in the Christ Church collection at Oxford. (†)

In my opinion one of Bacchiacca's best and most
mature works of this period is the carefully executed picture
in the Palazzo Giovanelli at Venice.   Until recently it was
regarded as the work of Dürer, and the present writer had
the satisfaction of being the first to recognise in it the
hand of Bacchiacca (†) (photographed by Naya at Venice).
It is painted on panel (3½ ft. by 2½), and contains about
forty principal figures besides many smaller ones in the
background.[1]   In the centre is Moses, with a golden staff
in his hand, kneeling before a high rock, from which a
spring gushes forth; the people press forward from all
sides to quench their thirst, and with them birds and
beasts of every description—lynx, cats, deer, parrots, goats,
oxen, martens, asses, &c.   Some of the heads, more especially those of the women, are executed with miniature-like
precision; the costumes are in part very fantastic, and
here again we find that Bacchiacca has borrowed occasionally from the engravings of Lucas van Leyden, which
may account for the picture having formerly passed as the
work of a German.   The landscape background, with
his characteristic grey rocks, is cold in tone.   Three studies
in black chalk, for different heads in this picture, are in
the Uffizi, under the name of Michael Angelo (Case 183,
No. 599). (†)  To the latter are also attributed seven drawings by Bacchiacca in the collection at Lille. (†)   They are
studies for masks in red chalk, and were probably intended
for decorative borders for tapestry (Braun 35).   The following I should also consider to be works of his middle
period.

    (n) The series of five panels in the Borghese gallery. (†)

---

[1] I would call special attention
to a youth on the right side of this
picture, to whom an old woman
offers water from a jar; the head
should be carefully studied, and then
compared with the portrait of the
boy in the Louvre, No. 1506.

A good red chalk drawing for the figure of Benjamin in two of them is in the Morelli collection.[2]

To Bacchiacca's third and last period belong:

(o) "The Preaching of St. John the Baptist," in the possession of the Marchese Bacciocchi of Florence. St. John stands on a slight eminence, his hearers are gathered round him—the men on his right, the women on his left.

(p) "The Adoration of the Magi," unfortunately somewhat repainted, lately in the fine collection of Herr Edward Habich at Cassel.

(q) A large painting (without a name) of the Madonna in the collection of Sir Francis Cook at Richmond. (†)

Vasari records (in his biography of Tribolo) that on the occasion of the entry of Eleonora of Toledo into Florence, Bacchiacca, in company with Bronzino, Pier Francesco di Sandro (a pupil of Andrea del Sarto), Battista Franco and others, was employed in decorating with frescoes the courtyard of the Medici Palace, and that he afterwards painted "The Journey of Lorenzo il Magnifico to Naples," and "The Return from Exile of Cosimo il Vecchio," for the poet Landi's dramatic representation in honour of the marriage of Duke Cosimo (see the biography of Aristotele da San Gallo). He further states that Bacchiacca was one of those employed in painting the triumphal arches used at public rejoicings. All which proves that this painter was very popular in the third and fourth decades of the sixteenth century. His figures, as a rule (with rare exceptions, such as in the picture in Sir Francis Cook's collection, and the portrait in the Louvre), are not much above a span in height and are often smaller still. Vasari

---

[2] Reproduced in Dr. Gustavo Frizzoni's publication, entitled *Collezione di quaranta disegni scelti dalla Raccolta del Senatore Giovanni Morelli, riprodotti in eliotipia,* *descritti ed illustrati dal Dott. Gustavo Frizzoni* (Milano, Hoepli, 1886). (This drawing is now in the collection of Dr. Frizzoni at Milan.)

says of this master, that he also painted many pictures for different people, which were sent into France and England: ' Fece anco molti altri quadri per diversi che furono mandati in Francia e in Inghilterra.' Hence we may infer that many of his works are dispersed abroad under other names.

Bacchiacca appears to have chiefly devoted himself to painting ' predelle ' for altar-pieces, and so-called ' Cassoni,' or large chests, which by the Italians of the fourteenth, fifteenth, and sixteenth centuries were used as wardrobes. In those palmy days art was welcomed everywhere in Italy, and had a share in all the concerns of men, and in all the events and festivities of daily life. The nobles took a delight in enriching their palaces, their country houses, and the chapels in their churches with painting and sculpture, and even required that their household furniture should, whilst useful, be graceful and beautiful in form. Yet at that date there were no galleries for the improvement of public taste, no lectures and courses of instruction, no guides to the right understanding of art, such as we are now so abundantly blessed with, and as to annual exhibitions of pictures, they were totally unknown to this untutored race. We must therefore assume, with a North-German philosopher, that the feeling of pleasure and satisfaction afforded to the mind of that generation by works of art was ' not conscious and positive, but merely an undefined perception, latent in them, and scarcely, if at all, affecting their intelligence.' Be this as it may, certain it is, that in the first half of the sixteenth century, Baccio d' Agnolo, a very popular architect in Florence, was constantly taken into counsel by the principal inhabitants whenever they were desirous of obtaining finely carved furniture. Thus we are told by Vasari in the life of Pontormo, that Pier Francesco Borgherini, the wealthy

Florentine, on his marriage with Margherita, of the house
of Acciajuoli, applied to Baccio to execute some 'Cassoni'
for him, which were then entrusted to Andrea del Sarto,
Pontormo, Franciabigio, Bacchiacca, and Granacci to be
adorned with paintings. All these artists, it appears, were
commissioned to execute scenes from the Old Testament.
It was for Pier Borgherini, most likely, that Pontormo
painted "Joseph and his Kindred in Egypt" (now in the
National Gallery, No. 1131). Two other episodes from the
life of Joseph were represented by Andrea del Sarto in his
most attractive manner; these fine compositions are now
in the Pitti (Nos. 87 and 88), while those painted by
Bacchiacca are probably the two 'Cassoni' panels in the
National Gallery (1218, 1219).

In reference to these 'Cassoni' I may quote a curious
anecdote related by Vasari, that most delightful and naïve
of art-historians, whose writings still remain the principal
source of information for all that relates to the history
of early Italian art. In his life of Pontormo, after vividly
describing the splendour of the apartments in the house of
the Borgherini, where the 'Cassoni' were placed, he says
that at the time of the siege of Florence, in 1529, Pier Francesco Borgherini, who was a partisan of the Medici, having
fled to Lucca, the Florentine picture-dealer, Giovanni della
Palla, succeeded in obtaining permission from the city
authorities to remove these chests from the Palazzo
Borgherini, on payment to the family of a certain com-
pensation, under pretext of offering them as a gift to
Francis I., but really that he might carry them off to
France and turn them to good account for himself. When,
however, accompanied by several officials, he presented himself at the house, and informed the wife of Pier Francesco,
Margherita Acciajuoli, of his errand, this outspoken lady,
furious at such shameless audacity, burst out as follows:

'Out upon thee, Giovanni! hast thou the insolence to lay violent hands upon the noblest ornaments wherewith our palaces are adorned ?   I marvel not at thy scandalous purpose, vile caitiff, for what are the honour and glory of thy country to such as thee, who wert born to nought better. It is not only thy villany which kindles my wrath, but the baseness of the Signoria in lending a willing ear to such a wretch.   This bed, that thou wouldest seize and barter to satisfy thy greed of gain, was the gift of my revered father-in-law at my nuptials ; these chests, adorned by the art of our greatest masters on which thou hast cast thy covetous eyes, were the bridal gift of my beloved husband ; and for the love and reverence I bear to those dear ones I will defend these treasures with my life's blood. Get thee gone ! thou and thy myrmidons.   Return whence ye came, and in my name bid them who sent ye know, that while I live, I will never suffer a finger to be laid even upon the meanest thing in my house ; and if their object be, as they say, to offer gifts to the King of France, why let them first despoil their own houses for that purpose.   As for thee, if ever thou shouldest so far forget thyself as to darken these doors again, by my troth thou shalt rue that day.'

The somewhat churlish behaviour of this old-fashioned dame may provoke a cynical smile from nineteenth-century readers ; they must bear in mind, however, that in those days, 'culture' being still in its infancy, our modern notions of turning family pictures into money were wholly unknown. Later, when these simple burghers were raised to the rank of barons, counts, marquises, and dukes, the della Pallas of Italy, as well as of other countries, would scarcely have met with so unfriendly and impolitic a reception from the owners of works of art.

We have already noted that, on the one hand, several

of Bacchiacca's paintings are given to Raphael (C and D of our series, and also F, the portrait of the boy in the Louvre), and, on the other, that some of his drawings are ascribed to Michael Angelo. It yet remains for me to point out a drawing, which, though bearing the illustrious name of Leonardo, unquestionably shows all the peculiarities of Bacchiacca. This is an attractive portrait in red chalk in the Uffizi (Case 103, No. 414, Braun 434) of a young and handsome woman, whose costume alone would point to a later period than that of Leonardo. The careful execution of the dress, the form of the hand and that of the ear (recalling his master Franciabigio), the long sleeves reaching to the knuckles, the characteristic V-shaped fold on the upper part of one of them, the small hard cross-folds on its lower part,—all incline me to think that Bacchiacca, and not Leonardo, was the author of this portrait. (†) I do not, however, vouch for the correctness of this attribution. Francesco Ubertini belonged, as we have seen, to that group of Florentine painters of the first half of the sixteenth century, such as Franciabigio, Ridolfo del Ghirlandaio, Bugiardini, and Pontormo, who were first trained under the guidance of Albertinelli and Granacci, and later under that of Andrea del Sarto, and who were also influenced, in some degree, by the art of Leonardo and Raphael, and finally by that of Michael Angelo.

## BERNARDINO BETTI, called PINTORICCHIO.

Before proceeding further with the Florentine school, we may examine two other pictures once in the first room (∗) (∗). These again are decorative works for 'Cassoni' representing events from the life of Joseph. The catalogue ascribes them to Pintoricchio; but the execution is far too coarse and unskilful for him, and we shall do better to attribute them, with Messrs. Crowe and Cavalcaselle, to his school.[3]

In imagination, we hear many a visitor exclaim, 'What! no work by Pintoricchio in the whole Borghese gallery?' On the contrary, two genuine works by this underrated and even maligned master are here; but, as usual with his works, they are attributed to other painters—a fate which has too generally befallen poor Pintoricchio. One of them, the Crucifixion, No. 377, bears the absurdly inappropriate name of the Venetian master, Carlo Crivelli. On the right of the Cross kneels St. Jerome, gazing upwards; on the left is St. Christopher bearing the Infant Christ on his shoulder. In this, the earliest work known to me by Pintoricchio, he still follows Fiorenzo di Lorenzo so closely that many a student of art might be led to mistake pupil for master.[4] As to my individual opinion, I may observe that I recognised both the spirit and the hand of Pintoricchio in this picture, without being aware that Vermiglioli, his biographer, had already pronounced it to be by him.[5] The other picture (∗), representing St. Bartholomew, belongs to a later period of the master's career. The catalogue ascribes it to Giovanni Spagna, but the type of the head, as well as the modelling, at once betray the spirit and the technical manner

---

[3] In one we find several times repeated: 'sogno di Faragone.' To this day, the inhabitants of the Abruzzi are wont to divide two successive vowels by a *g*, for instance; 'idega' for idea, 'lagonde' for 'laonde,' 'Magometto' for 'Maometto,' &c., from which I infer that this assistant of Pintoricchio came originally from that part of the country.

[4] In the abnormal length of the upper part of the Child's body and in the fluttering mantle of St. Christopher, we are reminded of his master, Fiorenzo; but the type of the saint, the form of his hand with the bent forefinger, the folds in his mantle, and the position of his legs, all betray the hand of Pintoricchio.

[5] See Gio. Battista Vermiglioli, *Memorie di Bernardino Pintoricchio*, pp. 109, 110. This picture was at that time in the possession of a Dr. Monaco.

of Pintoricchio. The hatching of the shadows is the same as in his pen drawings. (†)

The portrait of Savonarola (∗), incredible as it may appear, is here attributed to Filippino Lippi. This unimportant production is only one of the many feeble copies extant (there is one also in the Florence Academy) of the splendid portrait of the Frate by his friend and partisan, the young Bartolommeo della Porta, now in the possession of the heirs of Signor Ermolao Rubieri.[6] Another picture—a "Pietà" (∗)—is also unjustifiably given to Filippino; but as far as I can judge in its present condition, it is only of his school.

The gifted and delightful painter, Filippino Lippi, is well represented in Florence, Prato, and Lucca; but with the exception of his frescoes in the Caraffa chapel in S. Maria sopra Minerva, executed jointly with his pupil Raffaellino del Garbo, and not in his best manner, nothing else by his hand is to be seen in Rome. He is, however, admirably represented in Florence, where the Badia, the Carmine, S. Spirito, the gallery of the Uffizi, the Corsini gallery, and S. Maria Novella, offer ample opportunities for studying him. The Pitti gallery also includes an example of Filippino, not, however, as the authorities would have us believe, No. 388, the "Death of Virginia"—the work apparently of another and much feebler pupil of Botticelli—and still less No. 347, the "Madonna and Child with Angels"—more probably by some imitator of Ghirlandaio—but No. 336. This small picture is here catalogued as 'unknown,' but I must beg students to examine the elongated form of the ear, the hand with the long fingers broad at the tips, the type of head and the landscape, and I do not doubt they will agree

---

[6] It may here be noted that a pen drawing by Leonardo da Vinci in the 'Albertina' at Vienna (Braun 97), is not the portrait of Savonarola, as there stated, but of some other monk.

with me in recognising both the feeling and the technic of Filippino.[7] (†)

A good work by the master is a fresco in a tabernacle in a street at Prato ; another is in the church of S. Domenico at Bologna; and a third is in the Seminario Vescovile at Venice, there absurdly attributed to Crespi.

As Filippino's drawings are frequently mistaken by beginners [8] for those of his pupil Raffaellino del Garbo, it may be advisable to mention a few characteristic examples by both masters, so that the student may impress upon his memory the forms of feet, hands, and ears peculiar to each.

## FILIPPINO LIPPI.

### In the Uffizi.

(Case 37, Nos. 171, 172 ; Case 460, Nos. 1253 and 1257.)

1. Case 32, No. 139, study for the head of the Madonna in the Badia (ear).

Case 40, No. 186, sketch for one of his frescoes in the Strozzi chapel of S. Maria Novella in Florence.

### In the Ambrosiana.

3. Study for the head of one of the three kings in his " Adoration " in the Uffizi (ear)—attributed to Leonardo da Vinci. (†)

### In the Lille Collection.

4. A drawing under the name of Masaccio. (†)   Braun, No. 9.

---

[7] Alinari of Florence has good photographs of this picture.

[8] The small picture of the " Communion of St. Jerome," in the Casa Balbi a Genoa, which Dr. Bode (ii. 581) attributes to Filippino Lippi, is merely an old copy of one by Botticelli of this subject, belonging to the heirs of the Marchese Gino Capponi at Florence.

*In the Dresden Collection.*

5. Study for a St. John under the name of Cosimo Roselli. Braun 40. (†)

6. A seated male figure, attributed to Cosimo Roselli. (†) Braun 41.

*In the Louvre.*

7. A man seated, resting his head upon his left hand. (Reiset catalogue, No. 230, under the name of Fra Filippo Lippi.) (†)

## RAFFAELLINO DEL GARBO.

*In the Uffizi.*

1. Case 83, Nos. 350, 352.

*In the Christ Church Collection, Oxford.*

2. Photographed in the publications of the Grosvenor Gallery, No. 44.

*In the British Museum.*

3. Photographed by Braun, No. 113. (Hand and foot.)

*In the Lille Collection.*

4. Photographed by Braun, Nos. 23 and 24, as Domenico del Ghirlandaio. (+)

In the Borghese gallery hangs a female portrait (No. 371), the features of which will be familiar to many. The catalogue merely says that it is 'in the style of Perugino.' The picture is labelled 'Ridolfo del Ghirlandaio'—a name more nearly approaching the truth, and which I suggested when discussing these pictures on a former occasion. Neither the modelling, nor the scale of colour, still less the landscape background, recalls the school of Perugino, but rather that of Florence of the first decade of the six-

teenth century.[9]   The commonplace person represented in
this picture, with her inanimate expression, is none other than
Maddalena Strozzi, wife of Angelo Doni, the wealthy and,
according to ill-natured reports, rather penurious Florentine
citizen.   Most persons are familiar with Raphael's portrait
of her in the Pitti, the pen drawing for which is in the
' Salle aux boites ' in the Louvre.   Some able painter closely
resembling Granacci, if not Granacci himself, made use of
this drawing [1] for a picture of his own, in which the lady,
to please a relative, or some pious admirer, was transformed
into a St. Catherine.[2]   Similar canonisations of pretty
women, or those who passed for such, though unsanctioned
by the Church, are frequently met with in the history of
Italian art.   To quote one example among many, Arnol-
fini, in the year 1594, writes to his beloved nun Lucrezia
Buonvisi of Lucca, entreating her to send him 'a certain
canvas,' on which she is depicted as St. Ursula (' in figura
di S. Orsola '), ' that he might at least solace himself by its
contemplation ' (' perchè possa almeno bearmi nella vista
della immagine.') [3]

## PIETRO DI LORENZO, called PIER DI COSIMO.

A "Tondo" (No. 343) represents the Madonna wor-
shipping the Holy Child who lies before her, while
two angels join in adoration.   The catalogue describes

[9] The 'eye,' or point of origin
of the folds in the drapery, is not
roundish as with the pupils of Perugino and Pintoricchio, but square after
the manner more especially of Granacci and Ridolfo del Ghirlandaio.
The hair is treated with little grace,
and the cold tone of the landscape
recalls Granacci more than Ridolfo.

[1] In this picture we find the same
two columns on either side of the
window, which occur in Raphael's
pen drawing in the Louvre.   In the
portrait in the Pitti the master has
omitted them.

[2] See Passavant ii. 278.   This
picture formerly belonged to the
Marchese Letizia at Naples, and
passed for a Raphael.

[3] See   *Storia   di   Lucrezia
Buonvisi raccontata da Salvatore
Bongi*, p. 114 (Lucca, 1864).

MADDALENA STROZZI AS ST. CATHERINE.

*(In the Borghese Gallery.)*

To face p. 118.

this much injured picture as an 'Abozzo di Raffaello, fatto nei primi anni sulla maniera di Perugino,' to which we may apply the Italian proverb: 'Quante parole, tanti spropositi' ('As many blunders as words'). Both this interesting work (No. 343) and a smaller one (No. 329) now bear the name of Pier di Cosimo. The colouring, especially the bright red robe of the Madonna, recalls Filippino's fine work in the Badia at Florence, while the two *putti* remind us more of Sodoma, and of Cesare da Sesto, who were in Florence in the early part of the year 1500.[4] Studying the characteristics of this picture—the stiff, unpleasing hand, the type of head, the landscape, and the cast of the drapery—we soon discover its real author, Pier di Cosimo (†), of whom Vasari has left us a very scanty biography.

Pier di Cosimo (b. in Florence about 1462, d. there 1521) is known to have been a pupil of Cosimo Roselli, from whom he derived his name. He was probably thus brought into closer relations with Bartolommeo della Porta (b. 1475), and with Mariotto Albertinelli (b. 1474)—both his fellow pupils—and, being older and more experienced than they, he may have had a certain influence on their art, especially in landscape. His fine altar-piece at Florence, in the Stanza del Commissario degli Innocenti, shows a close connection with Filippino Lippi, in the types as well as in subordinate details. No painter of the fifteenth century, with the exception, perhaps, of Benozzo Gozzoli, Pintoricchio, and Lorenzo Costa, devoted himself to

[4] Cesare da Sesto must have been in Florence during the first years of the sixteenth century, and while there was probably influenced, to a certain extent, by painters of the Florentine school, more especially by Lorenzo di Credi and Albertinelli. This is evident in the following works: a circular panel in the possession of the Melzi d' Eril family at Milan (a copy of which is in this gallery, and another in the Uffizi, No. 1013, under the name of Luini), and notably an "Adoration of the Magi" in the Borromeo gallery, also at Milan. (†)

landscape with greater ardour than Pier di Cosimo. Of
this we have abundant proof in the Uffizi, where many of
his landscape backgrounds, though somewhat fantastic in
character, are always original and ably executed.[5] From
him Andrea del Sarto, his pupil, may have derived his
taste for landscape backgrounds. As Piero's works are
rare, I may mention two other pictures by him, one in
Rome, the other in the Louvre. The first, representing the
Magdalen (half-length with a dark background), is well-
preserved, and recalls Filippino's type of feature. The dress
is dark green, the mantle a deep red with dark hatched
shadows; the brownish hair, as usual with Piero, lies flat
on the temples, and is adorned with a string of pearls.
The expression of the beautiful penitent is of a mild and
tender melancholy. This fine picture belongs to Baron Giovanni Barracco of Naples, a member of the Italian Senate,
and one of the most cultivated connoisseurs of art in Italy.
He bought it at the Monte di Pietà in Rome, where,
strange to say, it was attributed to Mantegna   The
second picture, a Madonna and Child, is classed among
the 'unknowns' in the Louvre (No. 1528). The late
director of the gallery, Vicomte Both de Tauzia, affirmed
that the picture reminded him of Signorelli. Dr. Gustavo
Frizzoni, however, immediately recognised in it the hand of
Pier di Cosimo.[6]

---

[5] The landscape in Pier di
Cosimo's "Rescue of Andromeda"
(Uffizi, No. 1312) is in every respect
identical with the landscape in this
"Tondo" of the Borghese gallery.
The inventory of the Uffizi gallery
of 1580 mentions that the picture
was drawn by Leonardo da Vinci,
and only painted by Pier di Cosimo
(Vasari vii. 119–20). As a rule I
lay very small store by 'tradition';
in this case, however, it appears
to me to be worthy of some attention; for several of the heads
have not only Leonardo's *sfumato*,
but recall the "Gioconda" in expression. Piero may, therefore,
have painted the picture about 1506,
when Leonardo was finishing the
portrait of "Mona Lisa." There is,
however, no question about the composition, which is by Pier di Cosimo,
and not by Leonardo.

[6] Messrs. Crowe and Cavalcaselle

The second picture by Piero in the Borghese gallery (No. 329), though not described as an early work by Raphael, is, with equal inconsistency, given to a pupil of Piero's own scholar, Andrea del Sarto, namely, to Franciabigio, who, as we have seen, was the master of Bacchiacca, and may himself have been taught in the school of Pier di Cosimo. This small and pleasing work represents the "Judgment of Solomon," (†) and may have been destined for the decoration of some piece of furniture. The rich Florentines of the second and third decades of the sixteenth century were evidently in the habit of employing that group of painters comprising Andrea del Sarto, Franciabigio, Pontormo, Bacchiacca, and others, who directly, or indirectly, had been taught in the school of Pier di Cosimo, to execute work of this kind.

The earlier works of Piero all point to the influence of Filippino, and were probably executed in the last years of the fifteenth and the first of the sixteenth century. Among them I should class No. 31 in the Uffizi, the large picture in the 'Stanza del Commissario degli Innocenti' in Florence, the Magdalen, belonging to Senatore Barracco, the "Tondo" in the Dresden gallery, Nos. 107 and 204 in the Berlin Museum, the "Death of Procris," an admirable example, in the English National Gallery, and the

---

(iii. 421) assume that Pier di Cosimo had a hand in those altar-pieces in the church of S. Spirito at Florence, which are there variously attributed to Ghirlandaio, to Filippino Lippi, and occasionally, with more intelligence, to Cosimo Roselli. I cannot refrain from expressing some doubts as to the correctness of their view, especially as these critics do not appear to have formed a very clear idea of Pier di Cosimo. They could hardly otherwise have failed to recognise his genuine works, in this gallery, in Dresden, and in Berlin, whereas they preserve a discreet silence about them all. The three pictures in the church of S. Spirito appear to me to be productions of the school of Cosimo Roselli, and very far indeed removed from Pier di Cosimo. A charcoal drawing at Weimar—the Infant Saviour, lying undraped upon the ground (Braun 69)—is not by Piero, nor is the portrait once in the first corridor of the Uffizi. Why this latter should have been attributed to *Pietro* Roselli is a mystery to me—it is obviously by Ridolfo del Ghirlandaio. (†)

Madonna and Child in the Louvre. On the other hand, the picture in the Uffizi, No. 1312, which in parts recalls Leonardo, shows that lighter scale of colour which later was partially adopted by Andrea del Sarto, and more decidedly by Bacchiacca. A form of skull peculiar to Piero first appears in his later works, as, for instance, in Nos. 82, 83, and 1312 in the Uffizi, and in No. 329 of the Borghese gallery, all of which are small decorative panels, intended either for furniture, or for the walls of a room—for art, having already attained full freedom, was gradually becoming secularised, and no longer laboured exclusively in the service of religion.

## MARIOTTO ALBERTINELLI.

Amongst the remaining works by Florentine masters we find a "Madonna and Child with the little St. John" (No. 310), bearing the date 1511 in gold. The composition apparently is that of Fra Bartolommeo della Porta; but the careless execution is undoubtedly that of Mariotto Albertinelli (†). In addition to the date it is also signed with the well-known red cross and the two interlaced rings—the former referring to the convent of St. Mark in Florence, the latter to the two friends and co-workers, Fra Bartolommeo and Mariotto. Similar feeble productions, dating from the years 1510, 1511, and 1512, may be seen in private and public collections — in the possession of the Marchese Bartolommei at Florence, in the Casa Guerrini-Antinori at Rome, in the public gallery at Vienna (dated 1510), and in the Corsini gallery at Florence (dated 1511). (†) It is said that the convent of St. Mark furnished the materials for these joint-stock productions, and that the profits were divided equally between Fra Bartolommeo, i.e. the convent, and Albertinelli. A picture similar to this one in the Borghese gallery was formerly in the Sciarra-Colonna collection (now closed to the public), where, as might be expected, Fra Bartolommeo was made responsible for it. (†) Messrs. Crowe and Cavalcaselle would attribute all works signed in this manner to Fra Paolino of Pistoia (iii. 478 and 482). Again I find it impossible to share their views.

In his fresco of 1516 in S. Spirito at Siena[7]—the Crucifixion, with Saints on either side—Fra Paolino proves himself an extremely feeble and unskilful artist,[8] and even in his large painting of 1519 in the Florence Academy, the figures are awkward and ungainly. It is only in his later works of 1528 in S. Domenico and in S. Paolo at Pistoia, that he imitates Fra Bartolommeo with more success. Fra Paolino was, as Vasari states, the son of Bernardo del Signoraccio, an inferior scholar of Domenico Ghirlandaio, and in all probability he served his apprenticeship with his father before becoming connected with Fra Bartolommeo. The "Madonnas" of the years 1510, 1511, and 1512, mentioned above, should be compared with Albertinelli's carefully executed "Annunciation" of the same period in the Florence Academy, and even with the predella of 1503 in the Uffizi (No. 1259) containing a similar type of the Virgin. In all of them the same characteristics are apparent—the same modelling of the eyes with high lights

[7] The drawing for this fresco is in the Uffizi, Case 484, No. 1402.

[8] The head of St. John and of the Magdalen in this fresco are heavy and absolutely without grace, the hands with the short clumsy thumbs are hard, the folds in the sleeves coarse, and the body of the Saviour badly modelled. It is evident, in short, that in 1516 Fra Paolino was only a beginner, while Albertinelli's paintings of 1510-12 show a practised hand. Besides Fra Paolino's other well-known works at Pistoia, there is a Madonna enthroned, with SS. Jerome, Sebastian, and Mary Magdalen, the little St. John and another saint, in the small church belonging to the hospital. This building also contains a fine panel by Lorenzo di Credi—a Madonna enthroned with the Child. He is blessing the Magdalen who kneels before Him ; SS. Catherine, John the Baptist, and Jerome stand by.

on the edge of the eyelid, the same form of hand, with a short peculiarly shaped thumb and nails of a grey tone, and even the same kind of nimbus—with this difference, however, that the paintings produced in the workshop of the convent were extremely careless in execution, having probably been ordered by persons of limited means. By way of settling the difference between Messrs. Crowe and Cavalcaselle and myself I may here cite the large "Annunciation" in the Geneva Museum which bears the following inscription :

1511.  FRĪS. BARTHO. OR. P.

ET MARIOTTI FLORENTINOR

OPVS.

Had Dr. Bode been acquainted with it, he would surely have hesitated before again following in their steps (ii. 675). Both Fra Bartolommeo and Albertinelli, his fellow-student and senior by a few months, passed their years of apprenticeship with Cosimo Roselli, whose workshop was very popular between 1480 and 1490. Towards 1485 Pier di Cosimo may have assisted his master in his *bottega*, and it is highly probable that the teaching and guidance of the pupils was entrusted to him by Roselli. A comparison between the pen drawings by Fra Bartolommeo and Mariotto in the Uffizi, and the "Adoration of the Infant Saviour" (pen and ink) by Pier di Cosimo in the same collection (Case 80, No. 343, Braun 211), clearly proves that in technic the latter must have exercised a strong influence over the two former. Subsequently, however, Albertinelli followed his more able and gifted friend Fra Bartolommeo so successfully, that some of his early works still pass under the name of the latter—for example, the beautiful little Triptych of 1500 in the Poldi-Pezzoli collection at

Milan, (†) the Madonna in the Seminario Vescovile at Venice, (†) and the two panels with St. Catherine and the Magdalen (Nos. 445 and 451) in the Academy at Siena. (†) [9] On the other hand, the "Noli me tangere" in the Louvre (No. 1115), an early work by Fra Bartolommeo, (†) passes under the name of Albertinelli.[1]

In the last years of the fifteenth century Mariotto was working in the convent of S. Maria Nuova at Florence with his friend Bartolommeo della Porta. A considerable impression seems to have been produced upon him by Hugo van der Goes' large altar-piece then in the church of that convent, containing portraits of the Portinari family. It is evident from some of his paintings of that date, that he strove to imitate this Flemish master—hardly Memling, as Dr. Bode (ii. 676) seems to think. This tendency is seen not only in the scale of colour and in costume, as in the Triptych of the Poldi-Pezzoli Museum, but also in the careful execution of the landscape backgrounds, as in the "Expulsion from Paradise," formerly in the possession of Signor Basseggio in Rome.[2] In his works of the first years of the sixteenth century—for instance, the splendid "Visitation" of 1503 in the Uffizi, and the two fragments of Saints in the collection of the author [3] (St. John the Evangelist and the Magdalen)—Mariotto nearly approaches

---

[9] Messrs. Crowe and Cavalcaselle (iii. 473) ascribe these two panels to Fra Paolino.

[1] Messrs. Crowe and Cavalcaselle, who regard this picture as the work of Albertinelli, place it in the year 1494 (!). The form of hand here is very characteristic of Fra Bartolommeo, and the landscape recalls the one in the Frate's "Vision of St. Bernard" in the Florence Academy, of 1506 (?). The fine chalk drawing for St. Bernard belongs to the

Grand Duke of Weimar (Braun 25).

[2] Messrs. Crowe and Cavalcaselle took this little painting, which is now in England, for an early work by Raphael (!). Passavant, who recognised the hand of Albertinelli remarks with reference to it: 'Le paysage est riche, mais froid de ton' (that is to say Flemish), ii. 314.

[3] Now in the gallery at Bergamo.

Fra Bartolommeo; the figures, however, are less refined and noble than those of the 'Frate,' and the foliage of the trees is executed with miniature-like precision, which is never the case in the landscapes of the latter.

Shortly before the death of Filippino Lippi (1504), and when his friend Bartolommeo had already been many years in retirement in his convent, Mariotto must have entered into more intimate relations with the former painter. Some of his works of that date, for instance, the fine " Tondo " (No. 365) in the Pitti, and the altar-piece in the cathedral of Volterra, bear witness to the influence of Filippino. On the death of the latter, leaving his large panel, now in the Louvre (No. 1114), in a very unfinished state, it was Albertinelli who was commissioned to complete it; the figure of St. Jerome was apparently drawn by Filippino himself.[4] The Florence Academy contains some good works of Albertinelli's later period.

Fra Bartolommeo's best paintings are probably those at Lucca; but the greater part of them are entirely defaced by shameful repainting. This great master is only represented in Rome by one picture in the Corsini gallery. In Florence, on the other hand, we find several characteristic specimens of his art in the Uffizi, the Pitti, and the Academy. One of his finest early works—a circular panel representing the Madonna and St. Joseph adoring the Infant Saviour— passed from the collection of the late Count Baldelli of Florence, into that of the well-known statesman, the Marchese Visconti-Venosta, at Milan. The cartoon for this picture is in the Florence Academy.[5] The works both of

[4] It is not difficult to recognise Filippino in the type of head and the form of hand and ear.

[5] Fra Bartolommeo's early drawings are usually executed with a fine pen; several examples are in the Uffizi (Case 457, Nos. 1233–39), and in the British Museum (Braun, Nos. 1, 2, 3, and 4); those of his later period, on the other hand, are nearly all in charcoal or black chalk. Pen drawings by his imitator, Andrea del

Fra Bartolommeo and Albertinelli are extremely rare out of Italy.

## ANDREA D'AGNOLO, called ANDREA DEL SARTO.

From Fra Bartolommeo we are involuntarily led to Andrea del Sarto. Works improperly attributed to him may be seen in the Borghese gallery. One of them, No. 334, representing the Madonna and Child (life size), is provided with the master's genuine monogram—two interlaced A's. Prior to the discovery, by Vasari's Florentine Commentators, that Andrea's real name was not, as stated by Baldinucci, Andrea Vannucchi, but Andrea d'Agnolo (it would now be Angeli or de Angelis), it was usual to find on paintings attributed to him an interlaced A and V, which were of course supposed to denote Andrea Vannucchi. Subsequent to the discovery of the painter's true name this monogram was usually corrected by a stroke drawn through the V, which was then transformed into an A. Thus Andrea del Sarto's genuine monogram (the interlaced A's) was reproduced. These improved monograms, like the one on this picture, look remarkably modern.[6] The composition of this painting is excellent, and is certainly to be attributed to Andrea; but the execution is far too hard and feeble for him, and it can only be regarded as one of many copies. What has

ANDREA DEL SARTO'S MONOGRAM.

---

Brescianino, are not unfrequently attributed to Fra Bartolommeo himself, as in the Uffizi (Case 458, No. 1244) (†). The former painter not only copied his drawings but also his pictures; we have an example of this in the Turin Academy, No. 133 (†).

[6] In the Doria gallery there is a Madonna and Child and St. John the Baptist, with the monogram of Andrea del Sarto. This is apparently the work of a German painter, who copied the Madonna and Child from Andrea del Sarto, and the St. John, in his fur-trimmed mantle, in all probability from Dürer. The form of hand, and the head of the St. John, strike me as very *Düreresque*. (†)

been said of this picture applies equally to others here ascribed to Andrea, and I may therefore spare myself and my readers from wasting more time over them. An exception, however, may be made in favour of a charming picture of the Magdalen[7] (No. 328), which has repeatedly been copied.[8] It is the work of one of Andrea's most industrious imitators, Domenico Puligo, (†) by whom there are several other pictures in this collection, and one in the Colonna gallery (No. 17).

## JACOPO CARUCCI DA PONTORMO.

Another Florentine painter much influenced by Andrea del Sarto was Jacopo Pontormo (1494–1556). To him, and not to his pupil, Angelo Bronzino, as the catalogue informs us, should be attributed a good life-sized portrait (No. 74) (†) representing an elderly man in a red velvet tunic, holding a book.[9] But instead of lingering over these indifferent specimens of Florentine art, let us turn to a really fine work of this school which merits our undivided attention. I say Florentine school, although the catalogue ascribes this portrait of a Cardinal (No. 408) to no less a master than Raphael himself—and under his name it naturally receives more admiration and attention than it might otherwise obtain.[1] The Cardinal, a man of middle age, is seated ; his attitude is stately but perfectly unconstrained, and he looks at the spectator with an air of

---

[7] Belonging to the same period of Puligo's career as a female portrait in the possession of the Marchese Covoni in Florence.

[8] An old copy is in the Turin Academy.

[9] The present director has accepted my attribution of this portrait to Pontormo.

[1] Passavant (ii. 358) considered that the head and the hands (!) bore the stamp of Raphael, and that the remainder was by a pupil, and drew especial attention to the covering of the table, as revealing the same hand as the Turkey carpet in the portrait of Cardinal Inghirami in the Pitti. Other critics, however, regard this latter so-called Raphael as a Flemish copy.

calm decision. The table by his side is covered with a
Turkey carpet; on it is a richly chased hand-bell resembling the one introduced by Raphael in his classic
portrait of Leo X. in the Pitti. The harmonious
colouring is neither that of Raphael's Umbrian nor
Roman period, but is entirely Florentine. The more
closely we examine this picture the more we perceive in it
the genius of Pontormo—for that something of the artist's
own personality is contained in every genuine work of art,
is a fact that no one will deny.[2] The modelling of the eyes,
deeply sunk in their sockets, is altogether his; so too the
drawing of the hands and the defective modelling in the

HANDS IN PONTORMO'S PORTRAIT OF COSIMO DE' MEDICI.

first phalanx of the fore-finger—a peculiarity of this
master [3]—the 'spongy' flesh-tint, and the Florentine background recalling Andrea del Sarto, all these characteristics

[2] I can offer no information as to
the identity of the person represented. Passavant (ii. 358) thought
it might be Cardinal Borgia.

[3] This defective drawing Pontormo seems to have derived from
his prototype, Andrea del Sarto; but
like all imitators he exaggerated the
faults of his master. Jacopo may
very likely, as Vasari relates, have
visited the workshops of Leonardo,
Albertinelli, and Pier di Cosimo, in
his boyhood, and may perhaps have
served there as a *fattorino*; his real
master, however, being Andrea del
Sarto. His fresco in the outer Court
of the SS. Annunziata at Florence
points to this, as do also many portraits of his early period—for instance, the portrait of a man in the
Pitti (No. 249), and that of a young
artist in the Morelli collection (now
at Bergamo).

convince me that the 'Raphael' of this first-rate
portrait is no other than Pontormo. (†) If further proof be
needed, this painting may be compared with the portrait of
Cosimo il Vecchio de' Medici, in the Uffizi (No. 1267), an
undisputed work of Pontormo, and also with two other
portraits by him in the same gallery (Nos. 1270 and 1220).
Another picture by Pontormo in Rome—this time under the
name of Peruzzi—is the "Pygmalion" in the Barberini
gallery (Room II. No. 89). (†) His best works are in
Florence—in the Pitti and the Uffizi, in the palace of the
Marchese Farinola, in the churches of S. Michelino and
S. Felicità, and in the villa of Poggio a Caiano. Good
drawings by him are in the Uffizi (Case 224, Nos. 671
and 672 ; Case 226, No. 675). The pen drawing of "Noah
receiving the command to build the Ark" (Case 147, No.
526) is probably a copy by Pontormo of an original drawing
by Raphael. There are twenty-seven drawings by Pontormo
in the Corsini Library in Rome, among them some excellent specimens (especially Nos. 124173, 124182, 124183,
124187, 1241228, 1241254), and two at Chatsworth, under
the name of Michael Angelo—a Madonna and Child (black
chalk ; Braun 47) and a figure from the ceiling of the
Sistine chapel (red chalk ; Braun 25). (†)

Near this celebrated painting of the Cardinal hangs an
inferior female portrait (No. 79)—a very doubtful work by
Pontormo's eminent scholar, Angelo Bronzino, who prior
to his relations with his master received his first instruction
in art, as Vasari relates, from Raffaellino del Garbo.
Bronzino (1502–1572), who, from the elegance of his style,
might be called the Florentine Parmeggianino, had a great
number of pupils and imitators in his native city. It too
often happens that he is held responsible for works, especially portraits, by them, though in point of fact he is far
superior to them all, both in his spirited and elegant draw-

ing, and in the excellence of his execution. Such being the case, it may be advisable to name a few of his imitators —Cristofano dell' Altissimo, Lorenzo dello Sciorina, Stefano Pieri, and Alessandro Allori, Bronzino's nephew.

Bronzino himself is represented in the Borghese gallery by a fine "Lucrezia" (No. 75) and by a still finer "Cleopatra" (No. 337), both of which I ascribe to his first period. These early works are all very careful in drawing but black in the shadows. Among his best portraits I would include the following: Giannettino Doria in the Doria-Pamfili gallery; the Sculptor (No. 1266), and Bartolommeo Panciatichi and his Wife (Nos. 159 and 154), both in the Uffizi; and, pre-eminently, the portrait in the Salon Carré of the Louvre.

### PORTRAIT OF CESARE BORGIA.[4]

To whom should be ascribed the stately, elegant, but somewhat stiff portrait (∗) hanging near, called Cesare Borgia? Many of my readers may think such a query too bold and even impertinent, for this much-vaunted portrait, which has repeatedly been reproduced by engraving and photography, is universally held to represent the Duca di Valentino and to be the work of Raphael.[5] Several modern critics, indeed, have ridiculed such an attribution, and the most discerning among them, the late Mr. Mündler,[6] unhesitatingly ascribed the portrait to Parmeggianino. Burckhardt,[7] another gifted writer, considers it to be a first-rate German work, perhaps by George Pencz. To differ from such eminent connoisseurs seems the height of presumption, yet if there be truth in the Italian proverb 'fra due

[4] This portrait has recently been sold to Baron A. de Rothschild as a Raphael.—(Trans.)

[5] Herr Carl von Ruland only places it in the school of Raphael.

[6] *Beiträge*, &c. p. 30.

[7] See *The Cicerone*, first edition, p. 910.

liticanti il terzo gode,' I too may obtain a chance of being heard where the learned disagree ; and if I also err, at all events I shall be in good company.

Let us examine this portrait more closely.[8]  The most superficial observer may satisfy himself that it cannot be the work of Raphael, by merely comparing it with the " Entombment " by that painter hanging near.  The next point to decide is, whether the portrait can by any possibility represent Cesare Borgia.  The arrogant mien, the expression, which is empty and unrefined, nay, even coarsely sensual, render this portrait repulsive to me rather than attractive.  Yet the regular features are undeniably handsome, and as the notorious Duke of Valentinois was traditionally the handsomest man of his day, we may assume this to have been one reason for the directors of the Gallery having recognised in it the likeness of Cesare Borgia.  It is unfortunate, however, that they should not have taken into consideration the fact that the political career of that hero in Italy had already terminated in 1503. It is well known that he fell before the town of Viana in Navarre four years later.  Had these features been, indeed, portrayed by the hand of Raphael, both drawing and painting, leaving the conception altogether out of the question, should reveal the Peruginesque manner of the master. Yet of this there is absolutely no trace.  It may be urged that Raphael need not have painted it from life, but might have executed it later from some drawing or earlier portrait. This theory might be tenable if supported by any historical probability, and if—which after all is the gist of the whole matter—the painting itself showed the hand of Raphael.

The Duke, if he ever sat for his portrait at all, would

---

[8] Cesare Borgia was created Duke of Valentinois by Louis XII. in 1499, and married in that year Charlotte d'Albret, sister of Jean d'Albret, King of Navarre.

have been most likely to confer this honour on Pintoricchio, his father's court painter, who, after working in Rome in the service of Pope Alexander VI. from 1492–97, entered that of the Duke himself in 1501.[9]  In that year and in 1502, Leonardo da Vinci is known to have filled the post of first military engineer to Borgia.  It would, therefore, be only natural to suppose that he, in preference to any other painter, would have been commissioned to immortalise the features of his master and patron, though it is unlikely he ever executed such a work.

This personage, as we see on closer inspection, wears a cap with black feathers, and a black doublet with slashed sleeves.  His right hand rests upon the hilt of his sword, his left upon his hip.  The costume of this supposed Cesare Borgia shows him to be a Florentine noble of the fourth decade of the sixteenth century.  Were the thick coat of yellow varnish removed from the surface, my supposition, that the portrait nearly approaches Bronzino, would I believe prove to be correct.  We find in it the *smalto* peculiar to his paintings, the cold flesh-tints and the somewhat hard lines of the eyes, which are deeply sunk in their sockets after the manner of Pontormo.[1] (†)  The studied

---

[9] Vasari, in his Life of Pintoricchio, enumerates several portraits by this master in the Castle of S. Angelo—for instance, Isabella the Catholic, Niccolò Orsini, Gian Giacomo Trivulzio, and Cesare and Lucrezia Borgia, all in fresco.  The same writer also tells us (vii. 113) that Pier di Cosimo painted the portrait of the Duke of Valentinois: ' Ritrasse ancora poi il duca Valentino, figliuolo di papa Alessandro VI. la qual pittura oggi ch' io sappia non si trova, ma bene il cartone di sua mano, ed è appresso il reverendo M. Cosimo Bartoli, proposto di San Giovanni.'  What may have become of the cartoon here mentioned ?  Dr. Gustavo Frizzoni, the well-known Italian critic, claims to have discovered four portraits by Pier di Cosimo, two at the Hague (Braun 316², 316¹), one in the National Gallery, and, finally, the portrait of the "Bella Simonetta" in the guise of a Cleopatra, described by Vasari— now in the collection of the Duc d'Aumale.

[1] It is sometimes extremely difficult to distinguish portraits by Angelo Bronzino from those by Francesco Salviati.

elegance of the pose points more to Bronzino than to any
other contemporary Florentine, and recalls his portraits of
the Panciatichi in the Uffizi.   The modelling and position
of the hand are almost identical with the right hand in the
pretty little portrait of a boy (No. 649) in the English
National Gallery, which, though there attributed to Pontormo, appears to me to be an excellent specimen of Angelo
Bronzino. (†)   So-called portraits of Cesare Borgia may be
met with in various other Italian galleries.   At Forlì we
find one (No. 151) attributed to Giorgione, which has no
sort of connection either with that painter or with Borgia,
but is probably some likeness by Palmezzano da Forlì (†) ;
the " Cesare Borgia " by Leonardo da Vinci, presented to
the city of Venice in 1849 by the late General Pepe, and
now in the Museo Civico (Correr collection), more probably
represents Don Ferdinando Avalos of Aquino.   This feeble
profile is, moreover, so entirely repainted that it is unworthy of attention.   A third " Cesare Borgia " in the
gallery at Bergamo (Lochis collection) passes there for a
Giorgione.   It is an extremely spirited portrait, certainly
neither by Calisto da Lodi, nor by Romanino, as Messrs.
Crowe and Cavalcaselle conjecture (vol. ii. 163), but by a
painter of the school of Ferrara-Bologna, probably
Giacomo Francia.[2] (†)   But in portraits painted from
life it is, I may add, an extremely hazardous and difficult
matter, in this declining period of Italian art, to attempt
to identify the master in every case.   A fourth so-
called " Cesare Borgia " was formerly in the collection
of Count Castelbarco at Milan.   It was attributed
to Raphael, but I considered it to be by Andrea
Solario.

----

[2] This portrait should be compared with the two saints in armour
in Giacomo Francia's large painting
in the Brera (No. 175).

## BALDASSARE PERUZZI.

Not far from this Florentine portrait, our eye, in search
of better things, is riveted by the nude figure of a youthful
woman (No. 92), whose pose and expression are animated by
the truest artistic feeling. The catalogue calls it " Venus
emerging from the Bath," and names Giulio Romano as
the painter. Dr. G. Frizzoni, however, in an article on
Baldassare Peruzzi, claims it for that master and, as it
appears to me, with justice. This refined Sienese artist,
the friend of Agostino Chigi, distinguished himself more
in architecture than in painting. In this latter art
he should be classed among those brilliant decorative
painters, at whose head stand Bramante and Melozzo da
Forlì.

Three artists appear to me to have distinctly influenced
Peruzzi as a painter : first Pintoricchio, then more especially Sodoma, and lastly Raphael. Numerous specimens of
his decorative art more or less well-preserved may still be
seen in Rome, where the greater part of his artistic career
was spent ; for instance, frescoes in the choir of the
convent church of S. Onofrio quite in the style of Pintoricchio, possibly even executed from that master's sketches ;
the three Graces in the Chigi Palace ; several episodes
from Roman history in the Palazzo de' Conservatori on
the Capitol, showing Sodoma's influence (Roman ignorance
in matters of art has here immortalised itself in attributing
these works to Bonfigli of Perugia) ; and the frescoes in the
first chapel on the left in S. Maria della Pace, in which the
influence of Sodoma is most distinctly apparent, both in
the harmony of the colours, the types of the heads, and even
in the serpentine folds of the drapery, so characteristic of
that master.

Among his easel paintings, when under the influence of Pintoricchio, may be mentioned the two in the Madrid Museum (Nos. 573, 574)—the "Rape of the Sabines," [3] and the "Continence of Scipio." (†)

As works of his second period, when influenced by Sodoma, I should name, in addition to his fresco already mentioned in S. Maria della Pace, the two splendid pen drawings in the Louvre—the "Triumph of Vespasian" (No. 437, Reiset Catalogue; Braun, No. 363),[4] and another episode from Roman history exhibited on the screen in Room X. under the name of Sodoma (Tauzia Catalogue, No. 1967). (†) In the frescoes on the ceiling of the Farnesina, completed in 1511, Peruzzi's study of the antique is very striking. The female figures involuntarily recall Greek or Roman gems; but it is the influence of Raphael's genius which we perceive in the "Venus" of the Borghese gallery—a graceful undraped figure, probably studied from nature, seated on a stone, a pale silvery blue drapery falling from her right arm. This composition, conceived entirely in the classic spirit of the Roman Court at the time of Leo X., offended the sense of modesty of one of its later possessors; a ready restorer, however, was easily found to lengthen the drapery, which originally reached

[3] Dr. W. Bode (ii. 733, 1884) wrongly attributes the "Rape of the Sabines" in the Chigi Palace to Peruzzi; it is by Sodoma. But, as I have already stated, this palace does contain a fresco by Peruzzi. Sir J. C. Robinson, in his catalogue of the Malcolm collection in London, confounds Peruzzi with Sodoma in a drawing of Sibyls, No. 316 (†) (see *Descriptive Catalogue of Drawings, &c.* by J. C. Robinson, p. 113).

[4] M. Reiset is in doubt whether to attribute this drawing to Francia, to Costa, or to Pellegrino da S. Daniele. Passavant, with more insight, ascribed it to Sodoma. The latter painter, again, is confounded with Peruzzi in "The Fall of Phaethon" in the Uffizi (No. 1644)—a composition in indian ink for the decoration of a ceiling. Dr. Frizzoni first directed my attention to this fine drawing by Sodoma. Peruzzi is easily recognised by the defect, inherited from his first master Pintoricchio, who in his turn derived it from Fiorenzo di Lorenzo, of making the legs of his figures of disproportionate length.

only to the right hip, and in the interest of morality the left hip was also covered.[5]

## RAPHAEL SANZIO.

This notice of Baldassare Peruzzi leads us to Raphael, whose world-renowned "Entombment," the most celebrated work of his Florentine period, hangs in this gallery. The cartoon for this, his first, dramatic painting—the result of laborious and conscientious study—was probably executed in Florence. The picture itself, which was ordered by Atalanta Baglioni of Perugia, most likely as early as 1503, must have been completed in the summer of 1507 at Perugia, with the help of several assistants; for we may infer that Raphael had assistants already at that date, not only from the picture itself, but from several of the sketches for it, which he himself made in silver point, but which his pupils, for their better preservation, went over with the pen. This is plainly visible in the large "Entombment,' or "Lamentation over the Body of Christ," in the "Salle aux boîtes" of the Louvre; in the drawing in the Uffizi (squared over for enlargement), and in several other pen drawings for the same subject; as in those at Oxford, in the British Museum, in Mr. Malcolm's collection,[6] in that of the Duc d'Aumale, in the Albertina at Vienna, and elsewhere.[7] It appears to me that the touch of

[5] In the Seminario Vescovile at Venice, a picture by Beccafumi of Siena, representing "Penelope," is attributed to Peruzzi. (†)

[6] The drawing of a skeleton, which from the Antaldi collection passed into that of Mr. John Malcolm (Robinson's Catalogue, No. 179), is merely one of the many forgeries with which the former collection was so richly supplied (†); the other so-called Raphael drawing for this picture (in the same collec-tion) is probably only a copy. All the drawings and sketches above mentioned for this painting should be compared with the magnificent pen drawing belonging to the well-known collector, Herr Edward Habich of Cassel, who had the good fortune to obtain it from the Klinkosch collection at Vienna.

[7] See on this subject Dr. W. Koopmann's well-written article in von Lützow's *Zeitschrift für bildende Kunst.*

L

Raphael, and his refined feeling for line, are absent in many parts of this academic work, and I cannot but endorse the opinion of Rumohr, who saw in this laboriously composed picture evident traces of an alien hand.

Be this as it may, the " Entombment" certainly touches me less than any works by Raphael of this period, and other critics have experienced the same feeling. It is among the earliest acquisitions of this collection, having been bought by Pope Paul V. (Borghese), in 1607, from the Franciscans at Perugia. Winckelmann regarded it as one of the most perfect works of the master, and particularly notes the energy of movement, the truth of expression, and the dramatic power of the whole composition. The little effect produced upon me and others, by this so-called classic work, is possibly due to the elaborate preliminary study bestowed upon its composition by the young artist. In other works of this period—for instance, in the so-called " Madonna di Casa Colonna " in the Berlin Museum, and in the " Madonna di Casa Niccolini " in Lord Cowper's collection at Panshanger—discerning critics believe they can also detect the help of pupils, and I think they are right.

If I am not very much mistaken, there is another work by Raphael in this gallery; it is numbered 397, and was formerly assigned to Holbein. The present director has, however, adopted my view, and attributes it, though only doubtfully, to Raphael. It represents a man of about fifty, with long dark-brown hair, wearing a black tunic trimmed with fur, and a black cap. His features recall those of Pintoricchio, in his fresco in the library of the cathedral at Siena. It certainly requires some courage —perhaps people would say an uncommon amount of assurance—to lay claim to the discovery of a hitherto unknown Raphael in one of the most frequented picture galleries in the world. Yet I have no hesitation in affirming that this portrait struck me at once as a work of the master's early period, of about 1502, and I cannot share the opinion of the late Mr. Mündler, that it is the portrait of Perugino by himself. The hair is treated with true Raphaelesque feeling and grace; the eyes have a vivacity and lustre which are generally absent in the heads of Perugino, and the nose and mouth are more sharply modelled than is usual with him. Moreover, the luminous flesh tones are distinctive of Raphael. The portrait should be compared with several heads of the Apostles in this master's " Coronation of the Virgin," in the Vatican. (†) It has suffered considerably, and has been deprived of its original surface. The position of the cap was evidently altered by the master himself, and altogether the portrait appears unfinished [8]—the tunic being only laid in. There is not much to be said about the little portrait of a boy (No. 399), which is described as the portrait of Raphael by himself, it being entirely repainted. Messrs. Crowe and Cavalcaselle think it may be by Ridolfo del Ghirlandaio. If I were to propose a name for this inferior production it would be that of Domenico Alfani. (†) It should be compared with " The Nativity " by Domenico in the gallery at Perugia (No. 24).

## PERINO DEL VAGA.

From Raphael we pass to another of his contemporaries and imitators, Perino del Vaga, who occupies a very different position from that of Domenico Alfani in the history of art. After the death of Raphael, Perino, like Giulio

[8] Among recent writers on Raphael, only the late Signor Marco Minghetti and Professor Karl von Lützow have, as far as I know, accepted my opinion. The Berlin connoisseurs, to my regret, continue to protest against my views, and with them Professor Müntz also lifts up his voice.

Romano, degenerated rapidly, owing to the influence of Michael Angelo.[9] In order to become better acquainted with this very able and thoroughly Florentine painter, we must seek his early works, especially those executed under the direct influence of his master and friend Raphael. They consist entirely of drawings, and of frescoes in the Vatican, and nearly all pass, as I shall endeavour to show, under the name of Raphael. As the biographers of the latter are wont to base their opinion of Perino solely upon the works of his second Roman period, I shall take the opportunity of following the career of this interesting artist, whose genius ripened early, and of drawing attention to the works of his first Roman period, from about 1513–1527, one of which is, I think, in the Borghese gallery. (+) It is rightly catalogued ' School of Raphael,' is numbered 464, and represents " The Nativity ": St. Joseph supports the Infant Saviour, who lies on the ground whilst the Madonna presents the little St. John to Him. A good sketch washed with sepia for this picture is in the Albertina at Vienna, and was photographed by Braun (No. 53) as a Luca Penni. (†)

Perino del Vaga was born about 1500 in Florence, and died in Rome in 1547. Works of his first Roman period, from about 1513–1527, are scarcely known, as his biographers are wont only to refer to those at Genoa, and to those of his second Roman period (1535–1547), and upon them to base their opinion of the artist. The Dutch painter Franz Hals has been similarly treated ; his early works, up to about 1616, are still unknown, and in all probability pass under other names. Vasari, who knew Perino personally, and valued his powers as an artist, says

---

[9] His frescoes in the Palazzo Doria at Genoa afford a proof of this. On the other hand, a certain influence of the Venetian Pordenone is perceptible in Perino's " Adoration of the Shepherds " belonging to Lord Dudley. The picture is signed and dated 1534.

THE ADORATION OF THE CHILD.

(A Drawing by PIERINO DEL VAGA, in the Albertina, Vienna.)

To face p. 140.

that he entered the workshop of Ridolfo del Ghirlandaio when he was about eleven, and there devoted himself chiefly to drawing, in which he far surpassed all his fellow-students.[1] The result of this proficiency was, that the Florentine painter Vaga, who then required a skilful draughtsman to aid him in his frescoes at Toscanella, took Perino thither as his assistant, and when this work was completed the youth, who ardently desired to learn and to improve himself, accompanied Vaga to Rome. There, according to Vasari, he applied himself, under the greatest privations, to the study of art, working night and day with indomitable industry. The biographer goes on to say, that though Perino copied Michael Angelo's frescoes on the ceiling of the Sistine chapel, his work showed more of the manner of Raphael than of Buonarotti ('seguitava più gli andari e la maniera di Raffaello che non quella del Buonarotti'). And so it came to pass, he adds, that Perino was regarded as the finest and best draughtsman in Rome ('il più bello e miglior disegnatore che ci fosse ').

He appears soon to have become intimate with Giulio Romano, and especially with his fellow-countryman Francesco Penni, called il Fattore, and one or other of them may have procured some sketches and drawings by their own master and prototype Raphael for him to copy.[2]

[1] 'E fù fra tutti i giovani suoi pari ritenuto il miglior disegnatore di quanti studiassero con lui nella bottega di Ridolfo.'

[2] Vasari relates that Garofalo, with whom he was personally acquainted, having come to Rome in his nineteenth year (1499), entered into relations there with the Florentine painter Giovanni Baldini, who possessed some fine drawings by various first-rate artists ; many of these he lent to Garofalo, who sought to cultivate his eye by studying them, and to train his hand by copying them at night (*Vasari*, xi. 223). Again, in his *Life of Cristofano Gherardi* (xi. 2), he says, ' Capitò al Borgo il Rosso, col quale avendo il Gherardi fatto amicizia, ed avuto de' suoi disegni, studiò sopra quelli, con molta diligenza,' &c. See too the *Life of Michael Angelo*, xii. 159 : 'Amando il Granacci Michelangelo e vedutolo molto atto al disegno, lo serviva giornalmente de' disegni del Grillandaio,' &c.

Several such copies by Perino are still, I believe, in existence, and we shall consider them presently. Like nearly all his drawings, they are washed with water-colour, and recall the technic of Rosso Fiorentino. In company with the latter, and with many other Florentine artists, Perino studied and copied the nude figures in Michael Angelo's celebrated cartoon (for the so-called "Battle of Pisa")—distinguishing himself above all his fellows, as his biographer records. Before long the young Florentine acquired so great a reputation among Roman artists for his admirable drawings, that Raphael expressed a desire to know this youthful prodigy. Having seen the boy's work, he commended him to Giovanni da Udine, then superintending the painting and decoration of the Loggie in the Vatican, and commissioned him to give employment to this young and promising painter. The following frescoes in the Loggie are named by Vasari (x. 88) as having been executed by Perino from Raphael's sketches : [3] "The Israelites bearing the Ark across the Jordan;" "The Fall of Jericho;" "The Battle of Joshua;" "Joshua commanding the Sun to stand still;" the "Birth," and the "Baptism" of Christ; the "Last Supper," and many more. All these, more especially the "Last Supper," are so repainted that it is only as compositions that they can still afford us any pleasure. According to Vasari, the allegorical paintings below the frescoes in the Stanza d' Eliodoro were also by Perino.[4]

When Pope Paul III., at a later period, caused the fire-

[3] The following painters, who worked in the Loggie from Raphael's sketches, are enumerated by Vasari : Giulio Romano, Penni, Pellegrino da Modena (?), Bagnacavallo (?), Vincenzo da S. Gemignano, Polidoro da Caravaggio (?), and Perino del Vaga. In 1674 Titti added the name of Gaudenzio Ferrari to them, and

Taja, in 1754, tried to show that Raffaele del Colle had also been employed.

[4] See the sketch for one of these paintings, "The Expedition of the Argonauts," reproduced in Dr. G. Frizzoni's book, entitled *Quaranta disegni scelti dalla Raccolta del Senatore G. Morelli* (Milano, 1886).

SKETCH BY RAPHAEL FOR A FRESCO IN THE FARNESINA.

To face p. 143.

place to be moved from the ' Camera del fuoco ' [5] to the
' Camera della Segnatura,' it was Perino who was commissioned to execute, in chiaroscuro, allegorical subjects, like
those in the Stanza d' Eliodoro, beneath Raphael's frescoes,
and in place of Fra Giovanni da Verona's intarsias which
had been removed. If we compare these later works by
Perino, executed during his second stay in Rome, with those
in the neighbouring room which were completed under the
direct influence of Raphael, we shall see, I think, how
rapidly the school declined only a few years after the
master's death. Vasari was perfectly correct in his assertion that, though Giulio Romano and Francesco Penni were
called scholars of Raphael, and inherited his sketches and
drawings, they neither of them inherited the feeling and
grace (*l' arte et la grazia*) which Perino was able to give
to his figures. In technical execution both undoubtedly
approached their master closely both in drawing and in
painting—so closely indeed, that many paintings by Giulio,
and many drawings which both Giulio and Penni had executed from sketches by Raphael, are still attributed to the
latter.[6] But neither Giulio Romano, Francesco Penni, nor

---

[5] Namely, the ' Stanza d' Eliodoro,' not to be confounded with the
' Camera dell' Incendio di Borgo,'
called also ' Torre Borgia.'

[6] I shall here enumerate a few
of these paintings and drawings by
Giulio Romano.    Paintings : (1)
" The Vision of Ezekiel," in the
Pitti at Florence ; (2) " The Forna-
rina," in the Barberini gallery at
Rome; (3) the "Madonna del divino
Amore," in the Naples museum ; (4)
the  " Madonna della Perla," at
Madrid ; (5) the painting called " Lo
Spasimo di Sicilia," at Madrid ; (6)
the " Madonna della Rosa," at
Madrid ; (7) the  " Madonna di
Francesco I.," in the Louvre ; and

(8) the large " St. Michael," in the
Louvre. In the collection at Cologne
there is an extremely interesting pen
and ink sketch by Raphael (see illustration) for a lunette in the first
room of the Farnesina. This sketch
may serve to throw some light upon
the part taken by Raphael in these
frescoes, in those in the ' Stanza
dell' Incendio di Borgo,' in the
' Chiesa della Pace,' and elsewhere.
I believe that the first slight sketches
for these paintings were made by
Raphael ; from them his pupils and
assistants probably made drawings
which were afterwards enlarged
upon the cartoons prepared for
transferring them to the wall ; the

any other of his many scholars and imitators, knew how
to reflect the spirit and the charm of Raphael with such
purity and freshness as Perino del Vaga in his first Roman

cartoons were then subjected to the
master's approval and were corrected by him, after which the assistant immediately set to work. In
this way it is easier to understand
how Raphael, who was so much in
request both as the architect of St.
Peter's, and as an archæologist, was
able to execute such an immense
number of paintings and drawings
in the space of six years. Vasari
viii. 38) observes, with reference to
the frescoes in the 'Stanza dell'
Incendio di Borgo': 'Nelle quali
sale del continuo teneva [Raphael]
delle genti [i.e. assistants] che con i
disegni suoi medesimi gli tiravano
innanzi l'opera [that is, they executed
the painting], ed egli continuamente
rivedendo ogni cosa suppliva con
tutti quegli aiuti migliori, che egli
più poteva, ad un peso cosi fatto.'
And again, speaking of the frescoes
in the Farnesina (viii. 54), he says :
'Parimente non soddisfeciono affatto
gli ignudi [namely, the nude figures]
che furono similmente [that is, with
the help of his scholars] fatti da lui
[Raphael] nella volta del palazzo
d'Agostino Chigi in Trastevere
[Farnesina], perchò mancano di
quella grazia e dolcezza che fù propria di Raffaello, del che fù in gran
parte cagione l'avergli fatti colorire
ad altri col suo disegno.' Most of
these drawings, executed from
Raphael's sketches, I believe to be by
Giulio Romano ; for instance, for the
Farnesina—"Venus and Psyche,"
red chalk, in the Louvre (Braun
257); the "Three Graces," red chalk
Windsor (Grosvenor Gallery Publication) ; the nude figure of a youth

holding a vase, Ambrosiana (Braun
129); for the frescoes in the
'Stanza dell' Incendio di Borgo,' in
the Vatican—the "Water-carrier"
—red chalk, Uffizi (Braun 493—
Professor A. Springer first questioned
the genuineness of this so-called
Raphael ; the original, lightly
sketched with black chalk on blue
paper, is in the Morelli collection) ;
and two standing nude male figures,
red chalk, Albertina (Braun 176).
The inscription on this latter drawing is a forgery. The writing, in the
first place, is not that of Dürer ; and,
secondly, the cultivated painter of
Nüremberg would scarcely have
written, 'Raffahel.' He must also
have been aware that Leo X. esteemed Raphael no less highly than
his predecessor Julius II. had done ;
but the chief point is, that the drawing itself reveals the hand of Giulio
Romano, and not that of Raphael.
Add to these a red chalk drawing in
the Uffizi (Braun 491), for the picture at Madrid called "Lo Spasimo
di Sicilia" ; the red chalk drawing
for the so-called "Madonna di Francesco I." in the Louvre (Uffizi, Braun
486); and the drawing for the child
in the preceding picture, red chalk,
Uffizi (Braun 487).

Three red chalk drawings for the
"Transfiguration," in the Louvre,
(Braun 254), the Albertina (Braun
139), and the Ambrosiana (Braun
128) might be by Francesco Penni (?)
called il Fattore. The forms in
them are not those of Giulio
Romano, and still less of Raphael
to whom they are attributed. And
what, it may be asked, are the cha-

TRIUMPH OF SILENUS. BY PERINO DEL VAGA.

*(In the Albertina, Vienna.)*

*To face p. 145.*

STUDY BY PERINO DEL VAGA FROM DESIGNS BY RAPHAEL
FOR THE 'DISPUTA.'

*(At Windsor.)*

*To face p. 145.*

period. It is not surprising, therefore, that his drawings, though so different from those of Raphael, both in the forms and the technic, have yet, down to the present day, been almost without exception ascribed to that master—a further proof of the superficial manner in which the works of the Italian painters have hitherto been studied.

But to return to our theme ; let us first examine some of those drawings of Perino's middle period, which are recognised as such in public collections, and endeavour to determine their characteristics. In the Albertina we find the " Triumph of Silenus " (Braun 25) ; in the Louvre (Salle aux boîtes), the " Triumph of Bacchus " (Braun 70). Both these excellent drawings belong to the same period, and are, as M. Reiset states in his catalogue, drawn with the pen on greyish paper, shaded with bistre and heightened with white. The cranium is too strongly developed in proportion to the faces, giving the head a triangular form. Several of the figures in the background are conspicuous by the abnormally long oval of the heads ; the arms are unnaturally long and too fleshy, more especially in the upper part at the shoulder ; the forefinger is often bent like a hook. The shading of the eye-sockets is so dark that the eye itself is scarcely perceptible. All these charac-

racteristics which distinguish the drawings of Giulio from those of Raphael? Among the most apparent I may mention the following : a. In Giulio's drawings the ear is never so round or so fleshy as in Raphael's ; b. The upper lip is always thick as if swollen ; c. The knee and elbow joints are always strongly accentuated ; d. The form of hand differs from that of Raphael ; e. The edge of the folds in the drapery is harder than in Raphael's drawings. We find these characteristics more especially in drawings of his Roman period. This master should be studied in the following works : his painting in the church of S. Maria dell' Anima in Rome ; the " Madonna della Gatta " in the Naples museum ; the "Battle of Constantine" in the Vatican, and in his carefully executed drawing at Chatsworth, there rightly attributed to him (Braun 66)—his sketch for his " Presentation in the Temple," in the Louvre (No. 1,438), there given to Bagnacavallo (†).

teristics are apparent in another drawing in the Louvre
(Braun 275), which both M. Reiset in his catalogue and
Passavant (ii. 180 and 465) attribute to Raphael, though
even Vasari (x. 154) mentions it as Perino's drawing
for the painting he executed in 1522, for the church of
S. Lorenzo at Florence. It represents "Moses crossing
the Red Sea, and the destruction of Pharaoh and his
Host." (†) Those who accept the two first-named drawings
will scarcely dispute that the latter is from the same hand.

From these drawings of Perino's middle period, let us
go back to the sketches and drawings executed by him in
the first years of his sojourn in Rome. As the earliest
among them, I would name one at Windsor (in vol. i. of
the Raphael drawings), and one at Oxford (†) (University
galleries, Robinson, No. 60). Both are studies and sketches
for the "Disputa del Sacramento." I believe them to have
been copied by Perino for his own instruction, either from
the fresco itself, or from Raphael's sketches which may have
been lent to him. Even Passavant (ii. 491) is doubtful
about the Windsor drawing, whether to give it to Raphael
or not, while both he and other writers regard the one at
Oxford as a genuine work of that master. The right hand
of the figure on the extreme left in the Windsor drawing
should be compared with the left hand of a woman on the
extreme right in a drawing in the Albertina at Vienna
(Braun 25) ; this alone should prove that the two belong to
one master, the same feeling and technic being apparent
in both. We find the same in the following drawings ;
hence, though attributed to Raphael, I believe them to be
by Perino. They were unquestionably made from Raphael's
sketches, but it was perhaps Perino who executed them in
fresco in the "Loggie."

In the Albertina there are three : Abraham kneeling
before the three Angels. (†)     Passavant (ii. 176), follow-

THE DESTRUCTION OF PHARAOH AND HIS HOST.

*(Drawing by PERINO DEL VAGA in the Louvre.)*

To face p. 146.

JOSEPH INTERPRETING HIS DREAM.

(*Drawing by* Perino del Vaga *in the Albertina, Vienna.*)

*To face p.* 146.

ing tradition, ascribes the fresco to Penni, the drawing
to Raphael (ii. 430) ; Jacob and Rachael. (†)   Passavant
(ii. 177) ascribes the fresco to Pellegrino da Modena, the
drawing to Raphael (ii. 430) ;  Joseph interpreting his
Dream to his Brethren. (†)   Passavant (ii. 178) cannot
decide to whom to attribute the execution of this fresco ;
the drawing, however, he gives to Raphael (ii. 430).

In the Louvre are the four following drawings : The
Almighty giving Moses the Tables of the Law (†) (Passavant ii. 465 and ii. 180 ; Braun 270) ; SS. Peter and Paul
appearing to Attila (†) (for the ‘ Stanza d’ Eliodoro ’
Passavant ii. 470 ; Braun 235 ;—in Venice, as early as
1530, this drawing was regarded as by Raphael ; the
‘ Anonimo ’ mentions it as such, thus furnishing us another proof of the worthlessness of tradition) ; the “ Calumny
of Apelles ” (†) (Passavant ii. 469), and the “ Battle of
Constantine ” (Passavant ii. 470 ; Braun 236).

In the Uffizi four drawings by Perino are attributed to
Raphael : the “ Worship of the Golden Calf ” (Case 138,
No. 510 ; Passavant ii. 180) ; the so-called “ Morbetto ” [7]
(Case 146, No. 525 ; Braun 484), the composition of which
appears to me certainly to belong to Perino.   He probably
designed it after the death of Raphael, between 1520–1530 for
Marcantonio’s engraving, for at that time engravers appear
to have shown a special predilection for Perino’s designs.[8] (†)
Caraglio or Bonasone engraved the “ Marriage of Alexander
the Great and Roxana ” from a drawing made for the

---

[7] The other two drawings are,
No. 509, Case 138, and No. 536, Case
152.  A fifth, No. 533, Case 150,
belongs to his first period, and is
rightly ascribed to him.

[8] A gifted North German writer
Raphael remarks : ‘ I never
can look at this drawing without
a kind of shudder, but the ideal
conception raises me above such
weakness ; one feels that the artist
was superior to it all ’ (H. Grimm :
*Zehn ausgewählte Essays*, p. 101).
Would the drawing have produced
the same impression on his imagination had the writer been aware
that it was not by Raphael ?

purpose by Perino, and copied by him not from Sodoma's well-known fresco in the Farnesina, but from the red chalk drawing now in the Albertina, which was at that time in Rome, possibly in Perino's own possession. Only two feeble copies of Perino's original drawing for Caraglio's engraving have come down to us; the best of the two is in the Louvre, the other is at Windsor. (†) (Braun 144, 277.) At Chatsworth several good and characteristic specimens are rightly attributed to Perino (Braun 12, 17, 21), while the following, which are his also, pass under the name of Raphael: the "Raising of Lazarus," "Constantine address-ing his Soldiers" (for the chamber of Constantine in the Vatican), and a monarch crowned, seated on a throne, with two kneeling suppliants before him, and five other figures on the left and four on the right. (†) In the same collec-tion an interesting early drawing by Giovanni Bellini (four figures of Saints) is given to Perino, while a genuine Holy Family by the latter with SS. Elisabeth and Joachim is even ascribed to Leonardo. (†)

In conclusion, lest I should weary my readers by a list of undue proportions, I will only mention three pen draw-ings by Perino. Two of them bear the name of Raphael: one, the well-known drawing in Dresden, "Neptune and his Train," was, according to Passavant (ii. 450), for a bronze or silver salver, designed by Raphael for Agostino Chigi; the other, an "Adoration of the Shepherds," is in the collec-tion at Oxford (Robinson's Catalogue, No. 76, Passavant ii. 512); the third, a "Procession of Nymphs and Tritons" (†), is in the Taylor Institution. Neither Sir J. C. Robinson (Catalogue, No. 83) nor Passavant attributes this drawing to Raphael; the latter critic thinks (ii. 507) it may have been executed by Francesco Penni.

Aided by these few hints, students will doubtless succeed in identifying Perino's numerous drawings which are

usually attributed to Raphael in different European collections. Before quitting this attractive Florentine painter,
who for natural grace and lightness of touch is worthy to
be classed with his older fellow-countrymen, Leonardo, Fra
Bartolommeo, and Andrea del Sarto, I should like to mention a document which has recently been published by Signor
Bertolotti, referring in all probability to Perino del Vaga.
It is a letter sent by Pandolfo di Pico della Mirandola, the
Duke of Mantua's political envoy in Rome, to his employer,
the well-known Isabella Gonzaga. It is dated Rome,
January 29, 1520, a few months therefore before the death
of Raphael, and runs as follows:

'Illustrissima Madama: In Roma evvi un giovane de 20
anni, fiorentino, quale in arte de pictura, sotto l' opera de
Michelangelo,[9] s'è fatto grande che ognuno che se intende de
tal arte se meraviglia che in quella etade sia tanta suffi-
cientia, et perchè Raphaello cognosce quanto è per reusir,
lo tiene basso in modo che, avendo pigliato io sua amicitia,
l' ho persuaso a voler andar fuor de Roma, per farsi cono-
scere; esso mi ha promesso che, finite alcune cose [che]
ha nelle mani, che sarà a Kalende de Giugno, che ad ogni
modo vole andar fori, donde che io ho pensato che [se] V.
Exc. volesse far dipingere di posto come meriterebbe quel
loco, io lo invierò et sarà cosa da pochi giorni et da poche
spese, perchè se contenterà in pocha cosa. La professione
del ditto giovane è de dipingere a fresco sopra muro
ovvero a tempera, non havendosi usato a colorire a olio.

---

[9] Vasari (x. 139) says: 'E Perino
disegnando in compagnia d' altri
giovani, e fiorentini e forestieri, al
cartone di Michelangelo, vinse e
tenne il primo grado fra tutti gli
altri; di maniera che si stava in
quella aspettazione di lui,' &c. &c.
and p. 141 (as already noted):
' Perino comminciò a disegnare nella
Cappella di papa Giulio [the Sistine
chapel] dove la volta di Michelangelo Bonarotti era dipinta da lui
seguitando gli andari e la maniera
di Raffaello da Urbino,' that is, he
copied and rendered Michael Angelo's
figures in Raphael's style and
manner.

Nondimeno tanto è grande el disegno, ma che tutto fara
bene pur ch' el se exerciti.  Io gli facio fare un quadro
colorito a olio per mandarlo a V. Extia., acciò quello indichi
l' arte sua quanto è grande in quella età di 20 anni.'

The letter might be thus translated :

' Most illustrious lady : There is in Rome a young
Florentine, 20 years old, who has greatly distinguished
himself in painting under the influence of Michael Angelo,
so that all who understand art marvel at one so young in
years having gained such proficiency, and as Raphael perceives to what excellence this young artist is likely to attain,
he gives him only unimportant work.  As I am on friendly
terms with the youth, I have advised him to try his fortune
and to make himself a name elsewhere, and he has promised
me that, so soon as he shall have finished the work he has
on hand  (which will be about June), he  will assuredly
leave Rome.  Wherefore, should your Excellency contemplate having any paintings executed on the wall, of which
the place is certainly worthy, I would send him to you.
The matter would not require much time or money, as the
young man would be easily satisfied.  He is principally a
fresco, or tempera, painter, not having as yet accustomed
himself to the use of oil; nevertheless, as drawing is his
strong point, he is sure to succeed in everything when he has
once had a little practice.  He is now at work upon an oil
painting which I shall send to your Excellency, as a specimen of his art and of his capabilities at the age of twenty.'[1]

The drawings of Francesco Mazzola, called Parmeggianino, dating from the second decade of the sixteenth
century, prove how strong an influence Perino must have
exercised over this kindred spirit—the painter of Parma.[2]

[1] See Bertolotti, *Artisti in rela-
zione coi Gonzaga*, p. 155 (1885).

[2] Even P. J. Marriette, one of
the best French connoisseurs of
drawings and engravings, mistook a
drawing in the Louvre (a copy of an
indian ink drawing by Perino) for a
Parmeggianino (*Abecedario* i. 89).

After this long, but I trust not unprofitable, digression about Perino del Vaga, we will turn to

## THE LOMBARDS.

### GIOVAN ANTONIO BAZZI, called IL SODOMA.

No. 462 in the catalogue is rightly given to its true author, Sodoma; we will therefore begin with this master, who has scarcely been sufficiently appreciated, and discuss, in their proper order, those Lombard painters represented in the Roman galleries and in other Italian collections. The picture represents the " Pietà "—the Madonna supporting the Body of her Divine Son—it has darkened considerably, but is nevertheless an important work; once attributed to the school of Leonardo, it now bears the name of Sodoma, which the new director, adopting a suggestion of mine, has given to it. The forms, the type of head, the fall of the drapery, and more especially the landscape peculiar to Sodoma, conclusively prove him to be the author of this "Pietà." In his early works, from about 1501–1512, the shadows are light and clear; for instance, in the fine circular panel of the " Nativity " and the splendid " Descent from the Cross," both in the gallery at Siena (Nos. 85 and 343). We may therefore infer that this " Pietà," by reason of its opposite qualities, is a work of his mature period. I am quite of the opinion of Dr. G. Frizzoni, who first assigned this picture to Sodoma, that the master belongs to the Lombardo-Milanese school, and, moreover, to that branch which was under the immediate influence of Leonardo.

Towards the end of 1507 Sodoma was summoned to Rome, the fame of his works at Siena and Mont' Oliveto (of 1505) having preceded him. He was commissioned to

decorate with frescoes the ceiling of the 'Camera della Segnatura,' where Bramantino was then at work.    Bartolommeo Suardi, called Bramantino, who had known Sodoma
personally at Milan, may not improbably have been
instrumental in procuring this commission for him.    Documentary evidence proves that when Raphael came to Rome
in the summer of 1508, Sodoma was still working in the
Vatican, and the former thought so highly of his frescoes in
this chamber that he left them as far as possible undis-
turbed.    As a further mark of esteem, Raphael introduced
Sodoma's portrait, next to his own, in the "School of
Athens."[3]    In 1513 Sodoma was again in Rome, possibly
at the same time as Leonardo, his master and prototype.
In all probability he was summoned there by his wealthy
patron, Agostino Chigi, of Siena, to decorate a room on the
upper floor of his new villa, the 'Farnesina.'    I shall return to these frescoes later, but another important work by
Sodoma in this gallery must be mentioned (No. 434).    Like
the preceding, it was formerly only assigned to the 'school'
of Leonardo.[4]    It represents Leda with her twin children
and the swan.    The composition of this fine painting
certainly carries out the principles of Leonardo,[5] but is

---

[3] The man in white, with a white
cap, next to Raphael, is certainly
not, as commonly supposed, Pietro
Perugino (who fortunately had
nothing to do with the frescoes
in this room), but Bazzi, who
decorated the ceiling.  I am glad to
find that Dr. Bode (ii. 707, 1884)
appears to agree with me here.  In
the next room, the so-called 'Camera
d' Eliodoro,' Raphael paid the same
graceful compliment to Baldassaro
Peruzzi, for he, I believe, is represented among the Pope's bearers,
and not—as art-historians from the

time of Vasari have asserted—Giulio
Romano, then (1514) barely twenty-
two.  The head of the first bearer on
the left should be compared with the
portrait of Peruzzi in his large indian
ink drawing in the Uffizi (No. 438).
Much of the decoration in this room
is by Peruzzi; he must, therefore,
here be regarded as the assistant of
Raphael.

[4] The new director has concurred
in my opinion, and the picture is
now ascribed to Sodoma.

[5] Leonardo in his 'Trattato della
Pittura' (chap. lxiv.) observes : 'Le

"LEDA." BY SODOMA.

*(In the Borghese Gallery.)*

*To face p* 132.

conceived entirely in the spirit of Sodoma. (†)   In Lomazzo's "Trattato della Pittura" the following passage occurs: 'Fece [Leonardo] Leda tutta ignuda col cigno in grembo, che vergognosamente abbassa gli occhi.'   Lomazzo may be correct in his statement, though I myself have never come across a drawing by Leonardo which had the slightest reference to this subject; but, as Baron Rumohr thought he had discovered a "Leda" at Cassel by Leonardo, and a similar picture by him is said to be at Hanover, I have no wish to cast doubts on the possibility of the great Florentine having treated it.

In the foreground of the beautiful example in the Borghese gallery, we find the accessories usually introduced by painters of this school: daisies and violets springing up in the grass; a finch, a dove, and a thrush perching close to the young demigods, Castor and Pollux—an arch and merry little couple, though seemingly but just emerged from their shell.   In the centre of the picture stands Leda undraped; the swan approaches her with ardent devotion; she droops her eyes with a half-bashful smile.   Her beautiful, well-proportioned form is animated by a refined sensuousness, and is full of charm, vividly recalling the exquisite figure of Eve in Sodoma's fresco, "The Descent into Hades," in the gallery at Siena (No. 362).   The swan could not be more felicitously treated both in its eager impassioned gesture and in the modelling.   Compare its conception and treatment with the realistic representations by Hondecoeter, or even with the celebrated allegorical swan by Asselyn at Amsterdam, and the immensity of the gulf separating the great Italian masters from the realistic

---

donne si devono figurar con atti vergognosi, le gambe insieme ristrette, le braccia insieme raccolte, teste basse, e piegate in traverso.'  See, too, *The Literary Works of Leonardo da Vinci*, by J. P. Richter, i. 291, No. 583.

Dutch painters will be felt at once.     The luxuriant landscape in the background is quite in the spirit of Sodoma,[6]
and the children recall both the *putti* in the Farnesina and
those on the ceiling of the ' Camera della Segnatura.'     The
latter, however, are in a very damaged condition.[7]

Thus I thought and wrote on the subject of this " Leda "
about fifteen years ago, and when I studied the picture again
later I saw no reason for altering my first opinion.     As
my excuse I must plead that until quite recently it hung
some way from the window, and was, therefore, only seen
in a half-light.     The authorities of the gallery have lately
had it moved to a better place ; here Dr. J. P. Richter saw
it, and at once drew my attention to the fact that it was
probably nothing but an old, though good, copy of an
original by Sodoma.     When I again examined the picture,
the scales fell from my eyes, and I at once recognised the
justice of Dr. Richter's criticism.     This may serve as a
warning to critics never to pass judgment on any work of
art unless they have examined it in a good light.

I am unable to say if the original of this picture is still
in existence ; but I can mention several drawings which

---

[6] A comparison between Sodoma's landscapes and those in
early works by Cesare da Sesto and
Gianpietrino, will reveal at once how
closely these three painters were
connected.     According to Vasari
they all learned this branch of their
art from Bernazzano, an excellent
landscape painter.

[7] Some northern critics still per-
sist in saying that, as the drawing
for " Roxana " in the Albertina is by
Raphael, and not, as I have shown,
by Sodoma, so the *putti* on the ceiling of the ' Camera della Segnatura '
are not to be attributed to the
latter, but to Melozzo da Forli (!)
Principally, according to Dr. Bode

(ii. 596, note), because on the blue
sky are introduced the arms of the
' della Rovere,' to which family Pope
Sixtus IV. belonged.     But Julius II.,
I may observe, also belonged to the
house of della Rovere.     It seems
incredible that anyone should have
been reminded of Melozzo da Forli
in these *putti*.     Braun has photographed all Sodoma's frescoes on the
ceiling of the ' Camera della Segnatura ' (Nos. 111, 112, 113, 114, 115),
and an examination of these reproductions will    prove that the
*putti*, notwithstanding their damaged
condition, have the characteristic
type of all Sodoma's children.     See
more especially Nos. 113 and 114.

Sodoma made use of for it. Three are attribuced to Leonardo, one to Raphael, and a fifth is rightly given to Bazzi.
One of the three first-mentioned pen drawings, representing
Leda kneeling, her head turned towards the swan on her
left (Braun 148), is in the palace at Weimar, attributed to
Leonardo. (†) In a second, at Chatsworth, Leda also kneels,
with her left arm round the neck of the swan (Braun 51).(†)

A third pen drawing for this picture is at Windsor in
vol. ii. of the Raphael drawings (Grosvenor Gallery Publication, No. 50). In this remarkable example the pose of Leda
is very similar to that in the painting in this gallery. There
is certainly something Raphaelesque about the drawing, and
it is therefore excusable that amateurs should have regarded it as the work of the Umbrian master ; but to persons
familiar with the spirit and technic of Sodoma this drawing
must appear indisputably his. (†) It furnishes us with a
further proof that, when engaged upon the "Leda" and
the "Marriage of Alexander and Roxana" in Rome, the
Lombard painter must have entered into more intimate
relations with Raphael. The *putto* near Leda is extremely
Raphaelesque, though it reminds us also of Leonardo.[8]
Looking more closely at the drawing, we cannot fail to
recognise the spirit and the hand of Sodoma in the form
of the feet, the full fleshy knees, the almond-shaped eyes,
the arrangement of the hair, which is quite unlike Raphael,
and the fine strokes of the pen.[9] The modelling of the

---

[8] Drawings by Sodoma's master, Leonardo, are even occasionally attributed to Raphael—for instance, the pen drawing in the His la Salle collection in the Louvre. (Both de Tauzia's Catalogue, No. 2283.)

[9] The following are some of Sodoma's characteristics apparent to every observer : (1) The fingers are almost always tapering (*dita affusolate*) ; (2) the knuckles are often only indicated by a kind of dimple ; (3) the eyes are almond-shaped ; (4) the knee is full and fleshy ; (5) the landscape consists mostly of a broad well-watered plain, with groups of low trees. He often introduces on one side a hill, with buildings, towers, Roman temples and arches.

figure, which is not altogether faultless, coincides equally
with the modelling in the two preceding drawings, and
with other pen drawings and sketches which in public collections are regarded as undoubted works by Sodoma.
The pen drawing in the Esterhazy collection at Buda-Pesth
for the standing figure of Roxana, and the drawing for her
couch at Oxford (Robinson's Catalogue, 177) probably belong
to the same period, 1514. (†)    A fourth pen drawing for
the Leda (Grosvenor Gallery Publication, No. 50) is also at
Windsor, this time under the name of Leonardo instead of
Raphael. The sheet contains four studies for the head, seen
from the front and the back—the elaborate braiding of the hair
having received special attention.(†)    A fifth remarkably fine
drawing, in red chalk, for the head of Leda is in the Museo
Civico at Milan ; in treatment it recalls the drawing for
Roxana in the Albertina, and is rightly ascribed to Sodoma.
The arrangement of the hair is similar to that in the Windsor
drawing.

There is another picture by Sodoma in the Borghese
gallery, a " Holy Family," No. 459; the execution is good, but
the vigour and freshness of his early Lombard days are no
longer apparent. With the exception of his fine frescoes in
the Farnesina, the " St. Christopher " in the Palazzo Spada
(in a deplorable condition), and " The Rape of the Sabines "
in the Palazzo Chigi, I am not acquainted with any other
works by the master in Rome.[1]

Sodoma is a most able and gifted painter, worthy at his
best to rank with the greatest masters.  His finest works

---

[1] In the Barberini gallery there
is a much repainted Madonna (No.
54), bearing the name of Bazzi, but
those who have seen the picture will
not require to be told that such an
attribution is absurd. It is probably by the same painter of the
Bolognese school who, in the Doria
gallery, has received the name of
Lodi (does this mean Calisto da
Lodi ?), and who closely approaches
Innocenzo da Imola and Bagnacavallo.

LEDA AND THE SWAN.   DRAWING BY SODOMA.

*(At Weimar.)*

*To face p.* 156.

LEDA AND THE SWAN.   DRAWING BY SODOMA.

(At Chatsworth.)

To face p. 156.

LEDA AND THE SWAN.

*(Drawing by* SODOMA *for the Picture in the Borghese Gallery.   At Windsor.)*

*To face p.* 156.

HEAD OF LEDA. DRAWING BY SODOMA.

(*At Windsor.*)

*To face p.* 136.

are at Siena, and there he should be studied in the churches
of S. Spirito, S. Domenico, S. Bernardino, in the Academy,
and the Palazzo Pubblico, and at Mont' Oliveto near the city.
Florence also possesses some good works by him, especially
the splendid " St. Sebastian " in the Uffizi, and the fragment
of a fresco at Mont' Oliveto, near the city. As a fresco
painter, Sodoma when he chose was unrivalled. The only
fresco I know by him in north Italy is the so-called " Madonnone," attributed to Leonardo da Vinci, in the Casa Melzi at
Vaprio. The late Mr. Mündler always regarded it as the
work of that master ('Beiträge,' &c. p. 32), but it appears
to me undoubtedly by Sodoma, executed probably between
1518–1521, during his stay in Lombardy. (†) The conception is fine, the execution rather poor.

His panel pictures are more numerous; three good
specimens are in the Turin gallery, several in Milan in the
collections of Signor Cereda-Bonomi, Count Borromeo,
Signora Ginoulhiac, and Dr. Frizzoni. A male head treated
quite in the manner of Franz Hals is in the author's
collection,[2] and in the gallery at Bergamo there is a much
darkened picture of the Madonna by him (No. 136) attributed to Leonardo. In the Venetian territory he is represented only by a damaged " Tondo " in the Scarpa collection
at La Motta, representing the Madonna and St. Joseph
adoring the Infant Saviour, whilst the little St. John and
an angel kneel before Him. It passes for a Cesare da
Sesto.

When students examine the great number and variety
of works by this many-sided painter, I think they will agree
with me that Sodoma, taking him all in all, is the most
important and gifted artist of the school of Leonardo—the
one who is most easily confounded with the great master
himself. Jovial, careless, pleasure-loving, and almost licen-

[2] Now in the Public Gallery at Bergamo.

tious, he had neither ambition nor earnestness of purpose. On the other hand, a true artist, arrogance and self-assertion were foreign to his nature, and one who is deficient in these qualities rarely attains to celebrity. In his best moments, when he brought all his powers into play, Sodoma produced works which are worthy to rank with the most perfect examples of Italian art. Michael Angelo's influence, which carried all before it in his day, never diverted Sodoma, who was strictly an original painter, from his own independent course. His female heads, as even his adversary Vasari was forced to acknowledge, are unsurpassed. From a certain point of view he may be classed, with Lotto and Correggio, with that body of gifted artists who, like Leonardo, mainly strove to depict 'the sweetness of the soul.' In the "Ecstasy of St. Catherine" in the church of S. Domenico at Siena, the hands, more especially the left, are conceived and treated just as Correggio might have treated them; and the beautiful boy angels over the arch have quite the feeling of Lotto or of Correggio himself.

Giovan Antonio Bazzi, who was so unworthily treated by Vasari, shared the fate of Lotto and Moretto da Brescia —both the most unassuming of artists—of Bonifazio Veronese, and of other excellent masters of the first half of the sixteenth century, whose best works were all attributed to their more renowned contemporaries, and under their names became famous.[3] A few examples may be men-

[3] Most of Sodoma's drawings are in Italy; the Uffizi alone possesses over a dozen, among them Nos. 421 (scribed to Leonardo), 563, 565, 566, 1479, 1506, 1507, 1644; and in portfolios in the engraving department, Nos. 1932, 1935, 1936, 1938, 1943, 1944, 1945. Two are in the Royal library at Turin, and two in the author's collection (now in that of Signor Frizzoni). It is scarcely necessary to observe that the red chalk drawing of a female head at Lille, attributed to Sodoma, can only be a copy after him (Braun 43). In the Louvre I saw three genuine drawings by Bazzi, Nos. 87, 88, and 94 (Reiset Catalogue); Nos. 89, 90,

SKETCH BY SODOMA FOR THE MARRIAGE OF ALEXANDER AND ROXANA.

*(In the Uffizi.)*

*To face p. 158.*

tioned: four drawings for the "Leda," and the large fresco at Vaprio, are, as we have seen, ascribed to Leonardo; other drawings, again, are given to Raphael—for instance, all those referring to the "Marriage of Alexander and Roxana," at Buda-Pesth, in the Albertina and the Uffizi; a fine head of a man in the British Museum (Braun 94), and another in the Albertina. In the Städel Institute at Frankfort a beautiful female portrait by Sodoma (†) is still persistently given to Sebastian del Piombo.[4] As so many conflicting opinions with regard to Sodoma exist, it is to be hoped that some good connoisseur of the Italian schools will appear as his champion, and will give us a trustworthy account of this great artist.

## GIANPIETRINO, or GIANPEDRINO.

Under No. 456 in the Borghese gallery we meet with a picture which, though in bad condition, is still extremely beautiful; it is catalogued as a production of the school of Leonardo. The sweet smile of the Madonna certainly recalls the female heads of Leonardo and Sodoma, with the latter of whom Gianpietrino, its author, as I consider, is confounded.[5] (†) In dealing with the Milanese school of the end of the fifteenth century, and of the first decades of the sixteenth, it is desirable to draw a distinction between Leonardo's own pupils who were directly under his guidance, and those painters on whom the great

---

91, 92, and 93 are most erroneously ascribed to him by M. Reiset, solely, it appears, because on No. 93 the name of Antonius Vercellensis (the miniaturist?) occurs. (†) This is an example of the grave errors into which even practised connoisseurs may fall when relying solely on written evidence. A drawing for a Magdalen by Sodoma is in the Ambrosiana (Braun 191).

[4] Dr. Bode actually attributes it to Jan Scorel! (*Repertorium für Kunstwissenschaft*, xii. Heft 1, p. 72).

[5] In 1860 the "Lucretia" of the Turin gallery (No. 376) still passed for a Gianpietrino, till the author restored this fine painting to Sodoma. (†)

Florentine exercised a general influence, though more æsthetic than technical. In the first category should be included the following: Boltraffio, Marco d' Oggionno, Salaino, Giovan Antonio Bazzi, Gianpietrino, Cesare da Sesto, and, perhaps, also Francesco Napoletano;[6] in the second should be placed, Andrea Solario, Ambrogio de Predis, Bernardino de' Conti, Bernardino Luini, Gaudenzio Ferrari, the miniaturist Antonio da Monza, and others, whose works are known, but whose names have not yet been satisfactorily ascertained. Gianpietrino is called by Lomazzo, Pietro Rizzo, Milanese. Neither the date of his birth nor death is known, nor, so far as I am aware, are there any works signed with his name. His direct connection with Leonardo is most clearly proved, I think, by a fine charcoal drawing in the Christ Church Collection at Oxford (†)—the Madonna with the Child on her right knee—damaged unfortunately from the forehead upwards by restoration.

[6] Few works are known to me in Italy by Napoletano, an imitator of Leonardo by no means devoid of talent, and these are all of his early period, for in the first years of the sixteenth century he settled at Valencia, in Spain, and probably remained in that country. Signor Bonomi-Cereda possesses a signed work by him of his early period—the Madonna enthroned with the Child, between St. Sebastian and St. John the Baptist. Another small Madonna came by exchange into the Brera from the Venice Academy, under the name of Cesare da Sesto. Professor Carl Justi, a learned authority on the history of Spanish art, kindly informed me that several works by Francesco Napoletano are at Valencia, the best—in the cathedral—consisting of twelve Leonard-esque paintings with life-sized figures, forming the inner and outer wings of the large sculptured *retablo*. These scenes from the life of the Madonna were completed by Francesco Neapoli (*sic*) in conjunction with Paolo of Arezzo in 1506. 'The colours,' adds Professor Justi, 'are very rich—a warm, brown tone predominating in the foreground, in the buildings, and in the flesh tints. The whole series is full of gaiety and charm; in all, however, the treatment of the nude is poor.' According to the same competent authority there is a Madonna with St. Anne in the church of St. Nicholas at Valencia; a marriage of St. Catherine in the cathedral at Murcia may, he thinks, be also ascribed to Francesco Napoletano.

Gianpietrino as a rule painted only half-length figures, rarely large altar-pieces. Most of the works bearing his name are only of his school.[7] In his early period his flesh tints are cold, and his hands very life-like, contrasting with the stiff lifeless hands of Marco d' Oggionno, with whom he is often confounded.[8] A deep orange is noticeable in his paintings, and is characteristic both of him and of his school. Many old copies of the beautiful Madonna in this gallery are in existence ; one is in the Palazzo Rospigliosi, and a second in the Munich gallery (No. 1047), formerly ascribed to Luini, and recently catalogued as an original by Giovanni Pedrini (sic). A small and good picture by Gianpietrino is in the Villa Albani at Rome (†) (No. 59), there attributed to Salaino, and referred to as such by the late Professor Minardi.[9] It represents the Madonna holding some violets ; whilst the Child, on her knee, has a lily in His hand. His finest works are at Milan—a "St. Roch," belonging to Donna Laura Visconti Venosta ; a "Flora," in the Borromeo collection ; a lovely "Egeria," belonging to the Marchese Brivio ; two representations of the Magdalen, one in the Brera and the other in the Museo Civico ; a Madonna with the Child, and another with the Child and the little St. John in the Poldi-Pezzoli museum, there attributed to Cesare da Sesto. This last

---

[7] For instance, a St. Catherine, No. 381, in the Pitti ascribed to Aurelio Luini, and a large "Ecce Homo" in the Turin Academy, No. 240. (†)

[8] For instance, in the "Christ bearing the Cross," No. 107, in the Turin Gallery. (†) A similar subject by Gianpietrino is in Sir Henry Layard's choice collection at Venice.

[9] Minardi : 'Scritti delle qualità essenziali della pittura' (Rome, 1864). The writer characterises the picture as 'Di una esecuzione stentata, povera di sentimento e di sapere, mediocre del tutto.' As the same critic describes the head of "Medusa," in the Uffizi, as an 'excellent work by Leonardo da Vinci, I shall make no further comment upon his estimate of Gianpietrino. It is only on a par with the view taken by most modern painters of the works of the old masters.

is taken from Leonardo's cartoon for the so-called "St. Anne," now in the 'Salon Carré' of the Louvre.

One of his best works is perhaps a Madonna belonging to Mr. John Murray, the well-known publisher, in which Gianpietrino closely approaches Sodoma. In Sir Francis Cook's interesting collection at Richmond he is represented under the name of Leonardo (†). The so-called "Colombina" in the Hermitage at St. Petersburg, formerly ascribed to Leonardo and now to Luini, is an undoubted work by Gianpietrino (†), though Messrs. Crowe and Cavalcaselle cite it as one of the best 'productions' of Andrea Solario, and even of the whole school of Leonardo (ii. 58). In this painting, which I only know from a photograph,[1] the master may be recognised, more especially in the form of the left hand, which differs from that in the pictures both of Luini and Andrea Solario.

Among his larger altar-pieces should be mentioned that of 1521, in the church of S. Marino at Pavia, there called Salaino (†),[2] and the Nativity, with angels playing on musical instruments, in the sacristy of the church of S. Sepolcro at Milan. Gianpietrino's workshop was the resort, in all probability, of Flemish painters, who flocked to Italy after the death of Leonardo. We may mention several Flemish paintings in the manner of Gianpietrino which prove this; for instance, the portrait of Joanna of Aragon in the Doria gallery (No. 858), a similar Joanna in the Balbi collection at Genoa, and the St. Cecilia in the Munich gallery.

---

[1] Braun, No. 74, under the name of Luini.

[2] A red chalk drawing by Gianpietrino in the Louvre, is probably the sketch for this picture. It is ascribed to Leonardo da Vinci. (Braun 187.) (†)

THE 'COLOMBINA.' BY GIANPIETRINO.

*(In the Hermitage, St. Petersburg.)*

*To face p.* 162.

## BOLTRAFFIO.

There is not a single work by Boltraffio in central and southern Italy, with the exception of the much-damaged fresco in the cloisters of S. Onofrio in Rome. This was first pronounced by Dr. Frizzoni to be the work of Boltraffio and not of Leonardo, and with good reason. The long oval of the Madonna's face, so characteristic of Boltraffio, would alone testify to his hand. In its present condition it is a mere wreck. The best works of this noble artist, mostly of small dimensions, are in his native city of Milan—in the Poldi-Pezzoli collection, in the Casa Maino, in the possession of Count Sola, of Dr. Frizzoni, and of the author,[3] and in the Ambrosiana (drawings); in the Borromean palace on the Isola Bella, and at Bergamo, where there is a beautiful Madonna in the gallery, and a small St. Sebastian in profile belonging to Signor Federico Antonio Frizzoni. The series of female martyrs in fresco, in the gallery of the choir of S. Maurizio at Milan, may have been painted by Boltraffio's scholars from his cartoons. Some of these half-length figures are of great beauty. The master's best work is, I think, the Virgin and Child in the English National Gallery.[4] The Madonna in the

---

[3] Now in the gallery at Bergamo.

[4] Besides the fine pastels in the Ambrosiana ascribed to Leonardo I know of only one other drawing (in the Louvre) which appears to me to be the work of Boltraffio, but which is of course attributed to Leonardo. It is the head of a boy in profile crowned with a garland of oak leaves (in silver point, Braun 176) and is the sketch for the St. Sebastian mentioned in the text belonging to Signor Federico Antonio Frizzoni, at Bergamo. I may add that the male portrait ascribed to the master in the Ambrosiana, which Dr. Bode pronounces an excellent work by Boltraffio (ii. 746), does not even belong to the Milanese school, but more probably to that of Parma. The attribution to Boltraffio is purely arbitrary, dating, like so many others, from the last century, and it is entirely due to ignorance or indolence on the part of the Italian authorities that such names are still retained.

Esterhazy gallery at Buda-Pesth (175) approaches it nearly, and, if I recollect rightly, is attributed by Dr. Bode to Bernardino de' Conti.

## MARCO D' OGGIONNO.

There are no authentic works by Salaino ; those ascribed to him in public collections are all extremely doubtful. By Marco d' Oggionno [1470 (?)–1540 (?) ], on the other hand, we find a genuine work in the Borghese gallery—a carefully executed " Salvator Mundi " (No. 435). By placing it near a window the authorities testified to their appreciation of it. And no wonder, since for nigh three hundred years it had borne the name of Leonardo. As such it was regarded by Pope Paul V., over whose bed it hung, and who only reluctantly ceded it to his nephew, Cardinal Scipione Borghese, the founder of this collection, when the latter, after many years of fruitless effort, had failed to obtain a specimen of the great Florentine's art. It represents a half-length figure of the Saviour holding the sphere in His left hand, and blessing with His right. The pendant to this little picture, representing the same subject and of nearly similar size, by the hand of Boltraffio, is in the possession of the author [5] at Milan. Both were apparently executed by Leonardo's two pupils about the same time. The garment of our Lord in the Borghese picture is of a bright cherry red, a colour much used by Marco d' Oggionno, Boltraffio, and sometimes also by Gianpietrino ; the mantle is dark blue. The hand with stiff, bony, lifeless fingers, and the cheek-bones widely apart, are characteristic of the master, as are also the angular folds on the sleeves, and the black shadows and sharp lights. The background is dark, as in nearly all portraits and half-length figures of the Lombardo-

[5] Now in the gallery at Bergamo.

Milanese school. Most of Marco d' Oggionno's works are still in Milan or in the Milanese territory—in the church of S. Eufemia, in the Ambrosiana, the Brera, the Bonomi-Cereda collection, and elsewhere.

## NICOLA APPIANI.[6]

A contemporary and imitator of Marco d' Oggionno was Nicola Appiani, an inferior and little-known painter, by whom there are two works in the Brera—an "Adoration of the Magi," and the "Baptism of Christ" (Nos. 84 and 85). An altar-piece in the sacristy of S. Maria delle Grazie I believe to be by him (†), and not by Marco d' Oggionno, to whom it is there attributed, and the "Marriage of St. Catherine" in the Turin gallery, No. 104, is also more probably by Nicola than by Oggionno. (†) Other small paintings by this unimportant artist are in private collections at Milan.

## CESARE DA SESTO.

I have not met with a single work by Cesare da Sesto in Rome ; this is the more strange as he was in that city for some time. There is certainly a large Madonna in the Vatican collection, signed with his name and dated 1521, which M. Rio,[7] who was more at home in ecclesiastical history than in matters of art, regarded as genuine. It is, however, an extremely poor production by some late Lombardo-Milanese painter, as anyone even slightly acquainted with the north Italian schools must see. The signature, Cesare da Sesto, and the date are palpable

[6] The two pictures in the Brera are given to Appiani in the 'Ritratto di Milano,' by Canonico Carlo Torre ; I am unable to say whether correctly, as no signed works by this painter are known. Neither Vasari nor Lomazzo mentions him, but he is named by Carlo Amoretti in p. 156 of his *Memorie storiche sulla vita, gli studi e le opere di Lionardo da Vinci.*

[7] Léonard de Vinci et son école, p. 216.

modern forgeries.[8] (†)    The subject is the Madonna seated, the Child on her knee holding her girdle; on the right is a bishop, on the left St. John the Baptist.

Cesare da Sesto was probably born about 1480, at Sesto Calende on the Lago Maggiore; the date and place of his death are unknown.   Vasari mentions him in vol. ix. p. 22, as follows: 'Bernazzano, a good landscape painter, but with little aptitude for the treatment of figures, entered into partnership with Cesare da Sesto, who was skilled in that branch;' and in vol. xi. 274, he remarks, that besides Marco d' Uggioni (d' Oggionno) there were many others who successfully imitated Leonardo da Vinci, among them notably Cesare da Sesto, and cites a "Baptism of Christ,"[9] a "Salome," and a large painting of "St. Roch" by this artist.   The earliest work I know by him is an "Adoration of the Magi," in the collection of Count Borromeo, at Milan —a most interesting picture, probably painted in the first years of the fifteenth century.   In it we perceive the influence of different painters upon the young Lombard: of Lorenzo di Credi and Albertinelli when he was in Florence, and of Pintoricchio when at Siena.[1]   The "Tondo" belonging to the late Duke Melzi d'Eril, at Milan (the Madonna with the Infant Saviour and St. John the Baptist), is most likely also an early work.   A copy of this picture is in the Uffizi (No. 1013), under the name of Luini, and another was formerly in the Borghese gallery. (†)

The "Cesare Milanese," who about 1506 was executing frescoes in company with Baldassare Peruzzi in the "Rocca"

---

[8] Dr. Bode believes this picture to be by Cesare da Sesto (see ii. 751).

[9] In 1595 the 'Baptism of Christ' was, according to Moriggia (*La Nobiltà di Milano*), in the house of the Senatore Galeazzo Visconti. It now belongs to Duke Scotti at Milan.

[1] In this painting, which I think I am justified in ascribing to Cesare da Sesto, certain of the master's characteristics should be noted: the attitudes, the movements, and the form of hand and ear, which all tend to support my view. (†)

at Ostia (Vasari, viii. 221), was probably identical with Cesare da Sesto. The two painters were doubtless employed in the service of Baldo Magini (Vasari, x. 222), the *Castellano* of Ostia. From about 1507 to 1512 Cesare was probably working at Milan, under the direct influence of Leonardo da Vinci. Of this I think we have evidence in the following pictures: the so-called "Vierge aux Balances," in the Louvre, No. 1604 (ascribed by Passavant, ii. 345, to Salaino) ; the "Daughter of Herodias " (in the public gallery at Vienna); a "St. Jerome" in Sir Francis Cook's collection at Richmond ; [2] the beautiful Madonna in the Esterhazy gallery at Buda-Pesth (No. 172) ; and the large "Adoration of the Magi" painted by the master for a church at Messina, and now in the Naples museum. In all these Cesare appears as the imitator of Leonardo, while the large " St. Roch," which he painted for the church dedicated to that saint at Milan,[3] shows that Raphael had then become his prototype. According to Lomazzo, the two painters were very intimate in Rome. An interesting drawing by him in the Louvre—" A Combat with a Dragon "—in the so-called Vallardi album, No. 2015, would lead us to infer that Cesare was still in Rome about 1520. Lomazzo mentions this drawing, on the back of which are three figures—one being a copy of the Mother of the Demoniac in Raphael's "Transfiguration" (†), painted by the latter between 1519–1520.

Three panels, each representing the Madonna and Child with Saints, should, I think, be regarded as later works by Cesare. One is in the Hermitage at St. Petersburg, under the name of Leonardo da Vinci ;[4] a second belongs to Lord

[2] Cited by Moriggia, in *La Nobiltà di Milano*, 1595, as in the possession of Signor Guido Mazenta.

[3] Now belonging to the heirs of the late Duke Lodovico Melzi at Milan.

[4] Cited by Moriggia (*ibid.* v. 277) as a work by Cesare da Sesto in the possession of Senatore Galeazzo Visconti, 'Una Madonna col

Monson in London; and the third, rightly named Cesare
da Sesto, is in the Brera.    In this last, in addition to
the Madonna and Child, SS. Joseph, Joachim, and the little
St. John are introduced.    A second Madonna by him is
in the Brera—a very refined little painting of somewhat
earlier date.[5]    From all that has been said it will be
seen that, although skilled in technical execution, like all
Leonardo's pupils, Cesare da Sesto was not, like Sodoma,
an original and independent artist.[6]

The following paintings in the Borghese gallery
are also assigned to the school of Leonardo: an allegorical figure representing "Vanity" (No. 470)—a copy

figliuolo in braccio con San Giuseppe
ed una Martire.'  Its attribution to
Leonardo was therefore an error of
recent date.

[5] For the benefit of students I
may here mention a few drawings
by Cesare da Sesto, some of which
are given to Leonardo (see also a
recent article in the *Gazette des
beaux Arts*, "Les derniers travaux
de Léonard da Vinci"); a red chalk
drawing at Windsor, in which the
influence of Michael Angelo is undeniable, representing St. Sebastian
bound to a tree, with two soldiers on
his left (Grosvenor Society, No. 86).
(†) This was Cesare's sketch for
the fresco, which, according to
Moriggia, was still to be seen in
1595 in the villa of Count Resta,
near Milan. The fresco has since
perished, but an old copy is in the
Malaspina gallery at Pavia.  Another sheet, containing two studies
of children, in red chalk and bearing
the name of Leonardo, is also at
Windsor (Grosvenor Society, No. 66)
(†); in the British Museum there
are three fine drawings on one sheet

by Cesare da Sesto, attributed to
Leonardo (vol. 16, the page bearing the following marks: 1862, 10,
11, 196)—two pen and ink sketches
of the so-called "Madonna di Casa
'Alba," and, on the back, the head
of an old man in red chalk.  In
Vallardi's so-called Leonardo album
in the Louvre there is a sheet with
several studies for a Madonna,
and a seated allegorical figure
(Braun 189). (†) Two beautiful
studies for the Infant Saviour
are in the Library at Turin, rightly
attributed to Cesare da Sesto.  In
the Venice Academy there  are
several good red chalk drawings by
him; and also a pen and ink sketch
for his large picture, the "Adoration of the Magi," in the Naples
museum (Perini 196).

[6] The  gifted 'Improvisatore'
Andrea Sabbatini, of Salerno, was
more probably a pupil of Cesare da
Sesto than of Raphael(†), as Dominici
would have us believe; his works
are to be found at Naples in the
museum, and in some of the
churches.

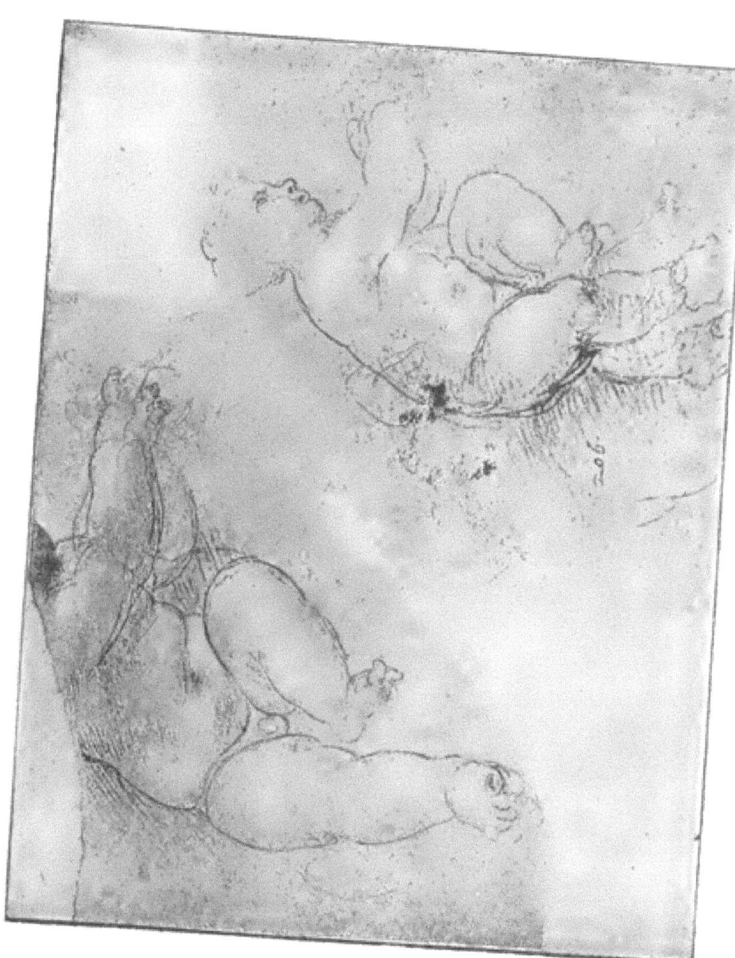

STUDIES BY CESARE DA SESTO

(At Windsor, in red chalk.)

To face p. 158.

MARTYRDOM OF ST. SEBASTIAN.

*(Sketch by* CESARE DA SESTO *at Windsor.)*

*To face p.* 168.

from Luini; an " Ecce Homo " (No. 286), which approaches
Andrea Solario in conception and technic; and a half-
length figure of St. Agatha (No. 429)—a late and feeble copy
from Luini.

## BERNARDINO LUINI.

The Borghese gallery contains no genuine work by
Bernardino Luini (born about 1475, still living in 1533);
but in the Sciarra-Colonna collection there is an exquisite
painting by the master (No. 43), unfortunately disfigured
by a thick coat of varnish. This, I need hardly say, is the
celebrated picture attributed to Leonardo da Vinci and
known as " Modesty and Vanity," though it might be more
appropriately named, " Sacred and Profane Love." It is,
perhaps, of the same time as Titian's version of a somewhat
similar theme in the Borghese gallery. This subject
appears to have been popular and frequently treated by
painters of the period—a fact not without interest, I think,
in the history of culture. It is painted in Luini's second
manner—the so-called *maniera grigia*—(from about 1508–
1520), when, under the influence of Leonardo and his works,
he was striving after more plastic modelling, especially in
the treatment of his heads. Another charming work by
Luini in the last room of the Palazzo Colonna must be mentioned, the Madonna holding the Infant Saviour, who bends
forward to embrace the little St. John—a motive often
repeated by this master—behind whom is St. Elisabeth.
It is finely conceived, but is in an unsatisfactory state in
consequence of excessive repainting. A female portrait in
the Corsini gallery has also received the name of Luini, but
only, I presume, by an oversight. Among the public collections of southern and central Italy, only the Naples museum
and the Uffizi contain examples of his art. In the former

we find a characteristic but unattractive Madonna ; in the latter the " Daughter of Herodias," much restored.

Luini was not gifted with any great powers of imagination, and as a creative genius he stands far below Sodoma, but he was an extremely conscientious painter and full of charm.[7] He can only be studied satisfactorily at Milan and in the Milanese district ; in the churches of the ' Passione,' of S. Giorgio in Palazzo, and of S. Maurizio ; in the Ambrosiana and the Brera, the Poldi-Pezzoli and the Borromeo collections ; at Legnano, Saronno, and Lugano, in the Cathedral at Como, and elsewhere. His forms are round and somewhat heavy, the feet usually too long, and the hands too broad and large, as with Giovanni Bellini. He had many pupils and imitators whose works, even in the Brera, are constantly attributed to him ; for example, the frescoes Nos. 13, 41–43, 51, 53 and others. (†)

## ANDREA SOLARIO.

In the Borghese gallery we find another work (No. 461) given to a Milanese painter of the ' golden age.' It bears the name of Andrea Solario, and represents Christ bearing the Cross, accompanied by two ill-favoured guards. Though cold in tone, too smooth in execution, and dark in the shadows, the picture is nevertheless finished with great care. The soldiers are caricatures, and have so decided a Flemish appearance that I have no hesitation in pronouncing it the work of a Fleming. (†) The figure of Christ is undoubtedly taken from Solario ; but it appears to me that the soldiers who show

[7] Drawings by this master are rare ; a few may here be enumerated. In the Ambrosiana : a sheet with three studies of children, in indian ink (Braun 175) ; " Tobias and his Father," in indian ink, heightened with white (Braun 179) ; and a Madonna, in red chalk. In the Venice academy, " The Expulsion from Paradise," in black chalk ; in the Uffizi a drawing washed with water-colour (engraving department No. 1940) ; and in the Louvre two heads of children (Nos. 237, 238).

their teeth—one of whom has a distinctively hideous thumb-nail—were added by some painter of the school of Antwerp sojourning in Italy.[8]

The same subject was often treated by Solario—for instance, in a small picture in the gallery at Brescia, and in two panels formerly belonging to the painter Galgani at Siena. In all these works the figure of Christ is more nobly conceived than in the example in this gallery; the tone is warmer and the colours are more thickly laid on—qualities which we find exemplified in his fine " Riposo " of 1515, in the Poldi-Pezzoli collection at Milan. Andrea Solario occupies a peculiar position in the Lombardo-Milanese school, and in technical execution he is, perhaps, its ablest representative. As writers on art have not yet succeeded in agreeing about this painter, I shall venture to give some further details respecting him.

The Solari, a family of artists (architects and sculptors), came, like the Lombardi of Venice, from the village of Solaro, in the province of Como. In the first half of the fifteenth century they settled at Milan, and here very probably Andrea was born about 1460. His elder brother, Cristoforo, was a sculptor and architect, and being somewhat deformed was surnamed *Il Gobbo* (the hunchback).[9] Andrea was much attached to this brother and seems to have been his companion in his many journeys. Hence the reason, perhaps, that the painter sometimes signed his pictures Andreas Mediolanensis, sometimes Andrea de Solario. The first signature he used on pictures painted

---

[8] Other Flemish copies after Solario, or imitations, may be seen in the galleries of Turin and Siena, and in the gallery at Vienna, all representing Herodias' daughter. The head of St. John the Baptist in the Louvre (No. 1533) is also a Flemish imitation of Solario. (†)

[9] M. Villot, in his catalogue of the Louvre, makes Andrea himself the hunchback, which was rather hard upon him. In the latest edition of the catalogue Cristoforo becomes the father of Andrea.

when he was absent from Milan ; the second on those
executed in that city.    All earlier writers call him ' Andrea
del Gobbo,' from which we may conclude that Cristoforo
stood in place of a father to his younger brother ; and by
some he has been confounded with Salaino, Leonardo's
amanuensis.    The first to throw some light on the character
of this master was the late Mr. Mündler, in his excellent
' Analyse critique de la Notice des Tableaux du Louvre.'
Messrs. Crowe and Cavalcaselle followed in his steps, but
added some new matter in their notice of the painter, in
which they appear to me to be quite mistaken.    Who his
master was has not yet been ascertained, but in the exquisitely delicate modelling of the heads the teaching of his
brother, the sculptor, is perceptible.[1]    No other Lombard
painter approached Leonardo so nearly, or succeeded in
treating heads with a like degree of finish—as, for example,
in the "Ecce Homo" in the Poldi collection at Milan.    In
the representation of the hand, however, Solario was far
behind Leonardo, Sodoma, and even Gianpietrino.    His
earliest works, so far as I know, are two small Madonnas,
one in the Poldi collection, the other in the Brera (No. 105
bis).    From the latter we might infer a certain connection
with Bartolommeo Suardi, called Bramantino.[2]

In 1490 Andrea accompanied his brother Cristoforo to
Venice, and there, between 1492–1493, may have painted
the fine portrait of a Venetian senator, now in the London

---

[1] Besides Cristoforo there was
another sculptor in the family,
Pietro Solari, by whom there
is a Madonna and Child in high
relief in the side entrance to the
church of S. Angelo at Milan.

[2] This picture formerly bore the
forged inscription ' Johannes Bellinus,' and was therefore regarded
by Vasari's commentators (v. 24) as
the work of Giovanni Bellini.    The
quaint headgear worn by the
Madonna is similar to that with
which Bramantino and Gaudenzio
Ferrari were wont to adorn the
heads of their female figures.    In
the collection of Prince Giangia-
como Trivulzio, at Milan, there is
a small portrait in bas-relief by
Cristoforo Solario, which recalls the
painted portraits by his brother
Andrea.

National Gallery (No. 923), in which the influence of Giovanni Bellini, and still more that of Antonello da Messina,
is visible. Formerly, when in the Casa Gavotti at Genoa,
this portrait passed under the name of Bellini. In 1493
the brothers appear to have returned to Milan ; two years
later Andrea executed a small altar-piece for the church of
S. Pietro Martire at Murano (now in the Brera, No. 106).
Whether he painted it at Venice or elsewhere I am unable
to say; it is, however, probable that he visited the city
of the Lagoons a second time and may then have executed
the picture. The type of the Madonna in this work is
entirely Leonardesque, and the drawing recalls Boltraffio ;
we may, therefore, infer that, in 1493 and 1494, after his
return from Venice, Solario was strongly influenced by the
great Florentine.

Besides the influence of Leonardo, Messrs. Crowe and
Cavalcaselle perceive in this picture that of Verrocchio, (!)
as also that of the Venetian school. In their eyes it is a
mixture of influences—Lombard, Florentine, Venetian, and
even Bergamasque—for in the landscape they are more
particularly reminded of Previtali, who in 1495 was barely
fifteen! Such theories of analogy and influence are fatal
to progress, and I shall not follow these critics further on
such slippery ground.

To return to Solario's works. We find in the Poldi
collection two small panels of 1499, representing respectively St. John the Baptist and St. Catherine (fragments of
a triptych), signed, 'Andreas Mediolanensis,' and therefore
not painted at Milan ; they came to that city from Venice.
The St. John is wholly Leonardesque, but the St. Catherine
is thoroughly Lombard in character.[3] Then follow, in
chronological order, the " Crucifixion " of 1503, signed

[3] A " St. Catherine " in a paint-
ing by Macrino d'Alba of 1506, in the
Turin gallery, vividly recalls this
" St. Catherine " by A. Solario

'Andreas Mediolanensis,' and a male portrait of about the
same period (1503–1504), both in the Louvre (Nos. 1532
and 1531). Recently the latter was pronounced to be the
portrait of Charles d'Amboise, the French governor of Milan,
and, strangely enough, was only *attributed* to Solario. It
represents a man between thirty and forty, wearing on his
cap the order of St. Michael; with a view of the Alps, as seen
from Milan, in the background. The execution is delicate,
but the details are almost lost in a thick coating of varnish.
It may have been painted by Solario at Milan, in the first
years of the sixteenth century. The work belonging to the
painter Galgani—" Christ bearing the Cross "—is of 1505,
and was probably executed in Milan, certainly not in
Florence, as Calvi, in order to draw his own conclusions,
conjectures; for in the same year, 1505, Solario painted
the portrait of his Milanese friend Longoni now in the
National Gallery (No. 734). To this his Milanese epoch,
that is, before his departure for France, I should further
ascribe the female portrait belonging to the Marchese
Emmanuele d'Adda at Milan. In the summer of 1507
Solario went to that country, provided with letters of introduction from the French governor of the Milanese, Charles
de Chaumont (known in Italy as Ciamonte), to his uncle
Cardinal Georges d'Amboise. For two years Solario
remained in the Cardinal's service. This ambitious prelate,
who on the death of Pius III. had cherished the hope of
obtaining the Papal dignity, had endeavoured, through his
nephew the governor of Milan, to secure the services of
Leonardo da Vinci, as he was desirous of having his chapel
at Gaillon decorated by that renowned artist. Leonardo,
however, was so occupied at that date with hydraulic
experiments and plans for the fortification of Milan that
he could not even find time to paint a Madonna for
Louis XII. (see Gaye, " Carteggio," ii. 94–96). Chaumont

therefore sent in his stead Solario, whom he considered, after the great Florentine, the best living painter in the Milanese territory. In September 1509 Solario brought his work at Gaillon to a close. Before his departure for France, or soon after his arrival at Gaillon, he may have painted the so-called " Vierge au Coussin Vert," now in the Louvre (No. 1530). It is not known whether he remained in France after his work at Gaillon was completed. I think he may possibly have spent some time in Flanders before returning home.

The school of painting at Antwerp was then in great repute, and it was likely that Solario had been acquainted with some of its representatives in Italy. Many of his paintings, more especially the "Riposo" of 1515, and the highly finished but cold "Ecce Homo," both in the Poldi collection, have so decided a Flemish character, and so strongly recall the school of Antwerp—notably Patinir in the composition and in the violet tone of colouring—that at first sight they might almost pass for Flemish works.[4] In 1515 Solario appears to have been in Italy again, if not in Milan. This may be inferred from the above-named "Riposo," which is signed 'Andreas de Solario Mediolanen : f. 1515.' After this date nothing more is known of him. It is more than probable that his large altar-piece for the Certosa of Pavia (now in the new sacristy there) was painted after 1515, particularly as, according to tradition, the upper part, left unfinished by Solario, was completed by Bernardino Campi about 1576. The truth probably was that the upper part, having suffered, was merely restored by Campi, as painters, I believe, are in the habit of beginning with the upper part of their pictures and not with the lower.[5]

[4] Dr. Bode (ii. 745) sees Roman (?) influences in the latter painting by Solario.

[5] Campi's repainting is still

Calvi repeats the statement, that Solario accompanied Andrea da Salerno to South Italy (but whence?) about 1513, and worked in company with him in a chapel of S. Gaudioso, at Naples;[6] but this surmise appears to me as improbable as the tale about Bernardino Campi. In this case we may assume that Solario was confounded with Cesare da Sesto.

Three portraits by Solario must still be mentioned. One is in the collection of Duke Scotti at Milan, under the name of Leonardo. It represents a man of refined features, with a keen eye and resolute mouth, and is considered to be the likeness of the chancellor Morone.[7] If this be so, the portrait must have been painted after 1515, as Morone, if I am not mistaken, was not raised to the office of chancellor till 1518. The second painting, attributed to Raphael, belongs to Count Castelbarco at Milan, and is said to represent Cesare Borgia. Both of them have been much repainted. The third, a magnificent portrait of a high-bred man, formerly in the Casa Perego, is now in the collection of Signor Crespi at Milan.

I know of only one drawing by Andrea Solario, the pen and ink sketch in the Venice Academy for his altar-piece at Pavia. It proves, I think, that Andrea's master in draughtsmanship was his brother Cristoforo. There are several pen drawings by the latter in the Ambrosiana at Milan.

visible, more especially in the heads of the Madonna and of the two angels who crown her.

[6] See *Notizie sulla vita e sulle opere dei principali architetti, scultori e pittori che fiorirono in Milano durante il regno dei Visconti e degli Sforza, raccolte ed esposte da S. Calvi*, p. 277 (Milan, 1865). The book is an example of the way in which a writer, devoid of all knowledge of art, and trusting implicitly to documents, may be led astray.

[7] Girolamo Morone was born in 1470, and died in 1529. The portrait represents a man of about fifty, and must have been painted about 1518–1520. It is, therefore, very possible that the portrait does represent the chancellor, and a comparison with the medal appears to confirm this supposition.

## LEONARDO DA VINCI.

By Leonardo himself there is a small unfinished painting, in the Vatican collection, of St. Jerome as a penitent—
to art-critics a work of the highest interest, but to the general
public an unmitigated horror. Besides this painting, I
know of only two other works in Italy which could seriously
be ascribed to the great Florentine — the unfinished
" Adoration of the Magi " in the Uffizi, and the world-
renowned, oft-repainted " Last Supper " at Milan.

As Dr. Bode's estimate of the Italian masters differs so
widely from mine, it will scarcely surprise my readers to
learn that I can only regard the drawing of a female head
in the Borghese gallery (No. 514), which he (ii. 668)
ascribes to Leonardo, as the production of some inferior
imitator of Bernardino de' Conti. There are no genuine
drawings by Leonardo either in Rome or Naples, and of the
twenty-seven attributed to him in the Uffizi, only *five* are
authentic in my opinion.[8] On the other hand, there are
about twenty-five genuine examples in the Venice Academy,
twelve in the Royal Library at Turin, and ten in the
Ambrosiana, exclusive of those in the *Codex Atlanticus*. In
all these drawings by Leonardo, the shading, as I have
observed on a former occasion, is from left to right—for
Leonardo both wrote and drew with his left hand, and only

---

[8] As some may be disposed to
be incredulous as to this assertion, I
feel bound to enumerate those drawings in the Uffizi which I consider
to be rightly assigned to Leonardo,
as well as those which are falsely
ascribed to him. The following
are genuine: Nos. 423, 436,
446, 449, and finally the pen drawing, with the landscape, of the year
1473—five in all consequently. The
following drawings I consider not
authentic: 414 (by a later artist);
419 (copy); 420 (far too poor for
Leonardo); 421 (Sodoma, Brau
448); 422 (by a pupil); 424 (copy);
425 (by a pupil); 426 (by a pupil);
427 (A. de Predis [?]); 428 (Flemish
copy after Verrocchio, Braun 429);
429 (by a pupil); 430 (by a pupil);
431 (by a pupil); 432 (copy after
Lorenzo di Credi); 433, 434, 435.
437 (imitations); 447 (forgery); 448,
450, 451 (imitations).

occasionally made use of his right when representing spherical objects. The drawings in the so-called *Codex Atlanticus*, and in Leonardo's various other manuscripts in Paris, in England, and in Italy, give abundant proof of this, as do also those judiciously selected by Dr. J. P. Richter for his admirable work on the master.[9]

Unprejudiced students will, I think, acknowledge that I have done well to protest against the persistent and arbitrary attribution to Leonardo of countless unauthentic drawings and paintings, due in some cases merely to their supposed ' geistigen Inhalt ' (inward qualities). The best of them are, as we have seen, by his pupils Boltraffio, Sodoma, Cesare da Sesto and Gianpietrino, or by his imitators Ambrogio de Predis (Venice) and Bernardino de' Conti (Ambrosiana, Louvre, &c.) ; the inferior ones, like the head in the Borghese gallery, are either late copies or *forgeries,* and of these last there are not a few.[1]

---

[9] *The Literary Works of Leonardo da Vinci,* London, 1883.

[1] For the benefit of students I will enumerate half a dozen of these false Leonardo drawings : (1) Windsor, pen drawing, the Madonna in a recumbent position with the Child, and four studies of a child playing with a cat (Grosvenor Gallery Publication, No. 57) ; (2) Albertina, a large sheet formerly in the collection of Vasari, later in that of Mariette. The six heads at the side are genuine, the female head and the little St. John in the centre are spurious (Braun 102–109) ; (3) Louvre ('Salle aux boîtes'), pen drawing, the head of a youth in profile turning to the left, and several caricatures, forgeries (Reiset Catalogue 382, Braun 172)—the drawing of the eye and of the hair should be specially noticed ; (4) Albertina,

pen drawing, five caricatures and two profile heads (Braun 98) ; (5) British Museum, pen drawing with three caricatures ; upon which is the name of Leonardo da Vinci and the date of 1476—by a Flemish master (Braun 49). In the same collection there is a head of an old man showing his front teeth, again the work of a Fleming (Braun 27) ; (6) British Museum, an allegorical subject, in indian ink ; the original is in the ' Salle aux boîtes ' in the Louvre (Braun 53). It is curious that even as far back as the sixteenth century the great masters should have been so little understood in their own country and abroad. Vasari himself had such a mistaken conception of Leonardo—an artist whose power is irresistibly felt even in his least important works—that he ascribed to him, as we have seen, the two

If we compare Leonardo's genuine works, viz. the " Adoration of the Magi " in the Uffizi, the " St. Jerome " in the Vatican, and the "Mona Lisa" and the "Vierge aux Rochers" in the Louvre, with those ascribed to him by Dr. Bode, viz. the " Annunciation " in the Uffizi, the " Resurrection" at Berlin, the female portrait and the unfinished head of a man in the Ambrosiana, the "Madonna and Child " in the Hermitage at St. Petersburg, and others, I think that even those who generally agree with this critic must admit that the same hand and the same feeling are not perceptible in all.

## GAUDENZIO FERRARI.

Neither at Florence, Rome, Naples, nor Palermo do we find a single work by Gaudenzio Ferrari, a further, if only a negative, proof that he never crossed the Apennines, and that his supposed apprenticeship with Perugino and friendship with Raphael are pure fiction. At some future time I hope to prove this.

The large "Apotheosis of S. Bernardino of Siena," so absurdly ascribed to Gaudenzio in the Sciarra-Colonna gallery, is neither his work, nor that of any north Italian master, but is more probably by some Sienese painter of the end of the sixteenth century. The small Madonna and Child in the Capitoline collection (Room I. 210) owes its remarkable attribution, I suspect, to an amusing *quid pro quo*. When the painting was brought from Ferrara to Rome, the name of the town Ferrara was most probably inscribed on the back of the panel, and the director of that day immediately jumped to the conclusion that it stood

drawings in the centre of the sheet which was in his own possession. A like fate befell Giovanni Bellini and Giorgione in Venice; for, as Michael Angelo had eclipsed all his predecessors in Tuscany, so the fame of Titian, Tintoretto, and Paul Veronese had thrown all other painters of Venice into the shade.

for the name of the painter Ferrari.   Even the most
superficial observer, one would imagine, must at once have
recognised the painting as of the school of Garofalo.  This,
however, was not the case.   The late Professor Tommaso
Minardi accepted this attribution, like so many others,
without question, and proceeded thereupon to discourse
about Gaudenzio Ferrari and the Milanese school.  I merely
allude to this writer here, because in his lifetime he was
regarded as the greatest authority on matters of art in
Rome and throughout the Papal dominions, and also because
there are many of his stamp in other countries, perhaps
even among the *savants* of Germany.   And Minardi, be it
observed, was no mere amateur, but a professional painter
and art-critic.

Two Milanese painters still remain to be mentioned,
namely, Ambrogio de Predis and Bernardino de' Conti.

## AMBROGIO DE PREDIS.

Some years ago I had the good fortune to light upon
an excellent Milanese portrait painter who, till then, had
been wholly unknown to students of Italian art—Ambrogio
Preda or Predi.   A portrait of the Emperor Maximilian
in the Ambras collection at Vienna, signed 'Ambrosius de
p̄dis (predis) Mēlanensis (Mediolanensis) 1502,' first directed
my attention, in 1873, to this hitherto neglected painter.
Messrs. Crowe and Cavalcaselle mention it, but speak of it
(ii. 50) as in the Schönborn collection, and ascribe it, not
with Nagler[2] to Bevilacqua, but to Ambrogio Borgognone.
After carefully observing all the characteristics in this somewhat repainted portrait,[3] I felt that I might make further

---

[2] See Nagler, *Die Monogram-
misten*, i. 414.

[3] When studying this portrait I
noted the following characteristics :

(1) The dark edge of the upper eyelid runs in a straight line to where
it is joined by the lower lid, from
which it is separated by a bright

THE EMPEROR MAXIMILIAN.  BY DE PREDIS.

*(Vienna.)*

*To face p.* 180.

discoveries of works by this forgotten artist elsewhere. My researches were not fruitless, and in 1880, in my critical studies of "Italian Masters in German Galleries" (p. 456–458), I was able, to my great satisfaction, to mention three portraits and a drawing, which, though bearing the name of Leonardo, appeared to me unquestionably by Ambrogio de Predis.

It may have been presumptuous of me to suppose that by this discovery I might have rendered a service, however trifling, to the history of art; nevertheless I must confess to having cherished this hope, and it was disappointing to find Dr. Bode once more strenuously opposed to my views.

The German critic even charged me, I regret to say, with having confounded the great Leonardo, whom he professes to know so thoroughly, with 'the dry Lombard portrait painter, Matteo de Pretis.' That he should have been unaware of the existence of the Milanese Ambrogio de Predis is very pardonable, since this painter was equally unknown to all other writers on the history of art until I

---

streak of light. This streak of light, between the dark line of the upper eyelid and the strongly marked shadow cast by it, I found in all profile portraits by Ambrogio de Predis, which had not been repainted. This is, consequently, very characteristic of the master. (2) Each eyelash is indicated separately; (3) the contour of the upper lip is stiff, the under lip full and heavy. In some well-preserved portraits by this master the lines on the latter are well marked, as in the profile portrait in the Ambrosiana, in the portrait of a page in the Morelli collection, and also in the portrait of the Emperor Maximilian. (4) The bridge of the nose is marked by a sharp line of light; (5) the heavy mass of loose hair is touched with separate strokes of light; (6) the collar of the Golden Fleece is painted in the manner of a miniaturist. All these characteristics which struck me in the portrait of the Emperor Maximilian, recur in the profile portrait in the Ambrosiana, in one in the Poldi-Pezzoli collection, in that of an old man belonging to Dr. G. Frizzoni, in those of Lodovico Sforza and his son Maximilian, in the "Libro del Jesus" in the library of Prince Trivulzio, and in the fine profile portrait of the same Maximilian Sforza, as Duke of Milan, in the Morelli collection.

rescued him from oblivion, and I will assume that it was merely a *lapsus calami* on the part of Dr. Bode mistaking him for Matteo Preti, an inferior Calabrian painter of the seventeenth century. His attack upon me ended with the following extraordinary statement:

'A genuine and exquisite portrait of about 1485, closely resembling the so-called "Belle Ferronière" in the Louvre, is in the Ambrosiana. It is supposed to represent Isabella of Aragon,[4] wife of Giovanni Galeazzo Sforza; the portrait of the latter being also there.[5] This profile portrait, simple and unpretending in conception, is yet surpassingly lovely and attractive, and of so high a degree of finish that only Leonardo himself, one would suppose, could be credited with it, even did it not reveal all the characteristics (?) of his earlier works.[6] Nevertheless this marvellous work has recently [that is, by Lermolieff] been ascribed to a dry Lombard portrait painter. The portrait of Giovanni Galeazzo, which hangs next to that of his wife, is also genuine. Unfortunately it is unfinished, but, as giving us

[4] The portrait is now said to represent Bianca Maria Sforza, wife of the Emperor Maximilian.

[5] Gian Galeazzo Maria Sforza died in 1494, aged twenty-five. In 1485, therefore, he was barely sixteen, whereas the man in this portrait looks about thirty. A little knowledge of general history might occasionally benefit even art-historians.

[6] In the edition of the *Cicerone* of 1879 (p. 626), Dr. Bode writes: 'The portrait of a goldsmith in the Pitti (No. 207) is a *fine and genuine* work of Leonardo's earlier period.' In the edition of 1884, four years after my *Critical Essays* had been published, in which I ascribed the "Goldsmith" to Ridolfo Ghirlandaio, the same critic wrote as follows (ii. 681): 'The striking analogy between this acknowledged altar-piece by Ridolfo Ghirlandaio and the "Goldsmith" in the Pitti, which is there universally admired as a Leonardo, proves this latter to be an undoubted work by Ridolfo.' 'Il tempo è galantuomo,' the Italians say, and I therefore feel encouraged to hope that, with time and study, and after testing my theories, the Berlin critic will come to recognise the merits of A. de Predis, and instead of stigmatising him as a 'dry mechanical' Lombard, will acknowledge him to be the painter of the profile in the Ambrosiana, which he at present continues to regard as a 'Wunderwerk' by Leonardo da Vinci.

an insight into Leonardo's technical method, it is of the highest interest.' [7]

In justice to myself and to those who agree with me, I felt bound to uphold my own views—the result of long and exhaustive study—against the opinion, so confidently expressed, of the northern critic. Once more, then, I would here repeat what I said in 1880 of the profile portrait in the Ambrosiana—that it is the work of Ambrogio de Predis. As to the unfinished portrait, I look upon it as the likeness of some unknown individual. It has no connection either with de Predis or with Leonardo, but is, perhaps, by the same pupil or imitator [8] of the latter master, who executed the copy of the " Vierge aux Rochers " (now in the London National Gallery) and the two angels belonging to it, in the possession of Duke Melzi at Milan. I may here quote the opinion, expressed many years ago, about these portraits in the Ambrosiana by the late Baron Rumohr, of Berlin, a very distinguished critic in his day. On p. 73 of his little book, " Drei Reisen in Italien," he observes : ' Two remarkable portraits in the Ambrosiana, of Lodovico Sforza [Dr. Bode's Gian Galeazzo] and his wife [Dr. Bode's Isabella]. His portrait, three-quarter face, somewhat violet in tone, still opaque in the shadows, belonging in style to an earlier period of art, but the forms are

---

[7] If an unprofessional critic like myself may be permitted to say a word about the method of the painting in Italian works of art, I would beg my readers to compare the technic of this unfinished portrait in the Ambrosiana with that of the equally unfinished "St. Jerome" in the Vatican, and the " Adoration of the Magi " in the Uffizi. They will then, I think, agree with me that the author of the Ambrosiana portraits cannot possibly be the same as the painter of these two unfinished works.

[8] To this distinguished anonymous imitator of Leonardo several drawings may, I think, also be ascribed : such as the silver point drawing of a female head in the Uffizi (Case 107, No. 426, Braun 436) ; one in the Ambrosiana with a string of pearls round her neck, three-quarter face ; a youthful head in the palace at Weimar (?) (Braun 149), and others elsewhere.

treated with refinement and intelligence.  His wife of less
importance.    Looking at these pictures, I began to surmise that Leonardo may have come into connection with
the painters of the Lower German schools, and have learnt
from them the use of oil as a medium, which was not
customarily employed in Florence; indeed, it was hardly
even historically known there before the period of his
journey to Milan.    A charming little painting of the
Madonna and Child, belonging to Count Alberto Litta [now
in the Hermitage at St. Petersburg], has confirmed me in
this opinion.    The *motive* of this picture is seen also in a
much-retouched drawing in the Uffizi (?).    The painting has
suffered in parts, and the hand of the Child has lost its glazes,
but this very fact renders an acquaintance with Leonardo's
method easier.    We see that he first laid in his shadows
with opaque colours, and altogether the carefully prepared
pigments, the light priming, the precision of execution,
display much of the early Flemish manner.' [9]

We can scarcely be surprised that in Cardinal Federigo
Borrommeo's day these portraits should have passed for works
by the same master; for art-criticism, like every other kind of
criticism, was then at its lowest ebb, and every drawing or
painting bearing the slightest resemblance to Leonardo's
manner was immediately ascribed to the master himself.
But that the portraits should have been taken to represent
" il Moro " and his wife Beatrice d' Este is quite inexplicable,
for in churches and in private collections in Milan and the
country around these personages are found frequently
portrayed in painting and in sculpture.    To tradition, that
time-honoured source, we are again indebted for these

[9] In my opinion this charming
little Madonna is certainly not by
Leonardo da Vinci, but by another
'dry' Lombard painter, namely,
Bernardino de' Conti.

astonishing attributions, and they were blindly accepted by
the most distinguished critics of this century. Not only
Amoretti and Lanzi in Italy, but Baron Rumohr and
Mündler in Germany, and, forty years later, Dr. Bode
himself, walked straight into the trap which perfidious
tradition had laid for them. In the opinion of all these
critics, the two portraits in the Ambrosiana and the Madonna at St. Petersburg are by the same master—
Leonardo da Vinci. Baron Rumohr, however, rightly
esteems the unfinished portrait of the man higher than that
of the woman. But there is another point on which the
Berlin critics come into collision, namely, as to the period
when oil painting was first practised in Tuscany. Dr. Bode,
on the strength of his newly-discovered painting by
Leonardo (!), "The Resurrection," maintains that in 1478
oil as a medium was already in use in Florence. Baron
Rumohr, on the other hand, asserts that it was scarcely
even historically known at that date in Tuscany, and I
should be disposed to agree with him.

Ambrogio de Predis was employed by Lodovico Sforza,
as his most favoured portrait painter, as early as 1482.
This may be gathered from the following document published by the late Marchese Campori. 'A di 22 Mazo
(May) 1482 : A Zoane Ambroso di predj de Milano (depin-
tore) de lo Ill. S. Lud. Sforza, Braza 10 de razo alexandrino
de campione de la Ex. de Madama, la quale gie dona la
Ex. del nro Sig.' 'To Giovanni Ambrogio di predj of
Milan, painter to his Highness Lodovico Sforza, ten yards
of Alexandrian satin of the same kind as that of her
Excellency the Duchess which his Excellency our master
gives him as a present.' (Archivio di Stato in Modena ;
Libro : Ricordi de la Salvaroba de Castello,' a. c. 65.) In
1482 Ambrogio de Predis was, therefore, a finished artist,
and we may infer that he was born between 1450-1460.

The earliest portrait I know by him is the portrait of the Duke.

I will now briefly enumerate those works which, I believe, may be attributed to Ambrogio de Predis, and Dr. G. Frizzoni, the Marchese Visconti Venosta, and the well-known picture restorer, Signor Cavenaghi, concur in my opinion.

1. The portrait of Gian Galeazzo Maria Sforza, Count of Pavia, belonging to Count Porro at Milan.[1](†)  2. The profile portrait in the Ambrosiana, already mentioned, is of about the same period. (†)  An attractive and sympathetic head ; the cranium is not quite correct in drawing, and the line from the neck to the back is too straight.  Leonardo himself would never have been guilty of such mistakes.[2]  3. The refined portrait of Francesco di Bartolommeo Archinto (b. 1474, d. 1551), governor of Chiavenna in the time of Louis XII.  It was formerly in the possession of the Archinto family at Milan, and now belongs to Mr. Fuller Maitland, as Dr. Frizzoni, who saw it in that collection, informs me.  It is dated 1494, and signed **MR** (Ambrogio Preda) F.  4. The profile portrait of Lodovico il Moro, a miniature in the so-called ' Libro del Jesus,' in the library of Prince Trivulzio at Milan. (†)  5. The profile portrait of Massimiliano Sforza at the age of five, in the same book. (†)  All the miniatures in this celebrated Codex are ascribed to Leonardo, but the characteristics of de Predis, which I have already described, should serve to convince

[1] This portrait should be compared with the medal of the unfortunate young prince. The boy in the portrait looks about twenty. Gian Galeazzo died, as is well-known, in 1494, in his twenty-fifth year. In 1489 he married Isabella of Aragon ; the portrait was probably painted about this time.

[2] Who this attractive portrait represents I do not pretend to say ; all I wish to contend for is that it is not Beatrice d' Este, the wife of il Moro, as has always been assumed in the Ambrosiana, and that it cannot be by Leonardo as usually asserted, but is by the forgotten Ambrogio de Predis.

FEMALE PORTRAIT. BY DE PREDIS.

*(In the Ambrosiana, Milan.)*

*To face p.* 186.

PORTRAIT OF LUDOVICO SFORZA.

*(In the Libro del Jesus, Milan.)*

*To face p.* 186.

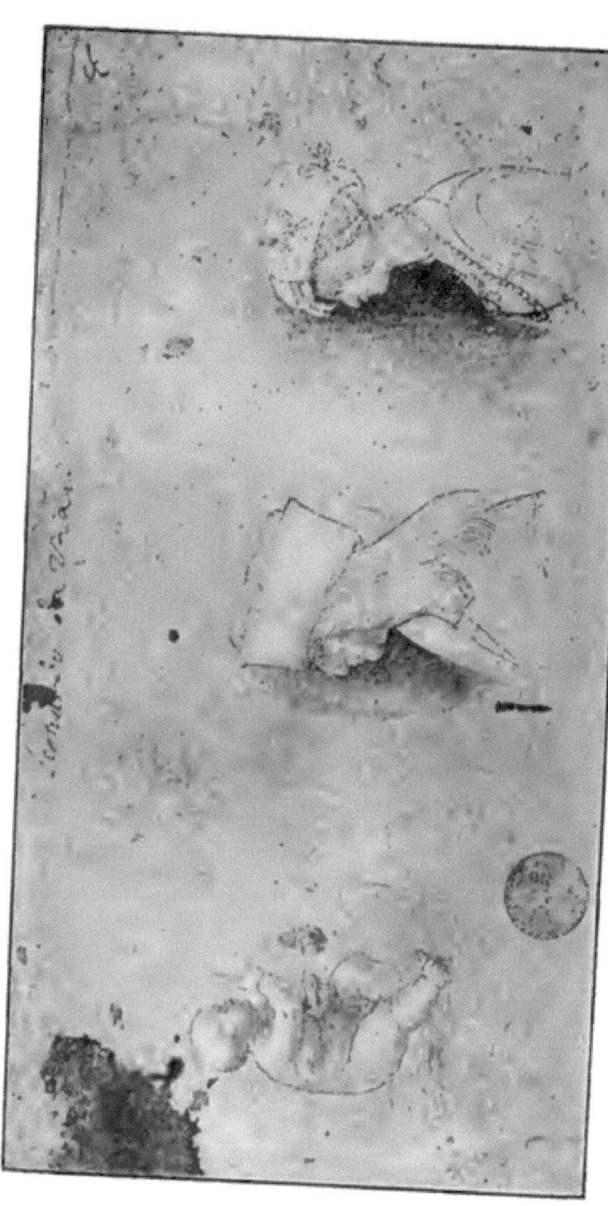

PORTRAITS OF THE EMPEROR MAXIMILIAN AND BIANCA MARIA SFORZA. BY DE PREDIS.

(In Venice Academy.)

To face p. 137.

every intelligent student of art that these two portraits,
executed about 1497, are unquestionably by that painter.
Mention is made in this Codex of a ' Messer Brunoro Preda '
who accompanied the ducal family in their flight from
Milan to Innsbruck in 1499. Whether Brunoro was a
relative of Ambrogio I am unable to say, but it appears to
me very probable that the ' Maestro Ambrosio,' spoken of
in the following verses, is no other than our painter : ' Qui
maestro Ambrosio dice : Dá de ughette al Conte, E lui con
lieta fronte, Dimanda del cappone.' [3]   Drawing was in those
days a necessary part of a young nobleman's education.
Ambrogio may have instructed the sons of ' il Moro ' in this
art, and it is not improbable that he accompanied them in
September 1499 in their flight to Innsbruck. He very likely
remained several years at the Court in that city, and would
there have painted the portraits of the Emperor and his
wife in 1502.[4]

To continue our list.   6. The portrait of a young man
with fair hair (head and shoulders). The background is
dark, as is always the case in Ambrogio's portraits. It
belongs to the Maggi family at Milan, and was formerly
attributed to Leonardo da Vinci. (†)   7. A youth with long
fair hair, in the dress of a page, full-face, in the collection
of the author at Milan.[5] (†)   On the back in old characters
is the following inscription : DI LEONARDO PITOR Fiorentino.
8. A young man with an arrow in his hand (St. Sebastian),
full-face, belonging to Dr. G. Frizzoni at Milan.   Formerly
it passed as a Boltraffio.   All these works, belonging to the
early period of de Predis, are light in the carnations, and

---

[3] ' Says Maestro Ambrogio—Give
raisins to the Count—And he with
smiling face—Asks for capons.'
The lines refer to young Massimiliano Sforza at table.

[4] The drawing for these portraits (see illustration) I afterwards
found in the Venice Academy under
the name of Leonardo.

[5] Now at Bergamo.

the *smalto*, resembling that of the profile in the Ambrosiana, is peculiarly distinctive.

The following works of his later years (from about 1510–1515) are superior in modelling, and display a browner tone in the flesh.   9. The portrait of Francesco Brivio, son of Jacopo Stefano, the Duke's counsellor, and, in 1514, lord of Melegnano ; in the Poldi collection at Milan, where it is ascribed to Vincenzo Foppa.   10. The profile of a refined-looking old man, in Dr. G. Frizzoni's collection.   This too passed at one time as the work of Leonardo —an attribution approved in 1848 by the Florentine Academy. (†)   11. The profile of a youth of twenty, wearing the ducal chain round his neck, in the Morelli collection. (†)   If I am not much mistaken, this splendidly modelled portrait represents Massimiliano Sforza, who reigned at Milan from 1512–1515.   12. The profile portrait formerly in the corridor of the Uffizi (30 *bis*), attributed to Antonio del Pollajuolo, might prove to be by de Predis, if the thick mask of varnish now disfiguring the face were removed.   The mouth appears to me modelled quite in his manner ; the way in which the heavy mass of hair is touched with light, and the detailed treatment of the eyelashes, recall his method.   The modelling of the eyes coincides with their treatment in all the before-mentioned portraits.   It is, however, so much repainted that it would be unwise to make any positive assertion on the subject.

Both the year of de Predis' birth and that of his death are unknown.   His first instruction in drawing he probably derived from Christophorus de Predis, the celebrated miniaturist, and very likely his relation.[6]   To judge from

---

[6] In the Turin library we find an excellent example of the work of this Modenese miniature painter, who settled at Milan. I is signed: GZ. MA. DUX MDL. QVINTVS OPVS XOFORI DE PREDIS MVT. DIE 3. APRILIS. 1474. Other miniatures by him are in the pos-

some of his miniatures in the 'Libro del Jesus,' he may later have been under the influence of the school of Foppa, and in the beginning of the sixteenth century more especially under that of Leonardo. De Predis is a conscientious and careful painter, though his drawing and modelling are often defective, particularly in the representation of the hand. In the portraits belonging to Dr. G. Frizzoni, in the likeness of Gian Galeazzo Sforza, and in that of Archinto, belonging respectively to Count Porro and to Mr. Fuller Maitland, the hands are coarse and wanting in life.[7]

session of the d' Adda family at Milan, in the church of the Madonna del Monte at Varese, and elsewhere.

[7] Some time after these lines had been written, Dr. Bode kindly sent me a copy of his article on the true portrait of Bianca Maria Sforza, in a private collection at Berlin (published in the *Jahrbuch der königl. preussischen Kunstsammlungen*, No. II. 1889). I am glad to be able to state that I entirely agree with him as regards both the person represented and his own estimate of the value of the painting. From the heliotype appended to the article I notice that nearly all the characteristics of Ambrogio de Predis, enumerated by me on p. 180, note 3, are present in this portrait. In addition to the distinctive drawing of the eyes with the detailed painting of the lashes, the stiff contour of the upper lip, the strong light on the bridge of the nose, and the dry miniature-like treatment of the accessories (jewels, &c.)—in addition to all these, I repeat, I had the satisfaction of observing that *bright streak of light* in the outer corner of the eye which may be seen in the portrait of the Emperor Maximilian, signed with the master's name, and in the profile in the Ambrosiana. This is a characteristic which we may vainly seek for in the profile portraits of other contemporary Italian masters. As Dr. Bode justly remarks, the face of the woman in the Ambrosiana is infinitely more attractive and intelligent than that of Bianca Maria. Might this not be owing rather to the nature of the subject than to the merits of the artist? The Berlin critic is decidedly not of this opinion. 'The contrast,' he writes, 'between the profile in the Ambrosiana and the portrait of Bianca Maria is about as great as it can be. It is but an example of the immense gulf separating the works of one of the greatest painters of all times from those of his plodding mechanical imitator.' The æsthetic estimate of works of art should always, I consider, be left to each individual observer; yet I must remind my readers that even in this particular Dr. Bode and I differ materially, and I am often forced to class his verdicts on Italian pictures in that category which M. de Pourceaugnac would term *sujettes à caution*. Thus, for instance, he cites two portraits as originals which I can only regard

## BERNARDINO DE' CONTI.

The earlier works of Ambrogio de Predis show a decided affinity with the later portraits of Bernardino de' Conti

as copies. One of these, belonging to Mr. George Salting in London, he discusses on p. 9 ; the other is the portrait in the Pitti (No. 371) of Beatrice Sforza, wife of il Moro, there attributed to Piero della Francesca. When I saw Mr. Salting's portrait I was accompanied by several good authorities on art, among them Dr. J. P. Richter. At the first glance we all recognised it as a very poor copy of the Ambrosiana portrait ; it certainly never occurred to any of us to ascribe it to A. de Predis. Similar copies, equally bad, of portraits by this once renowned painter may be seen in the Museo Civico at Milan, and elsewhere. I have since heard that after our visit Mr. Salting took steps to rid himself as speedily as possible of his supposed treasure. The portrait in the Pitti Dr. Bode describes (p. 6) as ' a beautiful Ferrarese work,' by the hand of Lorenzo Costa. I venture to think, however, that an examination of Costa's fine and genuine portrait of Bentivoglio on the same wall would induce the German critic to think differently of this uninteresting work. In support of his views about A. de Predis, Dr. Bode quotes against me the judgment pronounced upon the Ambrosiana portrait by my friend the late Mr. Mündler, whom he rightly characterises as ' that refined and astute connoisseur of Italian art.' I had the good fortune to know this gifted Bavarian critic intimately. For two years I was constantly with him in

Paris, and together we studied the works of art in the Louvre. I can testify that at that time—namely, about forty years ago—Mündler was almost unrivalled in his intimate knowledge of Italian painting. Yet his modesty was such that, when occasionally led into error by his enthusiasm, he was always willing to be corrected by less competent connoisseurs than himself. For, like all men of real learning, Mündler had a horror of self-assertion and dogmatising. Ever anxious to improve his own knowledge, he would never have thought of discoursing to others on what he did not thoroughly understand himself. I feel convinced that, were he still alive, he would openly admit his mistakes, all of them most pardonable, considering the state of art-criticism in his day, and that he would no longer regard the profile in the Ambrosiana, the fresco at Vaprio (il Madonnone), or the " Vierge aux Rochers " in the National Gallery, as works by Leonardo. For since the days of Mündler the science of art-criticism has advanced, if with no great strides, at least in some degree, and that not only in the knowledge of Dutch art, in which, as is well known, Dr. Bode has gathered many laurels, but also in that of Italian painting. A more assiduous study of the Italian schools has led to various discoveries, which, though still called in question, as is inevitable, will in the end, I believe, maintain their ground.

(from about 1505), which makes it probable that Bernardino, besides being influenced by Leonardo, was also affected by de Predis.   Works by this little-known Milanese painter, Bernardino de' Conti, are often confounded with those of Leonardo.   Only Lomazzo and Orlandi, two very untrustworthy writers on art, mention him.   He is said to have come from Pavia, and may, therefore, have received his first instruction from Vincenzo Foppa or from Civerchio. The brownish-red flesh tints, and the peculiar arrangement of the drapery in his painting in the Brera of 1496, seem to point to the school of Foppa.   Later, when at Milan, Conti must have felt the influence of both Leonardo and de Predis.   Messrs. Crowe and Cavalcaselle (ii. 67) simply name him as the pupil of Zenale, and enumerate a few of his works—the portrait of a prelate in the Berlin Museum, signed and dated 1499 ; a Madonna and Child, in Munich, formerly in the collection at Schleissheim ; a replica of this latter, and a " Marriage of St. Catherine," in the gallery at Bergamo, and a Madonna in the Poldi-Pezzoli collection at Milan.   The Madonna at Munich I consider to be an old copy, and the two pictures at Bergamo can only be regarded as works of the school; the inscription and date, 1501, on one of these is scarcely likely to be by the master's own hand.   Dr. Bode, following in the steps of Messrs. Crowe and Cavalcaselle, describes Bernardino, in a few slighting remarks, as a most inferior painter.   The æsthetic estimate of works of art is a subject on which much might be said, for as the peripatetics rightly observed : *omne quod recipitur ad modum recipientis recipitur.*

Adhering to our usual method, however, we will first particularise those characteristic signs which distinguish the paintings and drawings of this master from those of other contemporary Milanese artists, and from those of Leonardo, with whom Conti is frequently confounded, more especially in drawings.

1. In his paintings, dating from the fifteenth century— for example the large altar-piece in the Brera formerly attributed to Zenale, and the portrait of a prelate of 1499 in the Berlin Museum—the carnations incline to red; in his later works—for instance, the portrait of 1505, belonging to the Countess d' Angrogna at Turin, the one in Mr. A. Morrison's collection in London, and the Madonna and Child at St. Petersburg—the flesh tints are pale and cold, and of a *smalto* which recalls the portraits of de Predis' first period.

2. The antihelix of the ear is extremely broad, hence the opening of the ear becomes very narrow.

3. The shadow between the eye and the upper part of the nose is strongly marked.

4. In the heads of his female figures the hair is drawn down smoothly over the temples.

5. The fingers are ungraceful in their movements, like those of Antonio del Pollajuolo, and the nails are short and broad.

6. His drawings are nearly all neatly and carefully executed in silver point; the shading is not from left to right, after the manner of Leonardo, but from right to left.

7. The mouth is not so hard in modelling as in the portraits of de Predis.

Taking into consideration all these characteristics, I should ascribe the following to Bernardino de' Conti:

1. The large altar-piece in the Brera (No. 87)—the adonna enthroned with the Child, between the four Fathers of the Church, whose heads are caricatures of Leonardo's types. Ludovico Sforza and his family kneel at the foot of the throne. This picture is now rightly ascribed to

VIRGIN AND CHILD.   BY DE' CONTI.

(*St. Petersburg.*)

*To face p.* 142.

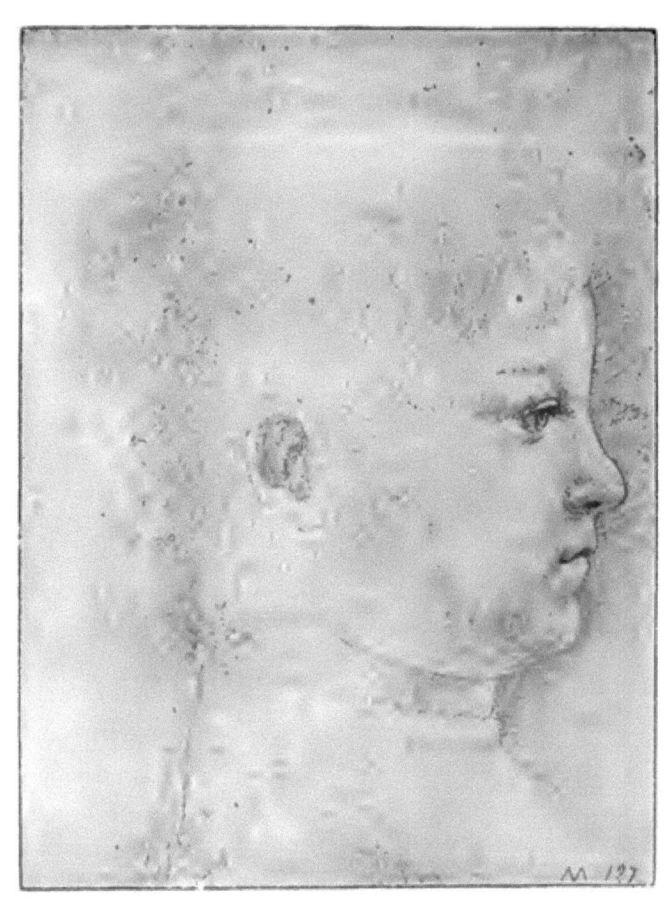

PORTRAIT OF MASSIMILIANO SFORZA.  BY DE' CONTI.

*(In the Ambrosiana.)*

To face p. 193.

Conti (†) ; at one time it passed as the work of Leonardo, and when it first came to the Brera was, for no reason at all, assigned to Zenale, much in the same way that Baron Rumohr's picture by Giovanni Santi, at Berlin, was suddenly transformed into Timoteo Viti's masterpiece.

2. The so-called portrait of Lucas van Leyden by himself, in the Uffizi (No. 444), appears to me an old copy after Conti, rather than an original. (†)

3. The female portrait belonging to Mr. A. Morrison in London. It was formerly in the Castelbarco collection at Milan, where it was ascribed to Leonardo. (†)

4. The portrait of Catellanus Trivulcius, signed and dated 1505, in the collection of the Countess d' Angrogna at Turin.

5. The charming little Madonna and Child, once in the Palazzo Litta at Milan and now at St. Petersburg, where it still retains the name of Leonardo. The small broad nails, the flesh tints, and the smooth hair of the Madonna drawn down over her temples, are characteristic of the master in this painting. (†)

6. The Madonna in the Poldi collection.

I shall now cite a few of the many drawings by Bernardino attributed to Leonardo in public collections, in order that students may test my attributions ; as in every branch of research the same principle holds good, that arguments unless well sustained are worthless.

7. In the Ambrosiana, the drawing for the profile head of Massimiliano Sforza in Conti's large altar-piece in the Brera (No. 87). The master's characteristic form of ear may be studied in the reproduction. (†) (Braun, No. 38.)

8. The large silver point drawing in the British Museum ascribed to Leonardo (Braun 45)—another study for Conti's altar-piece in the Brera. (†)

9. Head of a man ; three-quarter face, silver point. In

the Louvre.　Also attributed to Leonardo. (†)　(Braun, No. 169.)

10. The Leonardesque head of an old man.　British Museum, vol. 36, P. p. 1, 35. (†)

11. A splendid head of a man, silver point, in Mr. Malcolm's fine collection of drawings (No. 39), ascribed to Leonardo. (†)

12. A female head with long hair.　Christ Church collection, Oxford; ascribed to Leonardo. (†)

Like Ambrogio de Predis, Bernardino de' Conti was evidently very popular as a portrait painter at Milan in the first decades of the sixteenth century.　He cannot be classed with the great masters, but occasionally he succeeded in producing works which, like the Madonna at St. Petersburg, deceive even so-called connoisseurs of Leonardo and of the Milanese school.

I have devoted more space than I had originally intended to these two ' mechanical ' Lombard painters, as it has been said (' Deutsche Litteraturzeitung,' for 1886, No. 42) that, beyond the opposition which my opinions must provoke, I have done nothing towards furthering the knowledge of de Predis and Conti, two painters, I may observe, who were both equally unknown till I rescued them from oblivion.


## FRANCESCO FRANCIA.

We must now turn to Francesco Francia, to whom several paintings in the Borghese gallery are attributed. It would be difficult to name another work by this devout and excellent artist so deeply imbued with feeling as the St. Stephen (No. 65), which is of his early period, 1490–1496.　The saint kneels in a landscape with folded hands; blood flows from a deep wound in his head,

and he awaits his approaching end with an expression of
steadfast faith.   Few paintings are so full of the essence
of the purest art as this St. Stephen.   On a ' Cartellino ' is
the following inscription :—

VINCENTII . DESIDERII . VOTVM . FRANCIE . EXPRESSVM . MANV .

The " Madonna and Child in the Rose-garden " probably
belongs, in execution at least, to one of Francia's better
pupils or many imitators, while the " Lucretia " (*) is,
again, an excellent work entirely by the master's own
hand.[8]   The remaining Madonnas and the " St. Anthony,"
which pass under the name of Francia (Nos. 57, 34,
60a), are only works of his school ; the same may be said
of the Madonnas ascribed to him in the Vatican and
in the Doria gallery.

A genuine, though unfinished, work by him is the large
picture in the first room of the Capitoline gallery.   Francia
commenced it, and the part executed by himself is easily
identified ; some Bolognese artist of the seventeenth century
probably completed it, adding several figures, and the dog
and other accessories.   It may have been Francia's last
work, dating from the same year as the altar-piece in the
Facci chapel of S. Stefano at Bologna.[9]

In the same room is another picture attributed to this
master—the Madonna enthroned, with the Child ; SS.
Peter, Paul, and John the Baptist, on the right of the
throne, and SS. Andrew, John the Evangelist, and Francis
on the left.   The elaborately gilded architectural decoration
points to a painter who was influenced by Palmezzano.

---

[8] This Lucretia is probably the
painting described by Vasari (vi. 11):
' Il duca Guido Baldo parimente ha
nella sua guardaroba, di mano del
Francia, in un quadro una Lucrezia
romana, da lui molto stimata.'   An
old and good copy is in Lord Northbrook's collection in London.

[9] Messrs. Crowe and Cavalcaselle
ascribe this altar-piece to Giacomo
Francia.   (N. Italy, i. 574, note 3.)

The type of the Madonna, the form of hand and ear in the
Child, and the landscape, are apparently taken from Francia,
the types of St. Francis and of the remaining saints,
which are caricatures, recall Palmezzano, whilst the fruit
introduced about the throne reminds us of the school of
Crivelli.   The picture is dated 1513, and might be by
some painter of the March of Ancona.   As I have thus
mentioned one of Francia's latest works I may draw attention to one of his earliest attempts—the small St. George
and the Dragon in the Corsini gallery.   It has always been
looked upon as the work of Ercole Grandi di Giulio Cesare,
and years ago I myself cited it as such.   But after a closer
study I recognised it as an early work of Francesco Francia,
of about the same period (†) (1490–1494) as the following
pictures: the small " Crucifixion " in the Archiginnasio at
Bologna (†), the Madonna (No. 1040) in the Munich Pinacothek, and the paintings executed for the Bianchini
family (now in the Berlin Museum), and for the Felicini
family (now in the gallery at Bologna).    In the Tribune of the Uffizi at Florence we find an excellent, but
much-restored, portrait of Evangelista Scappi by the
master.

Most of Francia's best works are still in his native
city of Bologna—in the public gallery, in the churches of S.
Jacopo Maggiore, S. Martino, and S. Vitale, and in the chapel
of S. Cecilia.   Francia stood much in the same relation to
Lorenzo Costa as did Perugino to Pintoricchio.   Both Costa
and Pintoricchio are more imaginative, animated, and
dramatic than Francia and Perugino, who, however, in
their early works at least, are more correct as draughtsmen
and more conscientious as painters.   The single figures in
the pictures of the two latter are executed with greater
care, yet one pervading thought and purpose does not
inspire and animate them equally—in a word, each is

isolated and independent. Nevertheless they touch the spectator by their sweet and devout expression.

## SOFONISBA ANGUISSOLA.

We have still to mention a late, but at one time famous, Lombard painter to whom a small female portrait in the Borghese gallery is attributed. It is numbered 118, and is the work of a woman. The catalogue ascribes it to Sofonisba Anguissola, the friend in her old age of the young Van Dyck. She came of a patrician family of Cremona, and in her seventh year was sent by her father, Hamilcar, to the Cremonese artist, Bernardino Campi, to be instructed in painting.

When some years later (1550) Campi was summoned to Milan, the further training of the young artist was entrusted to Bernardino Gatti, called ' il Sojaro,' an imitator of Correggio and Parmeggianino, who was then living at Cremona. By 1559 Sofonisba had already gained so great a reputation that Philip II. sent for her to his court at Madrid. The earliest work known to me by her is the portrait of a dark-eyed nun, belonging to Lord Yarborough in London, signed, and dated 1551. She must therefore have painted this portrait, which has real merit, in her eleventh, or, at latest, in her twelfth year—very likely with the assistance of her master. In her own portrait in the public gallery at Vienna, dated 1554, and inscribed: SOPHONISBA . ANGVISSOLA . VIRGO . SE . IPSAM . FECIT, she looks about fourteen or fifteen. There are some half-dozen other portraits of herself in existence. One, in the Academy at Siena, represents her as a girl of about eighteen or nineteen, and must therefore have been executed about 1558. Beside her stands a man with a pencil in his hand— probably her former master, Bernardino Campi, who was

born about 1522, and looks about forty in this picture.
The figures are life-size. Another, much damaged, belonged to the late Duke Melzi at Milan. A still later one,
in the collection of portraits in the Uffizi, is signed :
SOPHONISBA . ANGVISSOLA . CREM[is] [Cremonensis] . AET.
SVAE . ANN . XX. It was probably painted at Madrid, as
the reference to her own home in the inscription would
also seem to indicate.

There are several portraits by Sofonisba Anguissola
in England—in the collections of Lord Spencer, of the late
Mr. Danby Seymour, and of the late Sir William Stirling
Maxwell. In the National Museum at Berlin (Raczynski
collection) there is a fine painting by her with the portraits
of three of her sisters ; another is in the Hermitage at
St. Petersburg, bought from the Leuchtenberg collection, and
one in the Naples Museum. A pretty little "Holy Family"
belongs to the author,[1] inscribed, SOPHONISBA . ANAGVSSOLA
[sic] . ADOLESCENS . P . 1559, and consequently painted in
the year when the young artist, aged eighteen or nineteen,
was summoned to Madrid by Philip II.[2]

She is decidedly an interesting artist, commended even
by Michael Angelo, and highly extolled by Vasari. Great
diversity of opinion exists as to the date of her birth and
death. She must have been born, I think, about 1539, at
Cremona. In her portrait of herself, of about 1554, she
looks, as already observed, about fourteen or fifteen. Had
she been born in 1530, as most of her biographers state,
she would scarcely have described herself as *adolescens*
in 1559 (as on the picture in the Morelli collection), for she
would at that time have been close upon thirty.

---

[1] Now in the gallery at Bergamo.
[2] Many years ago I saw a replica
of this picture in the collection of
the late Count Varano at Ferrara.
I am not acquainted with any other
Madonnas by this artist.

From about 1559 to 1570 Sofonisba appears to have remained at the Spanish Court. There she married a Sicilian noble, named Moncada, whom later she accompanied to Palermo, where he died. She married, secondly, a Genoese patrician named Lomellini, and settled at Genoa. In 1624 the young Van Dyck, arriving in that city from Palermo, made her personal acquaintance, and is said to have painted the portrait of the old lady, who was then blind, in 1625. A year later she died, aged about eighty-six.

Most of her portraits pass under other names; they are all fresh and spirited in conception and solidly painted. In Madrid I met with no work by her. The life-sized portrait in the gallery there, representing the Cremonese physician, Piermaria (No. 15), is signed : LVCIA . ANGVISOLA . AMILCARIS . F. ADOLESCENS. This Lucia was, if I am not mistaken, Sofonisba's second sister and her pupil. At Brescia there is a naïve little portrait by her of a third sister, Europa Anguissola, and it was Lucia, I consider, and not Sofonisba, who painted the small female portrait in the Borghese gallery. (†) The third sister, Europa, was also an artist, as Vasari, who visited her at Cremona in 1568, states (xi. 260), and so, too, was the youngest sister,[3] Anna Maria. Years ago I met with an unattractive little painting by her belonging to the *Vicario* of S. Pietro, at Cremona. The subject was a "Holy Family," with St. Francis presenting a basket of grapes and mulberries to the Infant Saviour. It was inscribed in gold letters : ANNAE . MARIAE . AMILCARIS . ANGVSOLAE . FILIAE. Italy was, I believe, the only country in Europe in which so many women once devoted themselves to painting as a profession,

---

[3] There were besides two other sisters, one of whom died young, the other became a nun. See Graselli : 'Abecedario biografico dei Pittori, Scultori, ed Architetti Cremonesi.'

and attained, moreover, to a certain degree of proficiency. Among others may be named : the devout Catarina Vigri,[1] of Bologna ; Titian's pupil, Irene of Spilimbergo ; the Sisters Anguissola ; Marietta Robusti ;[2] Barbara Longhi, of Ravenna ; Agnese Dolci, of Florence ; Lavinia Fontana, of Bologna ; and Galizia Fede, of Trent.

## THE FERRARESE.

HAVING thus glanced at the Florentine and other Italian schools, we will turn our attention to some Ferrarese painters who are well represented in the Borghese gallery.

### BENVENUTO TISI, called GAROFALO.

We meet with works by Garofalo and Dosso Dossi at every turn, and some of them are worthy to be regarded as among the greatest ornaments of the collection. We will begin with Garofalo and his school. He was a few years younger than his fellow-countryman Dosso, and I should consider him in many ways inferior as an artist to the latter, but we will give him the precedence, as he may be studied in Rome better than in any other place, for not even in Ferrara do we find so many specimens of his art showing every phase of his development. Most of these Ferrarese works were probably brought to Rome in the beginning of the eighteenth century, when, through the family of the Aldobrandini, the turn came for Ferrara to be annexed to the Papal States, for a political destiny sways the fate of pictures as of nations. Though Vasari knew Garofalo personally, his biography of him, as of most other

---

[1] A work by her is in the Venice Academy.

[2] Several portraits by her are in the gallery at Madrid.

artists, is full of anachronisms. In the main, however, it appears to be correct. It contains the following facts : that Garofalo was born at Ferrara in 1481, and died there in 1559, aged consequently seventy-eight, and that when about fifty he almost entirely lost the sight of one eye, which did not, however, in any way interfere with his activity in painting. His artistic life covered a space of close upon fifty years, and, being a man of immense industry, he must undoubtedly have executed a great number of works, as is proved by those seen in the Roman galleries. His father, Pietro Tisi (a shoemaker, like Sodoma's father), came from the little village of Garofalo in the province of Padua, hence the son is usually known as Benvenuto da Garofalo, or simply as Garofalo. About 1491, when ten years old, he was sent by his father to Domenico Panetti,[6] a dry and somewhat unpleasing Ferrarese artist, but thoroughly able and conscientious, as his works in the gallery of Ferrara prove, and at that time, no doubt, the most popular painter in that city. Panetti, Francesco Bianchi, and Costa appear to me to occupy about the same position in the history of the Ferrarese school as do Fiorenzo di Lorenzo, Pintoricchio, and Pietro Perugino in that of Perugia, and Francesco Morone, Girolamo dai Libri, and Bonsignori in that of Verona. Towards 1498, after about seven years of apprenticeship, the young Garofalo started on his travels. He first went to Cremona, where he seems to have had a friend or relative in the person of the painter Soriani, and where Boccaccio Boccaccino, whom he may have known previously at Ferrara, was also actively employed. The latter painter, a representative of the Venetian rather than of the Milanese

---

[6] In the school of Cosimo Tura, Panetti (d. 1512) was, I consider, a fellow-pupil with Francesco Bianchi (d. 1510), who, according to tradition, had the honour of being Correggio's first master.

P

school, was at that time rightly regarded as the first artist
in Cremona. Vasari relates, and the story has been repeated by Barrufaldi, that on this occasion Garofalo saw
Boccaccino's frescoes in the cathedral of Cremona, which,
however, is chronologically impossible. The paintings in
the choir were not executed before 1505 or 1506, and his
series from the Life of the Madonna, like the frescoes by
Romanino and his pupil Altobello Meloni in the same
church, were only produced between 1513–1518. According to a letter purporting to have been written by Boccaccino to the father of Garofalo, the young man appears to
have found employment with that master. It is probable,
therefore, that though he could not have seen the frescoes
mentioned by the biographer, he saw other paintings by
Boccaccino in the master's workshop at Cremona, and was
attracted by their splendid colouring. This letter is as
follows : [7]

'Highly honoured Sir !—Had your son Benvegnù learnt
good manners as thoroughly as he has learnt painting, he
would scarcely have played me such a shabby trick. For,
since the death of his uncle and your brother-in-law (?) Signor
Niccolò (Soriani), on the 3rd of January, he has never touched
a brush, though he knows well enough what a fine work he
was engaged upon. But this is not all. He has taken
himself off, I know not whither, and without a word. I had
procured work for him, but he has departed, leaving it all
unfinished, and moreover leaving all his own effects and
those of Signor Niccolò in my house. I can tell you nothing further about him. But this may be a clue to his
whereabouts that he said, if he is to be believed, that he
would see Rome, and it may be therefore that he has gone

---

[7] Some recent critics regard this letter as apocryphal, but I think
without sufficient reason.

thither. It is ten days now since he disappeared, in such bitter weather that the cold was almost unbearable. I salute you, and am yours in brotherly regard,

'BOCCACCINO.

'Cremona, January 29, 1499.'

To judge from this letter Benvenuto appears to have been of a somewhat unruly and determined character. On January 19, 1499, in the depth of winter, at the age of eighteen, he left the workshop of Boccaccino and Cremona for Rome. The journey was apparently a sudden resolve. Vasari tells us that on his arrival he lodged in the house of the Florentine artist Giovanni Baldini (probably a relation of the famous Baccio Baldini), where he had the opportunity of seeing and copying many drawings by great Florentine masters. The news of his father's severe illness recalled him suddenly to Ferrara. Here he appears to have formed a warm friendship with the brothers Giovanni and Battista Dossi, to have worked for a short time under their influence,[8] and, later, to have been employed with them in the service of the Duke Alfonso d' Este and his beautiful wife Lucrezia Borgia, then in her twenty-fourth year. The elder Dossi, Giovanni, was then also between twenty-four and twenty-five years of age and Garofalo about twenty-two or twenty-three—undoubtedly the best and brightest years in the life of a gifted artist. Masaccio, Filippino Lippi, Mantegna, Andrea del Sarto, even Raphael himself, were not much more than twenty when they executed some of their finest works, and at the court of the highly cultured Alfonso d' Este, we may be sure, employment for painters was not wanting.

Garofalo's large " Descent from the Cross " and Dosso's

[8] Much in his early work, the " Adoration of the Shepherds," in the Borghese gallery, recalls Battista Dosso more than Giovanni.

two works, the so-called "Circe," and the "Calisto"
—characteristic paintings in the Borghese gallery of both
artists—show how close must have been the connection between them. Whose influence, it may be asked, was the
dominant one? Was it Garofalo who influenced Dosso, or
the latter his younger fellow-countryman? In my opinion
the two stood in the same relation to each other as did
Francia to Lorenzo Costa—each may have taken from
and given something to the other. In all his works, both
good and indifferent, Dosso reveals himself as a highly
imaginative and, what we should in these days term, a
'romantic' painter. In the main he does not change, but
preserves the same artistic character throughout his life,
whether in the freshness and vigour of his early period, as
in the "Circe" and the "Calisto," or in his later years
when, after a sojourn in Venice, he had mastered the
manner of Giorgione and Titian. The same cannot be said
of Garofalo, who was more elegant, sober and restrained as
a painter. For though in all his works he too preserves
his Ferrarese character, yet in the different phases of his
development we can trace the influence of several masters
—of his older prototypes Panetti and Boccaccino, of the
brothers Dossi, and of Lorenzo Costa, and finally even that
of Raphael.

Let us first examine his large "Descent from the Cross,"
in the Borghese gallery.[9] In it are nine nearly life-sized

---

[9] In the Naples Museum there is
a modified copy of 1521 (?) of this
splendid painting by Garofalo; an
extremely feeble production which,
strange to say, is there considered an
original. The Magdalen, bewailing
the Dead Body of the Saviour, expresses her grief by exaggerated con-
tortions of the face; the women in the
middle distance are the very essence
of coarseness and vulgarity, the
whole picture is absolutely repulsive
and even defective in linear perspective. Dr. Bode (ii. 737) unhesitatingly accepts it as an original.
I must, however, assume that he is
not intimately acquainted with the
Ferrarese school, as he ascribes
Bagnacavallo's 'Cavalcade' in the
Palazzo Colonna to Garofalo. Life

figures, all showing deep emotion. In the background
is a fantastic landscape quite in Dosso's style, with St.
Christopher bearing the Holy Child across a river. The cold
tone of this landscape, the chalky light on the rocks and
on the flat reaches of country, contrast strongly with the
warm brown flesh-tints of the figures in the foreground; an
arrangement much in vogue with Venetian painters.
Garofalo's colouring is distinctive in all his early works.
He usually employed a full deep yellow, a red of a beetroot
shade, a bright blue, and a luminous white. It would
have been fortunate I think for his art, had he always
remained true to his Ferrarese instincts, as his best and
most powerful works were certainly produced during the
five or six years when he was constantly with the brothers
Dossi. We will now consider some of his pictures in
Rome, and as far as possible in their chronological order.

The earliest I know is the small "Adoration of the
Shepherds," No. 224, in the Borghese gallery. Both the
feeling and execution show it to be a very youthful
work. The stiff heavy folds on the Madonna's blue mantle
still belong to the *quattro-cento,* and the figure of St. Joseph
is abnormally long in the upper part. The flesh-tints incline to brown, as in the "Descent from the Cross," and the
fantastic landscape is similar to the one in that painting.
Following my method, let us first note the characteristics
in this early work of Garofalo so as to compare it with
his later pictures. 1. The type of St. Joseph's head often
recurs in works of Garofalo's early period; 2. The noses
are straight; 3. Stiff cross folds occur on the front part of
the sleeves; 4. The hand has the thumb turned outwards
and the forefinger bent; 5. The ear is long in form and

is too short and art a subject too
vast for one man, however able and
persevering, to grasp and compass it in all its many and varied
phases.

uniformly broad; and 6. The landscape shows a straight line of hills with a steep declivity on one side; a stretch of country in the middle distance illuminated with a chalky yellow light; the sky is red in tone towards the horizon; a group of dark trees is as usual introduced, behind which other trees with light brown foliage are seen, and in the foreground are numerous small round stones—all these particulars are very characteristic of the master's works of the same period.

Several years later than this picture I should place the spirited and beautiful " Adoration," or " Nativity," No. 312 in the Doria gallery (†), attributed to Ortolano.   St. Joseph is of the usual type, and besides we find in it all the other characteristics just mentioned—the straight nose, the same form of hand and ear, the peculiar distribution of light in the landscape, the redness of the horizon and the same treatment of drapery; but there is more skill shown than in the preceding picture. The choir of singing angels in the air, often met with in Garofalo's works, seems to me characteristic in this picture in the Doria gallery. On comparing it with a much later work by Garofalo in the same gallery, No. 206, we shall even find in that picture many of the characteristics of the " Nativity "—the same form of hand, the same types and general treatment, as well as the distinctive reddish-yellow tone of the horizon.  In the same gallery there is another large work by Garofalo, a " Visitation," of 1519 (No. 228), and here again we see the same round stones in the foreground, the same land-scape and treatment of drapery, with the stiff cross folds on St. Elizabeth's sleeves, the same arrangement of head-dress, &c.

After this " Adoration " follow, I think, in point of time the two panels with SS. Sebastian and Nicholas of Bari, in the Capitoline gallery (Nos. 70 and 87) (†), attributed without the smallest reason to Giovanni Bellini, although they contain all Garofalo's characteristics.

About 1508, in his twenty-seventh year, Garofalo may have painted the large "Descent from the Cross" in the Borghese gallery,[1] and a year later, perhaps, the splendid picture in the National Gallery (†) attributed to Ortolano, representing St. Sebastian between SS. Roch and Demetrius. The central figure recalls Dosso's St. Sebastian in the Brera. Garofalo's characteristics are apparent in the form of hand, the brown flesh-tints, the drapery, the landscape, and the small stones in the foreground.

A small St. Sebastian by the master in the Sala Veneziana of the Naples museum (No. 39) also recalls Dosso, and so does a beautiful little picture in the gallery at Bergamo—the Madonna enthroned with the Child between SS. Roch and Sebastian.

Immediately after executing these works, Garofalo may have painted the "Noli me tangere" (No. 244) in the Borghese gallery, and the "Santa Conversazione" in one of the rooms of the Doria gallery, there most erroneously ascribed to Basaiti. In the latter fine painting we find the same form of hand as in the "Adoration of the Shepherds" in the Borghese gallery; the same shade of straw-coloured yellow in the sandals of Zacharias, who has also the usual distinctive type of head; the same treatment of drapery, the same arrangement in the headdress of St. Elizabeth, the same long folds in the upper part of the Madonna's robe, and the same landscape with the small stones in the foreground. This picture, the "Noli me tangere," and "Christ at the Well with the Woman of Samaria" (No. 235) in the Borghese gallery, belong, I believe, to Garofalo's period of transition, from his manner resembling that of

[1] The Marchese Visconti Venosta has a Garofalo of the same period— a head of St. Anthony—in his collection at Milan.

Dosso, to his third manner when he was influenced by
Costa. In the Doria gallery we find a small "Holy
Family" by Garofalo attributed to Costa. The head of
the Madonna certainly recalls that painter, and it is
probable that Garofalo, who is known to have spent some
time at Mantua with Dosso Dossi in 1511, there felt the
influence of Costa's works. In 1512, a little later therefore, he painted the fine picture of "Poseidon and Athene," [2]
in the Dresden gallery.

Then follows the Holy Family of 1513 in the gallery
at Ferrara (No. 93), there attributed to Ortolano.[3] From
this time Garofalo's style remains almost unchanged, and
up to 1530, and even later, he produced excellent work.
It would be a tedious task to describe, or even to enumerate,
the many paintings, large and small, by Garofalo and
his imitators, contained in Italian collections. But for a
student it would certainly be worth while to trace the
development of this painter through the works of his
early, middle, and later period.

To return to his biography. We left him fully occupied
at Ferrara seeking to rival the brothers Dossi. Towards
the close of 1509 he was invited to Rome by his fellow-

[2] This painting, as well as the
"Holy Family," of 1513, in the gallery
of Ferrara, certainly recalls Lorenzo
Costa more than Raphael. Braun has
photographed the Dresden picture
(No. 156) as well as the one ascribed
to Ortolano in the National Gallery
(No. 669). Comparing these two
photographs, we shall find Garofalo's
characteristics in both; the landscape with the chalky lights, the
group of trees in the middle distance,
the round stones in the foreground,
the drapery, the form of the hands
and feet, and the types of the heads.
The picture in London belongs to
the period when Garofalo was working with the Dossi, the one in
Dresden to the transitional period
when he was under the influence of
Costa, about three years later.

[3] In this picture we find the
same small stones, the group of
trees, behind which the light brown
foliage of other trees is seen, and the
same form of hand and ear. It is
inscribed: M.DXIII., IVLI. This mention of the month is also characteristic of Garofalo. Close by there
is another picture by the master (No
65) dated December, 1514.

countryman Geronimo Sagrato.[4]   In the Eternal City
Garofalo saw the ceiling of the Sistine chapel, then
partly completed, and in all probability also the Cartoons
and the drawings on which Raphael was then engaged
for the frescoes in the 'Stanza della Segnatura,' even
if he did not see the frescoes themselves.   An artist's life
in Rome must indeed have been a stirring one in the days
when Garofalo, as a man of twenty-nine, returned thither.
Fierce rivalry and burning enthusiasm were rife among the
painters gathered round the throne of the aged pontiff
Julius II., and it is not astonishing that Benvenuto, contrasting the art-life of Rome with that of Ferrara, Bologna,
or even Cremona, should have given the preference to the
first-mentioned city.   It was for this reason, perhaps,
that Vasari said of him that he ' malediva le maniere di
Lombardia ;' and from this point of view the biographer
may be excused for having done so.[5]

The Florentine editors and commentators of Vasari have
sought, as usual, to exonerate[6] him from the reproach of
showing too great a predilection, or even partisanship, for
the Tuscans, and especially for the so-called Roman school.
As is often the case, however, with well-intentioned but not
particularly well-informed persons, they did a far greater
wrong to the Lombard and Venetian schools, than did even
Vasari himself by his thoughtless words, by adding the

---

[4] Vasari states that Garofalo
returned to Rome as early as 1505
(xi. 224). This was probably a slip
of the pen, as the painter could
scarcely have seen the works of
Michael Angelo and Raphael at that
date !

[5] Vasari's standard of excellence
induced him to stigmatise all art
which had not been formed upon
Michael Angelo as ' Minuta, secca e

di poco disegno.'   There are also
critics in the present day who, devoting themselves to the study of
one particular master of the quattro-cento, imagine that they can
detect traces of his genius everywhere, even where they are altogether absent. To these persons the
great artists of the best period are
positively intolerable.

[6] Le Monnier's ed. xi. 225.

following naïve remark : ' Certamente il Vasari intese di alludere alla grettezza delle scuole primitive (?) innanzi che Leonardo ne fondasse una nuova.' ' Troppa grazia, S. Antonio,' the Lombards and Venetians might reply, like the peasant who, after offering up prayers to the Saint for rain, was rewarded by a downpour of hail. ' Had we no painters then ? ' they might add, ' and were Giovanni and Gentile Bellini, Alvise Vivarini, Mantegna, Bartolommeo Montagna, Domenico Morone, Giorgione, and Titian, all of no consequence, to say nothing of many other great artists ? '

Vasari further says of Garofalo : ' per lo che mutò in tanto la practica cattiva in buona, che n'era tenuto dagli artefici conto.' In other words, during his second stay in Rome, like other painters greater than himself, he partially lost his local Ferrarese character, while his fresh and healthy vigour entirely disappeared. In some respects he certainly improved, more especially in his external forms and in refinement ; at the same time it cannot be denied that he became flat, insipid, and sometimes even empty and conventional. Dosso, on the other hand, who held to Venetian principles, and had studied the practice of his art at Venice, nevertheless developed his distinctive character with greater freedom, and therefore always preserved his own originality. In his early works, Garofalo reveals himself as a true artist—bold, resolute, at times even grand and impressive. He is equally removed from that narrow, prosaic realism, which appeals so strongly to a certain class of small-minded persons in the world of art, and from that shadowy idealism which to some pedantic philosophers and ' æsthetes ' is the principal attraction in a work of art, and stimulates them to many of their rhapsodical flights.

In the " Holy Family, with Saints," in the Borghese

gallery (No. 240)—a picture which generally receives a large amount of admiration—we already detect a change in Garofalo. He is still an attractive, conscientious painter; his technical execution, indeed, has improved in some respects, but his drawing is weaker, his touch less decided, and his conception of character is more trivial, insipid, and conventional. The scale of colour still resembles that of his early works, though it is more realistic, as we may see by comparing this picture with those already described—the "Nativity" in the Doria gallery and the "Descent from the Cross," and "Adoration of the Shepherds" in the Borghese. The shadows, which in Garofalo's youthful works were of a liquid brown, now incline to black.

Garofalo's stay in Rome lasted about a year and a half. In 1511 he was at Mantua, and in 1512 we find him settled at Ferrara, which city he never again quitted for any length of time. In the gallery there we find works by him ranging from 1513 to 1549.[7] The large altar-pieces on which he was often employed from this period to the end of his life are nearly all inscribed with the year, and often with the month, in which the painting was completed, though not always with the master's name. Some of them, executed in the second and third decades of the century, are extremely fine. It is from the great number of his works of this date that an estimate of the master has usually been formed.[8]

[7] As a painter, as we have already observed, Garofalo always remained a Ferrarese, even after his second visit to Rome—as an artist he brought away with him certain classic impressions. Rome refined his taste, but it also warped his genius. Raphael's influence is most clearly perceptible in his beautiful chiaroscuro frescoes (of 1517) in the Seminario at Ferrara, formerly the Palazzo Trotti, representing episodes from Grecian mythology and Christian legends. Few buildings in Italy are decorated with equal taste and intelligence.

[8] Garofalo signs some of his pictures, BENVEGNV; others,

Garofalo's fellow-countrymen have called him 'the Ferrarese Raphael,' in the same way that the Milanese have called Luini 'the Lombard Raphael,' and, if properly understood, both appellations have their meaning; for both these painters occupy much the same position in their respective schools as did Raphael in the Umbrian school, Francesco Carotto in the Veronese, Andrea del Sarto in the Florentine, &c., though the individual gifts of each were, of course, very different.

Benvenuto Garofalo died at Ferrara in 1559. His mother's name was not Girolama Soriani, as hitherto stated, but Antonia Barbiani. His wife was Caterina di Ambrogio Scoperti, called della Grana, widow of Niccolò Besuzzi. His youngest son, Girolamo, born in 1536, devoted himself to science, became a distinguished scholar, and was chancellor of the University of Ferrara in 1576. He wrote a biography of Ariosto for the edition of 1584 of the "Orlando Furioso." [9]

I have devoted a good deal of space to Garofalo, and have specified even the most apparently insignificant characteristics in his works. I felt bound to do so, among other reasons, because Dr. Bode refuses to acknowledge that the large "Descent from the Cross," and other pictures, which I hold to be early works of Garofalo, are by the master. Some years ago he ascribed them to Giovanni Battista Benvenuti, called l'Ortolano (ii. 737); later to an anonymous painter whom he calls 'the Master of the Borghese Descent from the Cross.' Vasari certainly has not a word to say about Ortolano, or of this 'Master of the Descent from the Cross,' to whom Dr. Bode ascribes what he terms the 'finest Fer-

BENVEGNV   DE   GAROFALO   again BENVENVTO GAROFALO.
MDXXXV.; others again, BENVEG-          [9] See *Memorie di L. Napoleone*
NV GAROFALO, MDXXXIV., and   *Cittadella*, Ferrara, 1872.

rarese work of that date ; ' nor do any other contemporary writers mention this 'most important Ferrarese painter of the beginning of the sixteenth century.' The lāte Count Laderchi, one of the most careful and intelligent writers on the school of Ferrara, went so far as to doubt the very existence of a painter named Ortolano, and was disposed to regard him as a myth.

What is even of greater weight than Laderchi's personal opinion is the fact that the conscientious keeper of the Ferrara archives, the late Signor Napoleone Cittadella, was unable to discover a single document in which mention was made of the supposed artistic career of Ortolano. According to the latter writer, a painter named Giovan Battista Benvenuti, whose brother was a shoemaker, and his brother-in-law a fruit-seller, was acting as a witness at Ferrara in 1512. In all probability the father was a market gardener ; hence the painter, his son, received the name of ' dell' Ortolano ' (i.e. the son of the market gardener). A few paintings ascribed to him in the second sacristy of the cathedral at Ferrara prove him to have been a weak imitator of Garofalo.[1] Had not the internal evidence of the paintings already convinced me that this splendid "Descent from the Cross," the "Nativity" in the Doria Palace, the two Saints in the Capitol, and the fine work in the English National Gallery, were early works by Garofalo, the proofs I have already brought forward ought to be sufficient to deter anyone from giving them to Ortolano.

I am quite aware that many works by Garofalo were

[1] The following works, corresponding with the panels in the second sacristy of the cathedral, might consequently be attributed to Ortolano : The fresco of the Madonna and Child in the Atrium of the Palazzo Crispi (there given to Girolamo da Carpi) ; the frescoes with half figures of Saints belonging to Cavaliere Santini, formerly in the convent of S. Giorgio ; frescoes with Saints in the Palazzo Massari (formerly in S. Francesco), and the "Annunciation" in the gallery at Ferrara (No. 44).

ascribed to Benvenuti, especially in the last century;
probably only because the signature of Garofalo's Christian
name (Benvegnù) was mistaken for Ortolano's surname.[2]

Except in Rome and Ferrara, Garofalo is not well represented in public collections in Italy. In the Pitti, an
Apostle's head (No. 5, a copy after Dosso) and the pretty
little "Zingarella" by Boccaccio Boccaccino (No. 246)
are attributed to him. There are some good specimens
of his art in the gallery at Modena and in the Brera at
Milan.

## GIOVANNI DI LUTERO, called DOSSO DOSSI.

It is strange that Garofalo is never mentioned by his
great compatriot Ariosto, while the poet in his "Orlando"
(though not earlier certainly than the edition of 1532)
praises the brothers Dossi even above their merits, in those
well-known stanzas in which he ranks them with Leonardo,
Mantegna, Giovanni Bellini, Michael Angelo, Raphael, and
Titian. This may be accounted for by Garofalo's rather
homely character, which had not much attraction for
the poet. Dosso's nature, on the other hand, had many
points in common with that of Ariosto,[3] though in his
works he is occasionally unpolished and even slovenly.
His fantastic and spirited "Circe," in the Borghese
gallery, might be the embodiment of one of Ariosto's

---

[2] It is scarcely necessary to observe that the sketch-book mentioned by Barrufaldi (Vite de' Pittori
&c. i. 168), under the title "Studio
di Me Zoane Bapta dᵉ Benvegnù
fatto in Bologna suxo le dipinture
del Bagnacavallo et del Sanzio da
Urbino a li anni MDVII et MDVIII,"
is in all probability nothing but one
of the many forgeries of so-called
documents, perpetrated at Bologna
in the seventeenth century. How
could Ortolano have seen paintings
by Raphael in Bologna at that date
(1507 and 1508)?

[3] Vasari says of him: 'Fù il
Dosso molto amato dal Duca
Alfonso di Ferrara, prima per le sue
qualità nell' arte della pittura, e poi
per essere uomo affabile molto e
piacevole' (ix. 22).

poems. I have good reason for supposing that it is an early work, painted by him probably in the second decade of the sixteenth century; it may therefore date from about 1516, when the first edition of the "Orlando" was published. Later, no doubt, Dosso produced more important works, which were unsurpassed in splendour of colour; yet I can scarcely recall one—the noble figure of St. George at Modena perhaps excepted—which struck me as being so fresh and full of poetic feeling and charmed me as much as this Enchantress.

In No. 220 of the Borghese gallery, Dosso, and not Garofalo, as the catalogue informs us, has immortalised the nymph Calisto.[4] (†) Here, too, the landscape background is most poetically conceived. There are several other works by Dosso in this collection under different names. In No. 1, Apollo is represented seated on a rock, and endeavouring, by the touching strains of his lyre, to stay the steps of the flying Daphne. (†) The catalogue is too modest to give this poetical but damaged work to Dosso himself, only assigning it to the school of Ferrara. The life-size figure of Apollo is vigorous and full of animation; the landscape is original in treatment and characteristic of the master, as are also the rounded forms of the hand and ear.

No. 22 is a large panel representing life-sized figures of a sick man and his wife imploring relief from SS. Cosmo and Damiano. (†) The catalogue gives this carelessly painted picture to the school of Paul Veronese.[5] It was very likely painted as a sign-board for an apothecary, and Dosso has introduced his name in a quaint fashion on a

[4] Already in the seventeenth and eighteenth centuries many works by Dosso were given to Garofalo, among others those which came to Dresden from Modena.

[5] The two last-named pictures have now, at my suggestion, been attributed to Dosso.

medicine pot, which is inscribed: 'ONTO D . . . .' *i.e.*
Unto D'Osso (bone-fat).

I will now examine a picture in this gallery under Giorgione's name, said to represent Saul and David. The colouring is certainly Giorgionesque. A warrior, fully armed, has near him the head of a giant, and behind him a page wearing a cap with red and white plumes. Whether it really represents Saul and David with the head of Goliath, or some episode from the "Orlando Furioso," is of little consequence. It is decidedly one of Dosso's later, and therefore less powerful, works.[6] (†)

From the researches of the late Signor Cittadella ("Notizie relative a Ferrara," 1864) it appears that Giovanni, son of Niccolò de Lutero, living in the Ducal Palace at Ferrara in 1528, had not then adopted the name of Dosso. It is not to be found in documents previous to 1532, in which year 'J. Nicolai de Lutero' is mentioned as 'Magister Dossus.' All his works signed with a 'D' traversed by a bone belong to his later period (1525–1540): for instance, the little picture of the "Money-changers driven out of the Temple," in the Doria gallery (No. 220). We may infer that this master is not much understood in Rome, as, out of his five paintings in the Borghese gallery, only one is rightly attributed to him.[7] In other

---

[6] Burckhardt mentions this picture as a Giorgione. As the same gifted writer describes the fine St. Sebastian in the Brera—which is unquestionably by Dosso, and not by the brothers Dossi according to Messrs. Crowe and Cavalcaselle—as a good work by Giorgione, he is at least consistent in his opinions. Ridolfi, with his usual uncritical judgment (i. 130), assigns both these pictures by Dosso to Giorgione. Messrs. Crowe and Cavalcaselle (ii. 164) consider that the example in the Borghese gallery betrays the touch of Pietro della Vecchia, more especially in the armour, in the head of Goliath, and in the hands of Saul. This picture was certainly several times *copied* by that painter, and such copies may be seen in the public gallery at Vienna, in that of Padua (No. 531), and elsewhere.

[7] The "Presepio" (No. 217) is not, I think, by Giovanni Dosso, as the catalogue states, but more probably by his brother Battista.

Italian collections, as well as in England and Germany, Dosso fares no better. In the Capitoline gallery several works, which are wholly unworthy of him, bear his name; for example, the feeble portrait of a man (Room I., No. 85) and the "Marriage of the Virgin" (Room I., No. 23), while the large "Holy Family" (Room II., No. 145), by no means one of his most attractive works, and spoilt, moreover, by unskilful cleaning, is given to Giorgione. (†)

In the Doria-Pamfili gallery, besides the small picture above mentioned signed with his monogram, there is a female figure by him conceived quite in Ariosto's vein—a young, handsome, and warlike woman, wearing a red mantle and a diadem on her forehead, and holding a colossal helmet in her hand (No. 549). She probably represents some heroine of the "Orlando Furioso." The following ridiculous description of the picture is given in the catalogue: "Portrait of Catarina, called Vanozza, by Dosso." This Vanozza was the mistress of Cardinal Borgia, afterwards Pope Alexander VI., and the mother of Cesare, Lucrezia, and his other children. She consequently lived about 1470, before Dosso was born. I do not recollect any other painting by the master in Rome, with the exception of the large altar-piece—a Madonna and Saints—in the Palazzo Chigi. There is nothing of importance by him either in the Uffizi or in the Pitti. A St. John the Baptist in the latter collection (No. 380) is by him, and not by Giorgione, as the catalogue informs us; and the portrait of Duke Alfonso (No. 311) is a copy by Dosso from one by Titian, though the catalogue would have us believe that it is the portrait of Charles V. by Titian himself! In what was once Venetian territory, I know of only two works by Dosso— a large and not particularly successful altar-piece in the gallery at Rovigo,[8] and a small composition, most poetically

---

[8] No. 135, ascribed to Garofalo. It represents the Madonna and Child enthroned between five Saints.

treated, in the gallery at Bergamo.[9]   In the Brera, there is
only the **St. Sebastian already** mentioned, formerly attributed to Giorgione.   An **uninteresting** picture in the
Ambrosiana—"Christ Washing the Feet of the Apostles"—
called by Dr. **Bode** (ii. 736) a work **of Dosso's** Roman (?)
period, is certainly not by him, but more probably by some
Flemish eclectic, who borrowed much from Raphael. (†)

Even Ferrara has little to show **of Dosso's art**; only
the large **and fine** altar-piece in the gallery, which **a** fatal
restoration **has** irreparably injured, and possibly the
frescoes (?) in **a** small room of what was once **the Ducal
Palace.   In** Modena, however, there are several excellent
**works by him.**   Nearly all his frescoes in the palace at
Ferrara and in the prince-bishop's castle at Trent **have**
either been destroyed **by fire or by the ravages** of time, or
have perished **through the apathy of** succeeding generations, **while such of his great works** as have come down to
us, damaged and fragmentary as **they are,** have only contributed to increase the fame of other másters—Giorgione,
Parmeggianino, Pordenone, Francesco **Penni** and Garofalo,
each having his share.   Yet **Dosso well deserves** to be
honoured and to be reinstated in his **proper** place.   **Gifted,**
healthy, cheerful, and often brilliant in his **art, no other**
artist approaches his renowned fellow-countryman and
friend Ariosto so closely **as he.**   Occasionally, however,
he allows himself too much licence, is careless **and** even
exaggerated; but no one can ever accuse him of being
coarse **or** commonplace.

Vasari, who is usually intelligent and appreciative in
his biographies, has given **a cursory,** biased and unjust
account of this painter, whom he **never** knew personally.
Two reasons might be assigned **for this:** one because Dosso

---

[9] Lochis collection, No. 218, representing the Madonna, before whom
**kneel** St. George and a bishop.

never saw fit to go to Rome in order to improve his
Ferrarese 'maniera secca'; the other because Vasari's
friend Girolamo Genga, who had been Dosso's rival in the
'Palazzo Imperiale' near Pesaro, most probably prejudiced
the mind of the biographer against him. In the same way
Beccafumi of Siena, another of Vasari's informants, maliciously libelled Sodoma. Vasari has not a word to say,
either about the brilliant and numerous frescoes with
which Dosso, the favourite of Alfonso d'Este, adorned the
palaces of that prince near Ferrara, or of his paintings
in that of the Gonzagas at Mantua. Later biographers
were of course not likely to correct Vasari's errors, or to
supply the deficiencies in his work. Few artists, moreover,
were probably so uncongenial and incomprehensible to succeeding generations as Dosso. Ariosto himself suffered
a similar fate when eclipsed by Tasso. Dosso died in 1541
and not in 1560, as is usually stated, seven years, therefore,
before his brother Battista. According to Cittadella, he
left three daughters. There are several works by Battista
Dosso in the Borghese gallery—one a small "Nativity";
another work by him will be found in the Doria
gallery.

A contemporary of, perhaps a fellow-pupil with, Dosso
in the school of Lorenzo Costa was that 'glow-worm'
among painters, the Ferrarese Lodovico Mazzolino, whose
father, Giovanni, was also an artist. He was principally
a *genre* painter, though in his early period he is said to
have worked much in fresco. His brilliant colouring made
him a favourite with art-loving prelates of succeeding
generations; hence his small pictures abound in Roman
collections. There are three in the Borghese gallery:
No. 218—an "Adoration of the Magi"—is clear and bright
in colour, and has a fine architectural background. In this
picture Mazzolino is less mannered than usual.

There are two paintings by Scarsellino yet to be mentioned—" Diana bathing " and " Venus emerging from the Bath "—and I have now, I think, touched upon most of the Ferrarese works in the Borghese gallery. But I must devote a few words to the world-renowned " Danae " by Correggio.

The unjust and superficial treatment accorded to Dosso is only an example of the way in which all the Ferrarese painters have been dealt with. A study of this interesting and vigorous school of painting, and an unprejudiced examination of its organic development, will prove that it was of far more importance in the second half of the fifteenth century than is generally allowed. Its three principal representatives at that time were Cosimo Tura, called Cosmè, a dry, angular, but serious painter ; Francesco Cossa or del Cossa,[1] naïve, vigorous, and attractive, notwithstanding his occasional tendency to moroseness ; and Ercole Roberti. The first of the three lived and worked entirely in his native city. To his school may have belonged Francesco Bianchi—surnamed in Modena, where he settled, Frarè (the Ferrarese) [2]—Domenico Panetti, and Lorenzo Costa.

Francesco Cossa left the court of Duke Borso in 1470, and settled at Bologna, where he died in his prime ;—not towards the close of the century, as I was once led to

[1] Most of Cossa's works in Italy pass under the name of Lorenzo Costa, with whom even Vasari confounded him. For instance, the fine seated figure of St. Jerome in the church of S. Petronio, at Bologna ; the standing figures of the twelve Apostles in the Marsilj chapel in the same church, probably executed after the master's death by one of his pupils from his cartoons, and the two painted windows in S. Gio-

vanni in Monte. Cossa's few paintings out of Italy are mostly given either to Mantegna or to Marco Zoppo.

[2] Many think his name was Bianchi-Ferrari ; but why should he have had two surnames ? As far as I know, the surname Ferrari never becomes *Frarè*, even in the Modenese dialect. It is, however, of no real importance where he was born ; as an artist he belongs to the school of Ferrara.

believe, but soon after 1480.[3] It was probably to him and his assistant at Bologna, Ercole Roberti, that Costa was indebted for his summons to that city. About 1483, while still a youth, he left Ferrara for the court of the Bentivoglios, and here he later formed a brilliant school, though Francesco Francia usually has the credit of being its founder. I am, however, quite convinced that, not only were Chiodarolo, Cesare Tamarozzo,[4] and others the pupils of Costa, but that even Francia, who in 1488 had attained great proficiency as a goldsmith, learnt painting from that artist, who was his friend. Costa's paintings of 1488 in the Bentivoglio chapel, and of 1506 in the chapel of S. Cecilia, decidedly recall Ercole Roberti, but do not show a trace of Francia's influence ; while, on the other hand, Francia's earliest works—for instance, the small "Crucifixion" (†) (in the library of the Archiginnasio [5]) and the altar-piece of 1494 in the public gallery—remind us very distinctly of Costa, both in tone and in many other particulars. I am quite willing to admit that Francia, eminent in plastic art, may have exercised a beneficial influence over the Ferrarese painter. I do not deny that he had a more refined feeling for line and greater anatomical knowledge, and that he was able, especially in his early works, to impart more depth and nobility of expression to his heads, than Costa—as, for example, in his "St. Stephen" in the

[3] Cosimo Tura, on the other hand, did not die in 1469, as usually supposed, but after 1495—a fact discovered by Cittadella.

[4] There are two frescoes by Cesare Tamarozzo in the chapel of S. Cecilia attached to the church of S. Jacopo Maggiore, wrongly ascribed by some to Giacomo Francia; also a fresco in the church of the "Misericordia" at Bologna—St. Augustine with some brothers of his Order (†)—and a Madonna and Child in the Poldi-Pezzoli collection at Milan inscribed with his name.

[5] Formerly attributed to Lorenzo Costa ; some ascribe it to Ercole Grandi di Giulio Cesare. Dr. Bode has, however, accepted my opinion of the picture, and assigns it to Francia's early period.

Borghese gallery. Costa, however, undoubtedly handled his brush with greater freedom and power. More fiery and excitable by nature, he was also more richly endowed with those gifts which characterise a great artist. Yet, while Cossa, Ercole Roberti,[6] and principally Costa must be regarded as the real founders of that school which flourished at Bologna in the last twenty years of the fifteenth and in the beginning of the sixteenth century, the influence of Dosso and Garofalo is also unmistakable in the early works of Bagnacavallo, Niccolò Pisani,[7] Biagio Puppini, and later even in those of Giacomo and Giulio Francia. In a word, it was the school of Ferrara which influenced the whole province of Romagna from about 1470 to 1520. I might have spared my readers these introductory remarks; but, as we are about to discuss Correggio's " Danae," I felt tempted to summarise in a few words my views upon a question in the history of Italian art, on which great confusion of opinion still exists—namely, as to the early years of Antonio Allegri da Correggio.[8]

[6] Amico, and not Guido, Aspertini, as stated by Vasari, was probably Roberti's pupil.

[7] An early work by him—a Pietà—is in the gallery at Bologna, signed 'Nicholo' and falsely ascribed to Niccolò Soriani; a later work by him is in the Brera; in the latter he appears as an imitator of Garofalo.

[8] Some interesting articles on the Italian pictures in the Berlin gallery have been contributed to the *Gazette des Beaux-Arts* by Dr. Bode. In one of them he observes: 'A. Venturi, dont les recherches ont posé les fondements de la connaissance des écoles de Ferrare, de Bologne et de Modène' (see No. V. February 1, 1889, p. 118). Signor Venturi is a young and promising writer, and I would not for a moment wish to depreciate the value of his researches, but the fact has, I think, escaped Dr. Bode's memory, that in 1875 and 1876, when I first published my articles on the schools of Ferrara and Bologna, information as to the history of both these schools was almost nil; a fact to which he himself testified in his edition of the *Cicerone* of 1879 (ii. 579-587). It was Signor Venturi indeed who succeeded in discovering the true author of the large painting in the Brera, which before had always passed as the work of an otherwise unknown painter, Stefano da Ferrara. In an old guide-book he found that before it reached

Writers on this subject, following Vedriani, allege that Correggio was first apprenticed to Francesco Bianchi at Modena, that on the death of that master in 1510 he went to Mantua in order to continue his studies under the great Andrea Mantegna ; and that in 1514 (in about his twentieth year) he was commissioned by the monks of Carpi to execute the altar-piece now at Dresden, in which conse- quently most critics plainly discern the influence of Mantegna, his master. The discovery, made later, that Mantegna died in 1506, told rather against this theory ; but the difficulty was ingeniously surmounted by assuming that one of Mantegna's sons, Francesco or Lodovico, must have become the guide and instructor of the young Correggio. Some frescoes, said to be still discernible at Mantua, in which every expert is expected to recognise the hand of Correggio, were supposed to corroborate this view and the theory of his sojourn in that city. The whole tale, however, is a mere supposition on the part of Vedriani. Not a single painting, still less any document, vouches for it ; but as it flattered the local patriotism of the Mantuans, it rapidly grew into a 'tradition.' Viewing the matter without any bias, I should say that the Dresden picture may have been completed by Correggio in 1515. As he was born in the

Milan, the altar-piece was in a church near Ravenna, and there had been attributed to one Ercole da Ferrara. On closer examination, the painting proved to be by Ercole Roberti. To Signor Venturi, again, we owe the discovery of many important documents which throw fresh light upon the painters of Ferrara, Bologna, and Modena. But when it came to defining the real connection between the early school of Bologna and that of Ferrara, to pointing out the importance of Francesco Cossa and Lorenzo Costa in that school, which was previously known as 'the school of Marco Zoppo and Francia,' and to tracing the development of Garofalo, Dosso Dossi, and Correggio, I fancy that I was in the field a little before either Dr. Bode or Signor Venturi. I trust my readers will pardon these few explanatory words, written not for self-laudation but in self-defence. An Italian proverb says: 'Chi pecora si fa il lupo lo mangia.' (He who makes himself a lamb is eaten by the wolf.)

last months of 1493, or in the first of the following year, he must have been about twenty-one when he delivered over his finished work to the monks, not of Carpi but of Correggio.   In those golden days of art, a painter had usually served his apprenticeship and mastered the technical and other difficulties of his work by his fifteenth or sixteenth year; and a nature so highly gifted as that of Correggio would naturally ripen early.   It may be therefore assumed that he had produced, prior to 1514, pictures of merit which had established his reputation, and had procured for him the flattering order from the monks of Correggio.

On examining this picture critically, we shall find that in the harmony and treatment of colours, and in the architectural form of the throne with its characteristic medallion in chiaroscuro, the influence of Costa and the school of Ferrara is more apparent than that of Mantegna.   Lord Ashburton's fine Correggio supports this view even more decisively, and those who doubt the genuineness of this picture show, I think, little knowledge of the distinctive characteristics of the master in conception and representation.

As a rule, indeed, writers on art are wont to form their opinion of a painter's mode of expression and of his character from his later works.   Hence those who judge Correggio from the " Notte " or the " St. George " in the Dresden gallery, or from the so-called " St. Jerome " at Parma, would naturally hesitate to recognise the same hand in Lord Ashburton's picture.   Yet, in both Correggio's early works—the " St. Francis " in Dresden and Lord Ashburton's picture—we already find indications of those qualities which partly attract and partly repel us in his later pictures.   The same forms, the same feeling in the treatment of the hands, and the same type of ear and arrangement of drapery, are apparent in them; only the colouring is different in his early works, both in tone and in harmony, and recalls Costa and his school. Lord Ashburton's picture appears to me earlier than the one at Dresden of 1515; the so-called "Flight into Egypt" in the Tribune of the Uffizi some years later—about 1517–1518. The tone in the latter is still wholly Ferrarese, but recalls not Costa and Ercole Grandi di Giulio Cesare, but rather Dosso and Garofalo. For the light straw-colour of St. Joseph's robe these two painters had a special predilection. In the Uffizi, in the room on the right of the Tribune, there is a small picture (No. 1002) which was formerly assigned to the Ferrarese school, and has lately been unhesitatingly ascribed to Titian. It represents the Madonna and Child, with two angels playing on musical instruments. The forms, especially those of the hand and ear, and the folds of the drapery (leaving the luminous colouring so distinctive of Correggio altogether out of the question) testify to the manner and the feeling of this master. The expression of the Madonna, of the Child, and notably of the angel on her right, confirms this view even more strikingly than do the outward forms, while the angel on the left reminds us more of early works by Giorgione and Titian.

I look upon this most interesting little picture, which has received but scant notice hitherto, as an early Correggio, produced under the influence of works by Giorgione, Titian, and Lotto. (†) For I have no doubt that, before settling at Parma, Correggio was in Venice, and must there have seen and studied many works by the great colourists of the Venetian school. To prove my theories yet more fully I should have liked to describe a little picture, formerly in the Costabili gallery at Ferrara, and recently acquired by Dr. Frizzoni. But as I am aware that the owner intends shortly to publish some account of it, as well as of several other early works by Correggio, I shall refrain from dwelling upon it here. It represents the "Marriage of St. Catherine," and the Ferrarese character of the colouring is so decided that several northern *amateurs* took it for a work of Mazzolino.

It matters little where Correggio learnt the technic of his art—whether from Francesco Bianchi at Modena, from Lorenzo Costa at Mantua, or at Ferrara itself, and whether he developed his knowledge later on by studying the works of Venetian painters. The point that I wish to prove is that he has nothing to do with the school of Andrea Mantegna, but belongs wholly and undeniably to that of Ferrara.[9] This is not the place to go further into the subject, but I trust that those who have made a conscientious study of Italian art in every stage of its development will be disposed to accept my views.

Let us now turn to the master's exquisite "Danae," a picture which has experienced many vicissitudes. From Italy it passed to Spain, whence it returned to Lombardy. Between 1580–1590 Lomazzo mentioned it as being at Milan, in the house of the sculptor Leoni Aretino. 'Danae e Giove che gli piove in grembo in forma di pioggia d'oro, con Cupido ed altri amori, co' lumi talmente intesi, che tengo sicuro, che niun altro pittore in colorire ed allumare possa agguagliargli; mandato di Spagna da Pompeo suo figlio statuario.' From Milan it went to the Emperor Rudolph at Prague, and thence for certain political reasons found its way to Stockholm. After enduring the hardships of that polar clime, poor "Danae" wandered southwards again, first to Paris, later to London, and then back again

---

[9] Correggio may have copied one or other of Mantegna's figures at Mantua, but this in no way tells against my theory.

to the former city. Here, as the picture then passed for a copy, Prince Borghese fortunately succeeded in obtaining it for a nominal price in the third decade of this century, and so, after two centuries and a half, " Danae " was once more restored to her own sunny southern home. Who knows where this much-travelled lady will find herself at the close of this century ? The picture has, of course, suffered severely from these repeated wanderings ; fortunately, however, it has escaped the fatal 'restorations' which have nearly deprived the much-extolled Correggios at Dresden, with the exception perhaps of the " St. Francis," of all their charm. The surface glazings have disappeared, but it is still perhaps the most ' Correggiesque ' work of Correggio, and a triumph of aerial perspective and chiaroscuro, as Mr. Mündler very justly observed. The representation of the naïve childlike manner in which the little Cupids busy themselves with sharpening their arrows, the somewhat startled, timid, yet unresisting air of Danae, and at the same time the sensuous bliss which thrills every fibre of her frame, have never, I think, been surpassed in painting. People of severe taste and austere morals may take exception to her artless undisguised expression of joy as being too sensual ; and I quite admit that Correggio's art in this picture narrowly escapes censure. It was painted for the Duke of Mantua, and according to Vasari, Giulio Romano declared that he knew no other picture to equal it. As to the consummate manner in which the artist has dealt with his subject, it is so true, so human, so chaste in the truest sense of the word, so far removed from the immoral prudery of the present day, that I may safely say I know no modern work which, in this respect, is more worthy to be ranked with Greek art. Needless to observe, however, that it is not exactly suited to adorn the walls of a girls' school. It is one of the gems of the gallery, and certainly the only

genuine Correggio in Rome,[1] for the exaggerated figure
called "Christ in Glory," assigned to him in the Vatican
gallery, is probably by some feeble imitator of the later
Bolognese school.   The "Danae," it is hardly necessary to
say, is on canvas, and not, like the much vaunted
"Magdalen" in the Dresden gallery, on copper. (†)
Painting on copper was first introduced into Italy by the
Flemings towards the close of the sixteenth century, but did
not meet with much favour.[2]

We must now leave this 'coarsely sensual' figure of
Correggio, as the "Danae" has been termed by an otherwise
highly-cultured German writer, and turn to the following
rooms, where we shall find Potiphar's wife variously
portrayed by several highly moral painters of the sixteenth
and seventeenth centuries, to the edification of the 'Lent
preachers' of art.   Admirers of art of this sort must seek
it out for themselves; it does not come within the range
of our present studies.   Works by the eclectics are of little
importance for them, although they have a certain interest
for the history of art and culture, and the public at large
find them far more attractive than those we have been discussing.   The finest work here of this class is undoubtedly
Domenichino's celebrated "Caccia di Diana"—a charming
picture which is worthy of a purer period of art.   Full of
cheerful animation and naïve and delightful details, it cannot fail to please.   With the exception of Guido's "Aurora,"
Caracci's frescoes in the Palazzo Farnese, and those of

---

[1] The Madonna belonging to
Prince Torlonia (Lungara) and the
one at St. Petersburg are merely
copies of the original in the Esterhazy gallery at Buda-Pesth. (†)

[2] As far as I know, it was not
till the second half of the sixteenth
century that Flemish artists, such
as Brill, Jan Brueghel the elder,
Pourbus, and others, painted on
copper.   I know of no Italian
painting of the first half of that
century which is on this material;
though I have come across many
later copies which pass for originals.

Guercino in the Casino Ludovisi, I know of no work of the seventeenth century which is so deserving of the popularity it enjoys. With it are hung Albani's " Seasons "—four good decorative works—and a large Madonna and Child (No. 110), by that unpleasing but remarkably able artist, Michael Angelo da Caravaggio.

In the gallery are some fragments of frescoes by three different painters. Those representing the history of Apollo and Marsyas are by Domenichino and came from the Villa Borghese at Frascati (*); the episodes from Roman history were formerly in the Villa Lante on the Janiculum, and have been ascribed by recent writers to Giulio Romano (*).[3] The Villa was built by this artist, and the frescoes were executed by his pupils and assistants, Pappacello, Pagni, and others, which explains the Raphaelesque feeling perceptible in them.

The remaining frescoes were ascribed by Passavant to Perino del Vaga,[4] by others to Raphael himself. They were in the ' Casino di Raffaello ' on the Pincio, till its destruction in 1849. One represents a group of archers, and another the " Marriage of Alexander and Roxana." Both are copies, I consider, by some late and feeble imitator of Raphael. The " Archers " are from a drawing at Windsor attributed to Michael Angelo. The " Marriage of Alexander " is taken from an engraving by Caraglio or, according to some authorities, by Bonasone,[5] executed from a drawing in indian ink made for the purpose by Perino del Vaga. (+)

---

[3] Passavant, *Raffael d'Urbin*, &c. i. 233. 'L'originalité grandiose de Jules Romain ressort aussi dans les petites fresques de la Villa Lante ; ce sont des sujets tirés des légendes et de l'histoire romaine qui se rapporte au Janicule,' &c.

[4] Passavant (ibid. ii. 236).

' L'exécution de cette fresque, en bon état de conservation, est traitée avec toute la délicatesse particulière (?) à Perino del Vaga.'

[5] P. J. Mariette (*Abecedario*, i. 89) mentions two engravings of this subject, one by Caraglio, the other by the elder Béatricet.

Vasari tells us (ix. 275) that, among Marcantonio's scholars, two were especially distinguished, namely Marco da Ravenna and Agostino Veneziano, and that both worked from Raphael's drawings.   In his casual manner, he mentions among Agostino's engravings the one representing the marriage of Alexander: 'Fece ancora Alessandro con Rosana, a cui gli presenta una corona reale.'   This careless statement gave rise to the grave and oft-repeated error, which extended to every drawing and sketch connected with Sodoma's fresco.   Only Raphael could have been their author, and poor Sodoma merely got the credit of having executed his splendid fresco from Raphael's designs.   In all this there is not, I am persuaded, a word of truth, and once more we are reminded of that significant parable, which was so admirably depicted by Brueghel in his painting in the Naples Museum.   Want of imagination was certainly not one of Sodoma's faults, whatever his other failings may have been.   This every unprejudiced student of his frescoes at Mont' Oliveto, and in the churches of S. Bernardino and S. Domenico at Siena, must admit. In addition to certain technical characteristics distinctive of the master, the well-known red chalk drawing[6] in the

The indian ink drawing for the engraving was at that time in the Crozat collection, and appears to be identical with the one mentioned by L. Dolce as by the hand of Raphael (bistre heightened with white), inscribed: 'Raffaello da Urbino.' This drawing, now in a portfolio in the Louvre, appears to me to be nothing but the *copy* of Perino's lost original. Mariette pronounced it to be by Parmegianino and so also did Zanetti. The Abbé Marolle, on the other hand, thought it was undoubtedly by Raphael, while M. Montaiglon and the Marquis de Chennevières pronounced it to be of the school of Raphael.

[6] Many of Sodoma's characteristics are apparent in this drawing — the right knee of Roxana is full and round, and resembles in treatment that in the drawings for Leda at Weimar and Chatsworth, falsely ascribed to Leonardo da Vinci (Braun 148 and 51); the big toe is of undue prominence; the form of hand and ear, the type of the children (distinctive of this master), the treatment of the hair — are all characteristic; so too is the

Albertina shows all the defects of composition that we find in Sodoma's fresco of the "Family of Darius before Alexander," and in this instance critics, so far as I know, have never doubted that both design and execution were by him. Four drawings by Sodoma for the "Marriage of Alexander" exist: the fine example in red chalk in the Albertina at Vienna (†);[7] the pen and ink sketch in the Uffizi (Case 495, No. 1479); a pen drawing in the Esterhazy collection at Buda-Pesth (†), representing Roxana as a nude standing figure, which Herr von Pulsky describes as a drawing by Raphael, in his article on the "Hungarian National Gallery" (p. 41–47); and a pen drawing for the couch of Roxana (†) in the University galleries at Oxford (Robinson's catalogue, No. 177, p. 311).

The first, third, and fourth of these drawings are attributed to Raphael. The sketch in Florence, formerly assigned to a pupil of Raphael, has recently been restored to Sodoma, accompanied by the extraordinary remark that it represents a part of the fresco which Sodoma executed in the Farnesina *from a drawing by Raphael.* This statement is doubly incorrect, for Sodoma executed his fresco with considerable modifications from the drawing now in the Albertina, and were the fine sketch in Florence

fine shading with the pen, differing wholly from the method employed by Raphael.

[7] Mariette remarks of this red chalk drawing: 'J'y reconnais tout le faire de Raphael; les expressions en sont bien plus fines (than in the other drawing which, as we have seen, he ascribes to Parmeggianino) et le détail en est excellent. Raphael le dût faire pour lui servir d'étude et de préparation au dessin drappé.' After passing through various other collections, this drawing finally came to the Albertina, and, of course, as a Raphael. Passavant (ii. 441) describes it in the following terms: 'Ce dessin que Rubens avait acheté à Rome, passa depuis dans la possession du Cardinal Bentivoglio, qui en fit présent au graveur en médailles Mélan. Crozat l'eut ensuite au sortir de la collection Vanrose, et le Duc Albert de Saxe-Teschen l'acquit d'un amateur. Il porte aussi l'estampille du prince Charles de Ligne. Toutes les figures sont nues et de la plus délicate exécution à la sanguine.'

a *copy*, it would have been taken, not from the fresco, but from the Albertina drawing.

Several years after the death of Raphael, the engraver of the "Marriage of Alexander" (whether Caraglio or Bonasone) may have applied to Perino del Vaga to make a drawing of the subject for him, for purposes of engraving. Two such drawings, recalling Perino's technic, have come down to us; the better of the two is in the Louvre; a very inferior one is at Windsor.[8] This, it appears to me, is the explanation of the confusion which has occurred.

Whether Perino's original drawing still exists, and, if so, where, I am unable to say. The two copies of it made use of by the engraver, as well as the engraving itself, reproduced the composition as we see it in the red chalk drawing in the Albertina, but not as it is in the fresco. Hence it follows that Perino copied this drawing and not the fresco, making slight alterations, such as adding drapery about Roxana's hips, and clothing Alexander and giving him a helmet.[9] One thing is, I think, beyond question, namely, that the four drawings having reference to the fresco are by Sodoma himself. (†)

The knowledge of original drawings may be said to be still in its infancy. It is only of late years that English, German, and Italian critics have applied themselves to the study of Raphael, and more especially to a careful examination of his early works. By this means the personality of the painter has been made clearer to us and has certainly gained by the process. The results of these critical studies

---

[8] Passavant is also of this opinion (ii. 493) : 'Les noces d'Alexandre et de Roxane : figures vêtues, dessin à la plume, et rehaussé de blanc. On connaît plusieurs esquisses de cette belle composition, mais dont aucune est l'original.'

[9] The form of this helmet should be compared with that of the helmet of the warrior on the extreme right in Perino's drawing in the Louvre (Braun 71).

greatly irritated the orthodox, who discharged their
harmless missiles against those who propagated these new
theories. But the storm gradually abated, and truth was
triumphant, regardless of the havoc she had wrought among
cherished traditions. As to the public, it made merry over
the discomfiture of gallery-directors and others, and was
disposed to doubt their infallibility and fitness for their posts.
As new combatants are constantly entering the lists, it
is to be hoped that these vexed questions may ere long be
satisfactorily settled.

I will now enumerate the drawings in the Uffizi which
I believe to be by Raphael, as well as those unworthy of
his name. This may, I trust, be an aid to students, and
afford them some instruction.

The following are *genuine* in my opinion :

No. 496. A Sketch.

No. 497. A Madonna.

No. 505. Madonna del Granduca.

No. 529. ⎫ St. George on horseback in combat with the
No. 530. ⎭ dragon.

No. 538. " The Entombment "—the sketch for the
picture in the Borghese gallery. This drawing was executed by another hand, but Raphael himself corrected it
in several places with the pen.

No. 539. Madonna and Child—for the unfinished painting at Buda-Pesth.

No. 541. " Adam "—for the " Disputa."

In the portfolio are two of Raphael's most splendid
black chalk drawings merely labelled " Umbrian School "—
one an executioner from the " Massacre of the Innocents,"
the other the " St. Stephen " of the " Disputa."

In all ten genuine drawings.

R

The following are wrongly ascribed to Raphael :

No. 531.

No. 509.⎫
⎬ Perino del Vaga.
No. 510.⎭

No. 514. Giulio Romano.

No. 525. Perino del Vaga.

No. 521.⎫
⎪
·No. 545.⎪
⎪
No. 544.⎬ Giulio Romano.
No. 543.⎪
⎪
No. 534.⎪
⎪
No. 535.⎭

No. 520. Enea Silvio Piccolomini going to the Cou
      of Basle—by Pintoricchio.

No. 57.   Timoteo Viti.

No. 540.⎫
⎬ Copy after Raphael.
No. 515.⎭

No. 516. By some Florentine master.

No. 524. Copy.

No. 498. Forgery.

No. 499.⎫
⎬ Imitations.
No. 500.⎭

No. 501. Forgery.

No. 504. School of Perugino.


## THE VENETIANS.

As I propose discussing the Venetian school more fully
when speaking of the Doria gallery, I shall content myself
now with mentioning those pictures in the Borghese gallery,
as to the authenticity of which I cannot always agree with
the compilers of the catalogue.

A male portrait (No. 97) is ascribed to Giovan Battista
Moroni of Albino. This Bergamasque pupil of Moretto—

the Brescian artist famed for his silvery colouring—was a very different person from the author of this uninteresting portrait, which does not even belong to the Venetian school. We will therefore pass on without further delay to a fine picture by Titian (No. 170) which has unfortunately been retouched in parts. According to the catalogue it represents the three Graces (?). Ridolfi mentions it as belonging in his day to the Borghese family. It is a magnificent piece of colouring and probably of the painter's maturest period. There is a fine though modified copy in the Palazzo Balbi at Genoa, and several other versions of it are in existence.

A small painting (No. 167), " St. Cecilia and her husband Valerian," is more probably by Domenico Feti (†) than by Paul Veronese, to whom the catalogue ascribes it. In this picture Feti sought to copy Veronese, as in a picture in the Sciarra-Colonna gallery he endeavoured to imitate Schidone. No. 185 is a fine and striking life-sized male portrait on canvas; although unprepossessing, and even common-place, in appearance, the subtle power of the artist succeeds in riveting our attention on this young man. He is clad in deep mourning, the lustre of his eye is dimmed by grief, for he seems to be brooding over the loss of one dear to him; his left hand rests on a table on which is an ivory skull, half hidden by jessamine and rose-leaves. These accessories tell a sad significant tale—even that death came upon her in the fulness of her youth and innocency ! In the beautiful landscape background St. George is seen slaying the dragon. The catalogue ascribes this portrait to Giovan Antonio da Pordenone,[1] but the late Mr. Mündler[2] gave it to its true author, Lorenzo Lotto. In the treatment of the hands, in the pose and movement of the head, which is quite

[1] Recently ascribed to Lotto by the new director.

[2] *Beiträge zu J. Burckhardt's Cicerone*, p. 58.

peculiar to Lotto, in the marvellous play of light on the drapery, and in the landscape, every characteristic of this gifted and original contemporary and fellow-countryman of Giorgione—his whole "tournure de l'esprit," in fact—is strikingly apparent.

An exquisite early work by the master is also in this gallery (No. 193), inscribed: LAVREN. LOTVS. M . D . VIII. It represents the Madonna, somewhat woebegone in appearance, holding the Infant Saviour ; on her right is a Bishop, on her left the venerable form of St. Onophrius. The Child wears a little shirt, hence probably the picture was painted for a nunnery either in Rome or in the March of Ancona, where Lotto was employed for some time. The dress of the Madonna is scarlet—a shade which Lotto's contemporaries Giorgione, Titian, Palma, and others never used, but which is found in the paintings of older Venetian masters—of Boccaccio Boccaccino, Marco Marziale, Lattanzio da Rimini, Rondinelli, and others. The scale of colour is original and characteristic of Lotto, and the movement of the Child is very naïve. In his later works Lotto often exaggerated his tendency to restless and impetuous gestures as seen in this Child, which then degenerates into affectation. The Madonna wears a greyish yellow drapery about her head and shoulders—a favourite shade with Titian in his early period, and sometimes with Palma. She looks towards St. Onophrius,[3] while the Child stretches out both hands to receive the heart offered him by the Bishop with an expression of devotion combined with a certain monkish moroseness. The drapery is hard and angular, but even in this early work we can trace that tendency to ample folds which later became characteristic of this attractive master. The right hand is treated quite in the manner of Bellini ;

[3] The head of this Saint recalls Dürer; it is not unlikely that both painters worked from the same Venetian model.

the lights are sharp and cold, the colouring is brilliant, the drawing very careful, the execution finished, and the whole evidently a labour of love. The expression of the two Saints is earnest and true to nature. They seem entirely taken up with what they are engaged in, and wholly regardless of the spectator. The late Professor Thausing justly observes, in his 'Life of Dürer,' that this St. Onophrius recalls that painter. Lotto, very likely, knew the German master in Venice in 1506, and may have studied the works produced by him in that city. Examples of this period of Lotto's career may be seen in the museum at Naples, in the parish church at Asolo, in the church of the Dominicans at Recanati, in the Munich gallery, and in the Bridgewater collection.

Lotto is an artist of much refinement, and was gifted with a lively imagination. His merits have hardly yet been sufficiently recognised ; to be adequately appreciated he should be studied in Venice and in the province of Bergamo. The Uffizi contains a Madonna and Child by him—not a favourable specimen of his art—and the Brera three splendid portraits. In the Borghese gallery there is a large picture (No. 157) vividly recalling the master, and apparently a good contemporary copy of some lost work by Lotto. The authorities formerly assigned it to the Venetian school, and they have not since improved matters by giving it to Previtali. It represents the Madonna beneath an orange tree, seated on a throne,the base of which is decorated with reliefs in chiaroscuro after the manner of Correggio. She holds the Child, whose movement is quite Correggiesque, with her right hand, whilst she blesses with her left the kneeling donor and his wife, presented to her by SS. Justina and Barbara. White drapery falls from her head about her shoulders, after the manner of Giovanni Bellini ; her mantle is sky-blue, lined with yellow, her dress of that shade of pinkish-red often employed by Catena. The landscape background resembles that in Lotto's altar-piece of 1506 at Asolo. On the ground, between the kneeling donors, lies an orange, and some rose-leaves are scattered about quite after the manner of Lotto. The portrait of the female donor is masterly in drawing and is painted with consummate skill. The original must certainly have been by Lotto, but I am unable to name the author of this fine copy, which has great merit. It is decidedly not 'a genuine Cariani,' as Messrs. Crowe and Cavalcaselle (ii. 553, note 1) appear to think.

The "Preaching of St. John the Baptist," a large picture (No. 137), fails to touch us, though it is the work of a good Veronese fresco painter, Battista Zelotti (†), a compatriot and fellow-worker of Paul Veronese, to whom the catalogue ascribes it.[4] Near it is a "St. Dominick" by Titian (No. 188). Ridolfi says of it that it belonged to one Gamberato: 'Fece il ritratto del suo confessore dell' ordine dei Predicatori; era tra le cose del Gamberato.' A good portrait of an old man with a white beard and a black cap, occupied in the agreeable task of counting his money (∗), is attributed by the catalogue to Giacomo da Ponte, but I am more disposed to regard it as an excellent work by his son, Francesco Bassano. (†) A feeble "Venus and Cupid" (No. 124), very erroneously given to Paul Veronese, is merely, I think, a copy after him.

We now come to one of the masterpieces of the gallery,

---

[4] The works of Zelotti and Paul Veronese are often confounded by amateurs. For instance, even in the public gallery of Verona (No. 277), an allegorical fresco of music by Zelotti is attributed to Veronese, and so too is the "Annunciation" in the Uffizi (No. 579), which was produced about the same time as this "Preaching of St. John the Baptist." It is to be hoped that Dr. J. P. Richter, the most competent connoisseur of the school of Verona, will shortly publish his views with respect to this painter and to the Veronese school in general.

Titian's "Sacred and Profane Love," which may be reckoned among the most celebrated pictures in the world. It was painted, if I mistake not, between 1510–1512, and is conceived quite in the spirit of Giorgione. It is an exquisite allegorical romance, with the most poetic landscape imaginable. Compared with the landscapes of contemporary Flemish artists—of Hendrik Bles, Mabuse, or Patinir, whom Dürer called the 'good landscape painter' in his "Diary of a Journey to the Netherlands" (p. 118)—we see how totally the Italians differed from the Flemings even in this branch of art.

The "Three Ages," in the Bridgewater Gallery, of which there is one copy in this collection, and another in the Doria gallery, belongs in all probability to the same golden epoch of the master's career. The face of the figure representing "Earthly Love" has been clumsily restored on the right side;[5] on the whole, however, this 'dream of beauty' is fairly well preserved. The long closely-disposed folds of the drapery involuntarily recall a fimilar arrangement of the folds of Salome's mantle, in another and no less beautiful work of Titian's early period in the Doria gallery, which was formerly ascribed to Giorgione, but is now catalogued and universally known as Pordenone's "Herodias."[6] The hair is similarly treated in both these pictures. It is strange that Vasari should make no mention of the magnificent work in the Borghese gallery. Ridolfi (1650), who never saw the picture, and described it merely from hearsay, refers to it as follows—'in Prince Borghese's possession is a painting of two women at a well, in which a child is reflected.'

[5] In this picture of Titian's, I would call attention to the right hand of the figure of "Sacred Love,' in which the ball of the thumb is too strongly developed. This is characteristic of the master.

[6] To my surprise, Dr. Bode agrees with me about this picture (ii. 738).

On a small picture of the Madonna and Child (No. 176) is a 'Cartellino' with : *Ioannes bellinus faciebat,* which has not the character of Giovanni Bellini's genuine signature.[7]   The picture has little merit and is only by some pupil or imitator of the master ; I should be most inclined to ascribe it to Francesco Bissolo. (†)   Messrs. Crowe and Cavalcaselle, however (i. 193), regard it as a genuine work by Bellini.[8]

No. 127, the "Trinity," is a large finely-coloured painting attested by the signature of its author, Francesco Bassano.   No. 241, the so-called "Birth of a Nobleman's Child," is not Venetian as the catalogue states, but a copy of a picture in the Pitti (No. 394) by Scarsellino of Ferrara.   It is scarcely necessary to add that Nos. 91, 10, 89, 168, 228, and 315 are all spurious productions.   A picture representing "St. Anthony of Padua preaching to the Fishes," when, according to the legend, the people of Rimini refused to hear him, is given to Paul Veronese, but is more likely a work of his school.

No. 106 represents "Lucretia" about to plunge a dagger into her breast—a fully-developed and strongly-built woman, with fair hair flowing over her shoulders.   Her expression is far too tame and indifferent for so tragic a moment.   The picture appears to have been painted from life ; and the

[7] There are several examples of these forged signatures on paintings by Bellini's scholars and imitators— for instance, No. 755, in the gallery at Padua ; on a Pietà in that of Bergamo (Lochis collection) ; on one in the Poldi-Pezzoli collection at Milan, and elsewhere. Dr. Bode, following Messrs. Crowe and Cavalcaselle, looks upon all these feeble productions as by Giovanni Bellini himself (ii. 634).

[8] Bellini's original was also copied by Rocco Marconi, but on a larger scale than by Bissolo. Marconi was honest, however, and signed the picture with his own name ; in 1888 it was in the possession of the well-known dealer Guggenheim, at Venice. Giulio Campagnola, of Padua, appears also to have copied many of Giovanni Bellini's pictures (see *Archivio Storico dell' Arte*, Fasc. v. 184).

catalogue rightly assigns it to the school of Titian.[9]  I consider it to be unquestionably by Palma Vecchio, (†) and of that period when he was closely connected with Lorenzo Lotto (1510–1514).

Another " Lucretia," belonging to a much later period of Palma's career, is in the Uffizi, and is probably the portrait of some coarse, unattractive Venetian woman, and a model he employed for other pictures.  This Bergamasque painter did not excel in depicting passionate emotion, and he was never successful in treating this subject, though he attempted it three times—the third example being in the Vienna gallery.  No 119, " Venus with Cupid and a Satyr," ascribed to the school of Titian, appears to me to be an inferior copy after Paris Bordone.  Three large pictures, Nos. 156, 186, and 149, are given to one painter, Bonifazio Veneziano.  No. 156 represents the mother of Zebedee's children bringing her sons to Christ, and appears to me to be the work of the elder Bonifazio Veronese.  It is in much need of cleaning, but the colour is still fine.  No. 186 represents the " Return of the Prodigal Son," and I should ascribe it to Bonifazio Veronese the younger.  No. 149, " The Woman taken in Adultery " is either a feeble work of the school, or an old copy.  The late Mr. Mündler, in his edition of Burckhardt's " Cicerone " (p. 62), drew attention to the fact that there was a family of painters called Bonifazio at Venice, who worked throughout the sixteenth century ; but the discovery is due not to him, but to the researches of two Italian writers. Moschini, a Venetian, observes, in his " Guida di Venezia " of 1815, that there must have been *two* painters called Bonifazio ; and the late Dr. Cesare Bernasconi pointed out, in his " History of the Veronese School," that, according to documentary evidence, at least *three* painters of that name had existed.  The eldest of them came from Verona, but

---

[9] It has recently been catalogued as Palma Vecchio.

settled at Venice while still young, and died there in 1540; the second and younger Bonifazio—a relation, perhaps a brother, of the elder, and in any case his scholar and imitator—died in 1553; while the third was still living in 1579. The two latter followed the elder so closely in composition and manner of painting, that an unpractised eye will be apt to confound the works of the three artists, as those of the three or four painters known as the Bassanos have been similarly confounded. The second, or the third, Bonifazio may have been born in Venice, and the existence of a *Bonifazio Veneziano* would hence be quite as possible as that of a *Bonifazio Veronese*, of whom the "Anonimo" speaks. The younger of the three, I may add, appears in his later works to be an imitator of Titian, whose influence was then dominant in Venice, while the elder, or great, Bonifazio is undoubtedly to be regarded as a scholar and imitator of Palma Vecchio. On another occasion I shall speak more fully of these painters.

We will now proceed to No. 163, the Madonna with the Child, who gives His benediction to a female suppliant, between St. Anthony—whose expression is fervent and natural—and St. Jerome. The light is treated quite in the manner of Lotto. The Madonna, however, looks like a Bergamasque peasant-girl. There is a lack of freedom in the drawing, and the drapery is hard and somewhat stiff. It is probably a work of Palma Vecchio's middle period (1514–1518)[1]—a few years earlier than his excellent painting in the Palazzo Colonna agli Apostoli at Rome.

The "Holy Family" (*) does not belong to the Venetian school, as the catalogue tells us, but is most likely

[1] The Madonna recalls the Madonna in the Duc d'Aumale's collection with the forged 'Cartellino' and the date 1500. This false inscription once threatened to cause dire confusion in the history of art.

by Ramenghi, called Bagnacavallo. No. 164, attributed to Giovanni Bellini, is the work of another Bergamasque—Cariani, the so-called pupil of Giorgione.[2] On the right is the Madonna; in the centre, the Holy Child standing on a parapet and giving His benediction to St. Peter; a grey curtain forms the background. The drawing is poor; the figures are trivial and plebeian; the Child is heavy, coarse, and without grace of movement; and the clouds are woolly; the colouring, however, is refined and glowing. Mündler (Beiträge zu Burckhardt's "Cicerone," p. 64) observed rightly that this picture was by the Bergamasque Giovanni de' Busi, called Cariani, whom I consider to have been a pupil of his fellow-countryman, Palma Vecchio, and an imitator of Giorgione. He must have been born between 1480–1490, at Fuipiano, in the Valle Brembana, near Bergamo, and was still living in 1541. Many works by this fine colourist are in the public gallery and private collections of Bergamo.[3]

No. 115 is a large painting with numerous figures—probably the family of the artist. In the centre is the mother—fair and buxom, and clad in white with sleeves of a brick-red tint. She holds an infant in her arms, the next youngest child is beside her, and five boys are grouped around, like a brood of chickens—one being apparently a sculptor in embryo. Behind stands the father, the artist, Bernardino Licinio of Pordenone, looking about fifty. The background, as in nearly all his paintings, is of a greyish-brown tone. This admirable group is signed

[2] Now rightly attributed to Cariani.

[3] Several paintings by Cariani are at Milan—two in the Brera, one in the Ambrosiana, one in the Museo Civico, one in the Bonomi-Cereda collection, and two in the collection of the author—a "Holy Family" in a landscape, and the portrait of a man (both now in the gallery at Bergamo). A Madonna by Cariani is in the public gallery at Vicenza, Room I., No. 41. (†)

*B. Lycinj opus.* The "Santa Conversazione," No. 171, is also by Bernardino, and not Bartolommeo, as the catalogue states. The Madonna is seated in the centre, wearing a brick-red dress and white drapery on her head; she holds the undraped and not very attractive Child; the little St. John, seated on a lamb, offers his cross to the Infant Saviour; behind are SS. Joseph and Anna; on the right, St. Jerome and the kneeling St. Catherine, with landscape background. It is one of his coarser works.[4] The flesh-tints in this, as in all the master's other pictures, are cold in tone with glazes of a rosy-red. He has introduced in the draperies his favourite colours—brick-red and sky-blue. In the Sciarra-Colonna gallery there is a "Daughter of Herodias" by him (†) under the name of Giorgione, and the portrait of a man under that of Carletto Caliari, which is probably by his pupil Francesco Beccaruzzi. Licinio is certainly not the brother of Giovan Antonio Regillo da Pordenone, as Mündler thought; he may have been his pupil, and possibly even some relation.

The pleasing little picture, "Christ among the Doctors" (∗), belongs to a good Venetian master of the school of Paul Veronese; it is a modified copy of a work in the English National Gallery, by Pedro Campaña, a Fleming who settled at Seville. (†)

A male portrait (No. 396) belongs to the Venetian school, although painted by a Sicilian.[5] The expression is most

---

[4] Messrs. Crowe and Cavalcaselle do not venture so far, and only recognise 'the style of Bernardino's school' (ii. 294); Mündler (Cic. p. 75) is of my opinion. How the latter keen-sighted critic could have taken Titian's beautiful early work, in the Palazzo Balbi-Piovera at Genoa, for a Licinio, is as incomprehensible to me as his judg-ment on the profile portrait by Ambrogio de Predis in the Ambro-siana.

[5] Formerly attributed to Gio-vanni Bellini—a further proof that Antonello owed more to the Vene-tians than they to him. Another and very fine portrait of his last period (1485-1493) is in the Naples museum erroneously ascribed to

unpleasant; but the eyes are full of life, as is usually the case in the portraits of Antonello da Messina, to whom this work unquestionably belongs. The flesh is of a reddish-brown tone, the eyebrows are executed with the care of a miniaturist, and the mouth is sharply modelled. In the catalogue it formerly bore the name of Giovanni Bellini, but Mündler restored it to its true author, and was followed by Messrs. Crowe and Cavalcaselle. To judge from the expression of the mouth, the Venetian here represented must have been an excellent man of business, though anything but amiable or agreeable in his domestic relations. This portrait may have been produced in the same year as that in the Palazzo Trivulzio at Milan, bearing the master's name and the date 1476. A portrait of a young man (No. 139) deserves some attention. It is incomprehensible that it should have been ascribed to the painter, to whom No. 97 of the Venetian school is given, to Giovan Battista Moroni. We have already seen that the latter painting had nothing to do with him, and the same may be said of this one.[6] It is a fine portrait and clearly the work of Girolamo Savoldo of Brescia, an excellent amateur, who was apparently first a pupil of

Bellini (large room, No. 16) (†). The form of ear, differing entirely from that of Giovanni Bellini, should

earlier portraits, and to this is probably due the present appellation of the picture.

EAR OF ANTONELLO DA MESSINA.

EAR OF GIOVANNI BELLINI.

alone have sufficed to identify the master. The drawing of the eye is not so exaggerated as in Antonello's

[6] It has now been given to Savoldo.

Romanino, then of Giovanni Bellini, and later more especially of Titian. (†) Savoldo's works are rare : a female portrait, with the attributes of St. Margaret, is in the Capitol ; one small picture is in the Uffizi ; two are at Turin ; and his most important work, a large altar-piece, is in the Brera.[7]

## NORTHERN MASTERS.

In the Borghese gallery are several fine works of the Dutch, Flemish, and even German schools. The picture which proves most attractive to the cultured public is a hen and chickens by Wenceslaus Peters, (∗) and the authorities were apparently equally enchanted with this *chef d'œuvre*, as they once assigned it a place close to a window and in the best light. We will pass on, however, to the works of more important masters. A "Venus and Cupid" (No. 326), almost life-size, is a fine piece of colour, inscribed with the well-known monogram of a good German master, Lucas Cranach the elder, and dated 1531. The small portrait of Charles V. (?) as a boy (∗) bears the name of Holbein, but is more probably the work of a Fleming. No. 253 represents the studio of a Flemish painter—perhaps that of the elder Franz Francken himself, who treated this subject several times. It is inscribed : Frans. Frank Inventor *et fecit*. To this somewhat stiff and formal painter Dr. Bode would attribute the Dresden copy of the Holbein Madonna. There are several good Dutch pictures. No. 273 represents a quack performing a surgical operation with much energy on the arm of a peasant. The unlucky victim is seated on a chair in

---

[7] The profile portrait in this gallery should be compared with the profile of one of the flying angels in Savoldo's picture in the Brera. Other works by this master are in the gallery at Brescia, in the Church of S. Maria in Organo at Verona, and in the Church of S. Giobbe at Venice.

the open air, yelling loudly under the professor's knife. An old woman, the surgeon's assistant, stands by, plying the sufferer with words of comfort and encouragement. This sprightly little painting is very unjustly attributed to Adrian Brouwer. It bears the name of its true author, G. Lunders, 1648. Evidently Gerrit Lunders sought to imitate Brouwer in this picture; eight years later, in his painting of 1656, now at Dresden, he took Dusart, or perhaps Ostade, as his model, and again, in 1660, followed Metsu and Mieris, as we see in a little picture in the Hausmann collection at Hanover (No. 283 (?),) also representing a surgical operation. No. 271 was formerly catalogued " Opera d'un Fiammingo." If I were to say to one of these Italian directors, ' My dear sir, it is not the work of a " Fiammingo," but of a Dutchman,' he would shrug his shoulders and reply, ' È tutt' uno' (' It's all the same '). And according to the gallery catalogues, it certainly is all the same, for apparently the only Dutch products known in Italy are herrings and stockfish. But what may this " Opera d'un Fiammingo " (No. 271) represent ? We see six soldiers in various attitudes, though it is impossible to guess what they are all about. It is a good example of the Haarlem School of Franz or Dirk Hals, and, on closer inspection, we discover the name of the painter, Pieter Codde, whom Dr. Bode has treated exhaustively, and with thorough knowledge of his subject, in his book " Franz Hals und seine Schule." [8] In No. 291, a little picture in the style of Teniers, we see a Flemish interior. A peasant is seated with his mug of beer beside him—the other inmates of the pothouse warm themselves at the fire. There is a copy of this picture, which I hold to be only a work of the

---

[8] Pieter Codde's works are often met with in Italian collections. Three are at Milan alone: in the Palazzo Trivulzio, in the collection of the late Count Lodovico Belgiojoso, and in that of Signor Bonomi-Cereda.

school, in the Corsini gallery in Rome, No. 28. A Crucifixion (No. 268) the catalogue ascribes to Van Dyck. It is certainly only a copy; and No. 411, the "Descent from the Cross," is also by some imitator of this refined but somewhat formal painter. No. 279, representing several female figures bathing, with a landscape background, should be ascribed, not to Poelenburg, but to his imitator, A. Cuylenborch (†). An expert will recognise at once that the picture attributed to Paul Potter (No. 285), "Cows grazing," can be nothing but a modern copy. The little work ascribed to Wouwerman (*) may be regarded as genuine. It appears to me to be too delicate in tone for a copy. Beside it is one of the numerous, somewhat uninteresting, sea pieces by Backhuysen. (*)

## GIORGIONE.

We will omit some more or less unimportant pictures, and, in conclusion, devote a little more time to a wonderful portrait (No. 143) which long attracted a large share of my attention, and is catalogued as the work of an "unknown master." It represents a woman of about twenty-eight; her dark eyes, full of fire and passion, are overshadowed by a low and intelligent forehead; the arrangement of the dark brown hair on the temples recalls in a measure that of the Knight of Malta in the Uffizi; there are hard long folds in the sleeves of her sombre dress. She stands at a window holding a white handkerchief, and gazing out with a dreamy yearning expression, as if seeking to descry one whom she awaits. The simple treatment of this mysterious figure reveals a great artist—but whom?

Before examining this attractive portrait critically, I thought of Dosso; but the dark background, the stone parapet, and the simplicity of the treatment did not appear to me to show the hand of this master. Then it occurred to me that it might be of Sebastian del Piombo's early period; but for him also the conception appeared too profound, and the form of hand too nearly akin to the *quattro-cento*. One day, as I stood before this mysterious portrait, entranced, and questioning, the spirit of the master met mine, and the truth flashed upon me. 'Giorgione, thou alone,' I cried in my excitement; and the picture answered, 'Even so.' Those eyes, with their profound and yearning expression beneath the slightly arched brows, that low straight forehead, that refined mouth, all testify to Giorgione, all are modelled as in the Knight of Malta. The painting has been retouched in the neck and other parts, but, on the whole, it is well preserved. The brownish-yellow head-dress which this charming figure wears resembles that often met with in Titian's early Madonnas. In conception it appears to me a very marvel of art, and to Giorgione alone was it given to produce portraits of such astonishing simplicity, yet so deeply significant, and capable, by their mystic charm, of appealing to our imagination in the highest degree. (†)

With this new-found work of Giorgione, to which I would here direct the attention of all who admire Italian art, I will close these studies on the Borghese gallery.

# THE DORIA-PAMFILI GALLERY.

THE long pontificate of Paul V., of the house of Borghese, was followed by the yet longer reign of Urban VIII., a member of the Barberini family. One would naturally suppose that as the Borghese gallery takes precedence of all the other Roman collections, by reason of its size and the length of its existence, the Barberini would rank second. This, however, is not the case.

Urban VIII., after annexing the castles of the Montefeltri and the Della Rovere, probably transferred many of their works of art to the Barberini palaces in Rome—for instance, the nine pictures of Apollo and eight Muses,[1] and the series of " Illustrious Men of Antiquity," formerly in the library of the Palace at Urbino, and now divided between the Palazzo Barberini and the Louvre.[2] But the heirs of

[1] These nine pictures were ascribed by Baldi (*Vita e Fatti di Federico, duca di Urbino*) to Timoteo Viti. When I first saw them, they were hung high in an ill-lighted room, and I took them for works of that mythical painter Francesco Bianchi, whom for many years I had confounded with the Ferrarese Cortellini. ' Es irrt der Mensch so lang er strebt.' On the death of Prince Barberini, Duke of Castelvecchio, the pictures were transferred to the Corsini gallery in Florence. On examining them in a better light, I came to the conclusion that Vasari was right in ascribing two of them, Apollo and one Muse, to Timoteo. The remaining six (one Muse is missing) appear to me to be by different feeble painters of the school of Giovanni Santi. The indian ink drawing for one of these Muses, ascribed to Botticelli, is at Windsor (Grosvenor Gallery Publication, No. 17). I am inclined to think that this drawing is by Giovanni Santi; if this be so, it proves that Raphael's father was also a pupil of Fiorenzo di Lorenzo. (†)

[2] When the possessions of the Colonna-Barberini family were

the Pontiff do not appear, on the whole, to have taken much interest in art.

It is the Doria gallery, and not the Barberini, which ranks second among the Roman collections. Shortly after the death of Urban VIII. (1644), Cardinal Giovan Battista Pamfili was raised to the papacy under the name of Innocent X. (September 29, 1644). His sister-in-law, Donna Olimpia, who came of the Viterbo family of Maldachini, is said to have been an ambitious and splendour-loving woman, who could not brook that her house should be eclipsed by any other in Rome. Hence this collection in all probability owes its existence, not to any love of art, but rather to the love of ostentation of this otherwise very

divided, half of the pictures, fourteen in number, fell to the share of the Sciarra-Colonna family. Later, they were sold to Signor Campana, and finally were bought by Napoleon III., with the whole Campana collection, for the Louvre. The Barberini share is still in the Palazzo Barberini in Rome. These fifteen pictures represent Homer, Scotus, Cicero, Petrarch, Moses, Hippocrates, Solomon, Euclid, Albertus Magnus, and others; and Federigo of Montefeltro, enthroned, wearing the ducal mantle over his armour and holding a large book. His hair is grey, his immense aquiline nose renders him unmistakable. His little son Guidobaldo, kneeling, presents the ducal sceptre to his father. The child was born on January 24, 1471, and looks about four years old in this picture. This painting is larger and better preserved than the others, but is by the same hand as the rest, namely by that of Justus of Ghent. This Justus (Josse Sneevoet) was at Urbino from 1464 to 1476, and in

addition to the pictures just mentioned, he painted a very poor "Cenacolo," which since 1865 has been in the academy at Urbino. The view of Messrs. Crowe and Cavalcaselle (ii. 565) that some of these portraits are by Girolamo Genga is inadmissible. There is not a trace of this painter's manner in any one of the twenty-nine pictures, and moreover the series was probably already complete in 1476, the year of Genga's birth. With regard to Justus of Ghent, I may take this opportunity of rectifying an error which has found acceptance among art-historians. Several recent writers, among them M. Alfred Michiels (*Histoire de la peinture Flamande*, iii. 149), have identified this Justus with Justus de Alemania, who in 1451 painted an "Annunciation" in the cloisters of S. Maria di Castello at Genoa. This painter was not a Fleming, but a Swabian from Ravensburg, and has nothing to do with Justus of Ghent, who only came to Italy in 1464.

avaricious woman, and to the fashion of the day. A few
of its most important acquisitions, however, date from the
time of the great Admiral Andrea Doria, and were removed
from Genoa to Rome at a later period. The Doria gallery
cannot, however, compare with the Borghese for the number
and value of its pictures; as regards their intelligent
arrangement and the light in which they are hung, it has
not much to boast of; all Italian galleries alike are victims
to ignorance and deplorable indifference.

In the large vestibule leading to the apartments
devoted to the pictures in the Doria Palace, we find among
many unimportant productions of the seventeenth century,
several finely composed landscapes by Gaspar Dughet, called
Poussin; " Noah's Sacrifice," a large and somewhat trivial
work by Pietro da Cortona; the " Deluge," by Scarsellino;
a landscape with many figures in the foreground by Battista
Dossi, the brother of Giovanni, and other decorative works;
but Italian art of the seventeenth century does not come
within the range of our present studies.

Before quitting this room, however, I cannot refrain from
saying a few words about the portrait of Pope Innocent by
Velasquez. This great Spanish artist was perhaps the most
original of all portrait painters, and this picture is world-
renowned. Professor Karl Justi, the able and gifted writer on
art, has observed, in his learned and standard work, " Diego
Velasquez and his Times " (ii. 183), ' It is a curious fact,
that, as in his own country it had been the great painter's
lot to portray the most gloomy-featured of ministers and
the most uninteresting type of princes, so in Rome he was
commissioned to paint the most ill-favoured among all the
successors of St. Peter.' And truly there is not a trace in
the features of Innocent either of the polished scholar, or
of the high-bred man of the world—types we are wont to
find among the princely ecclesiastical dignitaries of those

days. They are insignificant, even vulgar ; his expression is that of a wily lawyer, and it is a positive relief to forget his repulsive image. Yet cunning and suspicious as he was, Innocent X. was a mere tool in the hands of his sister-in-law Olimpia, a fact which it is difficult to explain. With the exception of a few of Rembrandt's finest likenesses, this painting surpasses all other portraits of that century. As Gainsborough has left us a " Blue boy," now in the Grosvenor House gallery, and Paul Veronese a " Green man," now in the Colonna Palace, so Velasquez, in Pope Innocent, has given us a red portrait.

According to some critics, there is another work by the Spanish master in Rome, namely, a portrait of himself in the Capitoline gallery. Even Professor Justi, the great authority on Velasquez, has not ventured to give a decided verdict, and I myself am not sufficiently acquainted with the Spanish school to express an opinion on such a delicate point. If it be by the hand of Velasquez, it must be a work of his first period.

The Venetians are particularly well represented in this collection, and I shall therefore discuss them at some length ; this will not deter me, however, from mentioning works of other schools when opportunity offers. The pictures, however, which strike us most on entering the second room are not Venetian but Florentine, namely, a fine " Annunciation " by Fra Filippo Lippi, (∗) and two little panels by his pupil Pesellino. We will therefore begin by examining a few works of the Florentine school.

## FRANCESCO PESELLINO.

Francesco Pesello, called Il Pesellino, to distinguish him from his uncle Giuliano Pesello, was born at Florence in 1422, and died there in 1457, having scarcely attained his

thirty-fifth year.    Masaccio's frescoes in the Carmine must
have made a profound and lasting impression upon him, as
on most of the other Florentine painters of the good period.
Many of Pesellino's figures testify to this, as also does the
simplicity of his composition.   His true master, however,
was Fra Filippo, as Vasari states ; but this by no means
precludes the supposition that Pesellino may have learnt
the first principles of his art from his uncle.   His earliest
known work,[3] in the Casa Buonarotti at Florence, is certainly not in the manner of Fra Filippo.   Vasari, indeed,
ascribes this panel to Giuliano himself, but most erroneously, and it is not improbable that Pesellino executed
it under the guidance of his uncle.   So far as I know,
there is no authentic work by Giuliano Pesello in existence.[4]   Vasari states that he painted an " Adoration of
the Magi," in consequence of which Padre Lanzi imagined
he had discovered the identical work in a picture representing this subject in the Uffizi.   Strange to say, Messrs.
Crowe and Cavalcaselle unhesitatingly agree with Lanzi,
and speak of this picture (No. 65) as by Giuliano.[5]

Pesellino is an extremely able artist who has been hitherto

[3] This picture, formerly in the
Cavalcanti chapel in Santa Croce,
represents  the  miracles  of  St.
Nicholas of Bari.

[4] A long low panel which passed
from the Palazzo Rucellai into the
collection of the author, might be
by Giuliano Pesello. It represents
the surrender of a besieged city to a
Florentine general. The landscape
and architectural background recall
Pesellino, while the remarkably
mild types of the soldiers have more
of the character of Fra Angelico.
The horses recall those usually met
with in Paolo Uccello's paintings.

[5] The present director has followed my suggestion, and restored
the picture to its true author, Cosimo
Roselli. Dr. Bode accepts the view
of Messrs. Crowe and Cavalcaselle.
In this picture, as in that of the
Baptism of Christ by Verrocchio,
the Berlin critic has observed what
he terms the ' Neue Firnismalerei,'
and he considers that in the latter
picture this new method is to be
attributed to the young Leonardo da
Vinci.   In the case of these two
pictures, however, I feel bound to
point out that their present condition is due entirely to the restorer,
who with his oil and his varnishes
has succeeded in disfiguring both.

much underrated. His two small panels in the Doria gallery (Nos. 508 and 514)—one representing Pope Sylvester before the Emperor Constantine, and the other the Saint binding a dragon to render it harmless—are both rightly ascribed to Pesellino, and appear to me to be of his later period Close to them are two small works which the catalogue most erroneously attributes to Pisano, the great Veronese painter, known as Pisanello. One represents the "Birth," the other the "Marriage of the Madonna." These two pictures, if I am not greatly mistaken, belong to the school of Siena and are probably by Bartolo di Maestro Fredi. ⸱(†) It has always been a mystery to me how such an astute connoisseur as the late Mr. Mündler could have supposed that these feeble productions showed the manner and even the colouring of Pisanello (see Cic. p. 6).

But to return to Pesellino, whose works are extremely rare. After years of research I have only succeeded in discovering about a dozen in addition to the two just mentioned. The panel in the Casa Buonarotti at Florence is, in my judgment, his earliest known work. That mentioned by Vasari: 'fece ai fanciulli della Compagnia di S. Giorgio, un S. Girolamo e un S. Francesco' (Vasari iv. 183), now in the collection of the author,[6] appears to me to be also an early work, though already entirely in the style of Fra Filippo. It represents St. Jerome in a cavern kneeling before a skull, with a stone in his right hand, and a crucifix in his left. The upper part of his body is nude; his red Cardinal's robe envelops the lower part. A monk in the grey habit of his order is seated near a rock caressing a lion; a lioness crouches beside him, her eyes fixed on the Saint; the red roof of the monastery is seen in the distance. Both composition and execution are extremely

---

[6] Now in the public gallery at Bergamo.

naïve and show a youthful hand. The type of St. Jerome's head is borrowed from Fra Filippo.

In the same collection is another panel by Pesellino, representing a Florentine patrician, one of the so-called 'borghesia ﾠgrassa,' arraigned by plebeian accusers, and brought before the judge, who is seated on a high throne—an excellent work, remarkable for life-like treatment and clever delineation of character, still showing the influence of Fra Filippo.

Not much later than these pictures I should place the three panels in the Palazzo Alessandri in Florence. One

"SAINT ANTHONY," FLORENCE ACADEMY.

represents "Simon the Sorcerer," another the "Conversion of St. Paul," and the third "S. Zenobio restoring a widow's son to life." Of two excellent panels,[1] originally forming the predella to an altar-piece by Fra Filippo, one is now in the Florence academy, the other in the Louvre (No. 1414). In the former is represented the "Nativity," a "Miracle of St. Anthony," and the "Martyrdom of SS. Cosmo and Damiano"; in the latter are the same two

---

[1] Of this predella Padre Lanzi has well observed: 'Che l'istorico (namely, Vasari) chiamò maraviglio-sissima, e forse non la lodò per quel secolo oltre il dovere (i. 103).

Saints healing a sick person, and St. Francis with the stigmata.

Among his later works I should class a panel of larger dimensions, representing the marriage of Griselda with the Marchese di Saluzzo—illustrating Boccaccio's well-known tale. This beautiful picture passed from the Palazzo Gherardi at Florence into the collection of the author.[8] It is one of the most characteristic and attractive of all the stories which this refined, gifted, and delightful chronicler, Pesellino, has left us. In it he shows himself completely independent. Scarcely a trace of his master, Fra Filippo is discernible either in this painting or in the two exquisite panels in the Palazzo Torrigiani at Florence, representing David's victory and his triumphal procession. The two latter are indeed ascribed to Benozzo Gozzoli, but every connoisseur of the Florentine school would, I think, at once recognise them as by Pesellino.[9] (†)

In addition to the thirteen pictures by Pesellino already mentioned, there is an altar-piece attributed to him in the English National Gallery. In ascribing it to Pesellino, the authorities have Vasari's testimony to support them, as the historian mentions it as the work of this master (iv. 182). It represents the Trinity with SS. James and Zeno, and was formerly in a church at Pistoia. I must confess, however, that to me it has nothing of Pesellino—neither his spirit, his style, nor his manner. He never, that I know of, painted large figures,[1] and this altar-piece appears to me more probably by his assistant, Piero di Lorenzo Pratese.

---

[8] Now in the Bergamo gallery.

[9] Like Hercules hesitating between two roads, Dr. Bode is undecided whether to ascribe these pictures to Pesellino, or to deprive him of them (ii. 575).

[1] An "Annunciation" in the Uffizi, No. 56, was formerly attributed to Giuliano Pesello and now bears the name of Pesellino. It is, however, an undoubted work of Baldovinetti. Dr. Bode (ii. 576) is also of this opinion.

There may be other works in private collections in Europe by this rare and thoroughly Florentine master; but not being acquainted with them myself, I am unable to furnish any information on the subject. As beginners in the study of Italian art are liable to confound the works of Pesellino with those of his master, Fra Filippo, and even with those of his contemporary, Benozzo Gozzoli—an error into which Messrs. Crowe and Cavalcaselle have also fallen (iii. 107)—I will briefly enumerate a few of the master's characteristics. Pesellino's figures are always slim, refined, and full of grace—quite the reverse of the rather heavy forms of Fra Filippo, with whom, nevertheless, he is sometimes confounded. In his colouring Pesellino has a predilection for grey, blue, and violet tones. In the form of his hands he resembles his master Fra Filippo, as he also does in the type of many of his heads in his early works. His ear is somewhat round in form, but is longer than that of Fra Filippo; the sharp dark brown outline of the helix of the ear is always characteristic of his pictures.

PESELLINO'S ROUNDED FOLDS.

Noticeable too are the rounded folds often seen in his drapery, especially at the elbow. The roofs of his houses are usually of a bright red; the floor, brick red; when he introduces pillars in his buildings, they are of a greenish tone. The works of this very attractive painter are, as we have seen, mostly in Italy. Two are in Rome, seven in Florence, three in the Morelli collection,[2] one in the Louvre, and a work of Pesellino's 'bottega' is in the English National Gallery.

[2] Now in the gallery at Bergamo.

## THE VENETIANS.

TURNING now to the Venetian pictures, it should be observed that they are scattered through the different rooms and corridors which serve as a picture gallery in the Doria Palace, and it therefore requires some patience and perseverance to discover them. We will begin with two masters whose names we find in the catalogue—Giovanni Bellini and Andrea Mantegna.

### GIOVANNI BELLINI.

Every great European collection in these days takes pride in being able to inscribe the name of Giovanni Bellini in its catalogue; yet from the end of the sixteenth century up to the middle of the present, he was but little esteemed. It was only his great pupils and followers who were sought after—Giorgione, Titian (more especially), Sebastiano del Piombo, Palma Vecchio, Paris Bordone, Tintoretto, Paul Veronese, &c.

The last thirty years of Bellini's life were devoted to the execution of large works, either for the Senate or for Venetian churches, so that even the art-loving Isabella Gonzaga, Duchess of Mantua, had to wait many years, notwithstanding her entreaties, before she succeeded in obtaining the picture which the painter had promised her.[3] To this is due the fact that at that time, even in Italy, the master's works were extremely rare out of Venice. With the exception of the following pictures, I could hardly name another which Bellini was commissioned to execute for persons beyond the limits of that city: a "Pietà," ordered by Sigismondo Malatesta of Rimini; the large

[3] See Gaye, *Carteggio d' Artisti*, ii. 71-82. The letters referring to this incident date from the years 1505 and 1506.

altar-piece, executed for the Franciscans of Pesaro; the "Bacchanal" for the Duke of Ferrara; the altar-piece for the church of Santa Corona at Vicenza, and the charming Madonna for a nunnery at Alzano near Bergamo.[4]

The following works by him still remain in Italy, out of Venice. In the Uffizi a "Sacred Allegory" (No. 631). This beautiful picture, full of grace and spirit, came to Florence as the work of Giovanni Bellini; later the name was changed to that of Giorgione, and quite recently, to the surprise of all connoisseurs of the Venetian school, to that of Marco Basaiti, Dr. Bode (ii. 641) also regarding it as a work by this master. The form of ear, however, and the excessive size of the hands, which is extremely characteristic of Bellini, reveal the master at once. The type of the Madonna, her pose, and the rocky landscape, recall the "Adoration of the Magi" by his brother Gentile in the collection of Sir Henry Layard at Venice.

The small head of an Apostle, also in the Uffizi (No. 177), and the so-called portrait of Giovanni Bellini by himself (No. 354), with a forged signature, are both by pupils. The "Pietà," No. 583, in the same gallery, which is only laid in, is so entirely disfigured by restoration that it is almost worthless. There is a genuine, though much damaged, "Madonna" by the master in the gallery at Turin, No. 779; the other painting ascribed to Bellini in that collection (No. 105) is merely a copy.

In the Brera at Milan we find three works of different

---

[4] The fine "Pietà" is in the Palazzo Pubblico at Rimini; the altar-piece at Pesaro in a church in that town; the "Bacchanal" in the possession of the Duke of Northumberland; the altar-piece at Vicenza is still in the church of S. Corona; the Madonna of Alzano, mentioned by Ridolfi, is now in the Morelli collection (at Bergamo). It is one of the best preserved of the master's works (of 1496-1498), and was twice copied by Giovan Battista Moroni. One of these copies belongs to the Agliardi family at Bergamo; the other is in a church in the Val Scrio near Albino.

periods of Giovanni Bellini's career. The earliest is the
" Pietà " (No. 284), dating from about 1464–1467. It
would be difficult to name another painting in which a
mother's grief for the loss of her son has been expressed
with such profound and touching pathos. The Madonna
(No. 261), painted for a Greek church, was probably executed about ten years later ; the treatment of the subject
is one of the most impressive I know—the expression of
tender melancholy in the face of the Child and in the eyes
of the mother is truly sublime. Another " Madonna " (No.
297), much damaged, is dated 1510. In Dr. G. Frizzoñi's
collection at Milan there is an extremely interesting early
work by Bellini recalling Alvise Vivarini, and in the collection of the author,[5] besides the picture already mentioned,
there is a second, of about 1475–1478.

In the gallery at Bergamo (Lochis collection) there is a
genuine but much repainted " Madonna " of his early period
(No. 140) ; another of his latest, about 1512, is in the
cathedral there. At Brescia, so far as I know, there is no
painting by Bellini. The " Descent from the Cross " ascribed
to him in the church of S. Giovanni Evangelista is
probably by Civerchio of Crema, a pupil of Foppa. (†)
Among the drawings in the Palazzo Tosi there is, however,
a sketch in pen and ink (a " Pietà ") by Bellini (†),
erroneously ascribed to Mantegna.

In the gallery at Verona there is a genuine and
beautiful Virgin and Child by Bellini (†), of about 1477
(Bernasconi collection, No. 77). It is unfortunately much
injured, and has actually been assigned to the Florentine
school.

At Vicenza the master's large altar-piece of 1510 is still
in the church of S. Corona, for which it was painted ; at
Padua, Ferrara, Bologna, Treviso, and in the Friulian district,

[5] Now at Bergamo.

I have not met with a single genuine work by Giovanni
Bellini. In the gallery at Rovigo, however, there is an
authentic but wholly disfigured painting by the master
(No. 109). Venice has had the good fortune to retain a great
number of his works, both large and small, though most of
them have been irreparably injured by the restoration, so-
called, which they have undergone. I will now enumerate
them. The Correr collection in the Museo Civico, which
has recently been rearranged with so little intelligence,
contains a few most valuable early works by the master :
a " Pietà " (Room IX., No. 27), which Dr. Bode (ii. 771) still
continues to ascribe to Pier Maria Pennacchi, I consider
to be a genuine work by Bellini, full of the most profound
feeling (†) ; a small " Crucifixion," with the Madonna and
St. John weeping at the foot of the Cross (Room IX. No. 46),
recalling his father Jacopo (†), and the " Transfiguration "
(Room VII., No. 23).

In the Academy we find an early Madonna (Room VI.,
No. 2) by the master, besides many interesting works of his
later periods ; such as the large altar-piece, dating from
the last twenty years of the fifteenth century ; several
Madonnas in the Sala Contarini (Nos. 17 and 24), and
four little panels with allegorical subjects (Room III., Nos.
47–51). The Madonna in Room V., and the two Madonnas
in Room VI., Nos. 33 and 44, probably date from the
last years of the fifteenth century. A splendid work of
1488 is in the sacristy of S. Maria dei Frari, and an early
Madonna is in the church of S. Maria dell' Orto, bearing a
' Cartellino' which has been mutilated by the restorer. In
the church of S. Zaccaria we find a large and celebrated
altar-piece of 1505, and in S. Francesco della Vigna a long
picture of 1507 with the Madonna and Child and four Saints.
The donor represented in it was probably an addition of
the seventeenth century. In S. Crisostomo is a splendid

work of 1513, one of the master's latest, and painted when he was eighty-five!

An altar-piece of 1488 yet remains to be mentioned— one which Giovanni Bellini executed by order of the Doge Agostino Barbarigo, now in the church of S. Pietro Martire at Murano. He is, of course, accredited with many other works in Venice, but I believe I have not omitted a single genuine one from the foregoing list. The Madonna ascribed to the master in the Borghese gallery I have already dealt with. In the Capitol no fewer than five pictures are attributed to him; the two figures of Saints (Nos. 79 and 87) are, as we have seen, by Garofalo; the pleasing portrait of a girl (No. 207) is, if I am not mistaken, by Amico Aspertini (†), a pupil of Ercole Roberti, of Ferrara, and the two other portraits (Nos. 129 and 132) are not by his hand. The same must be said of the pictures bearing his name in the Doria gallery. The "Circumcision" (No. 519) is merely one of the numerous copies of that unattractive subject which are frequently met with in Italy and elsewhere. The original is said to be in England.[6]

## NICCOLÒ RONDINELLI.

The second Bellini, so-called, is in Braccio II. of this gallery, No. 98. It recalls the master in a measure, but even the most superficial connoisseurs of the Venetian school would hardly think of ascribing it to him were it not for the misleading signature: IOANNES BELLINVS. It represents the Madonna, adoring the Child who lies on her knee; the little St. John standing by. A comparison between this picture and two works in the second room of this gallery by Niccolò Rondinelli, a pupil and assistant of Bellini, proves that these three pictures are by the same

[6] A similar copy, signed 'Marco BELLI,' is in the gallery at Rovigo.

hand. One of them, No. 111, is signed: NICOLAVS RONDINELO Both Nos. 111 and 315 are, however, so damaged that it is difficult to trace the artist's individuality. The hand in all three pictures is still very Bellinesque in form, the eyebrows are dark and thick, always a characteristic of Rondinelli; the broad gold border on the Madonna's red dress, and the stiff straight folds on her bodice, are also distinctive of his later manner. I could mention many similar paintings which, though bearing the signature of Bellini, are in reality by his pupils and imitators. For instance, a Madonna with SS. Peter and Sebastian in the Louvre (No. 1159), falsely inscribed with the name of Bellini, and the so-called "portrait of Bellini by himself," in the Uffizi, No. 354, which are both by Rondinelli. A portrait of a man in the Capitol, and a Madonna in the gallery at Padua (No. 1273), belong to this category. Francesco Bissolo, another pupil and imitator of Bellini, also inscribed his own paintings with the name of the master; but the signatures in his 'Cartellini,' unlike those of Bellini, are always in cursive characters—*Ioannes bellinus* —as, for instance, on the Madonna in the Borghese gallery, the picture of 1515 in the public gallery at Vienna representing a nude female figure arranging her hair, and others. These forgeries were in all probability perpetrated after the death of Bellini, in the hope of finding a better sale for the pictures—Marcantonio's copies, signed with Dürer's monogram, are examples of this practice. Some northern critics, misled by the fact that these forged signatures do not yield to chemical solvents, are inclined to assume, and to make others believe, that the master himself thus signed the works of his pupils and assistants. There is, of course, no reason why such beliefs should not be held if they give pleasure to those who hold them. Life is made up of delusions, and it is practically of no conse-

quence if an amateur, to whom a forgery is quite as
attractive as a genuine work of art, is disposed to accept
these views. We must consider, moreover, that, were it not
so, many a rogue would be reduced to beggary.

A Madonna very similar to No. 98 in the Doria gallery
belongs to the Senator Giovanni Baracco at Rome ; another
of the same period of Rondinelli's career passed from the
possession of the Buri family at Verona into the collection
of the late Prince Giovanelli at Venice. Other works of
this later period are at Ravenna in churches and private
collections—for instance, a large altar-piece in the church
of S. Croce—and a St. Sebastian is in the Cathedral at
Forlì. A very good work of the master's early period,
in the Brera (No. 177), represents St. John the Evangelist
appearing to Galla Placidia, who kneels before him. The
same gallery contains another altar-piece by Rondinelli
(No. 176)—the Madonna and Child with SS. Nicholas,
Augustine, Peter and Bartholomew, and three angel musicians. The catalogue ascribes it to Baldassare Carrari, of
Forlì ;[7] the late Mr. Mündler attributed it to Cristoforo
Caselli, of Parma (op. cit. p. 9). Neither the year of Rondinelli's birth nor that of his death is known. He belongs to
that group of artists who, like Cima da Conegliano, Cristoforo Caselli, Jacopo da Montagnana, Lattanzio da Rimini,
Pier Maria Pennacchi, Francesco Bissolo, and others, were
employed in the workshop of Giovanni Bellini during the
last twenty years of the fifteenth century. From Rondinelli's
school proceeded the brothers Francesco and Bernardino
Zaganelli of Cotignola, Girolamo Marchesi, also of Cotignola,
and Luca Longhi, of Ravenna. According to Dr. Bode

---

[7] Lanzi (iv. 35) gave this picture
to Baldassare Carrari. I am glad to
find that my views coincide with
those of Messrs. Crowe and Cavalcaselle, who attributed the picture to
Niccolò Rondinelli (i. 594, 2) before
I had expressed an opinion on the
subject.

T

(ii. 643), Rondinelli was influenced by Marco Palmezzano, the pupil and assistant of Melozzo da Forli, but this view appears to me hardly tenable. I should rather consider that the reverse was the case, and that the feebler artist, Palmezzano, derived much from Rondinelli.

To return to Bellini. With the exception of an entirely repainted Madonna in the collection of Prince Torlonia,[8] there is not a single picture by him in Rome. In the Museum at Naples we find a splendid early work by him—the "Transfiguration." It came there from Parma with other property of the Farnese family. The account of the Bellini family Vasari received from an informant was not only slight, but inaccurate. He mentions the portrait of Catarina Cornaro, queen of Cyprus, and the "Miracles by the Relic of the True Cross," as early works by Jacopo Bellini, while in point of fact they are by his son Gentile and of his later period.[9] Again, he ascribes the frescoes by Gentile da Fabriano and by Pisanello in the Doge's Palace to the brothers Bellini, whereas the latter, with Alvise Vivarini, were only commissioned to restore them in 1474.

Further, when the Sultan applied for a good Venetian painter, it was Gentile who was sent, because, according to Vasari, Giovanni 'on account of his great age could not have endured the fatigue of a journey from Venice to Constantinople'—the truth being that Gentile was the elder of the two, and at the time in question (1479) his brother was not much over fifty. This affords a proof that, even among Venetians in the middle of the sixteenth century,

[8] The Child stands on a pedestal in front of the Madonna; on either side are SS. Peter and Paul; signed: 'IOANNES BELLINVS.'

[9] The portrait of Catarina Cornaro in advancing years is in the Esterhazy gallery at Buda-Pesth. The pictures representing the "Miracles performed by a Relic of the True Cross," dating from the last decade of the fifteenth century, are in the Venice Academy.

all recollections of the Bellini were gradually dying out.

Taking him all in all, I consider that Giovanni Bellini was the greatest painter in North Italy in the fifteenth century, though undoubtedly Vittor Pisano was in his day, that is in the first half of the century, as great a pioneer in art, in a certain sense, as was Giovanni Bellini in the latter half. This is proved by his fine fresco of " St. George and the Dragon," in S. Anastasia at Verona, and by his most interesting pen drawings, which, with many other drawings of the early school of Verona, are contained in the so-called Vallardi album in the Louvre, to say nothing of his splendid medals.

Andrea Mantegna is certainly more impressive, powerful, and learned than Bellini, and depicts the moment of action with greater force and with a more truthful realism. Yet there is a certain monotony in the conception and mode of representation both of Mantegna and Pisano, whereas Bellini as an artist is versatile in the highest degree. Both Giovanni and his elder brother Gentile owed their artistic training mainly to their father Jacopo, whose great importance as an artist has only recently been proved by his sketch book, purchased not long since by the authorities of the Louvre. These pen drawings by their varied character prove Jacopo Bellini to have been one of the greatest Venetian artists of the first half of the fifteenth century.[1]

---

[1] Jacopo Bellini must have executed many frescoes, but all have either perished or been covered with whitewash. The only pictures by him with which I am acquainted are : " The Crucifixion," in the gallery at Verona (No. 344), a Madonna in the Venice Academy (No. 18), and another in the Tadini gallery at Lovere, in the province of Bergamo. All these have been greatly damaged by modern restoration. An "Annunciation" in the church of S. Alessandro at Brescia, and a Madonna in the Lochis-Carrara gallery at Bergamo (No. 230), remind me forcibly of the manner of Jacopo Bellini.

Giovanni Bellini was ever making progress and developing from his twentieth year upwards, that is from 1450 until his latest known works of 1513 and 1514 (the altar-piece in S. Giovanni Crisostomo at Venice and the "Bacchanal" belonging to the Duke of Northumberland), so that Dürer was right when, in 1506, he pronounced him the best artist in Venice. Bellini knew how to adapt himself to his subject, and was, as occasion required, grand and serious, graceful and attractive, naïve and simple. His women and children, his old men and boys, never resemble each other, and the same type and expression seldom recur. At times he is even fanciful, like his great pupil Giorgione, as, for example, in his beautiful allegory in the Uffizi (No. 631). We may admit all this without in any way detracting from the great importance of Mantegna. I certainly am not one of those critics who expect an exceptionally gifted nature to be endowed with every imaginable quality. I hold that certain gifts and endowments altogether preclude others, and that neither Mantegna nor Michael Angelo would have attained to the great heights they reached in their art had the Graces been among their instructors. To make my meaning plainer, I may say, that were Bismarck possessed of all those qualities in which his opponents affirm that he is wanting, the unity of Germany would scarcely have been accomplished. Among Bellini's earliest works is the very interesting little picture in the National Gallery, representing Christ standing and encircling the Cross with His left arm, while an angel, kneeling on the right, receives in a chalice the blood flowing from the Saviour's side ; in the background are numerous buildings in a hilly landscape

---

The former of these pictures is ascribed to Fra Angelico, the latter to Gentile da Fabriano. For notices of the works of Jacopo Bellini, see a paper by Professor Molmenti in the *Archivio storico veneto* for 1888.

—the light on the hills treated in the manner of Gentile da Fabriano. After this picture, in chronological order, I should place the Crucifixion in the Correr Museum (Room IX., No. 46). Bellini was, after Mantegna, the greatest delineator of character in North Italy, in an age when the portrayal of character was the principal aim of art. Later, when art sought to give expression to the affections and emotions of human nature, he shows himself second to none in depicting religious feeling, maternal love, and artless childlike joy, as well as pious awe and devout humility in his male and female saints. Bellini is never dramatic, but he always gives to his figures life, dignity, and power.[2] It is a curious fact that, whereas many school-pieces are often ascribed to the master himself, Bellini's own early works are constantly attributed, even by renowned art-critics, to painters far inferior to him; for instance, to Pennacchi, Zaganelli, Rondinelli, Lattanzio da Rimini, and quite recently even to Basaiti; while at times, and this is more excusable, Bellini is confounded in his early works with Mantegna or Ercole di Roberti.[3]

[2] The late Signor Cecchetti discovered a curious document (published in the *Archivio Veneto*, xxxiv. 204), according to which the widow of Giovanni Bellini made her will in 1554, thirty-eight years, therefore, after the death of her husband, who died at the age of eighty-eight.

[3] I have already had occasion to observe (p. 264, and Borghese gallery, p. 240) that all 'Cartellini' bearing Giovanni Bellini's name in cursive characters are forgeries, and that in his genuine signatures, one L is always taller than the other. In authentic 'Cartellini' which have been touched, we often find that the restorer has tampered with this peculiarity and made the letters of equal height.

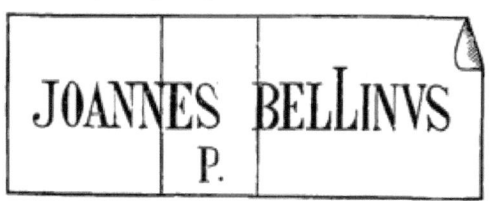

FACSIMILE OF A GENUINE 'CARTELLINO.'

I will now cite a few material characteristics, whereby
Giovanni Bellini may be distinguished from Mantegna, the
painter with whom he is most frequently confounded at a
certain period of his career (1460–1480). The form of
hand and ear is very dissimilar in the works of these two
masters. Bellini's ear is round and fleshy; that of Mantegna is longer and very cartilaginous. Mantegna's hand is
fleshy, with short fingers; Bellini's in his early period is bony
and nearly always unnaturally large, the fingers tapering
at the tips and the joints strongly accentuated. Bellini's
landscapes usually represent a well-watered plain with
fortified buildings in the middle distance, hills in the background and a winding road in the foreground and middle
distance. He adhered to this treatment up to the first
years of the sixteenth century, subsequent to which time
his landscapes became realistic. Originally the tones in
the foreground were of a subdued green with dark green
in the middle distance; gradually, however, these colours
became oxydised and are now very dark, almost black.
Mantegna had little feeling for line or colour in landscape.
In his backgrounds we usually see a steep hill surmounted
by a fortress with a path winding up to it; occasionally he
contents himself with introducing only jagged rocks.

Giovanni Bellini's pictures have for the most part
been much retouched and over-cleaned, in consequence of
which the master's characteristic and strongly developed
forms have been softened down in accordance with academic
rules. To become acquainted with his conception of form,
he must be studied in his early works; they are all in
*tempera* and have been less tampered with than his later,
which, being glazed with oil, have suffered most from
the restorer. This applies not only to Bellini's pictures
but to those of all the great Venetian masters of the
golden age of painting. In the early works of an artist,

all his peculiarities, both good and bad, are strikingly apparent. If the " Pietà " in the Brera (No. 284), and the " Transfiguration " at Naples, were not both signed with Bellini's name, they would undoubtedly have been ascribed to Mantegna. This has been the case with several other works of the same period of the master's career, for instance the " Agony in the Garden " in the English National Gallery (No. 726) and the " Transfiguration " in the Correr Museum at Venice (Room VII., No. 23).

A comparatively large number of Bellini's paintings have been preserved to us, but this is unfortunately not the case with his drawings, and of these I can only cite a very limited number. In the Venice Academy we find a " Pietà " (pen and ink), ascribed to Mantegna, and a drawing for a standing figure of an Apostle, which appear to me to be by Bellini. In the collection of the late Count Tosi at Brescia, there is an " Entombment " (pen and ink) by Bellini, again under the name of Mantegna. Another pen drawing for a " Pietà " is in the His la Salle collection in the Louvre (No. 2202). In the fine collection of drawings at Chatsworth, four standing figures of Saints (pen and ink), by Bellini, are strangely enough ascribed to Perino del Vaga. (†)

## ANDREA MANTEGNA.

According to a document recently discovered, Andrea Mantegna was not born at Padua, as hitherto supposed, but at Vicenza. There is not a single work by him in the public collections in Rome, though the catalogue of the Doria gallery very erroneously ascribes no fewer than four to him. One of these, No. 419, represents one of the many temptations whereby the faith of St. Anthony the hermit was tested. Two other works ascribed to the

master are in Braccio III. One represents St. Louis of
Toulouse distributing alms ; the other again a "Temp-
tation of St. Anthony." These three characteristic and
clever pictures were ascribed by Messrs. Crowe and Cavalcaselle (i. 359) to Parentino, a verdict I cannot accept.
They are thoroughly Veronese in character, and it seems
to me that Dr. Frizzoni has rightly recognised in them the
hand and the feeling of an artist closely connected with
Liberale da Verona (?). The fourth painting attributed
to Mantegna (No. 128) represents Christ bearing the
Cross. Signor Lombardi of Ferrara has a replica of this
painting on fine canvas, apparently by the same hand.
I am of opinion that both pictures are by a Flemish
artist who worked upon an Italian original.[4] (†)

The "Deposition" ascribed to Mantegna in the Vatican
collection must not be regarded as his work. It is probably
a copy of some lost painting by Bartolommeo Montagna,
executed by his imitator Giovanni Buonconsigli of Vicenza,
by whom there are several works in his native city. He
was a pupil of Giovanni Bellini and took Bartolommeo
Montagna for his model. Nevertheless in the Louvre he
is confounded with Mantegna in a drawing for a standing
figure of Christ (Braun, No. 409).

At Venice we find paintings by him in the churches
of S. Giacomo dall' Orio (representing SS. Sebastian,
Laurence, and Roch) and of S. Spirito (Christ between
SS. Erasmus and Secundus); in the Academy, the Madonna
between SS. Cosmo and Damiano; and a St. John the
Baptist in Sir Henry Layard's collection. A document[5]
published in the "Archivio Veneto" (xxxiv. p. 205) by the

---

[4] Messrs. Crowe and Cavalcaselle
look upon this picture as by Bonsignori, executed under the influence
of Palmezzano da Forlì (i. 478, 4).

[5] 'Io Vltruvio de bonconsejo

depentor q. miser Zuane de Vicenza
habitante qui in Venetia in contrada
de SS. Apostoli in casa propria
1539.'

late Signor Cecchetti, proves that Buonconsigli died previous to 1539.   Besides Giovanni Bellini and his pupil
Buonconsigli, Signorelli is also confounded with Mantegna
by amateurs—for instance, in his design for Marcantonio's
celebrated engraving, Mars, Venus, and Cupid (Bartsch
345), which is ascribed to Mantegna.[6] (†)

Two splendid works of Mantegna's middle period are
in the Uffizi (Nos. 1025 and 1111).   One represents the
Madonna and Child seated in a rocky landscape; the other
is a Triptych in the centre of which is the " Adoration of
the Magi," and on one side the " Presentation in the
Temple," and on the other the " Resurrection."   This is
one of the finest of his easel pictures.   A much damaged
portrait of a woman ascribed to Mantegna, is certainly not
by him, but more probably by Giovanni Francesco Carotto
of Verona.[7] (†)

The merits of this truly great master can only be fully
appreciated in his frescoes in the Eremitani at Padua,[8]
and more especially in those of the Camera degli Sposi in
the Ducal Palace at Mantua.[9]   There we see him at his
best and in the plenitude of his power.   In the Brera
we find three extremely interesting works by him, the
best being a Triptych with St. Luke, of the year 1452, a

[6] Passavant says of this engraving : ' Cette belle estampe, gravée
d'après un dessin du Mantegna,
porte la date de 1508 ' (Peintre-
Graveur, vi. 25).   Even in the engraving, Signorelli's manner is easily
recognised in the types, the form of
hands, the stiff and angular pose of
Venus, &c.

[7] Messrs. Crowe and Cavalcaselle
also ascribe this portrait to a
Veronese, namely, to Francesco
Bonsignori, but they regard it as
the likeness of Isabella d' Este (!)
(i. 479).   It should be compared

with a beautiful drawing by Leonardo da Vinci in the Louvre, representing Isabella in profile (Braun
162).

[8] One of these frescoes has been
completely destroyed by restoration.

[9] The series were nearly completed in the year 1474.   In 1876 and
1877 all, but more especially the
fresco representing the " Gonzaga
Family," were irreparably damaged
by ' restoration,' carried on under
the direction of the Government
Inspector General, Signor Cavalcaselle.

painting executed with scrupulous care and accuracy. The upper part is, I believe, earlier by a few months than the lower. In this early work no Flemish artist could have surpassed the realism of Mantegna.

One of his best works is the Triptych in the Church of St. Zeno at Verona. The public gallery in that city contains a Madonna and Saints by him (Bernasconi collection), and a similar subject is at Turin. In the Venice Academy we find a small and exquisitely painted full-length figure of St. George; in the Scarpa collection at La Motta (near Treviso) an unpleasing St. Sebastian, over life-size; in the gallery at Bergamo [1] a beautiful little Madonna; and at Milan, besides the two pictures in the Brera already mentioned, a large altar-piece of 1497 in the Palazzo Trivulzio and a small Madonna in the Poldi-Pezzoli collection.

These four last-named pictures are on canvas, and date from the last years of the fifteenth century.

## ANTONIO VIVARINI.

The Lateran and Vatican collections contain some good works by Mantegna's Venetian contemporaries, Antonio Vivarini and Carlo Crivelli. By Vivarini there is a large altar-piece in the former gallery; the centre occupied by a carved figure of St. Anthony, between SS. Christopher, Sebastian, Venantius, and Vitus, and above, the Almighty with SS. Peter, Paul, Augustine, and a Bishop, all half-lengths. It is dated 1464, and inscribed 'Antonius DE MURÃO (Murano) Pinxit,' a work therefore of the master's latest period. To gain a fuller knowledge of this early

---

[1] Dr. Bode (ii. 618) regards the portrait of Vespasiano Gonzaga in that gallery as a Mantegna. I consider it to be a fine work of the Veronese Bonsignori. The study in black chalk for it is in the Uffizi (†) (engraving department, No. 1702, Venetian school).

Venetian painter we must however seek him elsewhere—in the Sacristy of the Church of Pausola in the March of Ancona, and more especially in Venice, in the Academy and in the churches of S. Zaccaria, S. Pantaleone, and S. Francesco della Vigna (Sacristy). In the galleries of Bologna and Bergamo, and in the Brera at Milan, we also find a few of his works. In the Seminario at Brescia there is a picture representing St. Ursula and her Virgins, which, since the days of Ridolfi, has always been attributed to the Lombard Vincenzo Foppa, but which appears to me an indisputable work of Vivarini.[2] (†)    I consider that this master owes his artistic development to Gentile da Fabriano and Pisanello, or at all events to Giambono, who was influenced by the latter painter.

## CARLO CRIVELLI.

There are two works by this master in the Lateran,[3] and one, a Pietà, in the Vatican. Carlo and his younger brother (?) Vittore, spent the greater part of their lives in the March of Ancona, and chiefly in the neighbourhood of Ascoli. Nearly all Carlo's panels, executed with the help of his brother, and remarkable for their bright colouring, were formerly in that district. Most of them have now been removed to Rome, Milan, and London (National Gallery), but some few still remain in the March of Ancona —for instance, a small picture at Ancona itself, an early

[2] Passavant, in a very superficial article on the Lombard painters (in the *Kunstblatt*), also ascribed this picture to Vincenzo Foppa.

[3] One of these is an altar-piece in five compartments. In the centre is the Madonna with the Child, who holds a goldfinch by a string, and before whom kneels the donor; at the sides are four saints, inscribed: 1481, VLTIMA IVLII. It is powerful in drawing. The other picture is dated 1482, and represents the Madonna enthroned, with the Child, who holds an apple. At the foot of the throne a Franciscan monk is in adoration.

work of 1468 at Massa, others at Penna di San Martino,
Ascoli, and elsewhere.  The most historically interesting work
of Crivelli is in the gallery at Verona.   Messrs. Crowe and
Cavalcaselle (i. 82), and Dr. Bode, infer from this painting
that Crivelli was a pupil of Antonio and Bartolommeo
Vivarini of Murano.   The latter critic also considers (ii.
630) that the influence of Niccolò da Foligno and even of
Signorelli is perceptible in the works of Crivelli.  I find it
impossible to share these opinions.   To judge from the
picture at Verona, I should say that Crivelli's early training
was derived from Squarcione at Padua, for at the first
glance this picture looks like the work of Gregorio
Schiavone, whom all admit to have been a scholar and
imitator of Squarcione.  The angels, both in composition
and modelling, recall Schiavone's type and manner.   That
the painters of Murano exercised some influence over
Crivelli at a later date I have no wish to dispute ; but I
cannot admit that his works show either the influence of
Niccolò da Foligno or of Signorelli.   From Carlo Crivelli
proceeded Pietro Alemanni, by whom there are several unimportant paintings at Ascoli.   Lorenzo da Sanseverino the
younger, who is represented by a good work in the English
National Gallery, may also have felt the influence of
Crivelli.

There are some excellent works in the Doria gallery
by Bellini's scholars.  Among them, however, I should
neither include No. 521, nor a picture (No. 558) attributed
to Basaiti.

VIRGIN AND CHILD.   BY CRIVELLI, VERONA.

*To face p. 276.*

## CIMA DA CONEGLIANO.

The first of these pictures, No. 521, represents the Madonna with the Infant Saviour in her arms. It is merely one of the innumerable copies, so frequently met with in Italy, of an original painting by Cima da Conegliano.

Cima, the pupil and assistant of Bellini, was a serious and conscientious painter, somewhat monotonous perhaps, but occasionally attaining to great nobility. There are no genuine works by him in Southern or Central Italy. Recently, indeed, a picture bearing Cima's name has been exhibited in the first Venetian room of the Uffizi, but it is probably by Pietro da Messina, an imitator of the master, whose copies after different artists are often taken for originals. Thus we meet with him under the names of Antonello, of Bellini—as in the church of the Scalzi in Venice—and of Jacopo da Valenza in the gallery at Padua, Nos. 143 and 23. (†)

Cima's works are to be found at Bologna, Modena, and Parma—some excellent examples in the latter city ; in the Brera (No. 191, perhaps his finest work, and Nos. 300, 286, 289, 302) ; at Vicenza (his earliest signed work of 1489) ; at Conegliano, and above all in Venice—in the churches of S. Giovanni in Bragora, S. Maria dell' Orto, and the Carmine, and in the Academy. A fine early work by the master is a large altar-piece in several compartments in the church of the little mountain village of Olera, near Bergamo. Among those whose .works prove them to have been imitators of Cima may be mentioned Sebastiano del Piombo—as shown by his early work, the " Pietà," in the collection of Sir Henry Layard at Venice— Giovan Maria da Carpi, by whom there is a signed Madonna in the possession of Signor Antonio Piccinelli at Bergamo ;

Cristoforo Caselli of Parma ; Pietro da Messina ; Girolamo
da Santa Croce—a picture in the Venice Academy and
one at Bergamo (Lochis collection), bearing the forged
signature : BATT. CIMA. CONELIANENSIS. M . D . XV. ; the
unknown master who executed the good altar-piece in the
church of Sanfiore near Conegliano, and other painters of
this date. Cima is undoubtedly an excellent, though by no
means an original, artist ; most of his types being borrowed
from his master Giovanni Bellini. He had no dramatic
talent, but he is the best and most careful draughtsman of the
whole contemporary school of Bellini. Unlike his master
who was ever making progress even at the age of eighty,
Cima never abandoned the style of the *quattro-cento*. We
may see this even in his latest works—for instance, in the
beautiful picture in the Venice Academy, "Tobias and the
Angel."

We will now turn to the picture No. 558. It represents the Madonna and Child, with SS. Peter, John
the Baptist, Nicholas of Bari, and a female Martyr, and
is ascribed by the catalogue to Basaiti. In this gallery,
therefore, we find, first a work of Garofalo, and now
a Madonna with Saints of the school of Boccaccino,
both attributed to Marco Basaiti. How, we may well
ask, is an art-historian who is not at the same time
a connoisseur, to form any idea of the character of Basaiti
from these two pictures. He would be forced to take refuge
in theorising about the various influences to which this
painter must be supposed to have been subjected.

## BOCCACCIO BOCCACCINO.

This Lombardo-Venetian painter is unrepresented in
Southern and Central Italy, if we except the Zingarella
already mentioned in the Pitti at Florence (No. 246). In

Venice we meet him under the most varied names. In S. Giuliano he appears as Cordelgliaghi; in the Sacristy of S. Stefano, and in S. Pietro Martire at Murano, as Palma Vecchio, (†) (the latter picture is much repainted); and in the library of the Ducal Palace as Giovanni Bellini. (†) In the Academy he is alternately described as an early Ferrarese, as a pupil of Leonardo da Vinci, and as Pietro Perugino.[4] In his picture of the " Supper at Emmaus," belonging to Signor Sernagiotto, Boccaccino even passes for Leonardo da Vinci himself. This Cremonese painter was treated much as his countryman Bartolommeo Veneto, who signs one of his early works ' Bartolommeo mezzo Cremonese e mezzo Veneziano,' and whose paintings also pass under the most diverse names. Boccaccino is, however, an artist of a very different stamp, and endowed with far more character than that protean painter, Bartolommeo Veneto. He probably served his apprenticeship both in Ferrara and in Venice. All that is best in his art he derived from the school of the Bellini, from Alvise Vivarini and latterly from Giorgione. One of his finest works is in the Academy at Venice (Room II., No. 55)—the Madonna seated with the Infant Saviour, in a beautiful landscape, surrounded by St. Peter, St. Catherine, St. Rosa, and St. John the Baptist—

[4] This picture, " Christ washing the feet of His Disciples," is now assigned to Boccaccino. It is a very inferior production, and may have been partly the work of his brother. Messrs. Crowe and Cavalcaselle, speaking of it (ii. 447), observe : ' We are reminded in this picture of the schools of Lombardy and Leonardo, of Umbria and Pinturicchio, yet at the same time of those of Ferrara and Ercole Roberti, as illustrated by Panetti, Costa, Timoteo Viti, and the Zaganelli.' 'E se potran contarsi anco fian pochi ! ' says Ariosto. In order to follow these writers, my readers must know that Boccaccino was in Rome and Ferrara, and documentary evidence has also proved that he stayed for some time in Milan. In all these cities then, according to the historians of Italian painting, Boccaccino laid up a varied stock of impressions which he utilised for this picture in the Venice Academy.

signed 'Bochazinus.'[5] In addition to his fine frescoes in
the cathedral of Cremona there is also a good altar-piece of
1518 by him in his native city. Another still better work,
of brilliant colouring, representing the "Annunciation,"
belongs to Signor Giulio Princtti at Milan, and the gallery at Padua contains a Madonna with St. Lucy and
St. Catherine—an excellent and genuine work.

Boccaccino's son Camillo was also an artist, and his
large picture in the Brera (No. 426) proves that he deserves to
be classed among the better Lombard painters of the third
decade of the sixteenth century. This work also shows that
Camillo, like many other artists, fell under the influence of
Giovan Antonio da Pordenone, who was for a time at Cremona
and Piacenza. Padre Lanzi and Camillo's countrymen extol
him principally for his frescoes in the dome of the church
of S. Sigismondo near Cremona. I am inclined to think,
however, that it was fortunate for the painter's reputation
that his career was cut short by death soon after the completion of this work, at the age of thirty-one. The Boccac-
cini family has led me into a digression, and I will now turn
to another Venetian painter.

The Madonna (No. 558), as we have seen, is not to be
attributed to Basaiti. This gallery, however, contains a
genuine work by the master, a St. Sebastian (No. 495),
though falsely ascribed to Perugino. I see to my satisfaction
that Messrs. Crowe and Cavalcaselle also attribute it to
Basaiti.

---

[5] He signs himself variously
Bochazinus and Boccaccinus de
Boccacciis (see Grasselli, *Abecedario
biografico*, p. 54). There is a characteristic work by this painter in
the Correr museum (Room VII.,
No. 22).

## MARCO BASAITI.

Unfortunately, we know nothing of the early training of this master. In his later works he shows himself an artist of some importance. Vasari only notices him cursorily, and was moreover so ill-informed about him as to make out of the name two separate painters, Basarini and Bassiti (vi. 102), a proof that this painter, too, was almost forgotten by the middle of the sixteenth century, even by the Venetians.

Basaiti was principally trained in the workshop of Alvise Vivarini. His own works testify to this, as also does the altar-piece of 1503, in the church of the Frari at Venice, which, on the death of Vivarini, was completed by Basaiti,[6] who added the following inscription : QUOD VIVARINE TUA FATALI NECE NEQUISTI, MARCUS BAXITUS NOBILE PROMSIT OPUS. M . D . III. Considering that succeeding generations of Basaiti's own countrymen knew so little of his history, and that even in the present day art-historians have made him appear a species of chameleon, it is not surprising that the compilers of the Doria catalogue in the last century should have confused him with Garofalo, with Boccaccino (No. 558), and even with Perugino (No. 495). In other galleries the same occurs. In the Uffizi, as we have seen, he is confounded with Giovanni Bellini, in Milan and London with Cima da Conegliano,[7] and elsewhere with the

---

[6] Messrs. Crowe and Cavalcaselle (i. 261–263) discover the most varied influences in the works of Basaiti. In some they find reminiscences of Perugino, Timoteo Viti, Simone da Cusinghe, Matteo and Antonio Cesa, and of Antonio da Tisoio ; in others of the Vivarini, of Previtali and Giorgione—even of Lotto and Solario. At times again they are reminded of Cima, Carpaccio, the Bellini, and finally of the Lombards !

[7] Dr. Bode (ii. 641) regards the small picture in the Brera (No. 302, St. Jerome as a penitent) as a work of Basaiti. The form of hand and ear, and the landscape, in this picture, are all extremely characteristic

Veronese Gianfrancesco Carotto.    The large "Assumption" in S. Pietro at Murano is more probably the work of Bissolo, executed under the guidance of Giovanni Bellini, than that of Basaiti as Dr. Bode conjectures (ii. 641). (†)    In the Berlin museum there is a beautiful little painting by Basaiti (No. 40), which Messrs. Crowe and Cavalcaselle regard as an early work of Carotto (i. 482).    In the second edition of the catalogue, Dr. Julius Meyer came nearer the truth by placing it in the school of Alvise Vivarini.    I should venture to go a step further and to pronounce this charming Madonna, with the two angel musicians, to be undoubtedly by Marco Basaiti. (†)

Works by this master are by no means rare in Italy; they are for the most part in Venice: two in the church of S. Pietro in Castello; another in the Sacristy of the Salute; a signed Madonna in the Correr museum; two large works of 1510–1512 in the Academy—the " Calling of the Sons of Zebedee " and the " Agony in the Garden "; besides several smaller pictures in the same gallery. There are also works by Basaiti at Padua [8] and Verona, and in the Ambrosiana at Milan.    In the collection of the author [9] there is a fine male portrait, bearing the following inscription:  M . BAXITUS . F . M . D . XXI .   Its breadth of manner reminds one more of Cima and of Giovanni Bellini than of Alvise Vivarini.

In the gallery at Bergamo we find a much repainted

---

of Cima da Conegliano, to whom the director of the gallery has recently restored it. A similar picture by Cima under the name of Basaiti passed from the Hamilton collection into the National Gallery; but Sir Frederick Burton immediately recognised its true author and ascribed

it to Cima da Conegliano.

[9] No. 18; a good picture of the master's later time (1515–1520). It represents the Madonna and Child with SS. Peter and Liberale and three angels—signed MARCHVS BAXAITI.

[8] Now at Bergamo.

portrait of a man, signed; an "Ecce Homo" of 1517, and a St. Jerome as a penitent, signed MARCVS BAXAITI. The latter picture, which has suffered severely, recalls Cima. A Madonna with the same signature is in the possession of the Agliardi family, and a signed and much restored " St. Jerome " belongs to Signor Antonio Piccinelli.

It is probable that Basaiti was born about 1470, and died soon after 1521.

## GIROLAMO ROMANINO.

In the Doria gallery a large Madonna, of distinctly Venetian colouring, cannot fail to strike us; but strangely enough it has received no name. A picture without a name is worthless in the eyes of the public, as the directors of galleries are well aware, and I shall therefore take the liberty of bestowing on it that of Romanino da Brescia. I feel justified in so doing, as I have long been intimately acquainted with this splendid colourist. Were the picture properly cleaned, the master's peculiar and glowing tints would reappear.

Romanino is a powerful and original artist, often displaying great nobility, though at times excessively careless. He is well represented in the churches of his native city of Brescia, and throughout the whole of that district,[1] though beyond these limits his works are rarely met with. Hardly a collection out of Italy, the English National Gallery excepted, possesses an example of his art.

Few painters have so much character as Romanino, and few can equal him in brilliancy of colour and life-like treatment. His large altar-pieces in S. Francesco and S. Maria

---

[1] In the churches of Montechiari, Calvisano, Prealboino, S. Felice, Salò, Capriolo (under the name of Titian), and in other places.

Calchera at Brescia, and in the gallery at Padua, are among the finest specimens of Venetian art. His paintings on the shutters of the organ (of 1540) in S. Giorgio at Verona are also of a high order of merit. The same church contains a most charming altar-piece, also of 1540, by his younger fellow-countryman and rival, Alessandro Moretto. The merits of Romanino as a fresco painter may be studied in the cathedral of Cremona, in the lower church of S. Giulia at Brescia, in the gallery there, and also in various places in his native valley of Camonica.

Romanino's nature was simple in the extreme, and genuine and unaffected, hence the language of his art is of the same quality as the dialect of his native place. The few portraits he has left are models of simplicity and faithful reproductions of nature. We feel that the painter did not flatter those he portrayed, but represented them just as he found them, with the utmost truth. Romanino's portraits are simpler in conception than those of Tintoretto and Titian; the best among them, in the noble freedom of the lines, are scarcely inferior to the finest portraits of Titian or Velasquez; such for example is the portrait of a young man in rich attire, formerly in the possession of the Countess Fenaroli of Brescia, and now belonging to her heirs.

Romanino is to Alessandro Moretto much what Gaudenzio Ferrari was to Luini in the Milanese school. Romanino and Gaudenzio are more dramatic and powerful, and are endowed with higher imaginative faculties, than Moretto and Luini, who are perhaps more pleasing and attractive than their rivals.[2]

[2] Romanino's drawings are extremely rare; I am only acquainted with about four or five, all slight sketches in pen and ink. Two are in the Uffizi—a group of *putti*, No. 1465, and a male portrait. A very fine example is in the Ambrosiana, "The Woman taken in Adultery," (†) and another, extremely characteristic of Romanino, though bearing the name of Giulio Romano, is at Chatsworth—"Christ

## ALESSANDRO MORETTO.

The Vatican gallery contains the only work by this master in Rome—a picture so greatly defaced that it is scarcely possible to recognise in it the hand of the master, whose delicate silvery tones are, as a rule, very characteristic. To my surprise, Messrs. Crowe and Cavalcaselle extol this work on account of its excellent preservation.

A portrait of a young man with a dog is ascribed to Moretto in the Palazzo Colonna; but the attribution is purely arbitrary, since this work is not even of his school.

Moretto's portraits are extremely rare; beyond the two in the English National Gallery, I am only acquainted with a very small number. Those cited by Dr. Bode (ii. 779, 780) — a portrait in the gallery at Brescia, the so-called Doctor in the Brignole-Sale Palace at Genoa (signed A. B.), and the large equestrian portrait in the Casa Martinengo at Brescia —are only by some of Moretto's imitators. (†)

A small and excellent work by the master himself is in the Naples museum. The Uffizi can boast of no genuine example—the large " Death of Adonis " (No. 592), ascribed to Moretto, being, as we have seen, by Sebastian del Piombo.[3] The portrait of a man (No. 639) is more probably an early work of the Cremonese painter Giulio Campi; (†) and the small "Descent into Hades" reminds me more of the Veronese Felice Brusasorci, than of Moretto. (†)

Moretto's best works are still at Brescia and in its neighbourhood, and there this most attractive master must

with the Woman of Samaria." (†) In all of them Romanino shows himself a more able and spirited draughtsman than Moretto, whose drawings, though always very careful in execution, lack the vitality and decision which characterise each stroke of Romanino's pen.

[3] This is also the opinion of Messrs. Crowe and Cavalcaselle (ii. 416).

be studied.[1] I am not surprised that Messrs. Crowe and
Cavalcaselle, in accordance with their theories as to the
influence of one master on another, should have considered
that Moretto was greatly under that of Palma Vecchio, who
was then living in Venice; but it is inexplicable that Dr.
Bode, who is apparently so intimately acquainted with the
Venetian manner of painting, should have adhered to this
view, which in my opinion is absolutely erroneous and un-
justified by a single work of Moretto. I consider that the
master always preserved his Brescian character. After his
training under Ferramola was completed, he applied himself to studying the manner of his fellow-citizen Romanino,
and brought that style to its highest perfection.

Many foreign critics, and amateurs indeed, after taking
a hasty survey of some few works by the great Venetian
colourists, discern their influence in those of all contemporary painters of local schools connected with Venice.
An outward show of learning attaches to these theories, but
in reality they are mischievous and misleading, tending to
paralyse our intelligence and to cause the greatest confusion. I cannot sufficiently warn students against such
teaching. It may be compared to the glistening line
marking the path of the snail, which shortsighted persons
might mistake for silver, though a sound eye at once
perceives its true nature.

Near Romanino's picture we see a Madonna and Child
with St. Francis and the little St. John—a feeble production
of the Bolognese school, by some imitator of Bagnacavallo
or Innocenzo da Imola. The catalogue informs us that it
is the work of "Lodi"—I presume that Calisto da Lodi,
the well-known pupil of Romanino and a painter of considerable reputation in his day, is meant.

---

[1] In the churches at Castenedolo, Prealboino, Maguzzano, Orzinuovi,
Paitone, Calvisano, Auro, Mazzano, &c.

## CALISTO DA LODI.

Calisto Piazza, usually known as Calisto da Lodi, belonged to a family of artists at Lodi, bearing the name of Piazza with the addition of Toccagni.[5]  He was born about 1500, and died in 1561; his father's name was Martino, his uncle's Albertino.  Calisto had two brothers, Scipione[6] and Cesare, both painters, who usually assisted him.  His father appears to have sent him at an early age to Brescia to learn of Romanino.  Except in the districts round Brescia, Lodi, and Milan, this talented painter is hardly known.  In that neighbourhood he is frequently met with, especially in the Val Camonica—at Breno, Esine, and Cividate.  To judge from some of his early works, Calisto appears first to have followed Moretto closely—the latter being his contemporary and his fellow-pupil with Romanino.  This tendency is apparent in a long picture in the Poldi-Pezzoli museum, at Milan, which is there ascribed to Moretto.[7] (†)  The altar-piece in the gallery at Padua, signed with Romanino's name and dated 1521, is, I believe, a work of Calisto's early period rather later in date than the preceding. (†)  Calisto probably executed it in his master's workshop and under his directions.  The

[5] See *Memorie originali italiane risguardanti le belle arti*, serie prima, p. 171, by Michelangelo Gualandi, Bologna, 1840.

[6] In the church of S. Spirito at Bergamo, there is a signed picture by Scipione Piazza.  He died at Lodi in 1551.

[7] The landscape and the types of the angels are characteristic of Calisto in this picture.  Dr. Bode (ii. 778) ascribes it to Romanino; this is not surprising, for it is im-possible that anyone, however gifted, should be able to recognise a master in his early works without having himself lived in Italy, and there made a careful study of each painter's development.  A charming little Madonna in *tempera* by Calisto belongs to M. Paul Delaroff at St. Petersburg.  It proved to be a copy of an early work by Moretto belonging to Sir Henry Layard, and closely resembling the panel in the Poldi-Pezzoli collection at Milan.

"Adoration of the Shepherds" in the gallery at Brescia, signed and dated 1524 (formerly in the church of S. Clemente), shows the influence of both Romanino and Moretto. In the "Visitation," of 1525 in S. Maria Calchera, on the other hand, Calisto shows himself the imitator of Romanino alone, with whom, in the following years, he is constantly confounded. In the Brera this kind of confusion is so rife that the authorities actually ascribe a good work by Calisto (the "Baptism," No. 425) to Carlo Urbino, a feeble painter of Crema. (†)

After executing several altar-pieces in the Val Camonica, Calisto returned to Lodi in 1529 and received the flattering commission to decorate a part of the church of S. Maria Incoronata with frescoes, in company with his brothers Scipione and Cesare. A year later he painted in the same church the fine series from the life of St. John the Baptist, in the chapel dedicated to that saint. These frescoes are among the master's best works, and of such glowing colour that at a later date a fable was invented to the effect that Titian, on some occasion when passing through Lodi, painted several of the heads in them (Lanzi iii. 151). On the strength of this absurd tradition, some art-historian of the future, say, from Finland, will doubtless make out that Titian influenced Calisto. A good early work by him is in the Brera—a Madonna and Child enthroned, with SS. Jerome, John the Baptist, and an angel playing on a musical instrument (No. 225). He has also two other paintings in that gallery, one of which is the fine portrait of Lodovico Vistarini (No. 257). Another good work by him containing portraits of the Trivulzio family, is in a church at Codogno. In the year 1535 Calisto settled at Milan, and executed frescoes in the churches of S. Maurizio, S. Francesco, and S. Nazzaro e Celso.

I would observe that the unattractive portraits, Nos. 178 and 170, attributed to Holbein, are certainly not by that great painter; equally impossible is it, that the portrait of a high-bred woman, apparently discontented with her lot, should be the work of Tintoretto.[8] It is probably by Scipione da Gaeta. Several other portraits in this gallery are with an equal want of intelligence ascribed to Tintoretto.

## PARIS BORDONE.

In this gallery hangs one of Paris Bordone's fine decorative pictures (No. 321), its splendour of colouring hardly dimmed by the surrounding gloom. It represents Mars, Venus, and Cupid. Paris was born about 1495 at Treviso, and died soon after 1570; his life covers about the same space of time as that of Moretto and of Calisto da Lodi.

The following autograph entry was discovered by the late Signor Cecchetti in the Archives at Venice: ' Io Paris Bordon da Treviso, habitante in Venetia in contrà de S. Marcilian, 31 Agosto, 1563.' He had four children, Giovanni, Angelica, Cassandra, and Ottavia, and was in good circumstances. According to Vasari, Giorgione was his prototype; but undoubtedly he followed Titian even yet more closely, for in 1509, when about fourteen, he entered the workshop of that master, devoting himself principally to the study of works of Titian's Giorgionesque period. The "Baptism of Christ," in the Capitoline gallery (ruined by modern restoration), which has always been rightly regarded as an early work by Titian, has recently been ascribed by Messrs. Crowe and Cavalcaselle and by Dr. Bode (ii. 764,

---

[8] Several fine examples of Tintoretto's art are in the Colonna gallery. His merits as a landscape painter may be especially studied in that collection.

note) to Paris Bordone. This view appears to me altogether erroneous.[9]

In the Doria gallery is a picture representing the Holy
Family with St. Catherine of Alexandria (*); it is merely
an old copy of an early work by Paris Bordone, but it
shows how closely he followed Titian.[1] Another picture
by him is ascribed to Titian—a male portrait much restored but still revealing all the master's characteristics,
the distinctive rosy glazes in the flesh-tints and the peculiarly shaped hand with stiff fingers. It is apparently
the portrait of a poet, though, notwithstanding the crown
of laurel encircling his brow, his appearance is the very
reverse of poetical.

Paris Bordone is a noble, attractive, and refined artist,
and a splendid colourist, though of unequal merit and at
times superficial. Several of his works are in the Colonna
gallery; one, a Holy Family with SS. Elisabeth, Jerome,
and John the Baptist, is falsely ascribed to Bonifazio
Veneziano; another, a "Santa Conversazione," is one of
the master's finest works, though disfigured by barbarous
repainting. In the Pitti a "Riposo" (No 89) and "Au-
gustus and the Sibyl" (No. 257) are attributed to Paris
Bordone, though in reality these pictures are by one of the
Bonifazios, as pointed out by the late Mr. Mündler. There
are, however, two excellent portraits by him in Florence—
that of a youth in the Uffizi (No. 607), and the so-called
"Balia di Casa Medici," in the Pitti (No. 109); and the
Brignole-Sale Palace at Genoa also contains a fine portrait
by him.

---

[9] In this picture we find the
form of hand and ear so distinctive
of Titian's early works. The portrait of the donor too is characteristic
of Titian, so also is the Giorgionesque
treatment of light in the landscape.

[1] Dr. Bode (ii. 775) considers
this picture to be by Bernardino
Licinio, 'with reminiscences of
Paris Bordone.'

His principal works are still in Venice and its neighbourhood. Several are in the Academy, and among them
his best, " The Fisherman presenting St. Mark's ring to the
Doge "—a picture of the highest charm, to which its
exceptionally good state of preservation contributes not a
little. Another masterpiece by him, representing the
Madonna and Child with SS. George and Christopher, is in
the Tadini collection at Lovere on the Lago d' Iséo. Vasari
mentions it in vol. xiii. 50, and adds that St. George was
the portrait of the donor, Giulio Manfroni of Crema.[2] In
this work, which is singularly brilliant in colour, Bordone
appears to have been inspired by his fellow-citizen Lorenzo
Lotto.

About half a dozen of Bordone's works are still in his
native city of Treviso.[3] In the gallery at Padua there is a
much damaged but genuine painting by him which the
catalogue ascribes to his school—" Christ taking leave of
His Mother " (No. 67).[4] At Milan we find several of his
works—in the church of S. Celso, in the Brera, in the
Archbishop's Palace,[5] and some splendid portraits in private
collections. Vasari records that the Fuggers, some of
whom were established in Venice, persuaded Bordone to
come to Augsburg, their native city, and that he remained
there for some time in the employment of that family. He
further relates that in 1538 Francis I. of France sent for
the master and commanded him to paint likenesses of the
most beautiful women at his court. These portraits, however,
have not been preserved, and Bordone's works are extremely

[2] See also the *Anonimo*, p.
145, second edition, annotated by
Dr. Gustavo Frizzoni, Bologna,
1884.

[3] Among them a Holy Family in
the gallery (No. 53), there ascribed
to Palma Vecchio.

[4] It is curious that the same
subject was treated almost contem-
poraneously by Correggio, Lotto and
Bordone.

[5] This fine picture represents the
Holy Family with a bishop and the
donor.

rare in France, where I am not acquainted with any in private collections. Of the three ascribed to him in the Louvre, the portrait of Hieronymus Crofft of Augsburg (No. 1179) was only bought in the reign of Louis XIV., and the decorative picture of Vertumnus and Pomona (No. 1178) came to France as late as the beginning of this century. As to the third work, representing a "Man and a Child" (No. 1180), it is not by Bordone at all, but by a Flemish painter. (†)

## BONIFAZIO VERONESE.

The first Bonifazio[6] was a contemporary of Paris Bordone and akin to him in the nature of his art. In this gallery we find a most attractive painting by him (No. 886) —the Holy Family with two female martyrs—unfortunately ruined by some ignorant picture cleaner. Portraits by the hand of this cheerful and splendid colourist are rare, but I think I have been fortunate enough to discover one in the Doria gallery (No. 109). It is ascribed to Giorgione and represents a young man, wearing a black cap. (†)

The same barbarian who repainted Bonifazio's other work is probably responsible for having entirely destroyed the surface of this portrait; but it is still of great charm both for its graceful treatment and the simplicity of the composition. A beautiful Madonna with SS. Jerome and Lucy, by this brilliant artist, in the Colonna gallery[7] (Room I.)

---

[6] It appears from a document published by the late Signor Cecchetti, that the Bonifazio family also bore the name of 'de Pittatis': '1553, 26 luglio, De Pittatis Bonifacio, abitante nella contrà di San Marcuola, in le case dele monache di S. Alvise,' and 'Io Bonifazio di Pittati da Verona pitor, fò (fù) di Ser Marzio' (the son of the late Ser Marzio) (see *Archivio Veneto*, tome 34, p. 207).

[7] In the Doria gallery, Bonifazio is confounded with Giorgione, in

is ascribed to Titian. In this work Bonifazio's distinctive form of hand and ear may be studied. A small picture by him, of glowing colour, belongs to Prince Mario Chigi. It is surpassed by one of a still more brilliant and delicate colour in the Pitti (Sala di Saturno, No. 161), representing the "Finding of Moses," which is there ascribed to Giorgione. Masterpieces by this great painter are to be seen in the galleries of Venice and Milan.

## JACOPO PALMA, called PALMA VECCHIO.

Palma[8] is another great colourist of the school of Giovanni Bellini and of Giorgione, whose works are often ascribed to the latter, as also to Titian. We have already described two of his paintings in the Borghese gallery, but in the Doria Palace he is wholly unrepresented, either by genuine or spurious works. The Sciarra-Colonna gallery contains a fine picture by him, known as the "Bella di Tiziano." The portrait of this celebrated Venetian beauty, whose features so often recur in the works of Palma, Titian, and other contemporary Venetian masters, has only recently been ascribed to Titian. In the seventeenth century it was at Brussels in the collection of the Archduke Leopold William. David Teniers the painter, and the custodian of that collection, was commissioned by his master and patron, as is well known, to reproduce the more important paintings in it on a small scale. These copies were then engraved by Vorsterman, J. Van Kessel, and others for a large publication entitled "Théâtre des peintures de David Teniers, dédié au Prince Leopold-Guillaume,

the Colonna with Titian and Paris Bordone, and in the Pitti with Palma Vecchio and Giorgione.

[8] Signor Elia Fornoni of Bergamo, in a recent publication (*Notizie biografiche su Palma Vecchio*, Bergamo, 1886), maintains that Palma's surname was Nigreti, a question which need not detain us here.

archiduc, etc.," which appeared at Brussels in 1660. Many
of these Flemish reproductions of Italian paintings were
subsequently sent as a present to the Duke of Marlborough,
and some years ago I saw them in one of the upper rooms
at Blenheim. Among these copies was this "Bella di
Tiziano," with its rightful name inscribed on the back,
*i.e.* "Copie d'après Palma Vecchio."

In her youth this beautiful woman was undoubtedly one
of those notorious Venetians, the muses of Pietro Aretino,
who so often sat as models to the painters. Many a head
in Titian's pictures recalls this portrait, but even a superficial connoisseur of the school can hardly fail to recognise
in it the hand of Palma. It dates from that period when
he was closely connected with his fellow-pupil Lotto.[9] The
gay colouring, the light green shadows, and the modelling of
the hand recall that master. A similar portrait by Palma
is in the Poldi-Pezzoli museum at Milan, though it has
been so modernised by the restorer as to look almost like
a copy. The charming female portrait by Palma in the
Berlin museum (No. 197*a*) is, to my mind, far more attractive than this celebrated "Bella" of the Sciarra gallery.
A very characteristic work by Palma is in the Palazzo
Colonna agli Apostoli. It represents the Madonna and
Child, to whom St. Peter presents the donor. In this
picture we may study Palma's peculiar form of hand and
ear ; the landscape, with the red horizon, is also characteristic of the master. Another work by Palma, ascribed to
Titian, the "Woman taken in Adultery," is in the Capitoline

[9] Messrs. Crowe and Cavalcaselle
(ii. 478) also mention it as the work
of Palma. Vasari's Florentine commentators, on the other hand, continue to regard it as a Titian (xiii.
45). I must observe that although
these latter writers have done much
in other respects for the history of
Italian art, they have not shown
much judgment in their attributions
of pictures, more especially those of
the Venetian school. Hence their
notes to Vasari are not only feeble
but often full of errors.

gallery. The "Anonimo" mentions it as being in the collection of Francesco Zio (Giglio) at Venice in 1528.[1] These four pictures are the only works by Palma that I know of in Rome. The so-called "Schiava di Tiziano" in the Barberini gallery, which Messrs. Crowe and Cavalcaselle attribute to Palma (ii. 478), is probably one of the many imitations produced by Pietro Vecchia in the seventeenth century, for the admirers of Giorgione. One of Palma's most beautiful easel pictures, a "Santa Conversazione," is in the Naples museum, and is worthy to rank with his picture in the Louvre.

Of the four works ascribed to the master in the Pitti, not one is genuine, and the Uffizi has not fared much better, for, of the five works bearing his name in that gallery, the only authentic one appears to be the coarse-looking Judith (619) formerly attributed to Pordenone. The Holy Family with the Magdalen (No. 623) would probably, on closer inspection, prove to be only an old copy after Palma. The portrait of a "Geometrician" so-called (No. 650) is a copy, and not even after Palma Vecchio.[2] The small Madonna (No. 1019) can only be regarded as the production of some mediocre imitator of Titian. The "Supper at Emmaus" (No. 1037) is evidently of the school of Bonifazio. As to the much damaged female portrait (No. 1087), it would be no loss, I think, were it permanently banished from the collection. The galleries of Bologna, Ferrara, and Padua contain no works by Palma.

---

[1] See the *Anonimo* second edition, with notes by Dr. Frizzoni, p. 180).

[2] The original of this "Geometrician" so-called is in the collection of Sir Francis Cook at Richmond, where it passes for a Giorgione. I believe it to be by Bartolommeo Veneto. (†) It is evidently a portrait, and represents a man resting his right hand upon his sword-hilt, and holding a compass in his left. A copy of the picture in the Uffizi, dated 1555, is in the Correr museum at Venice. (†)

In the latter collection we certainly find a Madonna inscribed IACOMO PALMA, but the signature is a forgery, and the picture as unworthy of the name as is its counterpart in the Berlin museum (No. 31), (†) which was provided with a similar inscription, probably for the purpose of ensnaring future generations of art-critics and gallery-directors. In the gallery at Rovigo is a work of Palma's best period — a Madonna with SS. Jerome and Helena (No. 39)—though the restoration to which it has been subjected has almost destroyed the master's personality. Hence Messrs. Crowe and Cavalcaselle discreetly avoid all mention of it; they, however, bring forward a male portrait (No. 123) in the same gallery, in which they would fain recognise the hand of Palma (ii. 484). I can only regard this work as a copy. (†)

Two other copies after Palma are in the gallery at Modena—one (No. 129) ascribed to the master himself, the other (No. 123) to Giorgione. (†) The galleries of Parma and Turin are without works by Palma Vecchio. In the Brera we find a Triptych (No. 290), with SS. Helena, Constantine, Roch, and Sebastian, and a large altar-piece, "The Adoration of the Magi." The latter I believe to be the last work of the master, who at that date, 1526, was already suffering from the illness of which he died. The execution of the picture was consequently left almost entirely to one of his assistants. At Bergamo itself there is only a single work by this Bergamasque artist,[3] and that was not painted for the place. In his native valley of the Brembo, we find some beautiful examples of his art—the large altar-pieces in numerous compartments at Peghera, Dossena, and Scrinalta.[4] But the finest of all his large

---

[3] Now in the gallery.

[4] The altar-piece in the church at Scrinalta (Palma's birthplace) is in nine compartments. In the centre the "Resurrection," above it the "Presentation in the Temple;"

works is the altar-piece in S. Stefano at Vicenza, and that
in S. Maria Formosa at Venice. To these I should have
added the large picture in the Venice Academy (Room IX.,
No. 8), were it not entirely spoilt by repainting. Palma
appears to have painted few portraits. Two, almost
ruined by restoration, are in the Querini-Stampalia
collection (the Querini were Palma's patrons). Palma leads
us to his fellow-pupil Lorenzo Lotto, who was a few years his
senior, and influenced him at a certain period of his career
(1510–1515).[5]

## LORENZO LOTTO.

Lotto was the pupil of Giovanni Bellini, and was gifted
with a rich imagination. I believe that he was born at Venice
earlier than is usually supposed, namely, about 1475, and
not in 1480. In the first years of the sixteenth century he
appears to have settled at Treviso, and soon after to have
acquired the right of citizenship there. From that period
he nearly always signs himself 'de Tarvisio.'[6] Two
pictures by him are in the Doria gallery. One, No. 159,

at the sides SS. Joseph, Francis, John, James, Albert, Apollonia, and another saint. In addition to this altar-piece, Serinalta contains two other pictures of saints by the master, St. Peter Martyr and St. Adalbert. The altar-piece in the church at Peghera (Val Taleggio) is in seven compartments; in the centre SS. James, Roch, and Sebastian; above the Pietà—an angel lamenting over the Dead Body of Christ; on the right St. Anthony, and on the left St. Ambrose. In the upper part of the picture is the Almighty. The altar-piece in the church at Dossena is similar in character.

[5] This is very apparent in Palma's picture in the Louvre, and in the charming female portrait in the Berlin gallery (No. 197a).

[6] See Gustavo Bampo, *Spigolature dall' archivio notarile di Treviso.* '1504, 24 Febr. Tarvisii in domo habitationis Mag. Laurentii Loti de Venetiis pictoris Tarvisii, &c.' '1504, 25 Novb. Tarvisii—presentibus . . . et M. Laurentio Loto de Venetiis q. S. Thome, pictore habitatore Tarvisii.' '1505, 7 Aprilis. Tarvisii in domo habitationis M. Laurentii Loti de Venetiis, q. S. Thome, pictoris celeberrimi,' &c. From which we gather that as early as 1505 Lotto was a celebrated painter.

represents St. Jerome in a magnificently painted landscape, and is ascribed in the catalogue to Caracci (!). The passionate gesture of the old penitent, who is scourging himself, is wholly characteristic of Lotto. Another similar painting, of larger dimensions, is in the Madrid Museum, there ascribed to Titian. Mr. Mündler (*op. cit.* p. 58) recognised both these pictures as the work of Lotto, and in this verdict he was followed by Messrs. Crowe and Cavalcaselle. Years ago, in Paris, I saw another painting of the same subject belonging to this gentleman; it was signed in gold letters, and dated 1515. This picture is very likely the one mentioned by the "Anonimo" in the house of Domenico dal Cornello [7] (or Tassi) at Bergamo, as 'el quadretto de S. Gieronimo.' The other work by Lotto in the Doria gallery is described in the catalogue as 'the portrait of a Judge' (!) by L. Lotto. What this portrait has to do with a 'judge' I leave to others to explain; it is a question of no importance. The man represented is in the prime of life, but appears cast down by sorrow. His face is pale, and he presses his hand to his heart as if the source of his grief were there. His eye seems seeking one who is no more in this world. The figure is not elegant in our modern sense of the word, but the whole pose is in keeping with the grief expressed by the features. He is not more than thirty-seven, yet sorrow and care have already left their indelible traces on his countenance. Near him, on a small column, is a bas-relief representing Cupid looking heavenwards, standing upon scales and keeping them in equal poise—thus symbolising, perhaps, that as the scales were no longer set in motion by the god of love, so the heart of this sorrow-stricken man would never again vibrate beneath

---

[7] The Tassi owned a castle in the Brembo valley called Cornello, hence they were often called 'dal Cornello.'

his touch. This representation of Cupid standing on the scales, with the inscription *Nosce te ipsum*, recurs in the beautiful intarsia work by Capodiferro, in the church of S. Maria Maggiore at Bergamo, for which Lotto made the designs in 1523.[8] The late Mr. Mündler wrote in terms of the warmest admiration of this fine portrait, but I think he was mistaken in regarding it as that of the painter himself. Lotto was certainly born before 1480; if it were his own portrait therefore, it must have been executed about 1512. The technic of the painting, however, by no means coincides with his manner in other works of that period; neither does the signature, L. Lotto, for in all his works at Bergamo, from the year 1515 to 1524, his signature is in Latin, LAv. LoTvs, and it is only at a later period that he adopts the Italian form.

We have already discussed Lotto's works in the Borghese gallery, but there are several by this interesting forerunner of Correggio in other Roman collections. In the Colonna gallery, for instance, we find the portrait of Cardinal Pompeo Colonna, though in its present condition it appears more like a copy than an original. In the Casino Rospigliosi, which contains Guido's Aurora, there is a little painting by Lotto, giving us an example of the manner in which this religiously-minded man and devoted friend of the Dominicans treated mythological subjects. Mr. Mündler showed his appreciation of this finely conceived and carefully executed painting, and called it "The Victory of Chastity." It might with equal fitness be named Juno taking righteous vengeance on Venus. Juno wrapped in a green mantle, with a white drapery about her head, brandishes aloft Cupid's broken bow, and seems about to pour forth the vials of her wrath upon Venus. The goddess of

[8] See *Vite dei pittori, scultori e architetti Bergamaschi, scritte dal Conte Fr. Maria Tassi* (i. 64).

love—a violet mantle about her, pearls in her fair hair, a
brilliant star glowing on her brow, and gold chains round
her neck—seeks to shield Cupid from the fury of the
Queen of Heaven.  The little god, with his many-coloured
wings, cowers behind her with tearful face.  The name
Laurentius Lotus is still legible on a ' Cartellino.'  From
the technic of the painting the work would seem to belong
to his Bergamasque epoch, 1515–1524.  A fine picture,
splendid in colour, dating from the same period of Lotto's
career, 1524, was in the Quirinal previous to 1870.  It
represented the Madonna and Child with SS. Anthony,
Catherine, John the Baptist and Jerome, and a Bishop.
Considering the incredible indifference to art which prevails
in every department of constitutional government in Italy,
I should never be surprised to hear that this painting had
disappeared altogether.  The Capitoline gallery contains a
work by Lotto (†), though not recognised as such—a life-size
portrait in Room II., No. 74, representing a young and
refined-looking man, wearing a black doublet and cap, and
holding a musket; his left elbow rests lightly on a table
which is covered by a greyish-blue carpet.  It must once
have been a brilliant portrait, but is now a mere wreck.
Here again the peculiar pose is finely conceived and
skilfully represented.  The drawing of the hands is characteristic of this painter, and the ornamentation of the musket
is executed with minute care.  The portrait is catalogued
as the work of Giorgione, and described as " Ritratto di un
Monaco " (portrait of a monk) !

In the Spada gallery there is a copy of Lotto's painting in the Louvre—" The Woman taken in Adultery ; " a
Flemish copy of the same picture is in the Dresden
gallery.  The Naples Museum contains a most interesting
early " Madonna " (of 1507) by the master, and the Uffizi
one of 1534—by no means a favourable specimen of his art.

Baron Rumohr formed, to my mind, an entirely false estimate of Lotto. In order to understand and appreciate this refined, versatile, and highly-gifted painter, he should be studied at Recanati (works of 1508), Jesi (of 1512), Bergamo (of 1515–1524), Milan and Venice. At Alzano, at Trescorre, and more especially at Bergamo—in the gallery, and in the churches of S. Bartolommeo, S. Spirito and S. Bernardino—he is admirably represented. In the presence of these masterpieces we cannot but marvel that so few art-historians should hitherto have recognised his great merits, though it is not surprising that young students, and a certain class of connoisseurs who admire nothing but the austerity and simplicity characteristic of the *quattro-centisti* should not have done so. They would naturally be repelled rather than attracted by Lotto's works.

All reserved and sensitive natures should be met by sympathy and treated with consideration, if we would gain their confidence ; and we must deal in a like manner with Lotto's works, making allowance for his occasional failings. To narrow-minded pedants, who would judge him by rigid academical rules, the charm of his art will ever remain a sealed book. Lorenzo Lotto was a man of a melancholy temperament, and a vein of sadness, the expression of his own feelings, pervades most of his portraits. When not much over thirty, he exchanged the world for the solitude and retirement of monastic life. We must also bear in mind that as Titian eclipsed Giorgione, so Correggio eventually threw his forerunner Lotto into the shade.

### GIOVAN ANTONIO DA PORDENONE.

This painter was a younger contemporary of Lotto. Worldly, aristocratic, imperious, he was the direct opposite of the latter both in the sentiment of his art and in his manner of representation. He was born at Pordenone in 1483, and died at Ferrara in 1539. Mündler compared this Friulian artist with Rubens for the vivacious energy of his temperament and his predilection for colossal and well-developed forms. The simile is not inappropriate on the whole, but the nature of the Flemish painter was that of a pliant, politic, and calculating man of the world, while the organism of the Italian was passionate, excitable, ill-regulated, and swayed by pride and ambition. This it was, perhaps, which debarred him from ever attaining to a position of ease and luxury, such as that which Rubens won for himself in his artistic career, and continued to enjoy to the end of his life ; but this very instability also preserved Pordenone from ever degenerating into conventionality. Original, highly gifted, at times even strikingly grand, he at one period sought, not unsuccessfully, to rival Titian.

The changeableness of his nature is exemplified, even in his signature, which is sometimes *Sacchiense*, at others *de Cuticellis*, *Corticellis*, and *Regillo*. His great strength lay in fresco-painting, yet he has also left a considerable number of oil-pictures which may be classed among the finest examples of Venetian art ; for instance, his works at Pordenone ; two large altar-pieces in the Venice Academy (Room VII., Nos. 22 and 25)[9]; the Madonna in S. Giovanni Elemosinario, and the " St. Martin on Horseback " in S. Rocco, both in Venice ; the splendid altar-piece in the parish church of Sussignana ; the fine " Adoration of the Shepherds " in S. Maria de' Miracoli, at La Motta near Treviso, and the richly-coloured Madonna in the cathedral at Cremona, over the first altar on the right.

---

[9] The portraits contained in this picture of some of the Ottoboni of Pordenone, the family for whom Giovan Antonio executed this fine work in 1526, are worthy in my estimation to rank with the best portraits of all times. The picture is unfortunately in a damaged condition.

There is a good work by this rare master in the Doria gallery—a male portrait, No. 447. The catalogue describes it as " Ritratto di un Giudice ; " this portrait, therefore, is supposed to be that of a judge, like that by Lotto, presumably because the young man, who wears a red robe and a black cape, holds a roll of papers. It is just as likely, however, that these may refer to love as to law ; but this is of little moment. An art-critic of my acquaintance thought this painting should be ascribed to Dosso and not to Pordenone. The peculiar brilliancy of the carnations recalls the so-called portrait of " Catarina Vanozza " (No. 549) in a measure, but Pordenone's flesh-tints are always lighter than those of Dosso, and the drawing is more decided, as we may see by comparing these two portraits. This time, therefore, I fully agree with the compiler of the catalogue, who ascribes the portrait to Pordenone. In the vestibule of the Quirinal there was formerly an important work by this most eminent of all the Friulian artists, representing St. George on his white horse attacking the dragon with his sword. In a charming landscape the princess was seen kneeling beneath some trees, clad in an orange robe and returning thanks to Heaven for her preservation. The latest victim of the monster—a young knight—lay dead on the ground, and the bones of many animals were scattered around. The painting was full of fancy and had the qualities of the purest and best Venetian art, though its brilliancy was somewhat dimmed by restoration. It bore the following inscription : I . A . REG . PORD . F. (Joannes Antonius Regillus Pordenonensis fecit.) [1]

It is incredible that works by Moretto, an artist so totally dissimilar to this Giorgionesque painter, to use a

[1] The picture is said to be now in the anteroom leading to the private apartments of Pope Leo XIII.

stereotyped term, should so long have been ascribed to Pordenone. But to judge by the names recently bestowed upon pictures, it would seem that we must be prepared for still more astonishing mistakes. Not content with attributing to Pordenone Moretto's large altar-piece, formerly in the collection of Cardinal Fesch in Rome and now one of the gems of the Städel Institute at Frankfort, some writers have recently even seen fit to ascribe another yet finer altar-piece by Moretto in the public gallery at Vienna, the 'S. Justina,' to Pordenone;[2] and an Italian art-critic, who, in other respects, has proved himself worthy of consideration, pronounces the Saint to be the portrait of Signora Laura Eustocchia of Ferrara, and the kneeling donor to be the likeness of her lover, Duke Alfonso d' Este.[3] Another writer, M. Viardot, supposing both pictures to be by Pordenone, proceeds to point out the 'great analogy' between Pordenone's genuine work in the Venice Academy (Room VII., No. 25) and Moretto's picture at Vienna—a remarkable instance of the force of imagination.

Pordenone's most interesting frescoes are those in the chapel of the castle of S. Salvadore near Conegliano, belonging to Count Collalto; those in S. Maria di Campagna near Piacenza; and those in the cathedral at Treviso. To these I should have added the frescoes in the courtyard of S. Stefano in Venice, had they not been almost entirely destroyed.

Pordenone not being represented in any of the great

---

[2] The type of this saint recurs in several other pictures by Moretto, for instance in two altar-pieces in S. Clemente at Brescia, which renders the hypothesis that it represents some special character still more unlikely. At Vienna the picture formerly passed for a Titian.

[3] Even Count Pompeo Litta, a most careful and conscientious writer, thought the donor in this picture was Alfonso d' Este, and as such reproduced this figure in his well-known book, *Le famiglie illustri d'Italia.*

galleries out of Italy, I shall enumerate a few of his drawings, for by means of photographs of them, students may gain at least some superficial idea of his art. 1. In the Venice Academy there is a drawing washed with colour, the " Presentation in the Temple " (photographed by Perini, No. 155). 2. In the British Museum, an excellent black chalk drawing of St. Christopher with the Infant Saviour on his shoulder (Braun, No. 103). 3. A good red chalk drawing of the Madonna and Child by Pordenone (†) was sold in Paris some years ago. It was formerly in the possession of the Marquis de Chennevières, and was photographed by Braun as a Palma Vecchio (Braun, " Beaux Arts," No. 212). 4. A characteristic indian ink drawing of the master's early period was photographed by Braun under the name of Bellini. (†) It represents St. Mark (?) seated in a niche and preaching to a company of the faithful (Braun, " Beaux Arts," No. 144). 5. In the fine collection of drawings at Chatsworth there is a genuine work by Pordenone, (†) a red chalk sketch of St. Peter Martyr, ascribed to Giorgione.

## GIOVAN BATTISTA MORONI.

Near this fine portrait by Pordenone we see the likeness of a man, with a cast in his eye, holding a book. The compiler of the catalogue, as we have had occasion to observe, values the name of Titian above all others, and bestows it upon this picture, as upon so many in the collection. The error is a pardonable one, for in many galleries of greater renown portraits by Moroni are ascribed to Titian. There is only one other work by this Bergamasque painter in Rome—in the Colonna gallery (Room I.) The master is scarcely met with at all in South Italy, but Florence has several good specimens of his art. Two genuine portraits are in the Pitti (Nos. 121 and 128),

there ascribed, with extraordinary want of intelligence, to
the great Veronese painter Domenico Morone.  Five male
portraits by him are in the Uffizi.   No. 360, considered to
be of Moroni himself, was bought in Venice in 1684 for the
Florentine gallery, by Matteo del Teglia, the Duke of
Tuscany's agent.[4]  It, however, bears no resemblance to his
portrait in Bergamo.  We must, therefore, accept one or
other of the two, as the authentic likeness of Moroni,
though perhaps it would be wiser to reject both.  We
may seek vainly for works by Moroni in the galleries of
Bologna, Modena, Ferrara, Padua, Vicenza, and Verona, and
even in Venice,[5] but he is well represented in Bergamo
and its neighbourhood, and there we may follow him
through all the phases of his artistic development.  Several
of his finest portraits are in the English National Gallery.

## TITIAN.

In no other collection in the world do we find such
liberal use made of the names of Titian and Giorgione as
in the Doria gallery.  If we are to trust the catalogue, we
shall meet these two great masters at almost every step.
We must not, however, be too credulous, but bear in mind
that the worthy compilers of these catalogues, though
eminently respectable as a class, are often highly impressionable.  As soon as they have settled down to their
position and to the duties of their office, they gradually
devote themselves to the cultus of some one great master,
whose name is more or less familiar to them.  One selects
Raphael as the object of his especial veneration, a second
Michael Angelo, a third Leonardo da Vinci, or Verrocchio ;

[4] See *Nuova Raccolta di Lettere
sulla Pittura, Scultura e Archi-
lettura*, by Michelangelo Gualandi.
v. iii. 192. Bologna, 1836.

[5] The two portraits ascribed to
Moroni in the Academy have no
connection with him whatever.

others Giorgione or Titian. Carried away by their enthusiasm they end by recognising in almost every painting
or statue confided to their care, the characteristics of the
artist of their choice. This probably was the case with
the compilers of the Doria catalogue with regard to Titian
and Giorgione. I think I need hardly fear much opposition
if I assert that Giorgione cannot lay claim to any of the
pictures ascribed to him, and that to Titian only *one* of
the numerous paintings attributed to him can be given with
complete certainty ; this, however, may be accounted one of
the master's most attractive early works. It was formerly
regarded as the work of Giorgione and has recently been
ascribed to Pordenone. I consider it to be one of Titian's
most charming creations, fully compensating for the spurious
works, about sixteen in number, so arbitrarily attributed
to him here. It represents the " Daughter of Herodias,"
and bears the No. 517. (†) It is extraordinary that
Messrs. Crowe and Cavalcaselle, Titian's biographers,
should have attributed this beautiful woman of indescribable
charm, and of a distinctly Titianesque type, to that much
coarser painter Pordenone. Dr. Bode, on the other hand,
refuses to accept their verdict and agrees with me (ii. 758).
The type of Salome, as I have already observed, is wholly
that of Titian : the ear of her attendant is round in form and
characteristic, very different from the long ear peculiar to
Pordenone. The sharp angular fold in the drapery on
Salome's shoulder constantly recurs in Titian's works, and
the chords of colour are also characteristic of this master.
The same spirit and the same hand which conceived and
executed the " Three Ages "[6] in the Bridgewater gallery
undoubtedly produced this picture also. There is an old
and good copy of it in Lord Northbrook's collection—so
good, indeed, that Dr. Waagen pronounced it to be by

[6] See Vasari, xiii. 25.

Giorgione—and in the Doria gallery (No. 313) there is an old copy of the "Three Ages."[7] There is another work in this collection which always passes for a Titian (No. 361). It represents an old white-bearded man, clad in black, whose features are expressive of deep emotion; his right hand rests on a table, on which lie a white rose and some jewels —accessories probably referring to the death of his young daughter. It is an interesting picture, full of life and thoughtfully conceived. I am quite willing to admit that the portrait is not unworthy, as far as merit goes, to be classed in the long category of Titian's portraits, yet, at the same time, I cannot altogether recognise in it the hand of the master.[8] In order to invest it with greater interest, the name of Marco Polo was bestowed upon the subject, in the same way that another portrait (No. 131), certainly not a work by Titian, is said to be that of Jansenius. Portraits only received these absurd names in the seventeenth century when these collections were brought together, in order to give them more importance; the public, as a rule, taking more interest in the subject represented than in the artist's treatment of it. Thus, one was called Marco Polo, another Vanozza, a third Jansenius, a fourth "Titian and his Wife." So the study of a handsome female model in the Barberini gallery (whether by Guido or Guercino) would certainly never have been invested with such a halo of interest, were it not for the name of the unfortunate Beatrice Cenci by which it is known. *Mundus vult decipi*. Another large picture (No. 343) has received the name of Titian, though it is impossible to say why.

---

In Titian's "Three Ages" we see the same round form of ear and, in the young shepherd, the same type of head as in his "Baptism of Christ," in the Capitol. Both pictures probably belong to the same period of the master's career.

[8] It certainly recalls in some degree the so-called portrait of the physician Parma, in the gallery at Vienna, which is an indisputable work of Titian.

It is well known that it is the work of Jan Livens, by whom there is a similar painting in the collection at Brunswick.

The following, therefore, are the only authentic works by Titian in Rome : the three pictures in the Borghese gallery, the "Baptism of Christ" in the Capitol, the two well-known paintings in the Vatican, the exquisite "Daughter of Herodias" in this gallery, and the splendid portrait of Pietro Aretino in advancing years, belonging to Prince Mario Chigi, which is of the greatest simplicity both in conception and representation. In the Corsini and Barberini galleries there are several works ascribed to Titian, but the evidence of the paintings themselves in each case belies the name. The two attributed to him in the badly lighted rooms of the Barberini gallery are, the unpleasing painting known as the "Schiava di Tiziano," of which we have already spoken, and the portrait of Cardinal Pietro Bembo, No. 38. It is known that Titian was twice commissioned to paint that vain prelate before he received the Cardinal's hat. At the close of the last century one of these portraits was still in the palace once inhabited by Pietro Gradenigo, who had married Bembo's daughter Helena. Another portrait of smaller dimensions belonged to Paolo Ramusio at Venice.

According to the "Anonimo" Raphael also portrayed Bembo in his youth : 'el retratto piccolo de esso M. Pietro Bembo, allorchè giovine stava in corte del duca d' Urbino, in matita ' (' the small portrait in chalk of Messer P. Bembo in his youth, when he lived at the court of the Duke of Urbino '). In Bembo's own house at Padua there was also a profile portrait of him by the Venetian Jacometto : 'el retratto dell' istesso allora che l'era d' anni undici fù de mano de Jacometto in profilo '[9] (' the profile portrait of the

---

[9] See *Notizia d' opere di disegno*, &c., edited by Dr. Frizzoni, p. 46.

same Bembo, at the age of eleven, by the hand of Jacometto '). Later, Valerio de' Belli and Benvenuto Cellini were
commissioned to immortalise the prelate in silver and in
bronze. We may, therefore, infer that Bembo took delight
in bequeathing his features to posterity. The portrait in the
Barberini gallery appears to me to be only a feeble copy [1] (†) ;
the drawing is hard and the whole treatment wanting in
character. Another copy of one of Titian's portraits of
Bembo was left to the town of Bergamo, in 1673, by Marcantonio Foppa. It is now in the gallery of that city. Of
the paintings ascribed to Titian in the Corsini gallery, one
in Room VIII. (No. 30)—"The Woman taken in Adultery"—is evidently the work of Rocco Marconi, of Treviso. (†)
The subject was often treated by this painter, an imitator of
Bordone, who, though lacking in imagination, was a fine
colourist. The other is the life-size full-length portrait of
Philip II. This can only be regarded as a work of his school.
Titian painted his royal Spanish patron several times.
The finest, and undoubtedly one of the most splendid
portraits in the world, is in the gallery of the Prado at
Madrid (No. 454). I consider it even finer than the large
equestrian portrait of Charles V. in the same collection,
which is somewhat damaged. It is astonishing that Titian
was able to treat the feeble, insignificant, and even repulsive figure of Philip II. in such a manner as to render the
portrait one of irresistible power and charm. We never
tire of admiring the noble drawing, and the delicate and
harmonious colouring. Life pulsates in every part; the
refined hands alone seem to tell the whole history of the
man. The pale taciturn face, the gloomy reticent expression, the magnificent armour, the life-like drawing of the
lower limbs, the whole picture, in a word, is a very triumph

---

[1] Messrs. Crowe and Cavalcaselle regard this as an original. Dr. Bode is of the same opinion (ii. 761).

of art. Such portraits as these of Charles V. and Philip II.,
like Shakespeare's dramas, completely enthral our imagination, and render us forgetful of all else. For it is not the
individual alone which they depict ; they bring before us
an epoch of history—the whole moral atmosphere of his
age.

Leaving the Venetians, I turn for a moment to some
other works in this gallery which are ascribed to the
greatest Italian masters. Among them there is a portrait
(No. 358) of a young and refined woman in red velvet,
which, according to the catalogue, is by Leonardo da Vinci.
At a distance, the fine oval of the face recalls Raphael's
portrait of Joanna of Aragon, the wife of Ascanio Colonna,
in the Louvre ; the scale of colour in the dress points
not so much to the school of Raphael, as to that of Leonardo da Vinci at Milan, and more especially to that of
Gianpietrino. But the moment we approach the picture,
we see at once its origin. The lifeless, academic drawing
of the hands ; the weak, mechanical treatment and the
leaden tone of the white drapery ; the stiff curtain (recalling the curtain in the so-called Leonardo in the Dresden
gallery), the smooth, ivory-like flesh-tones, the hook-shaped
folds, all go to prove that the painting is one of the
many so-called 'pasticci,' which were produced, more
especially at Milan, in the third and fourth decades of the
sixteenth century—paintings which have deceived so many
art-connoisseurs. This picture was formerly as greatly
extolled as are the many so-called Leonardos in these days,
which are in reality the work of Flemish painters. Mr.
Mündler (*op. cit.* p. 41) was, I believe, the first who
pronounced it to be a feeble Flemish imitation. Passavant,
on the other hand, though not ascribing it to Leonardo
himself, considered it to be the work of one of his scholars.
In these days even a Roman cicerone would scarcely

venture to describe it as the work of Leonardo da Vinci.[2]
Perhaps the day is not far distant when more enlightened
critics will admit that these Flemish 'pasticci' and imitations of Italian originals are much more numerous in the
public galleries of Europe than has hitherto been supposed.

Another painting, equally renowned as the work of a
great Italian master, must detain us for a moment (No.
265); the catalogue describes it as "Virtue crowned by
Fame: a sketch by Correggio." As I approached the
picture one day, accompanied by some young friends,
a smooth-shaven gentleman was just taking a last look
at it. 'A charming picture, is it not?' observed his
companion, an elderly lady who was standing near, and
looking out of a window. 'Admirable,' he replied,
removing his eye-glass; 'after the "Moulin" by Claude,'
he added, as he offered his arm to the lady—'this is my
favourite picture in the gallery; here we see Correggio
as the forerunner of Prudhon.'

When this French couple had departed I placed the
picture in a better light, and we began to examine it critically. It is in *tempera* and unfinished in parts; the canvas
has rather a modern look. We were struck by the want of
transparency in the colouring, by the coarse clumsy folds
of the drapery, and by the heavy lifeless treatment of the
hair, especially that of the unpleasing boy in the foreground
on the right, though Correggio's delicacy and lightness of
touch in treating hair is particularly extolled by Vasari.[3]

---

[2] Even chronologically it is impossible that Leonardo da Vinci,
who left Italy in 1515, could have
painted the wife of Ascanio Colonna.

[3] Vasari, vii. 99. 'E oltra di ciò,
capegli si leggiadri di colore e con
infinita pulitezza sfilati e condotti,
che meglio di quegli non si può

vedere ' ('and moreover hair of such
a lovely colour, and arranged and
executed with so much care, that
nothing more beautiful could be
imagined'); and again, p. 103:
'perchè mostrandoci i suoi capegli
fatti con tanta facilità nelle difficoltà
del fargli, ha insegnato come e' si

'Just look at the girl in the foreground on the left,' I said to my companions, 'does she not vividly recall the shepherdesses on fans and porcelain cups of the time of Louis XIV. ? Yet,' I continued, 'in the eyes of the most celebrated critics of the last century and of our own time, this sketch has been looked upon as a masterpiece. Mengs, who in his day passed for the greatest connoisseur of Correggio's works, was struck by the fact that, "in this mere sketch, the grace of the master and his great technical endowments are no less perceptible than in his most highly finished works; the effect of nature being fully attained even in the parts which are only slightly laid in. Many paintings of Correggio," he adds, "are more beautiful than this one, but no other reveals the greatness of the master so strikingly." '

Even Mündler considered that this sketch surpassed the finished painting in the Louvre, in the inspiration of the heads, and in freedom of treatment. Dr. Julius Meyer, the former director of the Berlin gallery, in his well-known Life of Correggio, mentions it as a somewhat altered replica of the *tempera* painting in the Louvre, unfinished but undoubtedly genuine. Where so many distinguished art-critics have extolled a painting as a 'masterpiece' and 'undoubtedly genuine,' it is a dangerous venture to pronounce it to be merely a copy. Of course, however, I may be mistaken in this as in other instances. It is well known that the two originals (now in the Louvre) were painted by Correggio for the Duchess Isabella Gonzaga. Later, with Correggio's "Jupiter and Antiope" and Mantegna's "Triumph of Cæsar" (now at Hampton Court), they passed into the collection of Charles I. through the instrumentality of a

---

abbino a fare ' (' for he '—that is Correggio—' showing us with what ease he painted hair, which is so difficult a matter, has thus taught us how it should be done ').

Belgian agent. When that unfortunate monarch's works of art were sold by auction in 1650, these paintings were bought in Paris by the banker Jabach, of Cologne. Later he sold the two pictures by Correggio, consequently including the original of this so-called sketch in the Doria gallery, to Louis XIV. Mariette, whom I consider the most astute and intelligent art-critic the French have ever had, relates in his "Abecedario"[4] (vol. iii. p. 2) that Jabach had several painters in his house, among them the brothers Jean Baptiste and Michel Corneille, Pesne, Massé, and Rousseau; and in the article devoted to Michel Corneille, in vol. ii. p. 7, he relates that Jabach commissioned the young painter and his brother Jean Baptiste, as well as other young artists, to make copies of the original drawings of the great masters represented in his collection. These copies Corneille was wont to sell as originals. 'This deception,' adds honest Mariette, 'was most reprehensible, but Corneille found it decidedly profitable.'[5] It is surely within the range of possibility that this 'sketch by Correggio' may have been one of the copies produced in this way in Jabach's house. If my supposition prove correct, the Correggio in the Doria gallery has passed through vicissitudes very similar to those of the celebrated Holbein in Dresden. The originals of both these works fell into the hands of speculators in the middle of the

---

[4] *Abecedario de P. J. Mariette, ouvrage publié par Ph. de Chennevières et A. de Montaiglon* (Paris, 1854–56).

[5] 'Mais une des choses qui aidèrent davantage à lui' (Michel Corneille) 'former le goût, et à lui faire accorder la préférence aux ouvrages des meilleurs maîtres d'Italie et surtout à ceux des Carraches et de leurs élèves, fut l'occupation que lui fournit dans sa première jeunesse le sieur Jabach, qui avait la plus belle collection de dessins qui fut alors, et qui employait le jeune Corneille et son frère Jean-Baptiste, ainsi que plusieurs autres jeunes gens, à en faire des copies, que souvent il vendait pour des originaux. Cette supercherie était véritablement blâmable et honteuse; mais le jeune Corneille y trouvait son profit.'

seventeenth century. Holbein's Madonna came into the possession of Cromhart Loskart, the banker at Amsterdam —Correggio's painting into that of Jabach at Paris. Under their auspices both were probably reproduced, and the copies found their way later to Italy : the one after Holbein came to Venice, to the Casa Dolfin—the one after Correggio to Rome, to the Palazzo Pamfili, and both were then proclaimed 'wonderfully fine originals,' and were universally extolled as such. Since the Dresden Holbein, however, has been pronounced by the most competent German authorities to be a copy, a glance now suffices for every connoisseur to recognise in it a modern work, by the hand, moreover, of a Fleming. I am, therefore, not without hope that, in the course of twenty years or so, no one, having any pretensions to call himself a connoisseur, will regard this so-called Correggio as anything but the production of some French painter of the second half of the seventeenth century. To me the picture always calls up visions of Watteau or Lancret, and seems to betray the hand of a forerunner of these painters.

It is quite in accordance with experience, that both these copies, in Rome and Dresden, should prove more attractive to the public than the originals themselves, for it is in the nature of things that the more modern the copy of an old picture, and the more therefore it approaches to the taste and feeling of the spectator, the greater will be its attractions for him. We are told by Herr A. Teichlein, of Munich, the friend and companion of Wilhelm von Kaulbach, in his article on that painter ("Zur Charakteristik Wilhelms von Kaulbach," 1876), that the renowned artist, on seeing Raphael's "St. Cecilia" in the gallery at Bologna, criticised it severely and could find nothing to praise in it except the colouring. On the other hand, he was enthusiastic about Overbeck's frescoes in S. Maria degli Angeli, near Assisi. It is a well-known fact

that at the time of Napoleon I., Raphael's "St. Cecilia," then
in Paris, was first transferred from panel to canvas, and then
entirely repainted, *i.e.* 'restored,' in consequence of which
much of the charm of this splendid work has been irreparably destroyed. The only parts, therefore, remaining by
Raphael's hand—the composition and the drawing—were
underrated by Kaulbach, while the work of the modern
restorer met with his unqualified admiration. This confirms
the truth of what I have just observed, and proves also that
the most celebrated modern painters are no exception to
the rule.

As we turned away from this enigmatical 'sketch of
Correggio,' we again encountered the French couple. They
were evidently as much dissatisfied with the work of
Raphael they had just been examining, as we were with
the Correggio, and were coming back to have a last look
at their favourite 'pour la bonne bouche.' We on our
part proceeded to the double portrait by Raphael. We
were not able at first to examine it closely, as two German
gentlemen were standing before it engaged in a lively discussion.

'I tell you,' said the one, a Viennese to judge by his
accent—'I tell you the painting is Venetian.'

'And I can assure you,' returned the other, apparently
a North German, 'that this copy can only be the work
of Polidoro da Caravaggio.'

At that moment a Roman cicerone rushed past, followed by four fair Americans. At a little distance from the
picture he stopped and, waving his hand toward it, shouted :
'C'est Bartolo et Baldo, chef-d'œuvre de Raffaello
d'Urbin, peintre de Pape Leon dei Medici.' The
Americans all nodded and passed on, preceded by their
guide.

'These wretched ignorant Italian cicerones!' remarked

the North German; 'they seem to be here for the sole purpose of disseminating these silly traditions among the unlearned.'

'And are non-Italian cicerones any better?' inquired the Austrian. 'They, too, are wont to proclaim all the nonsense others have taught them with imperturbable assurance.'

'You think so?' returned the other in a piqued tone. 'Art-criticism, as practised now in Berlin, is apparently unknown in Vienna. The Austrians, as a nation, are far too superficial, or, if you will, too pleasure-loving, to take any real interest in the inner organic development of an artist.'

'What do I care for your inner organic development?' replied the Austrian. 'I can only tell you that Passavant, the greatest Raphael connoisseur the world has ever seen, who studied that master's works thoroughly for more than twelve years, and who must therefore have been more intimately acquainted with his manner than anyone else, pronounced this picture to be a Venetian copy.'

'Passavant's opinions are quite obsolete in Berlin now,' replied the North German drily. 'No educated Prussian in these days could possibly connect this picture with Venetian art. Just look at the dark-brown flesh-tints in the head of Navagero, look at the glazes of varnish over the glazes of oil about the eye, and at the broad touches about the mouth. The whole treatment is that of Polidoro da Caravaggio.'

'What can you have to say about Caravaggio's manner of painting, my dear sir?' said the Austrian; 'we know absolutely nothing about it. The few very unattractive specimens of his art in the Museo Borbonico prove him to have been a coarse painter with little feeling for beauty, and his frescoes on the façades of certain houses in Rome have little interest for us in their present damaged condition, though they show that he had a certain amount of inventive genius. Vasari much overrated the merits of this unrefined Lombard painter, probably because in his later years Polidoro followed in the steps of Michael Angelo, who was the idol of Vasari.'

'You may think what you please about Caravaggio in Vienna,' replied the other testily, 'but in Berlin we shall continue for all that to follow the view of modern critics, and to look upon Polidoro as an artist who was inspired by the spirit of Raphael.'

'I tell you,' reiterated the Austrian, 'that to my mind Polidoro is nothing but a second-rate decorative painter.'

'You must allow me to observe,' rejoined the gentleman from Berlin, 'that art-critics on the banks of the Danube appear to have formed very vague ideas of the true character of historical art.'

'What ! ' exclaimed the Viennese, 'do you think because you have an official position at Berlin that you are qualified to instruct the remainder of the universe ? '

'My dear Baron,' said the other, smiling, and in a condescending tone of voice, 'you must allow that you are only an amateur and absolutely unprofessional.'

'Professional or not,' replied the other warmly, 'I hold that amateurs who have a real love for art, and who, like myself, have a collection of their own, are quite as much enti led to express an opinion as—nay, even better entitled than—so-called professionals, who really care no more about the pictures than the anatomist cares about the dead body he dissects—people, in short, whose only object in taking up the study of art is to re-name every picture and statue.'

'My dear Baron,' said the North German, drawing himself up, 'allow me to remind you that in every department of science, hence, of course, in the science of art, there are critics and critics.'

With these words he buttoned up his overcoat and departed.

The Baron, who moved off in another direction, called after him : ' Undoubtedly, in the same way that some folk are clever and others unmitigated bores.'

As soon as they were gone, a fair-haired young lady, with a very intelligent expression, who had been listening attentively to this learned discussion, approached the picture with visible interest, and turning to me, smiling, observed : ' Excuse me if I venture to ask you a question. Do you agree with those gentlemen that this splendid head ' (pointing to Navagero) ' was not painted by Raphael ? If it is not by him,' she proceeded, without waiting for an answer, ' it can only be by one of the greatest painters in the world ! Or have I made a serious mistake ? '

' I fully share your opinion,' I answered, much delighted. ' The picture is a masterpiece—you will hardly find its equal the world over, and it is positive profanation to regard it, even for a moment, as a copy. The conception of these two heads is so noble, the execution so masterly, that I can name scarcely another portrait, whether by Titian, Velasquez, or any other renowned painter, which would be worthy to rank with it, save perhaps that unique portrait—Leonardo's " Gioconda " in the Louvre. I agree with you, that only a master like Raphael was capable of producing, thus *alla prima*, two human forms of such extraordinary vitality and truth.' (†)

' Indeed, yes,' she replied ; ' the longer one looks at these heads, the more marvellously life-like do they appear.'

' And see,' I continued, ' how delicately the mouth is modelled ; look at the wonderful play of light in the eye ; see how naturally the ear—the form of which is so characteristic of Raphael—is placed, and with what freedom and lightness of touch the beard is treated.'

'I am indeed delighted,' pursued the young lady, 'that you appear to approve, and even to confirm, my opinion, which is of course only the result of my own individual impressions, while you appear to be studying art as a connoisseur. Women, as a rule, I think, only measure works of art from the standpoint of their own feelings.'

'And for this very reason,' I rejoined, 'the opinion of a cultivated woman often approaches the truth more nearly than that of a pedantic art-critic.'

'Perhaps you are right,' she said, with a slight expression of satisfaction. 'Too much learning often destroys real enjoyment of art, as too much salt spoils the best cooking. In my country, and more especially in Berlin, people confine their studies far too much to books.'

'Berlin is undoubtedly the most learned city in the world,' I replied, 'and I am doubly gratified that my opinion of this portrait should be shared by a lady from Berlin of such cultivated tastes.'

At these words she glanced at me with some mistrust.

'This is not the first time,' I continued, 'that I have had occasion to observe that gifted and cultivated women, if they devote themselves to the study of art with zeal and assiduity, display a far keener perception than men. Women have one immense advantage over us, they come to this study unbiased by prejudice or preconceived theories.'

'Would you tell me,' said the young lady after a pause, 'the name of the critic who first pronounced this masterpiece a copy?'

'I believe it was Raphael's celebrated biographer from Frankfort,' I replied.

'Passavant?' she inquired.

'Yes, and nearly all his professional colleagues followed him. This is usually the way of the world, for most persons are glad to be spared the trouble of thinking for themselves. Passavant, who had rendered considerable services in his branch of research, discovered in an old Italian book, which is well known under the title of "Notizie di un Anonimo," that these portraits of Beazzano and Navagero were painted on panel. With this in his mind, he came to study the picture. Instead, however, of examining the painting itself, he first turned it round to make quite sure it was on wood. Finding to his horror that it was on canvas, he at once concluded it must be a copy, and, what was more, a Venetian copy.'

'Why Venetian and not Bolognese, as is usually assumed in such cases?' she inquired.

'Because the picture formerly belonged to Pietro Bembo at Padua, who, in 1538, gave it to Beazzano himself. Passavant's theory was, that a picture which had been for so long in Venetian territory could only have been copied by a painter of Venice.'

'But,' resumed the lady, 'was it not possible that the anonymous writer whom you have just mentioned might have made a wrong memorandum, and have mistaken canvas for panel?'

'Undoubtedly,' I replied, 'and I could tell you of many similar mistakes. Vasari even states that the "Madonna di S. Sisto" was on panel, but it is evident that this celebrated picture was painted on canvas.'

'Such mistakes, the result of a hurried examination, are pardonable enough,' said the young lady.

'Certainly,' said I; 'but the unpardonable part is, that such a masterpiece as this double portrait should have

been taken for a copy, and accepted as such ever since.
What are we to think of an art-critic who studied the
works of one master for twelve years, and finally came to
such a conclusion ? '

'It seems to me,' said the young lady, smiling, 'that
art-critics are rather apt to make such mistakes. May I
venture to ask you one more question ? Is it true, as
people say, that Raphael always painted his portraits on
panel ? '

'In his early period he undoubtedly did,' I replied.
'His portrait of his friend and master Pintoricchio in
the Borghese gallery is on panel, so are the portraits
of the "Doni" and the so-called "Donna Gravida" in
the Pitti, his own portrait, that of Leo X., and the splendid
portrait of Cardinal Bibbiena at Madrid. From 1516,
however, Raphael appears to have preferred canvas to
panel, and he employed this not only for the "Madonna
di S. Sisto" in Dresden, but also for the portraits
he painted in the last four years of his life—for those
of the so-called "Donna Velata" in the Pitti, and of Count
Baldassare Castiglione and Joanna II., both in the Louvre,
and for this double portrait of Beazzano and Navagero,
which he must have painted in April 1516.'

'How is that known ? ' she asked.

'From a letter,' I answered, ' written by Bembo to his
friend Cardinal Divizio da Bibbiena, referring to the presence
of these two Venetians in Rome.'

She thanked me and turned to study the picture again ;
then presently she resumed, 'How uninteresting the Berlin
portrait of Navagero appears to me now, compared with
this magnificent head ! The piercing eyes seem to read
our very thoughts and to inquire whether we are indeed
worthy to contemplate such a masterpiece. What would

these wise Venetians think,' she added with a smile, as she prepared to depart, ' if they could hear all the different opinions and learned remarks which are passed upon them every week ! '

And with a slight bow she disappeared.

# GENERAL INDEX.

# INDEX OF PLACES.

# WORKS RELATING TO ART, &c.

**EDWARD WHYMPER.**

**TRAVELS AMONGST the GREAT ANDES of the EQUATOR.**
With 140 Original Illustrations drawn by F. BARNARD, A. CORBOULD, F. DADD, W. E. LAPWORTH, W. H. OVEREND, P. SKELTON, E. WAGNER, E. WILSON, JOSEPH WOLF, and others. Engraved by the Author. With Maps and Illustrations. Medium 8vo. 21s. net. To range with 'Scrambles amongst the Alps.'

**A. S. MURRAY.**

**A HISTORY of GREEK SCULPTURE from the EARLIEST**
TIMES. With 130 Illustrations. 2 vols. Medium 8vo. 36s.

**HANDBOOK of GREEK ARCHÆOLOGY : Sculpture, Vases,**
Bronzes, Gems, Terra-cottas, Architecture, Mural Paintings, &c. Many Illustrations. Crown 8vo. 18s.

**C. HEATH WILSON.**

**MICHAEL ANGELO, Sculptor, Painter, and Architect : his**
Life and Works. By C. HEATH WILSON. Illustrations. 8vo. 15s.

**E. B. TYLOR.**

**PRIMITIVE CULTURE : the Development of Mythology,**
Philosophy, Religion, Art, and Custom. Third Edition. 2 vols. 8vo. 21s.

**PERCY GARDNER.**

**NEW CHAPTERS in GREEK HISTORY : Historical Results**
of Recent Excavations in Greece and Asia Minor. By PERCY GARDNER, M.A., Professor of Archæology in the University of Oxford. With Illustrations. 8vo.

**CROWE AND CAVALCASELLE.**

**TITIAN'S LIFE and TIMES. By CROWE and CAVALCASELLE.**
Illustrations. 2 vols. 8vo. 21s.

**H. B. WHEATLEY.**

**LONDON : Past and Present ; its History, Associations, and**
Traditions. By HENRY B. WHEATLEY, F.S.A. Based on Cunningham's Handbook. Library Edition, on Laid Paper. 3 vols. Medium 8vo. £3, 3s.

**CANON SCOTT-HOLLAND.**

**LIND (JENNY), THE ARTIST, 1820–1851 : her Early Art-Life**
and Dramatic Career. From Original Documents, Letters, Diaries, &c., in the possession of Mr. GOLDSCHMIDT. By Canon H. SCOTT-HOLLAND, M.A., and W. S. ROCKSTRO. With Portraits, Illustrations, and Appendix of Music. 2 vols. 8vo. 32s.

**L. J. JENNINGS, M.P.**

**FIELD PATHS and GREEN LANES ; or, Walks in Surrey**
and Sussex. Popular Edition. With Illustrations. Crown 8vo. 6s.

**SIR HENRY LAYARD.**

**KUGLER'S HANDBOOK of PAINTING : the Italian Schools.**
A New Edition, revised. By Sir HENRY LAYARD. With 200 Illustrations. 2 vols. Crown 8vo. 30s.

**NINEVEH and its REMAINS. With Illustrations. Post 8vo.**
7s. 6d.

**NINEVEH and BABYLON. Illustrations. Post 8vo. 7s. 6d.**

**EARLY ADVENTURES in PERSIA, BABYLONIA, and**
SUSIANA, including a residence among the Bakhtiyari and other wild tribes before the discovery of Nineveh. Portrait, Illustrations, and Maps. 2 vols. Crown 8vo. 24s.

**SIR J. A. CROWE.**

**KUGLER'S HANDBOOK of PAINTING : the German,**
Flemish, and Dutch Schools. New Edition, revised. By Sir J. A. CROWE. With 60 Illustrations. 2 vols. Crown 8vo. 24s.

**JAMES F. HUNNEWELL.**

**ENGLAND'S CHRONICLE in STONE ; derived from Personal**
Observations of the Cathedrals, Churches, Abbeys, Monasteries, Castles, and Palaces made in Journeys through the Imperial Island. With Illustrations. Medium 8vo. 24s.

**F. H. GUILLEMARD, M.D.**

The VOYAGE of the 'MARCHESA' to KAMSCHATKA and
NEW GUINEA. With Notices of Formosa and the Islands of the Malay Archipelago. New
Edition. With Maps and 150 Illustrations. 1 vol. Medium 8vo. 21s.

**JOSIAH GILBERT.**

LANDSCAPE in ART: before the days of Claude and Salvator.
With 150 Illustrations. Medium 8vo. 30s.

**T GAMBIER PARRY.**

The MINISTRY of FINE ART to the HAPPINESS of LIFE.
Revised Edition, with an Index. 8vo. 14s.

**DR. THAUSING.**

ALBERT DÜRER : his Life and Work. By Dr. Thausing.
Edited by F. A. Eaton. Illustrations. 2 vols. Medium 8vo. 42s.

**SIR CHARLES EASTLAKE.**

CONTRIBUTIONS to the LITERATURE of the FINE ARTS.
With Memoir by Lady Eastlake. 2 vols. 8vo. 24s.

**JAMES FERGUSSON.**

HISTORY of ARCHITECTURE in all COUNTRIES from the
EARLIEST TIMES. A New and thoroughly Revised Edition. With 1,700 Illustrations.
5 vols. Medium 8vo.
Vols. I. & II. ANCIENT and MEDIÆVAL. 63s.  Vol. III. INDIAN and EASTERN. 31s. 6d
Vol. IV. Modern. 2 vols. 31s. 6d.

**GEORGE DENNIS.**

The CITIES and CEMETERIES of ETRURIA.  20 Plans and
200 Illustrations. 2 vols. Medium 8vo. 21s.

**CHARLES DARWIN.**

An ILLUSTRATED EDITION of the VOYAGE of a NATURA-
LIST ROUND the WORLD in H.M.S. 'BEAGLE.' With Views of Places Visited and
Described. By R. T. Pritchett. 100 Illustrations. Medium 8vo. 21s.

**WILFRED J. CRIPPS.**

OLD  ENGLISH  PLATE : Ecclesiastical, Decorative, and
Domestic; its Makers and Marks. New Edition. With Illustrations and 2,010 Facsimile Plate
Marks. Medium 8vo. 21s.
⁎⁎⁎ Tables of the Date Letters and Marks sold separately. 5s.

**G. BALDWIN BROWN.**

The FINE ARTS. With Illustrations. Crown 8vo. 3s. 6d.
(University Extension Series.)

**LORD LINDSAY.**

SKETCHES of the HISTORY of CHRISTIAN ART.  2 vols.
Crown 8vo. 24s.

**H. BRUGSCH-BEY.**

A HISTORY of EGYPT under the PHARAOHS; derived
entirely from Monuments. A New and thoroughly Revised Edition. Edited by M. Brodrick.
Maps. 1 vol. 8vo. 18s.

**C. R. LESLIE.**

HANDBOOK for YOUNG PAINTERS.  Illustrations.  Post
8vo. 7s. 6d.

**SIR J. G. WILKINSON.**

MANNERS and CUSTOMS of the ANCIENT EGYPTIANS:
their Private Life, Laws, Arts, Religion, &c. A New Edition. Edited by Samuel Birch,
LL.D. Illustrations. 3 vols. 8vo. 84s.

JOHN MURRAY, Albemarle Street.